Refugees on the Move

FORCED MIGRATION

General Editors: Tom Scott-Smith and Kirsten McConnachie

This series, published in association with the Refugees Studies Centre, University of Oxford, reflects the multidisciplinary nature of the field and includes within its scope international law, anthropology, sociology, politics, international relations, geopolitics, social psychology, and economics.

Recent volumes:

Volume 45
Refugees on the Move: Crisis and Response in Turkey and Europe
Edited by Erol Balkan and Zümray Kutlu Tonak

Volume 44
Durable Solutions: Challenges with Implementing Global Norms for Internally Displaced Persons in Georgia
Carolin Funke

Volume 43
Mediated Lives: Waiting and Hope among Iraqi Refugees in Jordan
Mirjam Twigt

Volume 42
Outsiders: Memories of Migration to and from North Korea
Markus Bell

Volume 41
Latin America and Refugee Protection: Regimes, Logics and Challenges
Edited by Liliana Lyra Jubilut, Marcia Vera Espinoza, and Gabriela Mezzanotti

Volume 40
Un-Settling Middle Eastern Refugees: Regimes of Exclusion and Inclusion in the Middle East, Europe, and North America
Edited by Marcia C. Inhorn and Lucia Volk

Volume 39
Structures of Protection? Rethinking Refugee Shelter
Edited by Tom Scott-Smith and Mark E. Breeze

Volume 38
Refugee Resettlement: Power, Politics, and Humanitarian Governance
Edited by Adèle Garnier, Liliana Lyra Jubilut, and Kristin Bergtora Sandvik

Volume 37
Gender, Violence, Refugees
Edited by Susanne Buckley-Zistel and Ulrike Krause

Volume 36
The Myth of Self-Reliance: Economic Lives Inside a Liberian Refugee Camp
Naohiko Omata

For a full volume listing, please see the series page on our website:
https//www.berghahnbooks.com/series/forced-migration

Refugees on the Move

CRISIS AND RESPONSE IN TURKEY AND EUROPE

Edited by Erol Balkan and Zümray Kutlu Tonak

berghahn
NEW YORK • OXFORD
www.berghahnbooks.com

First published in 2022 by
Berghahn Books
www.berghahnbooks.com

© 2022, 2024 Erol Balkan and Zümray Kutlu Tonak
First paperback edition published in 2024

All rights reserved. Except for the quotation of short passages
for the purposes of criticism and review, no part of this book
may be reproduced in any form or by any means, electronic or
mechanical, including photocopying, recording, or any information
storage and retrieval system now known or to be invented,
without written permission of the publisher.

Library of Congress Cataloging-in-Publication Data

A C.I.P. cataloging record is available from the Library of Congress
Library of Congress Cataloging in Publication Control Number:
2021059045

British Library Cataloguing in Publication Data

A catalogue record for this book is available from the British Library

ISBN 978-1-80073-384-8 hardback
ISBN 978-1-80539-325-2 paperback
ISBN 978-1-80073-385-5 epub
ISBN 978-1-80073-652-8 web pdf

The electronic open access publication of *Refugees on the Move: Crisis and Response in Turkey and Europe* has been made available under a CC BY-NC-ND 4.0 license as a part of the Berghahn Open Migration and Development Studies initiative.

This work is published subject to a Creative Commons Attribution Noncommercial No Derivatives 4.0 License. The terms of the license can be found at http://creativecommons.org/licenses/by-nc-nd/4.0/. For uses beyond those covered in the license contact Berghahn Books.

https://doi.org/10.3167/9781800733848

For all those who are lost at sea trying to reach a safe harbor . . .

Contents

List of Illustrations   ix

Acknowledgments   xi

Introduction   1
   Erol Balkan and Zümray Kutlu Tonak

Part I. Different Perspectives on Migration: Migration and Neoliberalism

  1. The Political Economy of Migration   13
     Sungur Savran

  2. War, Migration, and Class   38
     Kemal Vural Tarlan

  3. Images as Border: On the Visual Production of the "Migration Crisis"   63
     Mariam Durrani and Arjun Shankar

Part II. Host Country Economies and Attitudes

  4. Why Do Employment and Socioeconomic Integration Have a Strained Relationship? The International Protection Context and Syrians in Turkey   93
     Saime Özçürümez and Deniz Yıldırım

  5. Welfare Nationalism and Rising Prejudice against Migrants in Central and Eastern Europe   111
     Anıl Duman

6. Vulnerable Permanency in Mass Influx: The Case of
   Syrians in Turkey   133
   Ahmet İçduygu and Damla B. Aksel

Part III. Europe and Migration: Past and Present

7. Legal Topography of the 2015 European Refugee "Crisis"   161
   Everita Silina

8. "The Preparation of Living Corpses": Immigration Detention
   and the Production of the Non-person   186
   David Herd

9. The Germans' "Refugee": Concepts and Images of the
   "Refugee" in Germany's Twisted History between Acceptance
   and Denial as a Country of Immigration and Refuge   209
   Marion Detjen

Part IV. Refugee Agency

10. "Without It, You Will Die": Smartphones and Refugees'
    Digital Self-Organization   239
    Stephan O. Görland and Sina Arnold

11. Processes of Wage Theft: The Neoliberal Labor Market and
    Syrian Refugees in Turkey   262
    Danièle Bélanger and Cenk Saraçoğlu

12. The Narratives of Syrian Refugees on Taking Turkey as a
    Land of a Long or Temporary Settlement   281
    Samer Sharani

Concluding Remarks   312
Erol Balkan and Zümray Kutlu Tonak

Appendix. Statement from the Association of Bridging Peoples:
   It Is Not a Refugee Crisis, It Is a Secret War against Refugees   314
   Cem Terzi

Index   323

Illustrations

Figures

5.1.	Salience of Immigration in CEE. © Anıl Duman.	121
5.2.	Salience of Economy in CEE. © Anıl Duman.	123
6.1.	Syrian Refugees and Policy Responses in Turkey. © Ahmet İçduygu and Damla B. Aksel.	144
10.1.	YouTube Language Tutorial. Source: YouTube.	250
10.2.	Verification of Information within the Chaotic Model. © Sina Arnold and Stephan O. Görland.	251
10.3.	Verification of Information within the Hierarchical Model. © Sina Arnold and Stephan O. Görland.	252
10.4.	Verification of Information within the Gatekeeper Model. © Sina Arnold and Stephan O. Görland.	253
12.1.	Projecting the Four Approaches on Two Dimensions, Place, and Identity-Agency. © Samer Sharani.	292
12.2.	The Four Poles of the Two Dimensions. © Samer Sharani.	293
12.3.	Representing the Narratives: (a) agency and self-identity exercised in the same place, Turkey (blurred boundaries between Turkey and Syria), and refugees prefer to stay in Turkey; (b) agency and self-identity exercised in different places, which have fixed boundaries (between Europe and Syria), and refugees prefer to leave for Europe. © Samer Sharani.	299
12.4.	The Mechanisms of (Non)Home Return Desire. © Samer Sharani.	302

Tables

5.1. Population and Stock of Immigrants in CEE–2018. Source: Eurostat. 119

5.2. Social versus Economic Fears in the CEE. Source: Author's calculations based on European Social Survey (ESS). 120

5.3. Welfare Nationalism in the CEE Region. Source: Author's calculations based on the ESS. 124

5.4. Welfare Nationalism in the CEE Region across Education. Source: Author's calculations based on ESS-2016. 125

5.5. Welfare Nationalism in the CEE Region across Income. Source: Author's calculations based on ESS-2016. 126

6.1. Determinants of Permanent Settlement in Mass Influx. Table constructed by the authors with the use of following studies: Kunz 1981; Jacobsen 1996; Koser and Black 1999; Castles 2006; Sert 2010; Harild and Christensen 2010; Schmeidl 2011; Scalettaris 2010. 139

10.1. Agreement to the Statement "I Use the Following Functions on My Smartphone" (n = 97). Table made by Sina Arnold and Stephan O. Görland. 244

10.2. Most Frequently Used Apps before, during, and after Migrating to Germany (n = 97). Table made by Sina Arnold and Stephan O. Görland. 245

12.1. The Four Approaches and Their Conceptualization of Place and Identity-Agency in Terms of Shaping the Home Return Intention. Table made by Samer Sharani. 291

12.2. Personal Attributes of Syrian Refugees. Table made by Samer Sharani. 304

Acknowledgments

First, we would like to thank our reviewers for their valuable comments. Their insights helped improve the manuscript. Thanks also to Neşecan Balkan, E. Ahmet Tonak, Barbara Kosta, Osman Balkan, Ahmet Dura, and Barbara Britt Hysell for all their suggestions and support.

Introduction

Erol Balkan and Zümray Kutlu Tonak

Since we started working on this book, the world has changed dramatically. First, the Covid-19 pandemic took the global community by surprise. The speed with which it spread was alarming. All borders had to be locked down, bringing refugee flows to a virtual halt. Meanwhile the disease entered overcrowded refugee camps in Greece, creating additional havoc and misery. Second, the global health crisis caused extreme vulnerability in both developed and developing host country economies as growing unemployment generated huge economic insecurity for most citizens and especially for the refugee population.

Refugees are a highly vulnerable population deserving utmost attention. Tragically, they were mostly ignored by the media and by host country governments during the pandemic. In this book we question this attitude and argue that the refugee crisis is still one of the most critical predicaments of our time.[1] It continues to be the most salient human indicator that demonstrates the deeply rooted contradictions inherent in the global capitalist system.[2]

The magnitude of this immense problem cannot be reduced to numbers, but it would be helpful to review some data on its sheer enormity. According to the UNHCR (United Nations High Commissioner for Refugees), 80 million people worldwide had been forcibly displaced due to wars, religious and political persecution, civil conflict, violence and famine, and environmental collapse by the end of 2019 (UNHCR 2020). Of this huge mass of people, approximately 26 million have fled their homelands. Most of these refugees are hosted in developing countries like Turkey, Jordan, Lebanon, and Bangladesh, and 6.6 million are Syrians (UNHCR 2020). Currently, Syria is in the midst of the tenth year of its civil war, and more than 11 million Syrians—nearly half the country's population—have been displaced either within Syria or to nearby countries.[3]

With an estimated four million Syrian refugees and more than three hundred thousand people of concern from other countries, Turkey hosts more refugees than any other country in the world (UNHCR 2020). The majority of Syrian refugees in Turkey live in poverty and are dispersed in densely populated urban settings in Istanbul, Izmir, and other major cities. Though the "temporary protection" status of Syrian refugees provides access to a range of free public services, including healthcare and education, refugees in Turkey lead a precarious life. The pandemic has further deteriorated their substandard living conditions. Food insecurities, lack of adequate sanitary conditions, insufficient access to online education, and loss of jobs are widespread problems among the refugee population.[4] The picture gets worse each day due to political volatility, growing tensions with the local populations, and increasing economic insecurity within the country.

Those who seek economic and political security in Europe also face considerable challenges. The European response to irregular migrants is brutal. In 2015, Europe was faced with the arrival of more than one million people in the EU zone, an overwhelming problem that Europe struggled to respond to. This development turned into a humanitarian and political crisis, as most EU countries erected fences and closed their borders. Later, the controversial EU-Turkey deal of 2016, designed to prevent asylum in Europe, sharply reduced the number of refugees reaching Europe.[5] Currently, getting to Europe is harder than ever.

Nevertheless, boats bound for Greek islands continue to fill up as economic hardships and limited access to basic rights persist for refugees. Among those who survive the journey, thousands are stranded in camps in Greece[6] and along the borders of Eastern European countries. Desperate to reach their destinations and in hope of getting asylum, they are often met with discrimination and violence. Currently, tens of thousands are being held in official detention centers and for long periods of time. Many European governments justify the need for containment and the closure of borders with reasons of national security against vilified "others."[7] One harrowing response to the refugee inflow has been the rise of populist right-wing movements.[8]

Meanwhile many scholars and activists have responded to the ordeal of the refugees in a most humane way, demanding solidarity. The sociologist Zygmunt Bauman described the current refugee issue as the crisis of humanity. In a 2016 interview, he said, "I don't believe there is a shortcut solution to the current refugee problem. Humanity is in crisis—and there is no exit from that crisis other than the solidarity of humans" (Evans and Bauman 2016).

Why This Book?

Refugees on the Move highlights and explores the profound complexities of the current refugee issue by focusing specifically on Syrian refugees in Turkey and responses from some European countries. Some of the issues we examine are the causes of the movement of refugee populations, the difficulties they face during their journeys, the daily challenges and obstacles they experience, and host governments' responses to managing and overcoming the so-called "refugee crisis."

Our decision to focus on Syrian refugees in Turkey and Europe stems from both our interest in the topic and our experiences in this area. We have had the opportunity to carry out projects with refugees and do research on different aspects of the issue in both Turkey and Europe. Our fieldwork and findings confirm the multidimensionality of refugee studies. In this volume, our goal is to bring together authors from a wide spectrum of perspectives who are grounded in disciplines such as political economy, anthropology, sociology, political science, and economics. We believe that methodologies such as fieldwork, interviews, and surveys specific to various disciplines enhance the book's scope and reach. The linguistic pluralism apparent in each chapter reveals the critical role each author's identity plays in the effectiveness of the narrative.

We must keep in mind that it is impossible to create a singular refugee narrative since refugee experiences are extremely diverse depending on the specific historical and geopolitical context. As research in this volume reveals, life experiences vary substantially even within this specific group of Syrian refugees in Turkey and Europe. The daily life of each person within displaced populations is different depending on class, occupation, location, gender, and age.[9] In addition, attitudes in developed host countries also differ toward educated versus uneducated, skilled versus unskilled, well-to-do versus ordinary refugees. Recognizing the refugees' individual stories is important.

Furthermore, to fully understand refugee issues, we need to analyze and question the international context in which the refugees arise.[10] The problem is not only the increasing number of refugees or the policies implemented to resolve this crisis but also the system that produces and reproduces refugees. We are encouraged to create solutions to the problems refugees face—housing, health, education, unemployment, xenophobia—and there is no doubt that these require urgent establishment and immediate response. However, awareness of the root causes of forced migration arising from systemic contradictions should also be on our agenda. Without having a rigorous political approach to address the root causes and material conditions in which refugees arise, remedial policies will not be sufficient to combat the ever-increasing number of refugees no matter how effective they are.

Finally, we would like to point out that while most research focuses on the refugee crisis in Europe, the majority of the world's refugees still lives in the Global South, frequently in countries bordering their own. The political developments in Europe suggest that Turkey and other developing countries will continue to bear the burden of hosting millions of refugees in the foreseeable future.

The Book

The book is divided into four sections:

Part I, titled "Different Perspectives on Migration: Migration and Neoliberalism" presents different approaches to migration and the refugee crisis.

In chapter 1, Sungur Savran uses a Marxist approach to describe the causes of migration flows and the refugee crisis. He argues that structural mechanisms—that is, the logic of capital accumulation—have been the root cause of all migratory flows since the nineteenth century. After examining the differences between migrants, refugees, and asylum seekers, Savran posits that refugees ultimately end up being part of the reserve army of labor within the capitalist system.

In chapter 2, Kemal Vural Tarlan argues that traditional migration models fail to explain some of the complex issues related to the status of refugees. He focuses on migrant and refugee labor, which he considers to be the only unchanging variable over time, and examines this variable within the formal and informal labor markets of host countries. Tarlan's chapter is based on eight years of fieldwork in Turkey, Jordan, and Lebanon, during which he interviewed refugees employed in the informal sector. What remains consistent in all these countries is that migrants perform low-wage labor. His observations point to the fact that migrants and refugees in these countries provide the most demanded form of labor in the informal sector where working conditions tend to be hazardous.

The tragic image of the body of Aylan Kurdi, a three-year-old Syrian-Kurdish child, that washed up on the Turkish shore in 2015 became iconic as it circulated throughout Western media. Many haunting images of children and adults on dinghies continue to bring attention to refugees and their hard and dangerous journey through the treacherous waters of the Aegean and the Mediterranean Seas.

In chapter 3, Mariam Durrani and Arjun Shankar focus on the colonizer-colonized relationships and show how images of suffering or dead refugee children like Aylan Kurdi are reproduced and circulated to garner empathy in the West. These images indicate that borders have become ever more hostile over time. The question the authors address most poignantly is, to what extent do images of suffering children perpetuate the stereotypic understanding of whose suffering should be redressed and whose suffering can be consumed as a matter of public voyeurism?

Part II, titled "Host Country Economies and Attitudes," deals with the problems of refugees in host countries.

In chapter 4, Saime Özçürümez and Deniz Yıldırım question why policies that aim at increasing the employability of refugees do not lead to a successful process of social integration. The authors conclude that several factors prevent the integration of refugees and claim that the international legal framework for refugees, the structure of the economies in host countries, and the socioeconomic profile of refugees are among the many barriers.

As mentioned above, in 2015 hundreds of thousands of refugees walked toward Europe, crossing dangerous terrain and ending up in remote areas on Eastern European borders. Although most of these countries prohibited the refugees' passage, their plight, broadcasted thorough various news media outlets, contributed to changing public attitudes toward them.

In chapter 5, Anıl Duman examines the changing sentiments toward migrants and refugees, the growing prejudice against them, and the evolving anxieties of nationals who fear the economic impact of this incoming flow of people. She discusses how these changing attitudes have strengthened the anti-immigrant populist ideologies in the context of Central and East European countries. Her findings suggest that the prejudices of the nationals are triggered by the perception that migrants will "steal" their jobs and benefit disproportionately from the welfare system.

The future of Syrian refugees in Turkey continues to be a topic hotly debated among academics, policymakers, NGOs, and government officials. It is also on the minds of many Turkish citizens. On the other hand, refugees need to evaluate the choices of returning home to Syria, permanently settling in Turkey, or, if possible, continuing on to European countries.

In chapter 6, Ahmet İçduygu and Damla B. Aksel examine these possibilities and address the likelihood of long-term or permanent settlement in the host country. They compare the similarities of and differences between Syrians in Turkey and Afghan refugees in Iran and Pakistan. Their research reveals that refugees continuously live in a state of "permanent temporariness." In the second part of their chapter, the authors provide an analytical and theoretical framework for permanent settlement.

Part III, titled "Europe and Migration: Past and Present," examines how European states respond to the inflow of migrants and refugees.

The huge refugee inflow to Europe in 2015 led to a dramatic increase in economic, legal, and social policy discussions and political decision-making within the European Union.

In chapter 7, Everita Silina investigates the patchwork of European policies aimed at containing the flow of refugees by critically examining the evolving legal guidelines. Her review of the efforts to establish refugee camps on five Greek islands and the practices regarding these refugee camps reveals the crisis of EU governance. Silina concludes that this so-called "hotspot approach" provides only short-term solutions to the problem. According to the author, this approach removes the refugees from public view solely to conceal the deeper crisis of EU governance.

An increasing number of refugees and asylum seekers are detained around the world and denied their basic rights, often living in conditions below international standards. Migration-related detention not only creates extraordinary hardships for the detained but also disrupts these communities through the separation of families. Nevertheless, keeping them in a state of perpetual waiting and uncertainty is still one of the instruments that states use to contain the flow of refugees.

In chapter 8, David Herd investigates the meaning of detention and its increased use by the state as a globalized response to human inflows. He examines the detention centers in the United Kingdom and the immigration policies that aim to create a "hostile environment" for undocumented immigrants turning them into non-persons.

The inflow of refugees to Germany following the opening of borders by Chancellor Angela Merkel in 2015 continues to dominate the political and social debate. That year marked the arrival of over a million refugees in Germany to be processed as asylum seekers.

In chapter 9, Marion Detjen explores the historical factors that led to the arrival of refugees in Germany and the resulting changes in the political and cultural landscape. At first, refugees were met with open arms, and volunteers offered resources and assistance to help them settle in their new "home." The volunteers secured housing, education, and work for the refugees with the support of the state and promoted social integration through language and culture courses. Yet, the large influx of refugees also sparked controversies regarding the challenges of integration and the impact of refugees on German society and culture. Taking 2015 as the starting point, Detjen traces the debates about what it means to be a migrant and refugee and how these attributes relate to the nation-state.

Part IV, titled "Refugee Agency," consists of chapters focusing on the decisions that refugees make and the actions they take to survive and continue living in the mostly adverse conditions they find themselves in.

The smartphone became a tool of survival for the refugee on the journey to safety. It mapped routes, charted roads, and helped navigate the seas that threatened to swallow those traveling in crowded, precarious vessels supplied by smugglers. The smartphone was also a means of communication among separated family members and friends while providing information on the passage ahead.

In chapter 10, Stephan O. Görland and Sina Arnold examine the role of smartphones as indispensable tools of flight. They argue that smartphones enable refugees to self-organize, share information, and achieve greater autonomy of movement. Equipped with smartphones, refugees inform themselves about their destinations. They chart specific routes and avoid the ones with border patrol and police presence. Moreover, smartphones can save lives in emergency situations. On arrival, refugees use these tools to overcome language barriers and negotiate urban spaces.

The Syrian refugees in Turkey do not constitute a homogenous population in terms of socioeconomic class. In fact, many Syrian refugees have no access to the formal employment sector and work instead in the urban informal sector. Most of these low-wage informal jobs are in textiles, construction, and manufacturing, often in various sweatshops.

In chapter 11, Danièle Bélanger and Cenk Saraçoğlu focus on the urban labor market in Turkey and look specifically at the social relations of production in which Syrian refugees participate. They address the complex relationships of Syrian workers with their employers and fellow Turkish and Kurdish workers. The results they present are from their fieldwork on small businesses conducted in Izmir from 2016 to 2018. Belanger and Saraçoğlu argue that Syrian refugees currently constitute an important segment of the working class in Turkey, and, as such, they should not be considered refugees but migrant workers.

In chapter 12, Samer Sharani presents fieldwork he conducted through interviews with Syrian refugees in Turkey, Germany, and Sweden. His chapter examines their narratives to understand how they make the decisions regarding where they would like to reside in the future. The interviews reveal the dilemma of the refugees in terms of whether they should stay permanently in their host countries or return home.

The book ends with the remarks of Cem Terzi, MD, the cofounder of the Association of Bridging Peoples, which is a nonprofit charity and solidarity association.[11]

It is our hope that the chapters contained in this collection will enhance the public debate and understanding of the refugee issue and contribute to the work of academics, policymakers, and various organizations active in the field.

Erol Balkan is professor of economics at Hamilton College and visiting professor at Sabancı University in Istanbul. His current research focuses on the impact of the pandemic on refugee communities.

Zümray Kutlu Tonak is lecturer at Smith College. She received her BA and MS in sociology from Middle East Technical University, her MA in theory and practice of human rights from the University of Essex, and her PhD in political science from İstanbul Bilgi University. Her teaching and research focus is on refugees, urbanization, and human rights.

Notes

1. The concept of "crisis" is used in three different contexts by the authors of this book: as the systemic crisis of capitalism that often leads to displacement of people, as the trauma and hardships of the displaced people, and as the crisis of the nation-state in dealing with the incoming refugees.
2. For an extensive analysis in this volume see Savran, chapter 1: "The Political Economy of Migration."
3. The post-9/11 U.S. wars have forcibly displaced at least thirty-seven million people in and from Afghanistan, Iraq, Pakistan, Yemen, Somalia, the Philippines, Libya, and Syria. See Vine et al. (2020).
4. For further discussions see Balcıoğlu (2018); Leghtas (2019); Kınıkoğlu (2020); Santana de Andrade (2020).
5. With the EU-Turkey deal, European leaders agreed that every individual who arrived irregularly on Greek islands—including asylum seekers—should be returned to Turkey. In exchange, Turkey would receive €6 billion to assist the vast refugee community hosted in the country, and Turkish nationals would be granted visa-free travel to Europe. The deal also stated that once the number of irregular arrivals dropped, a "voluntary" humanitarian scheme to transfer Syrians from Turkey to other European countries would be activated.
6. Refugees face high risks on their journeys including the capsizing of their boats and drowning in crossing to Greece. However, they still continue with these dangerous attempts in order to reach their destination. The facilities in Greece currently house more than 16,290 people. These overcrowded camps with substandard living conditions have always been a temporary and palliative solution. See General Secretariat for Information and Communication (2021).
7. For a critique of the "crisis" framework and its role in migration management, see De Genova (2016); Reece (2016); De Genova and Peutz (2010).
8. For a comprehensive description of this development see chapter 9 by Detjen in this collection.
9. For women's experience at all stages of forced migration, see Friedman et al. (2017).
10. For an analysis of the international context, see Haddad (2008).
11. The Association of Bridging Peoples promotes the development and strengthening of public friendships between people. It also facilitates solidarity during political and natural catastrophes with severe social consequences. The organization is known for its work with refugees in Turkey.

References

Balcıoğlu, Zeynep. 2018. *Sultanbeyli, Istanbul, Turkey: A Case Study of Refugees in Towns*. Medford: Tufts University, Feinstein International Center.

De Genova, Nicholas. 2016. "The 'Crisis' of the European Border Regime: Towards a Marxist Theory of Borders." *International Socialism* 150: 31–54.

De Genova, Nicholas, and Nathalie Peutz (eds). 2010. *The Deportation Regime.* Durham, NC: Duke University Press.

Evans Brad, and Zygmunt Bauman. 2016. "The Refugee Crisis Is Humanity's Crisis," *New York Times*, 2 May. https://www.nytimes.com/2016/05/02/opinion/the-refugee-crisis-is-humanitys-crisis.html.

Friedman, Jane, et al. (eds). 2017. *A Gendered Approach to the Syrian Refugee Crisis.* New York: Routledge.

General Secretariat for Information and Communication. 2021. "National Situational Picture Regarding the Islands at Eastern Aegean Sea (07/02/2021)." Retrieved 2 October 2021 from https://infocrisis.gov.gr/12125/national-situational-picture-regarding-the-islands-at-eastern-aegean-sea-07-02-2021/?lang=en.

Haddad, Emma. 2008. *The Refugee in International Society.* Cambridge: Cambridge University Press.

Kınıkoğlu, Suat. 2020. "Syrian Refugees in Turkey: Changing Attitudes and Fortunes." Stiftung Wissenschaft und Politik. SWP Comment C 05.

Leghtas, Izza. 2019. *Insecure Future: Deportations and Lack of Legal Work for Refugees in Turkey.* Refugees International Field Report.

Reece, Jones. 2016. *Violent Borders.* London: Verso Books.

Santana de Andrade, Glenda. 2020. "Beyond Vulnerability: Syrian Refugees in Urban Spaces in Turkey." *International Journal for Crime, Justice and Social Democracy*, 9(3): 34-46.

UNHCR (United Nations High Commissioner for Refugees). 2020. *Global Trends Forced Displacement in 2019.* Retrieved 14 November 2020 from https://www.unhcr.org/flagship-reports/globaltrends/globaltrends2019/.

———. 2020. "Figures at a Glance." Retrieved 14 November 2020 from https://www.unhcr.org/figures-at-a-glance.html.

Vine, David, et al. 2020. *Creating Refugees: Displacement Caused by the United States' Post-9/11 Wars.* Providence, RI: Watson Institute International and Public Affairs, Brown University.

Part I

Different Perspectives on Migration

Migration and Neoliberalism

1
The Political Economy of Migration

Sungur Savran

"Not so very long ago, the earth numbered two thousand million inhabitants: five hundred million men, and one thousand five hundred million natives." This is how Jean-Paul Sartre started his "Preface" to the rightly acclaimed *The Wretched of the Earth* by Frantz Fanon, first published in 1961 in French (Fanon 1963: 7). The times have changed. Decades have gone by, during which the international intellectual scene has been dominated by postmodernism, postcolonial theory, and identity politics. Politically correct language is the order of the day. No longer is any nation or ethnic group called "natives," unless even the word "native" is an improvement on the common appellation used for that group, as in the case of the "Redskins" or "Injuns" of America, who are now much more politely called "Native Americans." Whether they are treated much better, in objective and material terms, by the system that no longer disparages them subjectively and nominally is another question. All indicators suggest that not only native Americans but all the wretched of the world still carry on as miserable an existence as that described by Fanon, but the world now covers it up by niceties that are supposed to make their suffering tolerable or, perhaps more importantly, that work to soothe the conscience of those that are not and have never belonged to the wretched of the earth.

But, unfortunately for the intelligentsia, there remain spheres in which the dressing-up operation may not have been completed. The terms used are not as crassly discriminatory in a postcolonial environment as they were when colonialism raged with fury and violence, but nonetheless the nuances and the fine distinctions live on without being noticed by the partisans of politically correct language. When young Africans and Middle Easterners desperate for a decent life make it to Europe to find a job, or when unskilled Mexicans or Hondurans somehow cross the US-Mexican border and establish a new life in *el Norte*, they become "immigrant workers." But when a Canadian or an Australian moves to a less developed country to make a living, they are never called that: they are proud "expats," even when the person in question is not a company manager or computer expert but simply a young and adventurous unskilled worker who gets paid almost subsistence wages in return for the teaching of that lingua franca of our age, the English language, which happens to be their mother tongue. So the distinction between the citizens of the former colonialist countries and those of the formerly colonized countries lives on in this sphere, in a hardly noticeable guise and goes unchallenged. *Formal*–i.e., legal–colonialism survives in marginal form, but that is not decisive. What is decisive is that the *real* relationship between the imperialist countries and those that lead an existence in subordination to imperialism has not evaporated together with the more cumbersome and distasteful forms and practices of colonialism.

What is true of the purely economic category of immigration also applies to the more complex and confusing category of the refugee. The life of the ordinary refugee is fraught with such dire economic difficulties, and their fragile right to asylum is subject to such delicate conditions that nostalgia for one's own country probably takes last place among their worries. But not everyone is so desolate in a foreign country even if they have been banished from their own: not so the "émigré," not so the "exile," whether willingly or forcefully removed from their surroundings. These usually come from the privileged nations and are not even required to apply for any status–they are simply granted asylum almost automatically. A German intellectual such as Erich Auerbach who escaped the hazards of Nazi Germany and settled in Istanbul, Turkey, in the 1930s was honored and embraced and comforted in his new surroundings. Not so the intellectuals of the Turkish or Kurdish left who escaped to Western Europe under threat of torture and extinction at the hands of the officials of the military coup d'état in Turkey of 12 September 1980: they had to go through all the tortuous formalities of "seeking asylum" before being accorded or refused refugee status.

And the distinctions do not only apply to the dominant nations, the imperialist ones, as opposed to oppressed ones. They go even deeper and reproduce social distinction between people from different classes and strata originally from the same country. Most advanced countries have an entirely different disposition toward the skilled and the professional in terms of migration compared to their attitude to the unskilled, the uneducated, the unsophisticated. But, worse, refugees are also subjected to a sorting process that surreptitiously favors the educated and skilled. It should also be pointed out that many of the refugees that wish to cross over into their El Dorado, whether this is an EU country or the United States, are at least somewhat more well-to-do than the ordinary unskilled worker. Having amassed some money to pay off the human traffickers, the fees being counted in the thousands of euros or US dollars, they can at least hope to be transported, by some miracle, to the other side of the border. The unskilled and the uneducated simply cannot afford that much.

Going one rung up, all kinds of wealthy people are granted residence permits or even citizenship on the basis of the money they bring in to the country in question, buying real estate or investing in certain other assets, or starting up a business. In countries bordering Europe to the east and south– i.e., the Middle East and its eastern neighbors such as Afghanistan and Pakistan, as well as North Africa and those countries of sub-Saharan Africa close enough to the Mediterranean Sea to reach via land–where millions or even tens of millions of poor and destitute people, especially the youth, are dying to migrate to one of the EU countries, the wealthy and the select make their calculations of what country is most profitable to make one's investment in for a residence permit or citizenship. Some members of the European Union have made it their sphere of specialization to trade EU passports for investment in their country in return. Portugal and Malta offer the most inexpensive deals, and so many Turks, starting from the second richest family of the country (who own an industrial empire in Turkey) have bought their future security in such places, or so they think, in the eventuality of a thorough Islamization of their country or, God forbid, a proletarian revolution.

There is one country, though, that specializes in the upper end of the "market" for citizenship and residence permits. The superrich have been feverishly buying property in New Zealand for the last decade or even longer, as the country appears to be the uppermost candidate as a sanctuary in case World War III breaks out, which would, in all likelihood, involve the use of weapons of mass destruction, in particular nuclear arms. There is probably an implicit "gentlemen's agreement" between the great powers on turning New Zealand into a global version of what Switzerland stood for in Europe during the two world wars of the twentieth century. Modern science being the handmaid of wealth and capital, it has now been discovered that New Zealand's geological formation proves that it is a distinct continent from the rest of Australasia, which presumably will grant some special privileges to the geography that is called New Zealand.

Is it not clear that the dark reality of immigration and of asylum (and refugee status) does not apply to the citizens of New Zealand, or even to those of Portugal or Malta for that matter? Is it not clear that the social, political, and legal restrictions that apply to real, flesh-and-blood, dispossessed millions have no relevance when it is a question of the wealthy and the well-to-do? One can and should add to this the trials and tribulations of women who face the possibility of all kinds of sexual assault on their journey to the promised land and who, not infrequently, fall prey to the machinations of human traffickers, ending up as sex workers, living in a state of semi-servitude. The concept of servitude may perhaps sound exaggerated to those uninitiated in the area of migratory movements, but a quick check of the facts shows that at least in Libya, and at least during a certain period, slave camps were a reality to be reckoned with.

Overall then, migration, whether under its pure economic form or the more complex one of seeking asylum in other countries, is, as in all spheres of life, a class issue, an issue of inequality between different nationalities, and a gender issue. To approach the question as one alien to social differences, as if all nationalities and classes suffer in the same manner and to the same extent, is deception. Unfortunately, this is all too common among even those who, with the best intentions in the world and with the noblest of sentiments, engage in defending refugees and migrants in the face of the cruel treatment they are subjected to and more so among those who study the question and try to offer solutions. As we shall shortly see, the question of migration and of refugees is an economic and a political question through and through, and if one intends to help the millions of migrants and refugees who are in search of security and survival all around the world, one has to take a political stand that extends beyond the narrow confines of the question itself.

Migration as a Phenomenon of the World Capitalist System

To be able to come to terms with the very difficult questions posed by international migratory flows, one first needs to understand the structural mechanisms that lie behind these flows. Unless the driving forces behind a phenomenon are comprehended in their overall logic, one can only see the tip of the iceberg and fail to respond adequately to all problems relevant to the question at hand.

Most writing on the subject of international migration dwells on the immediate causes that set in motion the specific flow that is under scrutiny: a war between two nations, a civil war, ethnic cleansing of an "undesirable" minority, a natural disaster, abrupt changes in the political setup of a country that overnight criminalizes an entire portion of the population–on and on goes the list of diverse situations that are considered to be the root causes of different migratory waves. And there is no doubt that the events that are considered to be the root causes are all operational in bringing about the mass migration under scrutiny. Only they are not root causes but merely proximate ones. There is a fundamental structural mechanism in the modern world that is at the root of all the significant migratory flows for at least the period that extends from the nineteenth century to the twenty-first. It is that structural element that sheds light on the migratory movements of the modern age and makes it possible to understand the unity of these movements. This is the logic of the accumulation of capital on the world scale.

In order to understand the relationship between the accumulation of capital on the world scale and international migratory movements, one needs to turn to the concept of industrial reserve army or relative surplus population that Marx examines toward the end of volume 1 of his major opus, *Capital*, and integrate the analysis he lays out there with his study of what is commonly called "primitive accumulation." (The term is somewhat misleading since the original German term used by Marx implies the connection of this special type of "accumulation" to the origins of capital, to its genesis, and has nothing to do with being "primitive." This is why I will use the term "original accumulation" in the rest of this chapter.)

Marx's discussion of the industrial reserve army is one of the areas that have proven to be most difficult for a full comprehension of the author's intentions, for a reason that I will explain shortly. What is not understood is not the concept of the industrial reserve army. That is one of the concepts peculiar to Marx that is most readily understood and even accepted without hesitation, since the term refers to unemployment, which is such a commonplace scourge under capitalism. However, there are several propositions in Marx's treatment of the industrial reserve army that provide an entirely different picture of how capitalism functions. One of these is the idea that unemployment is not a problem that capitalism, through certain unfortunate circumstances, has very frequently failed to resolve but a mechanism that is *necessary for the reproduction of the capitalist economy*. According to Marx, because capitalists have the possibility of choosing a more machinery-intensive set of technologies when wages rise, they can always resort to those techniques and bring down the demand for labor, leading to rising unemployment, a more intense competition among the workers, and, hence, lower wages. Moreover, in addition to this deliberate action on the part of single capitalists, the cyclical movement of capital accumulation characteristic of capitalism, with periods of rapid growth being followed each time by slumps, causes the demand for labor to fall periodically, hence creating an industrial reserve army that will act to check any rise in wages that will prove cumbersome for capitalists. Thus, the labor market is not like any others. In any other market, supply and demand are shaped as the result of forces independent of each other. Not so in the labor market:

> It is not a case of two independent forces working on one another. Les dés sont pipés. Capital works on both sides at the same time. If the accumulation, on the one hand, increases the demand for labor, it increases on the other the

supply of laborers by the "setting free" of them, whilst at the same time the pressure of the unemployed compels those that are employed to furnish more labor, and makes the supply of labor, to a certain extent, independent of the supply of laborers. The action of the law of supply and demand of labor on this basis completes the despotism of capital. (Marx 1968: 640)

The existence of a reserve army of labor becomes, thus, perhaps the major economic mechanism for keeping the results to be obtained through workers' collective struggles (unionization, strikes, occupations, etc.) at a level acceptable to capitalists, i.e., at a level that will not hamper capital accumulation.

However, there is a second function of the reserve army of labor. As capitalism is, by its very nature, an extremely complex but unplanned system of production, there is no reckoning before the fact how rapidly capital accumulation will proceed at any given moment in time. There are of course attempts at forecasting the rate of growth, and many institutions have developed subtle techniques in predicting the performance of capitalist economies for the short term, both internationally and at the level of individual countries, but anyone who has remotely followed the relationship between forecasts and the realized results will know that there are times when the forecasts are wide off the mark in both directions. Thus, capital always needs a reserve army of labor for an eventual rapid acceleration of accumulation and growth. Here we come to the crux of the matter regarding the relevance of the concept of the industrial reserve army for international migration:

> Capitalist production can by no means content itself with the quantity of disposable labor-power which the natural increase of population yields. It requires for its free play an industrial reserve army independent of these natural limits. (Marx 1968: 635)

And where is this industrial reserve army to be found? Even the structure of the sentence above immediately points beyond a "national economy" toward the world economy. Those economists who are accustomed to thinking of the functioning of the capitalist economy as within a nationally bounded entity, with international trade, investment, and finance being brought in only later as additional factors, have a difficulty understanding, even under the conditions of the eulogistic celebration of the so-called phenomenon of "globalization," that the conceptual structure of Marx's work is different. Marx's *Capital* was planned as a series of volumes rising from the abstract to the concrete, and the last volume was to take up the world market as a synthetic expression of all the laws developed in the previous volumes. The world market is, in Marx's view, the only arena in which the fundamental laws of the functioning of the capitalist economy can be understood. Because economists, including latter-day Marxist economists, regarded Marx's analysis on the reserve army of labor as the depiction of the functioning of a nationally defined economy, those who were by disposition inclined to dismiss Marx's contribution simply chafed at his further propositions, and even those who took him seriously found themselves scratching their heads in bewilderment.

What are these "further propositions" developed on the basis of the centrality of the industrial reserve army for the functioning of the capitalist economy? There are two such propositions that seemed to fly in the face of the realities of the modern capitalist economies, such as those of the United States, the European Union, Japan, and similar ones elsewhere. The first is that the reserve army of labor is made up of several components. Of these, the one Marx calls "floating" is perfectly acceptable to economists of all stripes, since it is but the expression of the rise and fall in the level of unemployment depending on, respectively, the onset of recessions and slumps and the recovery of growth. The second component is the rise in surplus agricultural population as capitalism takes hold of the rural economy, which Marx calls "latent." This part of the reserve army is "constantly on the point of passing over into an urban or manufacturing proletariat, and on the lookout for circumstances favorable to this transformation" (Marx 1968: 642). So far this is not an outrageous statement for orthodox economists, since the long-term diminution of the rural population and the swelling of the ranks of the urban proletariat as a result of urban-rural (domestic) migration is a commonplace phenomenon in all countries. But already there is a first corollary that may disturb the observer of the modern-day advanced capitalist economy: in Marx's rendering, because the transition from the rural labor force to the urban one is not a smooth one, there is a permanent element of unemployment here, and "the agricultural laborer is therefore reduced to the minimum of wages, and always stands with one foot already in the swamp of pauperism" (Marx 1968: 642).

The third component lends itself immediately to criticism: this is the so-called "stagnant" component of the reserve army that suffers from "extremely irregular employment," with conditions of life that "sink below the average normal level of the working class." Its lowest strata are placed squarely within what Marx calls pauperism, including "the demoralized and ragged, and those unable to work, ... the mutilated, the sickly, the widows etc." (Marx 1968: 644). This is the first proposition that rings alien to the ears of the economists given the state of advanced capitalist societies of the late twentieth century and early twenty-first. Some others may rightly retort that the last few decades are testimony to the fact that Marx was right, as unemployment became an almost permanent condition in the advanced capitalist countries and soup kitchens and food coupons became more and more popular. But Marx is not talking only about situations of deep economic crisis, as is the case in particular with the period since 2008, when all economists started to compare the situation to the 1930s. For Marx, the stagnant component and its strata that have sunk into pauperism are *permanent* features of the reserve army of labor.

The second proposition follows from here. We need to quote Marx at length once again in order to understand the real import of the proposition in question:

> The same causes which develop the expansive power of capital, develop also the labor-power at its disposal. The relative mass of the industrial reserve army increases therefore with the potential energy of wealth. But the greater this reserve army in proportion to the active labor army, the greater is the mass of a consolidated surplus-population, whose misery is in inverse ratio to its torment of labor. The more extensive, finally, the lazarus-layers of the working class, and the industrial reserve army, the greater is official pauperism. *This is the absolute general law of capitalist accumulation.* (Marx 1968: 644, emphasis in the original)

This bold overarching statement has baffled many a Marxist economist, let alone orthodox economists. The latter only rejoiced to see Marx's prediction brought to its knees by the historical levels of prosperity that were allegedly attained by the advanced capitalist economies. Whatever our reservations with respect to the celebration of the level of welfare attained in the advanced economies, the picture of the "lazarus-layers of the working class" depicted by Marx cannot be sustained for these societies, not even for times of crisis, let alone for times of a booming economy. The "misery" of the kind that Marx is talking about seems to be alien to these societies. So much for Marxist economics then. If this is the "absolute general law of capitalist accumulation" that derives from the Marxist analysis of the capitalist mode of production, one is then permitted, so the reasoning goes, to discard the whole Marxist economic framework as pointless.

But as soon as one broadens the perspective and looks at the entire capitalist system as it has developed over the twentieth century, uniting the already existing world market into a single world economy under the laws of the imperialist system, the objections become so many pieces of shattered glass, and the criticism directed at Marx is transformed into a parochial protestation in denial of a capitalist juggernaut that unites the world in combined but uneven fashion. Then the rural laboring population of the entire "Third World" of yesterday and the "Global South" of today becomes the "latent" component of the reserve army of labor on the world scale, and the urban poor of Africa, of the Indian subcontinent, of Haiti and Bolivia and similar countries in Latin America, etc., become the "stagnant" component, and the lower strata of these two components are the layers that have sunk into pauperism. These are the people who are said, by all commentators as a matter of fact, to have to work every day to eke out a living for themselves and their families. These are the people whom international statistics register as living on less than two dollars a day. What other "lazarus-layers" does one need to seek when these masses of millions, nay hundreds of millions or even billions, suffer from malnutrition, from uninhabitable dwellings, from lack of the basic elements of sanitation, even from outright starvation? Not only has capitalism not brought prosperity to these regions of the world except for the few, but it also reproduces this miserable existence day in and day out. So, it turns out that the "general law of capitalist accumulation," so outlandish in the eyes of many economists, proves to have been confirmed by historical development.

And why is this the case? One need not go any further than Marx's analysis of original accumulation ("primitive accumulation") in the last part of *Capital*, volume 1, immediately after the part (part VII) that takes up the accumulation of capital and the concluding chapters of this part on the "general law of capitalist accumulation." Original accumulation is simply the process through which the direct producers are separated from the means of production that they had access to under different forms in precapitalist societies (I use "form" in the plural to make clear that before capitalism took over, there was a variety of social relations that were dominant in different parts of the world). This process was completed in England and Scotland very early on. It was later accomplished in the countries of continental Europe. It was brought to many parts of the rest of the world through white settler colonialism and colonialism tout court. Remember that Marx, in discussing the impact of the introduction of capitalism in agriculture, stressed that this process led to a significant loss of economic activity for the laborers. This is precisely what happened to the petty producers, tribal networks, etc., in those countries that were economically conquered by capitalism and, later on, capitalist imperialism. Subsequently, this led to the swelling of the urban poor as the rural labor that was set free through dispossession moved into towns and cities. So, although the historical process differed, the outcome paralleled the formation of the latent and the stagnant components of the industrial reserve army in the original capitalist countries. Original accumulation played the role of midwife in the birth of a worldwide industrial reserve army. Now they had an additional problem to overcome in their quest for survival, beyond the original "lazarus-layers" in the original capitalist countries. The world had become a patchwork of nation-states, and hence they had to cross national borders in order to survive.

These are the people who are the big armies of potential immigrants and refugees.

Contradictory Manifestations of the Law

The most obvious objection that could be made to the proposition that international migration is subject to the working of the general law of capital accumulation is that although this law implies that the capitalist class of the imperialist core of the world capitalist economy is in constant need of the supply of labor power from the less-developed and poorer countries, albeit to a varying degree over time, the cross-border movement of labor is, as a rule, rendered almost impossible by the very same states that serve the interests of those capitalist economies. There is nothing in this seemingly contradictory situation that would pose a problem for the analysis laid out in the previous section.

The need capital feels for a reserve army of labor does not automatically imply that all national restrictions will be lifted on migratory flows and that the circulation of labor will be made free across nations. There are, as in the working of each socioeconomic law, mediations of a social and political character that act to translate the law into more concrete corollaries and, furthermore, concrete factors that are at play in determining the course of things at each concrete moment and for each specific country or region.

There *are* moments in the course of the accumulation of capital when all advanced economies opened up deliberately to an inflow of immigrant labor. The most striking such moment is the period that followed World War II, when the so-called postwar boom that accompanied the reconstruction of the war-ravaged advanced countries, and in particular the European countries, required an immense extra labor force lest a bottleneck should arise from a lack of labor supply. The United Kingdom granted the citizens of the British Commonwealth special rights for settlement and work, leading to a significant flow of population from its former colonies, which lies at the root of the presence of sizeable populations of Pakistani, Indian, and Caribbean, even Greek and Turkish Cypriot, origin to this day. The continental powers followed suit, with North African Arabs from the Maghreb and Black Africans from the sub-Saharan former colonies taking the pride of place in France, Indonesians in the Netherlands, and even Mozambicans, Angolans, and others in Portugal, a minor and rather poor economy within the overall European context. And what did Germany do, that latecomer on the imperialist scene without a substantial colonial empire? It first depended upon a tolerant policy regarding the latent reserve army from the Mezzogiorno, that peculiar region of Italy that was like an internal colony of the rich industrial north. Once that flow started to slow down, Germany turned to other predominantly Christian European countries such as Yugoslavia. It finally struck up a special agreement with Muslim-majority Turkey in the mid-1950s, which was to give it the largest minority population in the country and a never-ending clash of cultures that has lasted to this day.

The postwar boom was thus a classic case of the general law of capitalist accumulation manifesting itself in the replenishment of the ranks of labor in the advanced centers of capitalism through migratory flows of labor from the underdeveloped regions of the world. It was almost a laboratory experiment that showed the connection between the need for surplus labor created by rapid accumulation and the reserve army of labor ever present in the poorer regions and countries of the world.

There are also certain countries that historically have made immigration relatively easy, almost, but not entirely, independent of the cyclical movement of capital accumulation at a given moment. Such are some of the countries formed on the basis of white settler colonialism, the United States first and foremost, but Canada, Australia, and others as well. The reason is clear: as Marx quite early on made clear in the very last chapter, titled "The Modern Theory of Colonization," of volume 1 of *Capital*, once white settlers reached these sparsely populated lands, and even the sparse population that existed was later decimated by the newcomers, they easily got possession of small plots of land and became independent farmers. Thus, in the course of its historical development, the capitalist class of these countries was in constant starvation of a sufficiently large reserve army of labor and had to look abroad to migration from other continents and, later, in the case of the United States, the countries of Latin South America and the Caribbean. Tens of millions of emigrants are estimated to have moved from Europe, including czarist Russia, and from China to the Americas, North and South, throughout the nineteenth century. Naturally, smallholding ownership has weakened over the centuries. Yet throughout the twentieth century as well, America has been much more open to foreign migration than Europe.

These two prominent examples show clearly, one in time and the other in space, that there is a *definite* relationship between the needs of the capitalist class for additional labor and the influx of a laboring population from other, poorer regions, countries, and even continents. It would then be easy to say that national restrictions on the inflow of labor are the result of a lack of need for additional labor in times when the pace of accumulation of capital slows down. The capitalist class does not feel the necessity for the reserve army of labor to be replenished from other countries, since a sizeable part of the working class of the country in question has been laid off and is therefore acting as the reserve army of labor. In other words, the expansion in times of crisis of the domestic reserve army of labor, of what Marx calls the "floating" component, makes it unnecessary for the capitalist class to dip into the "latent" and "stagnant" components that are to be found in poorer countries.

That would be a rash judgment. For the two examples that we looked at–one temporal and one spatial–are based *exclusively* on the need for an absolute expansion of the labor force of the country in question. In those two cases, capital accumulation is in dire need of expanding the pool of labor; otherwise, the lack of a sufficient labor force will act as an absolute barrier to the further expansion of capital accumulation. It is for this reason that the capitalist states in question relax restrictions on the inflow of foreign labor to such an extent.

However, the need for additional labor so as to expand the scale of capital accumulation is, as we have already seen, only one aspect of the reliance of the capitalist class on a reserve army of labor. There is a second aspect, it will be remembered, that relates to the reserve army of labor acting as a lever in the hands of the capitalist class to hold back an upward push of the wage rate in times of rapid growth and to bring wages down perceptibly in times of crisis. The reserve army of labor does this by pitting the unemployed part of the working class against the employed sections, putting all workers under fiercer competition and creating a downward spiral in wages. (Let me add here, once and for all, that the wage rate in reality stands as the most significant aspect among a series of other matters that lend themselves to class struggle between the capitalist class and the working class, such as working hours, conditions of work, intensity of labor, aspects of unionization [the closed shop or otherwise, for instance], and sick leave. I will use the wage rate as an indicator that stands for all these different variables.)

It may be concluded that a reserve army of labor is necessary even when there is already an expansion of the "floating" domestic component of the reserve army of labor. However, it is most direly needed for the interests of the capitalist class when rapid capital accumulation tends to decrease the ranks of the reserve army and thus, by reducing competition among the workers, makes possible a significant upward drift of the wage rate. Hence almost under all circumstances, the expansion of the reserve army, in addition to the already existing domestic "floating" component, is good for the capitalists. So, we cannot explain the national restrictions imposed on the inflow of immigrant workers simply by referring to the size of the domestic reserve army of labor. There is an additional factor here that is very important to understand.

Or, rather, there are several other factors one needs to understand. The one that comes immediately to mind is the resistance put up by the domestic working class to a lax immigration policy. It is almost common sense for the domestic worker to resist the expansion of the reserve army of labor through immigration, whether of the purely economic kind or under refugee status. For if it is true that capital enjoys benefits from the competition of workers through an expansion of the reserve army, first and foremost manifested in the pressure on the wage rate, then ipso facto the worker stands to lose in the face of additional competition from the immigrant laborer. And even though the state is a class state controlled by the capitalist class, it does not act in a vacuum but in constant attention to the response and reaction of other class forces, and it has to make certain concessions to the widespread sentiments in the ranks of the working class under most circumstances. Thus, working-class hostility to foreign workers is one factor that tends to create barriers in the way of a loose regime of immigration.

There is another, much more purely political factor that tends to bring additional restrictions to immigration. This partially preys on the aversion within the ranks of the working class to immigration. Certain political movements harp on the fears and insecurity of not only the workers but other plebeian elements of the population, and they attack immigration as the fundamental root cause of all the ills that the country in question faces. Movements of this kind grow rapidly in times of deep economic crisis in the advanced and semiadvanced countries, since such times create conditions in which all resources tend to dry up, lots of cuts in social services occur, and society experiences a generalized scarcity in all areas, such as housing, education, healthcare, etc. In such times, a rabidly nationalistic discourse that blames immigration for all of the scourges that the country faces gains support from the masses. Fascism grew rapidly in the 1930s, which was precisely the decade of the Great Depression. The period since 2008, in our opinion, deserves the same characterization of "great depression," which once again has given rise to ultranationalist movements that are completely hostile to immigration: Le Pen's movement in France, Salvini's Lega in Italy, or Nigel Farage, the champion of Brexit, and his followers in Britain are only the most prominent ones. Donald Trump is, of course, the paradigmatic instance of this political orientation. The appellation widely used for these movements is "populism." I choose to point to their roots in the fascist movements of their respective countries (with some exceptions, such as Trump and Farage), regard them as incomplete fascist movements or lone fascist figures, and propose to call them "proto-fascist" for reasons that would take me too far afield to explain.

There are also more particularistic factors at play in this or that country, into which we need not go. However, we have not yet touched upon the decisive factor. To understand that decisive factor is of capital importance, for it is this that gives us the basis for a class-based progressive political attitude to be adopted toward international migration.

The restrictions that hit immigration are, first and foremost in our opinion, the result of efforts that aim to create a situation that works toward the highest impact of the competition within the working class in favor of capital. The reasoning here is quite simple: if you allow for a rather lax regime of migratory inflows or even encourage them, this implies, by the very nature of things, that the foreign newcomers will enjoy the same kind of rights as workers as the domestic workforce (although not perhaps as citizens for a very long time). Turkish workers in Germany had, from the beginning, the same rights, with respect to unionization or social services, as their fellow

German workers. So, after a period of adaptation, these workers, German and Turkish, were able to protect their interests in their relation to the capitalist as unionized workers. The paradigmatic example for this situation is the case of the United States around the turn of the twentieth century. Filled with workers from a variety of countries thanks to the liberal regime of immigration that was in place, the US working class created one of the strongest and most radical unions in its own and in world history: International Workers of the World, better known by its initials, IWW. Hence competition within the working class during an expansion of the reserve army of labor does not necessarily lead to defeat; there is a countertendency in the organizing drive of the working class that can, at least partially, neutralize the impact of the high level of joblessness by canceling competition.

The way capitalists can overcome this prospect of unity among the workers—among, that is, the domestic and foreign elements—suggests itself immediately: let the foreign workers come into the country as illegal immigrants, thus leading to a status that curtails their rights, puts them in a precarious situation where they are beholden to the constant pressure of being apprehended, and thus makes them thankful for getting even the lowest-paying job. This is the best formula for the interests of the capitalist class one can imagine. These are the situations when the workers, facing the alternative of poverty and destitution back home, will bow to any conditions as long as they get a job in a sweatshop or a farm or as home help under any conditions, including giving up a part of their freedom of movement and turning their passport over to the middlemen, who constitute another category of beneficiaries, along with the capitalist class, of the irregular and shady deals of employment created under such murky regimes of immigration.

If this argument is correct, then it leads to the necessity of a total inversion of the commonsense response of the domestic working class. Common sense is usually not a good guide for action since things are hardly ever the same as they seem to be when viewed superficially. The "latent" and the "stagnant" components of the industrial reserve army on the world scale—i.e., the billions who live from hand to mouth in the underdeveloped and poor countries of the world—form an almost inexhaustible source for the needs of the world capitalist class. They are good for simply replenishing the ranks of the working class in advanced and semiadvanced capitalist countries quantitatively when the natural increase in population cannot meet the domestic pace of capital accumulation. They are also good for increasing the number of "hands" in times of prosperity as a check against the push for higher wages as unemployment shrinks. They are even good for creating additional competition in times of crisis, times when capital is going through hardships and needs to push down wages drastically. But the best fix is to keep them in a miserable state even as they have moved geographically in space and are now living in an otherwise affluent society. Illegal immigration does the job. If illegal immigration is the best scenario for the capitalists, then it is obviously the worst for the workers. Hence making immigration legal is to the best interests of the working class of the advanced country. This is what unions, along with the political parties that claim to side with or organize the working class, should fight for.

If such is the case, there is another implication. Humanistic and altruistic language of the type adopted by NGOs and charities might seem to help in an immediate sense. This approach is obviously incomparably superior to any degree of chauvinistic or hateful attitude toward immigrants. However, it is, as are many other such abstract discourses, self-defeating. For the humanistic discourse is one that implies that the citizens of the advanced country must treat immigrants well out of kindness, out of a consideration for their plight, out of a humane attitude that preaches that "we, citizens of a rich country" all give, privileged as we are, a small part of what we have to "these poor fellow human beings." We are not saying that the discourse in question is couched in these terms. What we are saying is that the underlying argument has this kind of structure.

This is doubly wrong. To the immigrant it insinuates a relationship of superiority on the part of the speaker, a benign attitude that is mixed with pity and compassion. Worse still in terms of its consequences, to the underdog of the advanced society—already living in fear for their job, for their child's education, dreading possible eviction from their housing, sharing with immigrant populations, legal and illegal, the insecurity and the dilapidation of their urban surroundings—what is being said is, "Share some of what you have with these poor souls." That may sound nice to the ears of people with a secure job and a safe home who do not fear for their future, who may even soothe their conscience for any qualms about the global inequity they enjoy the fruits of, but for the working class that has been suffering the consequences of neoliberal globalism for the last four decades and those, even more devastating, of the great depression that set in in 2008, they sound like just another attack on their interests. The idea that "we should sacrifice to a certain degree from our standards for the benefit of these poor souls" plays directly into the hands of the proto-fascist chauvinists. It is the obverse of their discourse, i.e., the proposition that these people take away what "we" deserve.

The only correct solution to the quandary born of the existence of a worldwide reserve army of labor is to fight together, citizen and foreigner, as fellow workers against the real culprits who play the unemployed sections of the international working class, those who live in misery, against the sections that have acquired certain rights and gains and positions in the past so as to take away from both.

The Migrant and the Refugee

It is now time to assess the extent to which this general analysis regarding the forces that govern international migration is relevant for the category "refugee." It is certainly true that the category "refugee" and the predicament of seeking asylum in a foreign country has certain specific characteristics that set it apart from the general concept of international migration. For one thing, it has its special place in international law through conventions that accord special rights to refugees not enjoyed by the migrant who crosses borders for mostly economic reasons. Also, migration is in general independent of a special traumatic experience such as war or civil war, religious or racial discrimination, or political persecution, while asylum is in principle predicated on that kind of event that abruptly and brutally changes the situation in the lives of individuals and families. Finally, this difference is the source of another: asylum and refugee status are usually not considered as economic in their nature but mostly political, while migration per se without any qualifying terms is strictly of an economic nature. So how is what I have said thus far of international migration relevant for refugees?

The author of these lines is of the opinion that, despite the clear differences that originally existed between the categories of migrant and refugee, over the decades and centuries these positions have converged so closely in the real world that it is no longer useful or even possible to distinguish between the two.

Before going on to explicate this process of convergence, I would like to point out one fact: in the two most important migratory events of the last decade, the entire world media constantly used the two categories of refugee and migrant interchangeably. The events I am referring to are, respectively, the 2015 mass exodus of Syrians and other Middle Eastern peoples toward Europe, via the sea route of the Mediterranean and later the land journey into the heart of Europe and the so-called "migrant caravans" of Central American origin, mostly Honduran but also Salvadoran and Guatemalan, that marched from the Guatemala-Mexico border in the south to the Mexico-US border in the north. In the first case the overwhelming majority were Syrians, who are considered to be refugees by everyone, although the media constantly referred to "migration" and "migrants" when discussing them. In the second case, a serious debate took place as to whether these were "migrant caravans," as they came to be commonly called, or in truth "refugee caravans." This debate was important because, within the last two decades, Central American countries (and Honduras most acutely) have become hotbeds for gang criminality, reporting some of the highest homicide rates per capita internationally, and many of those joining the caravans based their claim of a right to entry into the United States on incidents of persecution.

What both cases show is that in actual fact the two categories have become inseparable.

Let us now dwell on the reasons why it is no longer useful or even possible to distinguish between the two. Let me immediately make clear that I am not, or at least not yet, debating the utility and possibility of a legal distinction. That may appear on the agenda once the collective debate clarifies the issues involved in objective terms.

The first point to establish is that the meaning of asylum and refugee status has changed over time. Granting asylum to democrats fighting against tyranny was considered to be a paramount duty for democratic governments in the age of the democratic revolution in the Western Hemisphere, roughly the period extending from the American Revolution of 1776 through the Great French Revolution all the way to the so-called "spring of nations" in 1848, when there was a concatenation of revolutions all over Europe. This tradition has survived to this day. The figure of Karl Marx finding asylum as a German revolutionary successively in Paris, Brussels, and London (his lifelong co-thinker and friend Friedrich Engels had the advantage of being employed at a family concern in Manchester and did not need asylum) is all too well recognized. The same is true of Bakunin, Marx's nemesis in the First International, who was granted asylum in Switzerland as a political opponent of the czar. There are many other illustrious cases of such political opponents of repressive regimes seeking asylum in the more democratic countries of the continent. Refugees of yesteryear were single individuals or at most groups of people, even sometimes very large groups such as the Armenians in World War I and the Jews in the 1930s, who were, by the very nature of their activities or their position in society, direct targets of the repressive regimes they were escaping.

Not so today. The refugees of our day, most typically represented by the millions of Syrians that have fled the country in the course of the civil war that has gone on for close to a decade, are simply "the Syrians" or "the Palestinians" or "the Sudanese," etc. They are not tested to see whether they have indeed been or are likely to be persecuted or discriminated against. Being a Syrian caught in the midst of a cruel war that has gone on and on is deemed sufficient for the person to be considered a candidate for asylum. This conversion of the figure of the refugee or the exile from a single individual or a group that is known to have been specifically targeted by repression to immense crowds of people has totally changed the position of refugees. Because they are an enormous mass of people from a certain country, they are, as a general rule, the same group of people that belong to the economic position of the "latent" or the "stagnant" components of the industrial reserve army in their country, or even the "lazarus-layers" of that section of the population. They become lazarus-like even if they were not before.

It is not that mass-scale asylum is alien to history—persecuted populations have long sought safety in foreign lands. Examples include the temporary Hegira of the prophet of Islam, together with his followers, from Mecca to what was later to be called Medina in the seventh century; the migration of the Jews of Spain persecuted by the Inquisition to Istanbul at the end of the fifteenth century; the flight of the Huguenots, the Protestants of France, to Britain in the late seventeenth century; the flight of the Armenians from what had been their homeland in Anatolia since time immemorial to escape the genocide; and the hounding of the Jew under the Nazi boot in Europe, the last two both in the twentieth. What is relevant here is again the fact that these were all religious groups that were persecuted simply because they belonged to that religious group. Not so with the Syrians today, who are a mixture of ethnic (Arab, Kurdish, Turkmen), religious (Muslim, Christian, Druze), and denominational (Sunni and Alevi) groups, who, regardless of whether they or their family were under threat of persecution or oppression, have fled the country. Other cases of mass exodus can be found in the twentieth century. In the first of two examples, the Greco-Turkish exchange of populations totaled close to two million souls leaving their ancestral homes after the war between the two countries between 1919 and 1922; in the second, an immense population movement occurred after the Partition of India and Pakistan in 1947. But these were national (or binational, if one wishes to call them that) affairs that did not lend them to a more general internationalized solution.

The second point follows on directly from the first: because the masses in question are candidates for asylum and the status of refugee not by virtue of the fact that they have suffered any particular practice of persecution but simply because they have found themselves in the midst of a vortex that would cause an upheaval in almost anyone's life, their plight does not differ qualitatively from many migrants who set out on the road because of extreme adverse economic conditions. What is the difference between Congolese or Sudanese escapees of civil war and Indian peasants fleeing their homestead because of an invasion of locusts, or Mozambicans who can no longer survive as a result of unprecedented hurricanes destroying their sources of livelihood? (By the way, the two latter examples are likely results of the fast-approaching climate catastrophe and can be considered part of the "great climate migration," a new category that will make the status of refugee even more difficult to situate.) Although there is a difference in the proximate cause of the problems, the final consequence from the point of view of the masses that are sent fleeing their ancestral habitats are the same— i.e., the impossibility of self-reproduction and of sustaining their families.

Whether masses on such a large scale migrate for political or economic reasons, the end result turns out to be exactly the same: miserable wages and work conditions for the refugees or migrants as the case may be, with additional hazards for women, in particular the younger ones, that include regular prostitution or being married to older men already in wedlock (in most cases a disguised form of partial servitude). The bosses who buy their labor power are purchasing extremely cheap labor, and the intense possibility of exploitation manifests itself in work days extending beyond classical nineteenth-century standards and work conditions that would break the back of even the sturdiest laborer. So, whether these masses are considered as refugees or migrants, the economic consequences are the same. Hence all that has been said from the beginning to the end of this chapter is equally valid for both categories.

So, there is a very perceptible process of convergence between the categories of migrant and refugee, and the general law of the accumulation of capital applies to the mass of refugees as well as to migrants.

To make this observation is different from determining whether identifying the two categories is to the benefit of the groups in question. Here, in our opinion, the choice is very clear: of course, identifying refugees with migrants may play into the hands of the enemies of international migration by allowing them to reduce refugees to ordinary (economic) migrants and thereby assail the well-established legal rights of refugees enshrined in international law. However, even leaving aside the fact that when it is a question of such large masses the legal rights in question immediately become theoretical, as demonstrated by the experience of the 2015 exodus of Syrian refugees into Europe, there is an obverse side to the reasoning that says, "Let us not give up the hard-won legal rights of refugees by equating them with migrants." The question can easily be turned around: should we defend the acquired rights of refugees and thereby turn them into a (theoretically) privileged mass as opposed to the migrants, or should we perhaps defend, on a broader platform, the right of every economic migrant and, *a fortiori*, of every refugee to a decent life in the country of their choice? The question is up for debate, and I will leave it there.

Wars and Civil Wars as Triggering Factors

As I have already said, there is a widespread tendency to see wars, whether international or civil wars, as the main cause of migration. In a certain sense, there is nothing wrong in doing so. After all, wars are among the proximate causes of migration. However, the tendency I am talking about of focusing on wars also involves attributing, albeit in somewhat latent fashion, the responsibility for these wars purely and simply to local political forces. In other words, received opinion in the advanced countries really lays the responsibility of the flow of refugees and migrants into the richer parts of the world exclusively to forces that reside in the countries themselves.

The policy prescription that flows from this perception is to bring in the "international community" to set right whatever has gone wrong in the poorer regions of the world. Let the United Nations stop the wars, adjudicate between opposing claims, and thus protect our pristine cities and neighborhoods from being swamped by hordes of poor and uneducated foreigners. This is the kind of logic that perhaps unconsciously exonerates the vested interests and governments of the advanced imperialist countries from all responsibility.

What I am discussing here is not the role of the specialized agencies of the United Nations such as the United Nations High Commissioner for Refugees (UNHCR) or the United Nations Relief and Works Agency (the agency for Palestinian refugees). This is a topic unto its own, and any discussion should also include the role of NGOs and charities, religious or otherwise, in particular the large and ever-present international organizations and the relations of these to the poorer and less-influential regional or national ones, usually established ad hoc for each particular crisis. No doubt this is an important topic, because as long as the problem of refugees and migrants exists, there are things to be done to improve their lot and alleviate their suffering. What is debatable in this area is how best to do this. There is a voluminous literature on this area, and the reader might benefit from a survey of that literature, in particular if they are working in the field. I am no expert myself in this sphere and will as such pass on to the main topic: wars as the main triggering factor in refugee and migrant flows.

This is of course not the place to delve into a general discussion of the causes of war in our day and age. What I will do instead is to try and provide a brief panorama of twenty-first-century armed conflicts in the Middle East and North Africa (MENA) region so as to evoke in the reader a sense of how laying the blame for wars, international or civil, at the foot of the regional peoples and polities is fundamentally vitiated in an understanding of the real situation. The reason I am choosing the MENA region is that this is the region from which the largest convoys of refugees have been flowing into the richer regions of the world.

In the two decades of the twenty-first century, there have been four successive waves of wars in the MENA region. The first wave, which still lives on, was started by the United States as a reaction to a new type of transnational Islamism that can best be characterized as *takfirism*, an ideological current in Islam that arrogates to itself the authority to judge the entire world, including those who consider themselves Muslims in terms of its own self-styled Islamic precepts, and violently eliminates those it considers as a barrier to the spread of its own brand of Islam. The two outstanding organizations exemplifying *takfirism* are Al Qaeda and the Islamic State. The US administration under George W. Bush reacted to the 9/11 events by declaring war, under the slogan of "war on terror," immediately on Afghanistan (2001) and somewhat later on Iraq (2003).

The sagacity of initiating these two wars may be seen in the following facts. After almost two decades of conflict and tens of thousands of casualties (3,500 US soldiers, 72,000 Afghan National Army forces, and up to 90,000 Taliban and Afghan civilians) and an estimated 2.3 trillion dollars spent on the war by the US, the war in Afghanistan has resulted as an inglorious debacle for the US. As for Iraq, it would be a pity if we silently passed over one of the most ironic twists of recent history. It will be recalled that there were two different reasons cited for the US assault on Iraq. One was that Saddam Hussein was collaborating with Osama bin Laden, the leader of Al Qaeda. Saddam, as anyone who knows a bit of Iraqi history will testify, was one of the most secular leaders of the MENA region by Arab standards, so the story cannot withstand even the most cursory scrutiny. However, as the Bush administration knew that this would hardly be credible, it also claimed that Saddam had amassed a dangerous number of weapons of mass destruction. Weeks before the invasion of Iraq by the United States and what was then called the "Coalition of the Willing," former general Colin Powell, then US secretary of state, stood at the Security Council of the United Nations and made a presentation using state-of-the art technology with the aim of proving this. The occupying military forces, first and foremost those of the United States and the United Kingdom, would later search frantically for these weapons of mass destruction without being able to discover a single cache, finally admitting that there were none.

This first wave has continued most conspicuously in the war waged by the United States, with the assistance of Kurdish ground forces, on Islamic State. It should be added that this self-declared Caliphate of all Muslims was itself a direct product of the war on Iraq. The organization, an offshoot of Al Qaeda, found the strongest support among the Sunni population of Iraq, in particular the tribal structures in the north. This population had been totally alienated by the US occupying forces since the latter bet on the Shia and Kurdish segments of the population at the expense of the Sunni.

The second wave has consisted of the response of the United States and its closest allies to what has commonly been called the "Arab Spring." The succession of uprisings in 2011 in Tunisia, Egypt, Yemen, Bahrain, and Syria were, in our opinion, genuine revolutions that brought down long-reigning dictators in at least two of these (Tunisia and Egypt), partially in one of them (Yemen), and posed a real challenge to a king and a republican dynasty respectively in Yemen and Syria. (Libya, usually considered akin to these five cases, was no revolution but a tribal and regional settling of accounts from the very beginning.) America and the former colonial powers (Britain, France, and Italy) were caught off guard and vacillated at first in their policy response. But their regional allies, in particular Saudi Arabia, Qatar, and NATO member Turkey, spearheaded the struggle against revolution in the MENA region. The response varied from country to country. In Tunisia, the luckiest of all since in the end it at least gained a parliamentary regime replacing an autocratic one, the European Union absorbed the revolution into channels acceptable to imperialist domination. (At the time of writing, even Tunisian democracy seems to be menaced by the single-handed suspension of all parliamentary activity by the president of the republic.) The others went through hell. Saudi Arabia occupied Bahrain militarily (under the guise of the forces of the Gulf Cooperation Council, the GCC) to crush the revolution. It acted as the financier of the Bonapartist coup d'état by al-Sisi, the chief of staff of the Egyptian army, in 2013 and has since been economically propping up the new dictatorship. And the Saudis again intervened heavily in neighboring Yemen, first by fanning the flames of civil war and waging since 2015 one of the most ruthless wars, together with the United Arab Emirates (UAE), the newly rising local power, on the country.

But the neuralgic center turned out to be Syria. As we are now past the tenth anniversary of the uprising against Beshar al-Assad's regime, which was set off on 15 March 2011, the younger generations might not even be aware and the older generations may have forgotten that the Syrian turmoil started out as a people's rebellion, or even a revolution, that had nothing to do with armed conflict and nothing to do with sectarian religious feuds. For close to six months, it was the regime versus the unarmed ordinary people, the workers and peasants of Syria struggling over economic problems, unemployment, hunger, social services, etc. For the first six months, neither the United States and Israel nor the Muslim majority powers of the region worked against Assad, particularly since during the last years before the Arab Spring Assad had been negotiating indirectly for a rapprochement with Israel through the intermediation of Erdoğan's Turkish government, all under the benevolent gaze of the United States. It was only when the troika–Saudi Arabia, Qatar, and Turkey–from September 2011 on and particularly in early 2012, decided to bring down Assad that the Syrian situation turned from a popular rebellion into a civil war. The conflict progressively took on the allure of sectarian war from the point of view of the Sunni armies that were fighting what they considered to be the Alevi government of Assad but was in fact a secular government that, along with the Alevi minority of the country, relied on the support of the Sunni and Maronite bourgeoisie and the Druze as well.

To call the decade-long Syrian war a civil war is one of the most misled characterizations of recent history. Roughly one-third of the approximately two hundred countries in the world are engaged in the war in Syria. The anti–Islamic State coalition included around sixty-five countries. Add to this countries such as Russia, Iran, Israel, and Lebanon (in the form of Hezbollah) involved in some way in the Syrian war and you certainly have an explosive mixture. To call this a civil war tout court is, as I said at the beginning of this section, a handy way of attributing the Syrian catastrophe and the accompanying refugee flow to the ineptitude of the Syrian people and thus exonerating the "international community." However, the civil war aspect here is only a minuscule aspect of the overall conflict.

Libya is the other striking example of the responsibility of the rich world in striking up what is falsely perceived to be a "civil war." The immense hydrocarbon riches of this sparsely populated country have always whetted the appetite of the oil companies, which were highly frustrated over four decades–from 1969 all the way to the Arab Spring–by the idiosyncratic rule of Colonel Gaddafi, a minor Nasserite. As soon as the uprisings in Tunisia and Egypt caused a tremor in Libyan society, leading to a series of tribal and regional revolts against Gaddafi, the imperialist countries–with France and Italy at the forefront and the United States, under then-president and Nobel Peace Prize awardee Obama, "leading from the back"–immediately turned against the dictator, not only to cast off the close control on Libyan oil but also to establish control over this country geographically located precisely between the two most powerful revolutions in the Arab world, giving them the possibility of intervening in either country should either revolution get out of hand. The brutal, inhumane treatment given to Gaddafi's corpse, only matched by the grisly killing of the US ambassador to Libya sometime later, are but minor incidents when compared to the mutual slaughter of tribal and regional warlords in the years since then. Libya is now Syria in 2015 or 2017. It is a powder keg waiting to ignite, and a score of countries lurk there and play the warlords as puppets from behind the scenes.

To understand the importance of Syria and Libya, the reader should realize not only that the MENA region has been by far the major source of refugees since 2011 but also that these two countries are precisely the two major routes through which all the peoples of the Middle East and beyond (for Syria) and those of Africa all the way to Sudan and Congo (for Libya) offload their human suffering. Overpowering as the Syrian flow of refugees may be, when the Erdoğan government opened Turkey's borders to Europe at the beginning of 2020 in retaliation to Western policies vis-à-vis Turkey, it was not only, or even mostly, Syrians that flocked Turkey's frontier with Greece but Afghans, Iraqis, Kurds, Yemenis, and many from other nations. As for Libya, to the best of our knowledge, the overwhelming majority of the migrants who try to reach the shores of Europe, first and foremost Italy, are non-Libyans, since the Libyan state has collapsed and left the country free for all kinds of avaricious elements that wish to profit from human trafficking. There are, as I pointed out earlier, slave camps for would-be immigrants and refugees. So, what I am discussing here when I talk about Syria and Libya are not two countries but the entire geographies of Western

Asia, on the one hand, and Northern Africa all the way down to Congo on the other.

The third wave of wars is in fact already contained in the second wave. The Sunni-Shia divide in the Middle East has a long history, but in the last decade this has almost become a casus belli. The rivalry is led by the two rich and powerful states of Saudi Arabia and Iran, respectively Sunni and Shia. The struggle over hydrocarbon resources between these two countries finds an ideological expression in this age-old sectarian divide in the Islamic world. The divide was partially responsible for the events in Iraq, in Syria (where the ally of the Shia is the Alevi minority), in Yemen, and in Bahrain. However, after Trump took office, things have taken another turn. Trump has established a front led by Saudi Arabia, the UAE, Egypt, and, to top it all, Israel and targeted Iran, withdrawing from the nuclear deal signed in 2015 when Obama was president. Since then, all wars in the Middle East (though not in North Africa, since Shia presence there is very weak) are also, or even primarily, Sunni-Shia wars. The potential danger is immense. The Iran-Iraq war in the 1980s lasted eight years and took an estimated one million lives. So, a generalized Sunni-Shia war cannot even be imagined in terms of the overall toll. At the time of writing, the Biden administration has started to renegotiate the nuclear deal with Iran, which reduces the risk of belligerence, but has not reversed other policies established by Trump.

The fourth wave of wars in the MENA region comes as a result of the relationship of Israel to the entire region. In 2006 Israel heavily bombed Lebanon, causing immense damage, but was then repelled by Hezbollah. In the winter of 2008–9 Israel again bombed the Gaza Strip, causing devastation. These attacks leave their scar not only among the Palestinian people but also across the Arab world, later becoming the source of other wars or warlike activities.

Apart from the waves so far discussed, there are also some other armed conflicts in the MENA region that lack regional importance, however vital they may be to the contending parties, such as that which has confronted the Turkish army and the Kurdish guerrilla of the Workers Party of Kurdistan (PKK) for close to four decades or the conflict that has pitted the Moroccan army against the Polisario Front for the Liberation of Western Sahara.

It should be clear that an overwhelming responsibility for wars, civil or international, in the MENA region lies with the imperialist countries of the West, in particular the United States and the European Union and their close local allies, Saudi Arabia, Israel, and Turkey. With the MENA, from Iran in the east all the way to Algeria in the west, being the central hub of hydrocarbons, the long shadow of oil companies and rich countries has been cast over the entire region for more than a century. The well-meaning citizens of these Western countries ought to take a closer look at the foreign and military policies pursued by their own governments because in the end these wars tend to come home in other disguises. And the plight of refugees and migrants cannot be overcome unless we understand the causes that create the suffering.

Need for a Broader Perspective

In conclusion, all that has been said in this chapter on the question of migration and asylum seeking invariably leads us to broaden our perspective as we look at the suffering and exploitation of the millions who set out on the road for a better future. Both the economic dynamics and the political and military drivers of migration as a solution of last resort find their roots in the inequalities of the imperialist world economy, in the class dynamics of the capitalist mode of production, and in the wars that are ignited in the name of greed and domination. It is, without a shred of doubt, necessary to attend to the wounds opened by each and every episode of refugee flight or migration caravan, but it is as important to turn our eyes to the root causes of the misery and exploitation involved in these cases. The wounds must be healed, but the weapons used by those who inflict the wounds must also be wrested from their hands and destroyed.

Sungur Savran is an author and political militant based in Istanbul, Turkey. He received his BA in politics from Brandeis University and completed his PhD in economics at Istanbul University, where he also taught for ten years until resigning in 1983 in protest against military repression of Turkish universities. He has taught as visiting professor at various universities in the United States, among them the Graduate Faculty of the New School for Social Research in New York City. He is the author of several books in Turkish and the coeditor of two volumes in English on Turkey: *The Politics of Permanent Crisis* and *The Ravages of Neo-liberalism*, both published by Nova (2002). He has written for various US and British journals, including *Monthly Review, Capital and Class, Socialism and Democracy,* and *Khamsin.*

References

Fanon, Frantz. 1963. *The Wretched of the Earth.* New York: Grove Press.
Marx, Karl. *Capital.* Vol. 1. 1968. Translated by Samuel Moore and Edward Aveling. New York: International Publishers.

2
War, Migration, and Class

Kemal Vural Tarlan

Introduction

The mass migratory wave that has flowed from the Middle East to neighboring countries and thence to the heart of Europe requires us to take a new look at the "phenomenon of migration." Although theories of migration once considered valid are renewed every several decades, the causal relationships regarding the phenomenon of migration have become much more complex with this most recent wave. Migration became a mass phenomenon all around the world as a result of armed conflicts in the 1990s, which forced millions to relocate and formed a new peak in the history of migration. Having started during the time when the countries of the center developed on the basis of the exploitation of those in the periphery, migratory movements in the twentieth century were mostly due to differences between countries, the periodic crises of capitalism, income differentials, and world wars. These movements were held at a level that was kept under control by the core countries, and they were at times even encouraged. Migrant labor was frequently used particularly in the labor markets of these countries in the wake of World War II in order to resuscitate the economy.

The new wave of migration centered in the Middle East was triggered by the "people's rebellions," dubbed by some the "Arab Spring." However, one needs to go back in time to analyze the causes thereof. With the process of "globalization" that started in the 1990s, neoliberal capitalism spread across the planet to reach the farthest and the deepest points possible, also capturing the most strategic and profitable industries of the periphery. Without analyzing the last three decades of those countries that experienced these popular rebellions, it is very difficult to assess the migratory movements of the recent years, for, in contrast to its promises, neoliberalism brought widespread poverty to the local communities.

This new system, which saw sharpened income inequality, increased monopolization of the means of production, and property changing hands, led to ruptures in the social and economic structures in Syria, the subject of this chapter, and other Middle Eastern countries. On the one hand a new bourgeoisie was coming into being, centered in the Gulf countries, aligned and integrated with global capital; on the other hand, however, a young and educated but unemployed middle class, one that dreamed of entering the global labor market and used digital technology and social networks and media, was on the rise. This middle class in the Middle Eastern countries, which recently filled the Arab street, on the basis of the spread of new communication technologies, the internet, and social media, established links with the sectors of the Western world that had themselves gone on the streets, as in Syndagma and Puerta del Sol and flowed into its own squares (Tahrir Square in Cairo, the Pearl roundabout in Bahrain, Taksim Square in Istanbul). Those who formed the vanguard and experienced the greatest damage were the youth, in particular young women. Within the last decade before the rebellions, approximately 30 percent of the young population had been pushed outside the regular work force. Unemployment was very high among college graduates. It was particularly high among graduate women (Hanieh 2015: 133–35). From the point of view of the governments that ruled the Middle East and the elites clustered around them, neoliberalism, apart from brief interludes in which they experienced difficulties of adaptation, signified the construction of a system of privatization, wage cuts, tax increases, cuts in social expenditures, and skyrocketing food prices.

On the other hand, from the point of view of the bourgeoisie, a market was created where capital saw all barriers in its way removed. Just how fragile this newly created system was became obvious under the impact of the global crisis of 2008. The Gulf countries, with their economies greatly dependent on oil and other hydrocarbons, experienced disruption as a result of the fall in price of these products, and the crisis spread to peripheral countries such as Tunisia, Libya, Egypt, Bahrain, Yemen, and Syria, dependent on the Gulf states. In these countries, with economies based on industries that work on the basis of unregistered labor, such as agriculture and textiles, the labor market was encouraged toward flexibility as well as increasing the share of the unregistered industries. The growth of unregistered industries is one of the most important indicators of structurally growing poverty. The crisis resulted in large masses of people, dispossessed, unemployed, and becoming helpless with each passing day, emerging on the streets and bringing down, one by one, the authoritarian regimes that ruled the Middle East for decades and the dictators that led them.

When we come to the present, this is what we see in the Middle Eastern countries: although the Gulf states, which we can define as the core countries, and their ruling classes are still holding on, they have not come out of the quagmire of economic crisis. In those that are regarded as the peripheral countries, on the other hand, the new despots that have replaced the regimes ousted by the rebellions are divided and socially fragmented as a result of economic crisis and the deepening of domestic conflicts. In the cases of Yemen, Syria, and Libya, the countries in question find themselves divided, and the conflicts have evolved into civil wars.

These conflicts and civil wars have resulted in severe disruptions for the peoples of these countries, leading to the greatest migratory movements within a century, both domestically and abroad. In the countries that experience conflicts, close to half the population abandoned their homesteads and moved abroad. In the decade of the 2000s, Libya, Egypt, Yemen, and Syria joined the migration wave from the South to the North. Today, millions of emigrants, who leave these countries, cross seas, and make it to the Northern Hemisphere, are fighting to open up a niche for themselves to cling to in the labor markets of the countries they have reached. When considered from the point of view of the labor movement, it can be seen that migration is the consequence of globalization and the neoliberal economy. The root cause of the migratory movements triggered by globalization is the migration of impoverished, dispossessed, excluded human beings with the hope of a new beginning in life (Delgado 2013).

If we survey the last century of migration literature, we see that theories of migration have become ever more complex and have taken up the sociocultural context as well as taken up those factors that move labor such as wage differentials that set labor in motion (Toksöz 2004 :10–44). However, in its general lines, there is an increase in the direction of migratory movements resulting from the uneven geographic distribution of capital and labor flows toward the unlimited demand for labor created by the domination of capitalism and the markets. Also, there is mobility from the traditional sectors to the better-paid jobs in the modern sectors, where the expected net gain is the highest. The factors that provide momentum to migration set cheap labor in motion for capital. Whether voluntary or forced upon the immigrants, these factors have made labor migration a significant part of the capitalist world economy. During this period, as the land, raw materials, and labor in the peripheral countries have come under the control of world markets, large masses of people have become dispossessed and forced to migrate in order to survive.

For instance, in opposition to liberal theories of migration, Delgado Wise says that the fundamental reason for migration in our day and age is the impact of globalization and neoliberal policies. He then lists the sources of forced migration under four headings:

1. Violence, conflict, and disaster
2. Human trafficking
3. Layoffs, exclusion, and unemployment
4. Overqualification or over competence and lack of opportunities (Delgado 2013)

In short, theories of migration were developed from varying ideological perspectives and have evolved in such a manner as to cover very complex situations, with each trying to explain a different aspect of the phenomenon. As I pointed out initially, the process of emigration from Syria that started with the people's rebellion will have to be explained in terms of causality under a new perspective. This chapter will take up this process in terms of "labor migration."

In the writing of this chapter, the field observations I made in Jordan, Lebanon, and Turkey, in the context of the work I have carried out with Syrian refugees and my readings geared toward understanding the process of the people's rebellions in the Middle East and the attitude of workers within this process, have proven essential. The chapter covers the interviews I carried out and the observations I made in the last eight years with workers employed in workshops and factories in the production zones within the provincial borders of, first and foremost, Gaziantep but also Şanlıurfa, Kilis, and Adana, as well as with seasonal agricultural laborers working in the plains of Çukurova (Cilicia), Amik, and Harran, again within the frontiers of the same provinces. In Lebanon, the observations I made and the discussions I had during my visits to the rural regions in the north of the country, in particular Tripoli and the Bekaa Valley, and in Beirut, and the observations and talks I had in Jordan and the fieldwork in northern and western Jordan and in Amman made this chapter possible.

Labor Migration

Migrant labor has always been kept on the side as a subservient source of reserve labor convenient for employers with a view to keeping labor costs low, meeting the shortcomings of the labor supply, attaining flexibility, and disposing of cheap labor. As long as they could be controlled and their presence kept within certain limits, migrants were put to use by the capitalists as a mechanism to pressure their own working class and the labor market at large.

Since World War II, the capitalists have planned migratory processes meticulously, holding each component process under control. In the immediate aftermath of the war, a migratory wave of 15 million souls was experienced in Europe as a result of the changes in the borders. This was in fact a reorganization of the labor force that had suffered immense losses during the war. Then came the period that extended until the mid-1970s, during which capital grew rapidly, solved the labor shortage by using "contract labor," and rapidly enriched itself. Germany, France, and the United Kingdom at first met their labor shortage from Italy, Greece, Portugal, and Spain. Growth that exceeded 5 percent then made them turn to workers from countries like Turkey and Yugoslavia. Later the admission of workers was stopped, but rather than the present workers returning, they welcomed the arrival of their families, and a new period set in. Under the impact of the second oil shock in the 1980s, controlled labor migration came to an end. Those who came later were classified as asylum seekers, refugees, and undocumented migrants. With the dissolution of the Soviet Union and the speedy collapse of the Eastern Bloc countries, hundreds of thousands of people penetrated core Europe, and asylum seekers from Turkey, the Middle East, and other peripheral countries followed suit.

During this period, the major causes of migration from the periphery to the core were cited as the scarcity of jobs, escape from poverty, and the search for a better life. But especially in peripheral countries, economies were driven to crisis, and military coups were staged to manage the process. Şevket Pamuk and Roger Owen predicted that the process of economic change in the Middle East at the end of the twentieth century would inevitably upset the social order and that in certain situations there would arise strong popular opposition to government policies. They pointed to two aspects with respect to the future of the region: ongoing wars that never cease haunting many Middle Eastern countries and the imbalance between resources and population (Pamuk and Owen 2002).

As in other peripheral countries, migration acted as a safety valve in the Middle East as well in the absorption of regional unemployment. With the two oil shocks that occurred before the 1980s having led to Europe shutting the doors to immigrants, there was an attempt at finding a solution to the labor surplus through meeting the need for labor in the oil-rich Gulf countries (Kuwait, the UAE, Qatar, etc.). More than 70 percent of the migrant workers in the Gulf were Egyptians, Yemenis, Palestinians, Jordanians, Lebanese, and Syrians (Hanieh 2015: 313–14). In this sense, within the last three decades, migration was transformed into an instrument to balance out labor supply and demand on the overall scale of the region, but this was not sustainable. Migrant workers that had been working primarily in construction and agriculture had turned to other industries as their industries began to shrink and, with incoming families, the need for new migrant labor declined. New jobs were not forthcoming for the younger generation that came in as a result of rapid population growth. On the other hand, the Gulf bourgeoisie had promulgated new legislation to prevent the inflow of migrant labor: for instance, children who were not citizens were not permitted to enroll in the state school system. The gulf countries thus established a heavy system of exploitation that imposed lines of discrimination between citizens and non-citizens. The immigrant could only enter the country with the visa provided by the agencies and was compelled to pay a part of their revenue to these intermediaries for years on end. Under this system, dubbed *kafalah*, each worker had to hand over their passport to their employer. Despite all these hardships, the remittances sent home by the immigrant worker exceeded foreign capital inflows for many countries.

Immigrant workers lived under an integral system of exploitation combining poverty, cheap labor, long working days, and deprivation of basic human rights. This system was in fact the same in all Middle Eastern countries: the population was dispossessed, large masses of the people were impoverished, and a powerful system of exploitation was established as the shackles of feudal exploitation were consolidated by modern methods of production. Low employment, in particular among the youth and women, increased the rate of unemployment among graduates.

Although mass struggles against this system emerged, led by the youth and strongly supported by women, the arrest and exile of political activists, dotted by violence on the scale of massacres, quashed these struggles. On the other hand, the collapse of the bipolar world swiftly changed the political balance of forces in the region. The period of conflict opened up by the invasion of Kuwait by Iraq deepened ethnic, religious, and sectarian fault lines and created social polarization after the occupation of Iraq. As a result of rapid population growth, poverty, the monopolization of the economy by a small minority thanks to despotic regimes, inept administration, and other problems of the capitalist system in the Middle East, the Arab youth started to flow into the squares.

Gilbert Achcar, in his quest to shed light on the social, economic, and historical background of the "Arab Revolt" in his book *The People Want*, sums up the social situation that confronts the population in three words: "poverty, inequality, and insecurity" (Amar and Prashad 2014). In tracing the *Lineages of Revolt*, Adam Hanieh says that it is impossible to isolate a single factor such as authoritarianism, poverty, food prices, unemployment, etc.; there are many different factors at play in these revolts, and these factors are directly linked to the path of development of capitalism in the region. Underlining the extreme problems created by capitalist development within the last few decades, the author points out that whereas the dispossession of masses mired in poverty was advancing rapidly, a very small section of the population controlled the key moments of accumulation, served its own interests, and sustained close relations with international capital (Hanieh 2015: 313–14).

"The People Want the Fall of the Regime"
(*Eş-şaab yurid ıskat'en-nizam*)

The self-immolation of a street peddler, a college graduate, on 17 December 2010 became the signal flare of the popular uprisings of the Arab Spring. The violent repression against these uprisings and the period of conflict that accompanied them resulted in a profound disillusionment among Middle Eastern populations. Whatever term we use, whether "spring" or "uprising" or "revolution," what happened was an electrifying display of force on the part of the oppressed classes against despotic regimes from one end of the Arab-speaking geography to the other, from the Maghreb to the Mashriq. Having started in 2010, the uprisings were gradually replaced by violence and chaos. It was an excruciatingly painful process for the rebelling masses (Kassir 2011).

Ever since the beginning of the popular rebellions, the entire region has been drawn into spiraling violence. A large section of the population of those countries, in the belief that peace was never going to be restored, stuffed their hopes for the future and their minimal necessities in their backpacks and started to migrate toward "new lands" where they could lead a humane existence. It seems that the "profound sense of misfortune" that Samir Kassir says has penetrated every pore of the Arab soul will be transported to all corners of the world in those backpacks (Kassir 2011).

The predicament of the refugee as both rootless and rooted is characterized by Iain Chambers as "striking roots into rootlessness" (Chambers 2005). Becoming a refugee opens deep wounds in the soul and body of these people who can never go back to what they regard as their home. They march for days on end through barbed wire and minefields, facing weapons, crossing rivers and seas, and, somehow surviving, traversing borders as they look for asylum in other countries. These "new lands" will perhaps never become the destination of their dreams, but they will never be able to return to where they came from. Everything that they have left behind rapidly vanishes from their memory and disappears. Youssef, who has two university degrees and now labors as an unskilled worker, said, "However much I try to hold on to the past in my mind, souvenirs become hazier by the day." When I asked him why, this was his answer:

> We receive news every day, news of deaths, news of our homes being arsoned, news of the streets where I was born and grew up being destroyed. Seeing photos of the souk of Aleppo, so colorful, so full of people, filling me with such wonders when I was a child now fall into ruin, witnessing the destruction of our past and our cultural heritage gives me great pain. Perhaps it's best to forget the past.

A Syrian teacher who was working as a seasonal migrant worker in the Amik plain showed me the key hung around his neck and said:

There is no longer any door that this key can open. They bombed down my house to inexistence. I have visited the site and seen the rubble with my own eyes. But I will carry this key around my neck until the day I die, for I feel the warmth of my house in the cold of this iron key.

The Labor Market in Countries Neighboring Syria and Syrian Refugees

According to UN data, the number of Syrian refugees registered in countries neighboring Syria is as follows: Turkey: 3,576,396; Lebanon: 916,113; Jordan: 654,692; Iraq: 245,810; and Egypt: 129,426, the whole totaling 5,558,123 (UNHCR n.d.). In other words, since 2011, a considerable number of immigrant workers have been added to the labor market of the countries neighboring Syria. How did this affect the labor market of these countries? When we look at their economies, we see that the effect of the 2008 crisis is still continuing, that the economies in question are to a great degree dependent on inflows of foreign capital, that both unemployment and unregistered employment practices are quite high. So how are the labor markets of these countries reacting to the hundreds of thousands of newcomers? Research conducted on this question shows that the rate of unemployment as a ratio to the active population of the host countries is still high but declining; hence, the newcomers have become a part of the labor markets (Errighi and Griesse 2016; İçduygu and Diker, 2017: 12–35). The same studies also show that the Syrian refugees who have sought asylum in these countries work for low wages in the unregistered sectors of the economy. Immigrant laborers have become the basic element of the market for unskilled labor and accept work under terrible conditions. Unregistered employment practices have also flourished. The refugees who have become part of the labor market in their country of asylum are mostly concentrated in agriculture (seasonal migrant labor), construction, textiles and knitting, plastics and footwear, and the service industries, and they are employed as unregistered labor (Errighi and Griesse, 2016).

According to the Office of the United Nations High Commissioner for Refugees, 662,010 Syrian refugees have been registered in Jordan (UNHCR 2019. It is common knowledge that since no registration has been practiced since 2015, this does not reflect the real figure, which has reached 1.364 million. The Zaatari Refugee Camp has turned into a city with a population of 80,000. The work done shows that 360,000 registered Syrians of working age are now living in Jordan. If you add those that have not been registered, this figure doubles. We see that a great majority of these refugees are active on the labor market (Mercy Corps 2019).

In the agricultural fields of Irbid, Jarash, Mafraq, Al Zaqra, and the Jordan Valley, the Syrians form a considerable part of the workforce. The international organizations and the NGOs who work with refugees support the employment of Syrian refugees in the Jordanian labor market with the projects and programs that they conduct (ILO 2018). In 2019, the number of Syrian refugees with work permits in Jordan exceeded 138,000 (UNHCR 2019). This corresponds to approximately 45 percent of the three-hundred-thousand-strong registered workforce of Syrians in the country. These permits are valid in construction, first and foremost, and agriculture, textiles, and the services. They are not accorded to more technical staff such as healthcare workers, educationalists, or engineers.[7]

Since the 1970s, Jordan has hosted an abundance of immigrant labor in low-wage jobs. This is particularly a result of the inflow of Palestinians into the country, who have been forced to abandon their homes as a result of the Israeli-Palestinian conflict. Egyptian workers comprise the other significant immigrant labor demographic. Workers from Southeast Asia and China started to flow in on the basis of the *kafalah* system before 2011, and with the Syrian crisis that started that year, Syrians became the new immigrant workers of the labor market. In 2016, the Jordanian government and the European Union signed the Jordanian Compact in order to ameliorate the life standards of both the Syrian refugees hosted by Jordan and the vulnerable host communities. This compact, signed to strengthen the cooperation between Jordan and the European Union, covered the period of 2016–18 and contained provisions aimed at facilitating the temporary stay of Syrians in the country, to improve the life standards of both Syrians and vulnerable host communities, and to increase the socioeconomic expectations and resilience of Jordan (European Commission 2016).

In Jordan it can be observed that the increasing number of Syrian refugee workers, particularly in the construction industry, increase unemployment and, concomitantly, competition between workers for existing jobs; as a result of this, Jordanian workers are pushed out of the labor market. For instance, the rate of unemployment, at around 13 percent in 2011, rose to 19 percent in 2019 (CEIC Data 2019). Youth, in particular, have difficulty entering the job market. In the same period of 2011–19, the ratio of Jordanian workers employed in the construction industry started to decrease, whereas the employment of Syrians was on the rise. Outside of construction, a high number of Syrians are also employed in the retail and wholesale trades. The rate of unemployment for Jordanian workers in these industries has reached 18 percent. This whole situation results in a loss of opportunities for Jordanian workers (Stave and Hillesund 2015; ILO 2015). There are enormous problems regarding the employment of women. The ratio of women among those Syrian workers having received a work permit is only around 5 percent. Reports published show that working age for refugee children goes down below twelve, even pushing them into hazardous industries (ILO 2019).

For many years Lebanon was the country to host the highest number of displaced persons per capita. Palestinians and Syrians make up close to half the population of the country. The number of Syrian refugees in the country is 926,712. From 6 May 2015 on, the UNHCR suspended any new registration work upon the instruction of the Lebanese government. Accordingly, those waiting to be registered are not included in this figure (UNHCR 2019). According to some observers, this figure has now exceeded 1.6 million as a result of the influx of new refugees since then. Around 25 percent of the country's total population is made up of Syrian refugees. This share goes up to 37 percent in the Bekaa region. Syrian refugees are at the bottom of the ladder with respect to the relationship between working hours and wages. Northern Lebanon and the Bekaa are regions where Syrians work in the agricultural sector at a high level. These were in fact regions where Syrian seasonal migrant laborers worked in agriculture during part of the year even before 2011. The share of children working particularly in agriculture is quite high, and these are the regions at the forefront for the use of immigrant women's labor.

The last decade has been a period of grave problems for the Lebanese economy. The political situation in the country has progressively deepened these problems. Highly dependent on the central Gulf economies, Lebanon experienced considerable division as a result of the Syrian crisis. Hezbollah, the significant Shia political movement of Lebanon, stood by the Syrian regime and even opted to fight alongside it. This led the Gulf countries supporting the opposition groups inside Syria to cut their economic assistance and investment in Lebanon. Notwithstanding Lebanon's effort to make up for this through international aid and support, the gradual decline in this assistance is putting the country in a greater quandary by the day. The country, home to conflicts for decades and wielding a weak economy to begin with, is hosting over one and a half million refugees. The life standards of both the local people and the refugees are in constant decline. Approximately 59 percent of the refugees declare they are unemployed (David et al. 2019). Those who do have a job usually work in industries such as cleaning, construction, and agriculture in which employment takes the form of unskilled day labor; they work longer hours than the Lebanese workers and get paid less. The Lebanese labor market is increasingly characterized by the spread of women's and child labor. Women are paid approximately 40 percent less than men. The level of unregistered work is estimated by the World Bank to be 50 percent (UNHCR 2020; David et al. 2019). Child labor has spread like wildfire (UNHCR 2018). Street peddling, small agricultural enterprises, and family firms are the most common venues for the employment of child labor. The worsening of socioeconomic conditions generates school absenteeism. Studies show that 8 percent of children between the ages of ten and fourteen are employed and that an overwhelming majority of these are absent from school on a permanent basis. Moreover, 60 percent of refugee children of the same age group do not attend school. This will leave them vulnerable to labor exploitation in future. Half the children in this age group are looking for a job. The ratio of children who work is much higher among those who have lost their parents in the war. Parents make their children work so that they can further support the family financially (Calı et al. 2015).

The greatest sphere of employment for Syrian children in the countries they have sought asylum in is seasonal agricultural labor. A great majority of the seasonal laborers that work in the Çukurova (Cilicia), Amik, and Harran plains in Turkey currently consist of Syrians refugees. Girls and women in particular find a place in informal jobs in the agricultural sector. The same is also true for the agricultural regions of Lebanon such as Tripoli and Bekaa and the Jordan Valley and the agricultural areas of northern Jordan.

Syrian Participation in the Labor Market in Turkey

On the basis of UN data, according to unofficial figures, as of 31 July 2019, close to 4 million Syrians, 3,639,248 of those registered, are now living in Turkey, both inside and outside of camps. Refugee workers will in all probability have an impact on the labor market in Turkey for a long time. Due to lack of sufficient data, research conducted in this area has shortcomings regarding the adaptation of refugees to the labor market in Turkey (Akgündüz, van der Berg, and Hassink 2015). In the studies that have been carried out, it has been determined that the pace of wage increase for workers from Turkey experienced a fall and that the domestic worker has suffered a loss due to this (Del Carpio, Wagner, and Christoph 2015).

Because of the attitude of the Turkish government to keep its Syria policy and the refugee question away from the public gaze, the analysis and research regarding the impact of refugees from other countries on the labor market do not provide us with detailed data. Our field experience over the last eight years provides ample evidence. In effect, research carried out in other countries reflects the current situation of the labor market in Turkey. For it must be admitted that refugees who flee violence and oppression are potential members of the labor force in the host countries. In Turkey, with its approximately four million refugees, the increasing downward pressure on wages due to the increase in the labor supply led to a fall in wages and a sense of fear of economic insecurity in the minds of Turkish citizens. The Syrian refugees are blamed as the source of many problems, such as rent hikes, unemployment, lower wages, long workdays, etc., in particular in cities close to the Syrian border. However, the real crux of the matter with respect to the relation between migration and labor is the fact that it has the power to render labor less powerful relative to its original situation (Öner and Öner 2012: 90). With migration, thanks to the surplus population, capital is able to establish a control regime over labor through which it can hire whenever it wishes from this surplus labor pool and fire whenever it fits its needs. It is a familiar fact that Turkish capitalists express their understanding on the issue by saying at every opportunity, "These people will form the labor market for unskilled labor force in Turkey in the future, and this should make us happy." I witnessed a conversation between two employers within the first year of the arrival of Syrian refugees in Turkey. One of them said: "May Allah bless Assad! So good to have these Syrians over. Our workers did not even agree to work for 1,000 Turkish Lira, but now there are plenty of people who are ready to work for 500 or 600."

The Ansar-Muhajir Fraternity

When the first group of Syrian refugees arrived on 29 April 2011, the calculation was that they were going to return home in just a few months. An "open door" policy was implemented, which was, incidentally, perhaps the single most correct policy of the Turkish government. The "guests" started to flow to other cities, without any planning at all. The lack of foresight embodied in the judgment that the Baath regime would crumble in the space of a few months implied the strategic shallowness of partisanship toward the Muslim Brothers and those who sided with an Islamist ideology. That is why the camps were referred to the Disaster and Emergency Management Presidency (AFAD) and Syrians living within cities to Islamic NGOs, so much so that all information and data regarding the refugees were opened up to these organizations. Islamic NGOs and fraternities formed a "muhajir network" that was very widespread and powerful. All assistance was channeled through this network. Even when municipalities or other public agencies provided the assistance, reference was demanded from the Islamic NGOs. At the Islamic grassroots level, the question was conceived in terms of the "ansar-muhajir relationship." The intellectuals of the Islamic front theorized the question as the sociological dimension of migration and the Hegira.[2]

What was being stressed here beyond the claim that Syria is an Alevi state was the idea of a powerful Turkey as Islamic territory. After all, the Islamic element had been in power for approximately a decade, and the territory of Anatolia was being Islamized by this government. The mighty days of the Ottomans were back, and they were the only ones who had the correct words about the Middle East. All the scholars of Cairo, Damascus, and Baghdad, historic centers of Islamic civilization, were struck with admiration at the strategic depth of Turkey's vision and were bracing to kneel before Turkey. In fact, these were simply illusions: below the shallow neo-Ottoman discourse, there was no depth but rather a baseless vanity.

The swamp through which the country was wading was gradually sucking it in.

In practical life, from the point of view of the people and of the bourgeoisie, the situation conformed precisely to the rules of capitalism. The immigrants were exploited to the marrow. Everyone knows who got rich benefitting from the assistance collected for them and how the aid parcels were sold on the market. Here is how the system worked: the immigrant from Syria first had to stop by an association. There he or she was referred to a small enterprise located in the industrial zone. The owner of the enterprise laid off the worker he had been employing for many years and hired his poor co-religionist for half the wages of the earlier worker. He also engaged in another act of beneficence toward the immigrant, sending him or her to a member of the fraternity. This member also committed a charitable act, evicted his previous tenant, and rented his house or apartment to the immigrant for twice the previous lease. This story may be heard as a typical summary of that narrated by thousands of immigrants arriving from Syria. The ansar-muhajir nexus has in fact established a powerful system of exploitation within the last eight years.

When we come to the present period, both the government and the political and civil society organizations under its domination have realized that things are not going as they should, that the economic crisis is rapidly deepening, and that the hostility to refugees within the population is growing. Having conducted the affairs relating to migration and asylum in a nontransparent manner for eight years, the government now sees that under the impact of the anti-immigrant populist wave all around the world, and it is now moving away from playing the part of Ansar and is instead starting to intimidate the refugees. The Syrian refugees are dispersed all around the country, even the remotest corners, working on farms, in workshops and sweatshops, without job security, as a fresh source of cheap labor.

As of 2019, we know that Syrian refugees are dispersed to almost all cities, working predominantly as cheap labor. Having lived off scavenging from trash dumps, worked on farms and lived from hand to mouth, served in construction as day laborers at the cheapest rates, labored in factories and workshops for twelve or thirteen hours on end before being laid off without even being paid their arrears, these people now stand at the bottom rung of the labor market. In Çukurova (Cilicia), in Amik, in the greenhouses of the coastal areas, in the red beet weeding and harvest in Central Anatolia, it is the Syrian refugee that does the job. The employer in Beypazarı batters the Kurdish seasonal migrant workers and invites Syrian refugees in their stead (Köse 2016; Güler 2015).

The same situation manifests in the factories and workshops of the cities, which are filled with adolescents or with women workers. The men, who worked any job when they first arrived so that they could pay the rent or put dinner on the table for their children, are now being replaced by children and women. Children who cannot go to school are placed in jobs with the hope that they will at least learn some craft. In place of the husband who can no longer find a job, the woman becomes the provider of the whole family. The woman who has lost her husband to the war takes all kinds of risks in order to make ends meet and look after her children.

A refugee woman talking about the job-seeking process in the poor neighborhood where she had taken refuge with her children—feeling, with an intuition characteristic of her gender, that it was up to her own will to reach the light through the darkness—said the following:

> To men whose door I have to knock on looking for a job as a single woman, I am simply a woman in want. For them "poverty breeds poverty," whereas I wish to work and get my fair share. I am offering not my body to him but my labor. In return I'm asking for bread for my children. Because if I am to live in dignity, that is the only way.

In the history of labor migration, women have always provided the most vulnerable and the most flexible labor in the least skilled jobs under the worst conditions and received the lowest wages in return. Women are now replacing men, especially in the labor-intensive industries. Immigrant women are very commonly employed in farm labor, seasonal agricultural enterprises, daily labor, and domestic services. The fact that they are women and immigrants and from a different ethnic group and that they belong to the working class magnifies the degree of their exploitation. Thus, a female immigrant worker is at a disadvantage vis-à-vis a native woman worker because she is an immigrant, vis-à-vis a male immigrant worker because she is a woman, and vis-à-vis a skilled immigrant worker because hers is simple labor (Toksöz 2004: 10–44). Working women receive around 40 percent less in wages.

The number of refugees who are living in Turkey as of July 2019 exceeds 3.6 million, and those between the ages of eighteen and sixty number 1.8 million. If one adds children between ten and eighteen, this figure rises to 2.5 million. The research conducted shows that, leaving aside child labor, the number of Syrian workers who have become part of the labor market as of 2019 exceeds 1.2 million and the overall Syrian refugee labor force surpasses the mark of 1.6 million (Çoban 2018). In a country like Turkey, where unregistered employment stands at 34.4 percent, it might easily be guessed that with the entry of Syrian refugees as cheap labor into the market, unregistered unemployment has grown even further (TÜİK 2019).

According to some studies, the share of Syrian farm workers in the field of agricultural production, first and foremost in the plains of Cilicia (Çukurova), Amik, and Harran, is nearing 80 percent. Kurdish workers, who became seasonal farm workers after their villages were evacuated and they were forced to migrate mostly to cities in the western part of the country, have now been replaced by immigrant workers from Syria and other countries (Development Workshop 2016). In the past, families who worked as seasonal farm laborers would move to their places of employment in the spring, work there for a certain period, and then return home to the city after the harvest was done. Today, because the Syrian families who do the farm work have no homes to go back to and because the money they make is hardly enough to make ends meet, these families lead a nomadic existence. Many families move around during the sowing period, regular maintenance, and harvest. For this reason, within the last five years, seasonal farm labor has been transformed and is no longer seasonal but performed year-round. This state of things implies that, particularly for families, children's access to education becomes impossible. Although there are no official data regarding the number of Syrian child workers, there are claims that child labor is the most common recourse for fighting economic problems for Syrian families living in Turkey (Hayata Destek 2016). In many textile, knitting, and plastics workshops in many provinces, the number of Syrian refugee workers has surpassed the number of workers from Turkey. In labor-intensive workshops, starting with cities such as Istanbul, Denizli, Bursa, and Gaziantep, the unregistered employment of refugee workers is very common.

In provinces such as Gaziantep that are close to the Middle Eastern market, the footwear industry has undergone a period of revival thanks greatly to refugee labor. Because of its proximity to Syria, Gaziantep has become an industrial city that supplies the domestic market of Syria in essential industries such as textiles, knitting, footwear, and food to a considerable level. The number of small and medium-sized enterprises set up by Syrian entrepreneurs is increasing rapidly.

The construction industry, another sphere of employment, has also grown rapidly in the last two decades, thanks to the incentives provided by the AKP government, and has survived the last seven years by relying on refugee labor. The crisis that has gripped the Turkish economy for the last three years (and the construction industry is seen by some as one of the sources of the crisis) has manifested its effects on this sphere of activity as well. Despite the support provided by the government in the form of interest rate cuts in housing and other measures, the industry has been shrinking rapidly. It may be predicted that the construction industry, relying to a significant level on migrant labor, will become a source of increasing unemployment. According to the latest data, the rate of unemployment in Turkey has approached 13 percent (Anadolu Ajansı 2019). This figure does not cover the unemployed among the 3.6 million refugees.

According to UNICEF, it is held that while approximately 650,000 Syrian and other refugee children are registered at schools in Turkey, an estimated 400,000 Syrian children remain outside of the school system (UNICEF 2019). It has been determined that the foremost obstructions in children's access to education is the language barrier and socioeconomic problems. Human Rights Watch identifies three fundamental obstacles that Syrian children living outside of camps face in accessing the school system, namely language, peer bullying, and economic hardship. This is what the report has to say on the issue—we paraphrase:

> Economic hardships: families cannot meet expenses such as transportation, pedagogic material, and, when it is a question of educational centers, school fees. Child labor is a very common phenomenon within the Syrian refugee population, whom Turkey refuses to supply with work permits lest this has adverse impact on its own population of unemployed. Parents who are thus refused labor market security cannot hence receive a fair income that would be the counterpart of their labor and remain beholden to the income brought into the household by the children. (Human Rights Watch 2015)

Syrian children are employed in knitting workshops, textile factories, dried fruit factories, footwear production workshops, as mechanics in garages, on farms and in agricultural enterprises, and on the streets as vendors of tissue, bottled water, or dates (Lordoğlu and Aslan 2018).

The New Poor, the Recasting of the Middle Class

The work permits given out in Jordan, Lebanon, and Turkey do not permit the exercise of their profession by middle-class graduate Syrians. This presents a great obstacle to professional continuity for graduate Syrians. It may be observed that most middle-class Syrians who live in these three countries leave them, move to countries such as Germany, and become part of the labor market there as skilled workers.

Because educated middle-class Syrians that have sought asylum in Turkey do not have work permits, and because there is no legislation that provides them with the opportunity to practice their profession, they face great difficulties in finding jobs in their own area of specialization. Medical doctors, academics, lawyers, engineers, and other educated professionals in their mold who finished university in Syria survive under great hardships. It is very common to meet many professionals with that kind of background in workshops, sweatshops, or farms. They work twelve or thirteen hours a day and yet make a meager 1,500 to 2,000 liras per month. Because they have never before worked as manual laborers, they are hard pressed to sustain themselves under such conditions because they are not familiar with kind of labor process inherent in unskilled work, and in many cases they are laid off without their arrears being paid them because their employer is not content with the work they are doing.

The Syrian refugee community living in Turkey is of course divided into classes and strata within itself. There is a capitalist section of the community that has transferred its business to Turkey, as well as a new middle class, supporting the opposition inside Syria, that has started up in Turkey factories and workshops with the goal of exporting goods to Syria. This sector shares the rent created by the war by taking their stand within the opposition forces. This new stratum of entrepreneurs has a large share in the rise in enterprises belonging to Syrians in provinces such as Gaziantep, Urfa, Mersin, and Antakya.

Another sector is a younger generation that has become politicized with the civil war, some of whom have grown up in Turkey. A great majority are versed in a foreign language, work for international donor organizations, communicate with the new activist generation around the world, and share the same network as their own generation in the Middle East. Even if they set out on the road to Europe, they are bracing to become the new middle class of the Syrian diaspora. The number of young Syrians who somehow make it to the United States, Canada, or European countries by using these networks in order to continue their studies in those countries is increasing by the day.

From Camps to Day Labor Markets: The Reshaping of Labor Markets

Syrian immigrant workers will continue, for the present and the future, to be the unskilled and cheap labor force of the Turkish labor market and, in particular, of its unregistered segment. Even today, you can see "intermediaries" lingering before the gates of the camps, run by AFAD, in order to fill lorry dumpers or tractor trailers with thousands of refugees and take them away for daily jobs. Even factory owners have started to meet the daily labor needs of their factories by sending out intermediaries to day labor markets. You can witness the unemployed refugees who fill the day labor markets of border provinces, such as Gaziantep, Urfa, and Kilis, competing between themselves for jobs that pay twenty or twenty-five Turkish liras a day. You can also come across scavengers preying on garbage bins, children working in decrepit workshops, and cleaning ladies who work on a daily basis.

The Ünaldı region, which was the weaving and textiles production center of Gaziantep in the late Ottoman period, has now been transformed into a production zone consisting of hundreds of unregistered workshops where tens of thousands of Syrians work. A large part of the active workshops in this zone are subcontractors to which large textile firms outsource part of their production. Syrian employers oversee unregistered production activities in hundreds of workshops. Small enterprises that are active in textiles and knitting and rely mostly (to the level of 80 percent) on migrant labor have collectively turned into a special industrial zone. By the 1970s the Ünaldı region had become the center for the production of tapestry. Then it became a gigantic working-class neighborhood where Kurdish migrants who were forcibly evacuated from villages came and settled. The Kurdish workers that filled the workshops and the streets of Ünaldı in those years have now been replaced by Syrian workers. And the street vendors that used to sell local wraps filled with chickpeas have now been replaced by vendors of hummus and falafel. During noon recess you can hear Arabic rather than Kurdish on the streets. Not much has changed, though, in the subterranean mazes, where workers toil for twelve to fourteen hours a day. Piece work is the rule, wage payments are weekly, and it is children who cling to the lowest rung of the labor hierarchy. And in the surrounding neighborhoods, Syrian refugees coexist with the other indigent populations of the city (Gültekin 2019).

Another area in the center of the city is the historical zone of tanning yards. This zone has now turned into another unregistered workplace center. Nizip Avenue and the surrounding streets are predominantly filled with workshops, and the labor force flows in from the neighboring Karşıyaka area. Although filled with plastics and footwear workshops, the area, situated at the base of the historic Antep fortress, seems abandoned during the day in its deafening silence, only to come alive at sunset when thousands of migrant workers and children step out of the underground world where they toil the whole day and start walking toward Karşıyaka.

Syria and the Syrian refugees will be one of the major items on the agenda for Turkey in the years to come. Long-term plans and policies are needed in order to solve the problems accumulating by the day. How can the official participation of the Syrian workers be accomplished in the labor market of the host countries? This is easier to do as long as the international interest and assistance is sustained. It is important to maximize the coordination of the international community and the host countries now. One has to start somewhere in order to achieve all this. That somewhere is the determination of the legal status of the Syrian refugees.

Exclusion from the Labor Market and Future Threats

The high rate of unemployment among Syrian refugees also poses a serious threat for the future of the labor market of the host countries. In Turkey, within the scope of the Social Adjustment Assistance Program (SUY), established thanks to the support of international organizations, a sum of 120

Turkish liras is handed out to over 1.5 million Syrians each month through the Kızılay (Turkish Red Crescent) card system (Turkish Red Crescent Directory of Migration Services 2019). This is an important contribution to the finances of the refugees, who work for low wages in unregistered industries. Although the assistance and the support delays the entry of a part of the refugee population into the formal labor market for the moment, when this financial support starts to wind down, the situation will change, and a higher number of refugees will enter the labor market. The prolongation of the conflict in Syria is an indicator of the fact that in the future even more Syrians will seek asylum in neighboring countries. In recent days, news has spread that the more than 250,000 people who have amassed in the region as a result of the aggravation of the conflict in the Idlib area are bracing to seek asylum in Turkey. It seems that countries neighboring Syria will not be able to prevent the influx of Syrians despite the walls that have been erected and other security measures. Short of a secure system within the country itself through which refugees can build their future in tranquility, people will flee the country no matter what. They will become part of the labor market in the countries they go to as a source of cheap labor.

The fact that Syrian refugees are willing to work for low wages and under more difficult and adverse conditions is the source of a decline in work environments and labor market standards, the spread of the informal market, an increase in the tendency toward unregistered work, and a disregard for conformity with labor standards. Deterioration of work standards implies more difficult enforcement of the minimum wage and of compliance with labor legislation (ILO 2015). For instance, in interviews done with citizens of Turkey who work as farmhands in agricultural regions, I was informed that wages changed very little during the last four years. A Kurdish worker cultivating peppers in the Amik plain said, "When the Syrian workers arrived six years ago, there was a great wage differential between them and us, our wages being almost twice as high as theirs. In the last three or four years, the daily wages of the workers from Turkey have almost totally stagnated, but that of the Syrians has increased so as to nearly equal ours. The employers used this opportunity really well. It is true that wages are now equalized, but at our cost."

In interviews with workers in the knitting industry in the Ünaldı region of Gaziantep, they also pointed out that the wage differentials between refugee workers and those native to Turkey were recently reduced significantly but that this worked to the disadvantage of the workers from Turkey. Said one: "When they first came, the Syrian skilled workers received almost half of what our skilled workers received. Same for the semiskilled. The workers in package dyeing, apprentices, errand boys, etc., almost worked for nothing. Over the years, our weekly pay increased very little while they gradually raised theirs, and very rightly so because they could not have subsisted on those wages."

A Syrian skilled textile worker for his part said:

> I came here from Aleppo in 2013. What else could we have done? War, unemployment, starvation, the children's education, so we came here. I did the same thing that I'm now doing in Gaziantep, I worked on the machine. In Aleppo we have the requisite skills, I did not learn them here. When we first arrived, we rented a house together with the family of my sister. We were five and they were four, and so we lived nine people in two rooms for two years. My sister's husband, my son, and myself, the three of us were working and hardly brought in enough to look after the nine of us. We adults received four hundred [liras] per week, that makes eight hundred, and the young boy received seventy-five. We thought at that time that we would go back soon, so we stayed with two families in the same house. But we were not able to go back, and two families together was not possible, so we moved into two houses. I said we already did this job back in Aleppo, so we were skilled workers, but we were not able to make ends meet on those low wages. I changed jobs frequently, and each time my wages increased a bit more, finally to become equal to native workers. Anyway, they no longer wish to work in these jobs. They wish to go to the industrial estates and find a job with social security in large factories. Now, thank God, we're fine. The children were not able to go to school, so I'm teaching them the job. We get along.

In those countries where unregistered work is common, and employers opt for the cheaper kind of labor, it turns out that the longest employed native workers in the unregistered areas are rapidly replaced by refugee labor. The research conducted shows that the unemployment rate for refugees diminishes over time as they stay in the host country. In other words, their rate of penetration in the labor market increases. Refugees displace workers who work in unregistered areas, in particular the less educated, the women, and the elderly from the labor market. On the other hand, as refugees are increasingly hired in unregistered jobs, the citizens of the host country move up toward registered sectors. Furthermore, it has been determined that upon the entry of refugees in the labor market, women workers withdraw from the market (Suzuki et al. 2019).

Compared to the initial period when refugees arrived in Turkey, wage rates for refugees have now become more balanced, with the rate of wage increase for the host country workers decelerating. The new situation is hence a kind of equilibrium point that creates a disadvantage for workers. This is not universally true, though. In particular, wage raises for seasonal farm work have been very low during the last three or four years, and the wage differential between workers from Turkey and those from Syria has been eroding.

In Turkey, people under temporary protection have been accorded work permits since early 2016. According to a statement of 31 March 2019 made by the Ministry of the Family, Labor and Social Services, of the 96,972 aliens who have been accorded work permits, those from Syria number 31,185. The prohibition on the exercise of some professions—e.g., lawyer, pharmacist, dentist—for aliens is also valid for Syrians.

As the economic crisis has deepened in Turkey, the rise in unemployment increases poverty among the population. In a country where the middle class is rapidly crumbling, the population is increasingly impoverished; the competition between toilers is increasing, and a system is coming into being in which the Syrian poor are being pushed to the very bottom of the social hierarchy. Indigent Syrians, who have now become dispersed over all the provinces of Turkey, are now taking refuge in the poor working-class neighborhoods of the cities. These neighborhoods are becoming zones where the laborers are competing among themselves and hostility toward refugees and hate speech are becoming common occurrences.

In a country where the economic crisis is politically polarized and deepening by the day, opposition to Syrian refugees has become widespread among the Turkish population. Pumped by the media and social media, hostility toward immigrants can also be observed among workers at workplaces. At a time when unemployment is on the rise due to the economic crisis, refugees are held responsible for the problem. The right-wing populist wave that has gripped the world in recent years bases itself on hostility to immigration. In Turkey as well, political groups and parties compete with each other in order to ride this populist wave. As in previous elections, and also in recent elections, populist politicians frequently used hostility toward Syrian refugees as a theme on the streets as well as on social media simply to attract votes from the electorate.

In Jordan, approximately one-half of the refugees have reported that they have reduced the quantity and quality of the food consumed by the household, and they have also reported skipping meals. In Lebanon only 7 percent of refugees subsist at an acceptable level of food security. In Turkey, a report prepared by the association Hayata Destek (Support to Life) in Istanbul states that 12 percent of the refugee population cannot feed itself at a sufficient level and is under the threat of starvation. The same report points out that various strategies for coping with this situation have been developed, the most common being, with a share of 89 percent, turning to food products that are cheaper and less preferred. Also, 59 percent of families reduce the number of meals consumed every day, 58 percent resort to borrowing food from others, 29 percent reduce the serving size of dishes, 14 percent reduce the food intake of adults so as to be able to feed babies and children, 6 percent send family members elsewhere to eat, and 3 percent limit the amount of food women consume (Kaya and Kıraç, 2016).

Conclusion

One of the facts that has persisted throughout the centuries of experience with migration and stands out is that international migration is managed in such a way as to serve the interests of the core countries. In the last decade, we have seen that this fact has remained the same as Syrian refugees have forced the gates of Europe. Western countries started to spend billions of euros for border security while limiting the number of refugees to be admitted in line with their own needs; bribing, so to speak, peripheral countries like Turkey for the rest to stay there simply confirms this proposition. It seems that from now on Syrian refugees will be used as pawns against the Western countries. The recent steps taken in this direction seem to indicate that "days of servitude" await the Syrians. Rather than keeping the refugees away by paying out and making concessions, the international community should be preparing the conditions that create an environment in which Syrians and their children can lead a secure existence in dignity in their new countries before their hopes for the future wither away completely.

Kemal Vural Tarlan is a researcher and documentary photographer. Since 2000 he has been conducting visual sociology and anthropology research among Roma communities living in the Middle East. He lives in Gaziantep and is the general coordinator of Kırkayak Kültür and the head of the Center for Migration and Cultural Studies for the Middle East. He has been conducting cultural and anthropological research on the Gypsy communities living in the Middle East. He is visiting lecturer at Gaziantep University Communication Faculty

Notes

This chapter was translated from Turkish by Sungur Savran.

1. 138,000 Syrian refugees obtained work permits. See Turnbull (2019).
2. *Hegira* as a term signifies "migration from non-Muslim territories to the land of Islam." Although it is impossible to know the extent to which this network reached out to Syrian refugees, it will without doubt require a new chapter in the study of the labor market, labor migration, the theory of migration networks, and the sociology of migration. See Tatlılıoğlu (2013: 124).

References

Akgündüz, Yusuf, Marcel van der Berg, and Wolter Hassink. 2015. "The Impact of Refugee Crisis on Host Labor Markets: The Case of the Syrian Refugee Crisis in Turkey." *IZA Discussion Paper* 8841.

Amar, Paul, and Vijay Prashad (eds). 2014. *Arap Baharından Kesitler* [Scenes from the Arab Spring]. Istanbul: İntifada Yayınları.

Anadolu Ajansı (Anatolian News Agency). 2019. "İşsizlik Rakamları Açıklandı" [Unemployment statistics have been announced]. Retrieved 12 September 2019 from https://www.aa.com.tr/tr/ekonomi/issizlik-rakamlari-aciklandi/1556837.

BBC News in Turkish. 2019. "Türkiye'de Kaç Suriyeli Var, En Çok Suriyeli Nüfusu Hangi Şehirde Yaşıyor?" [How many Syrians live in the urban areas in Turkey?]. 31 July. Retrieved 24 August 2019 from https://www.bbc.com/turkce/haberler-turkiye-49150143#.

Calì, Massimiliano, et al. 2015. *The Impact of the Syrian Conflict on Lebanese Trade*. Washington, DC: World Bank Group. Retrieved 27 August 2019 from http://documents.worldbank.org/curated/en/2015/04/24424427/impact-syrian-conflict-lebanese-trade.

CEIC Data. 2019. "Jordan's Unemployment Rate." Retrieved 21 August 2019 from https://www.ceicdata.com/en/indicator/jordan/unemployment-rate.

Chambers, Iain. 2005. *Göç, Kültür, Kimlik* [Migrancy, culture, and identity].Translated by İ. Türkmen and M. Beşikçi. Istanbul: Ayrıntı Yayınları.

Çoban, Bilge. 2018. "Türkiye'de İşsizlik Profili Bağlamında Suriyeli Gençlerin İstanbul İşgücü Piyasasına Katılım Sorunları" [The challenges of Syrian youth to access in Istanbul labor market in the context of unemployment profile in Turkey]. *Çalışma ve Toplum* 56: 193–216.

David, Anda, Mohamed Marouani, Charbel Nahas, and Bjorn Nilsson. 2019. "The Economics of the Syrian Refugee Crisis in Neighboring Countries: The Case of Lebanon." *AFD Research Papers Series*, No. 2019–102, March. Retrieved 17 December 2010 from https://www.afd.fr/sites/afd/files/2019–04–05–33–32/Syrian percent20refugees percent20in percent20Lebanon.pdf.

Del Carpio, Ximena, Vanessa Wagner, and Mathis Christoph. 2015. *The Impact of Syrian Refugees on the Turkish Labor Market*. Policy Research working paper, no. WPS 7402. Washington, DC: World Bank Group. Retrieved 26 August 2010 from http://documents.worldbank.org/curated/en/2015/08/24946337/impact-syrians-refugees-turkish-labor-market.

Delgado Wise, R. 2013. "The Migration and Labor Question Today: Imperialism, Unequal Development, and Forced Migration." *Monthly Review* 64(9).

Development Workshop. 2016. "Fertile Lands, Bitter Lives." *The Situation Analysis Report on Syrian Seasonal Agricultural Workers in the Adana Plain*, Ankara.

Errighi, Lorenza, and Jörn Griesse. 2016. "The Syrian Refugee Crisis: Labor Market Implications in Jordan and Lebanon." *European Commission Discussion Paper*, no. 29. Retrieved 24 December 2019 from https://ec.europa.eu/info/publications/economy-finance/syrian-refugee-crisis-labor-market-implications-jordan-and-lebanon_en.

European Commission. 2016. "EU-Jordan Partnership: The Compact." Retrieved 12 September 2019 from https://ec.europa.eu/neighbourhood-enlargement/sites/near/files/jordan-compact.pdf.

Güler, Halime. 2015. "İşçi gitti mahsul kaldı" [The workers left, harvest on the ground]. *Hürriyet,* 12 September. Retrieved 10 January 2020 from http://www.hurriyet.com.tr/isci-gitti-mahsul-kaldi-30057162.

Gültekin, Mehmet N. 2019. "Kent ve Yeni Sosyal Etkileşimler: Gaziantep'teki Suriyelilerin Genel Örüntüsü, Mevcut Durumu ve Muhtemel Geleceği" [New social interactions in the city: The current and future social fabric of Syrians in Gaziantep). *GAUN Journal of Social Sciences* 18(1): 163–75.

Hanieh, Adam. 2015. *İsyanın Kökenleri* [The roots of revolt]. Istanbul: Nota Bene Yayınları.

Hayata Destek [Association to Support Life]. 2016. "Türkiye'de Çocuk İşçiliği Sorunu" [Problems of child labor in Turkey]. Retrieved 12 October 2019 from http://turkishpolicy.com/files/articlepdf/syrian-child-workers-in-turkey_en_3252.pdf.

Human Rights Watch. 2015. "Geleceğimi Hayal Etmeye Çalıştığımda Hiçbir Şey Göremiyorum: Türkiye'deki Suriyeli Mülteci Çocukların Eğitime Erişiminin Önündeki Engeller" raporu. [Report on Syrian children's access to education]. Retrieved 15 October 2019 from https://www.hrw.org/sites/default/files/report_pdf/turkey1115tu_web.pdf.

İçduygu, Ahmet, and Eleni Diker. 2017. "Labor Market Integration of Syrian Refugees in Turkey: From Refugees to Settlers." *Journal of Migration Studies* 3(1): 12–35.

ILO (International Labour Organization). 2015. *Regional Dialogue on Market Impact of Syrian Refugee Crisis in Jordan, Lebanon, Turkey, Iraq, and Egypt: Summary Report and Conclusions.* http://www.ilo.org/beirut/publications/WCMS_408999/lang--en/index.htm

———. 2018. "Response to Syrian Refugee Crisis." Retrieved 21 August 2019 from https://www.ilo.org/beirut/areasofwork/employment-policy/syrian-refugee-crisis/lebanon/lang--en/index.htm.

———. 2019. "Addressing Worst Forms of Child Labor in Jordan's Agricultural Sector." Retrieved 2 October 2021 from https://www.ilo.org/beirut/projects/WCMS_711788/lang--en/index.htm.

Kassir Samir. 2011. *Arap Talihsizliği* [Being Arab]. Translated by Ö. Gökmen. Istanbul: İletişim Yayınları.

Kaya, Ayhan, and Aysu Kıraç. 2016. *İstanbul'daki Suriyeli Mültecilere İlişkin Zarar Görebilirlik Değerlendirme Raporu* [Vulnerability assessment report of Syrian refugees in Istanbul]. Hayata Destek Derneği [Association to Support Life]. Retrieved 12 January 2020 from https://www.hayatadestek.org/wp-content/uploads/2019/06/istanbuldaki-suriyeli-multeciler-zarar-gorebilirlik-raporu.pdf.

Köse, Türey. 2016. "Nefret Mayası Tuttu" [Seeds of hatred flourished]. *Cumhuriyet,* 2 January. Retrieved 24 August 2019 from http://www.cumhuriyet.com.tr/haber/sokak/457625/nefret-mayasi-tuttu.html.

Lordoğlu, Kuvvet, and Mustafa Aslan. 2018. "Görünmeyen Göçmen Çocukların İşçiliği: Türkiye'deki Suriyeli Çocuklar" [The invisible working force of minor migrants: The case of Syrian children in Turkey]. *Çalışma ve Toplum* 3(2): 715–32.

Mercy Corps. 2019. "The Syrian Refugee Crisis in Jordan and Its Impact on the Jordanian Economy." Retrieved 23 August 2019 from https://www.mercycorps.org/sites/default/files/1_SyrianRefugeeCrisisImpactJordanEconomyExecSummary.pdf.

Öner Ihlamur, Aslı Ş., and Gülfer Öner. 2012. *Küreselleşme Çağında: Göç Kavramlar, Tartışmalar* [Migration, concepts and debates in the age of globalization]. Istanbul: İletişim Yayınları.

Pamuk, Şevket, and Roger Owen. 2002. *20. Yüzyılda Ortadoğu Ekonomileri Tarihi* [A history of Middle East economies in the twentieth century]. Translated by Ayşe Edirne. Istanbul: Sabancı Üniversitesi Yayınları.

Stave, Svein Erik, and Solveig Hillesund. 2015. *Impact of Syrian Refugees on the Jordanian Labor Market*. ILO. Retrieved 24 August 2019 from https://www.ilo.org/wcmsp5/groups/public/---arabstates/---ro-beirut/documents/publication/wcms_364162.pdf.

Suzuki, Ken, Paul Saumik, Maru Takeshi, and Motoi Kusadokoro. 2019. "An Empirical Analysis of the Effects of Syrian Refugees on the Turkish Labor Market." Retrieved 25 January 2020 from *ADBI Working Paper* 935. Tokyo: Asian Development Bank Institute. https://www.adb.org/sites/default/files/publication/491661/adbi-wp935.pdf.

Tatlıloğlu, Durmus. 2013. *Göç Sosyolojisi Açısından: Hicret* [Pilgrimage: Sociology of migration]. Sivas: Asitan Yayınları.

Toksöz, Gülay. 2004. *Uluslararası Emek Göçü* [International labor migration]. Ankara: Imaj Yayınları.

TÜİK. 2019. *İşgücü İstatistikleri, Mayıs 2019* [Labor statistics, May 2019]. Retrieved 21 August 2019 from http://www.tuik.gov.tr/PreHaberBultenleri.do?id=30691.

Turkish Red Crescent Directory of Migration Services. 2019. *Suriye Krizi İnsani Yardım Operasyonu Raporu* [Syrian crisis: Report on humanitarian operation]. Retrieved 25 February 2020 from https://www.kizilay.org.tr/Upload/Dokuman/Dosya/kasim-2019-suriye-krizi-insani-yardim-operasyonu-raporu-31-12-2019-28050091.pdf.

Turnbull, Elizabeth. 2019. "138,000 Syrian Refugees Obtained Work Permits–UNHCR." *Jordan Times*, 8 July. Retrieved 21 August 2019 from https://www.jordantimes.com/news/local/138000-syrian-refugees-obtained-work-permits-%E2%80%94-unhcr.

UNHCR (United Nations High Commissioner for Refugees). 2018. "Syrian Refugee Unit Work Permit Progress Report." Retrieved 21 August 2019 from https://data2.unhcr.org/en/documents/download/64904.

———. 2019. *Operational Portal Refugees Situations*. Retrieved 20 January 2020 from http://data.unhcr.org/syrianrefugees/country.php?id=107.

———. 2020. *The Lebanon Crisis Response Plan 2017–2020*. Retrieved 21 January 2020 from https://data2.unhcr.org/en/documents/download/68651

———. n.d. Operational Portal, Refugee Situations. Syria Regional Refugee Response. Retrieved 12 January 2020 from https://data2.unhcr.org/en/situations/syria.

UNICEF (United Nations International Children's Emergency Fund). 2019. *Turkey Humanitarian Situation Report*. Retrieved 10 January 2020 from https://www.uniceturk.org/public/uploads/files/UNICEFpercent20Turkeypercent20Humanitarian percent20Situation percent20Report_Mid-Year percent202019.pdf.

3

Images as Border
On the Visual Production of the "Migration Crisis"

Mariam Durrani and Arjun Shankar

Introduction

In 2015, there was a marked increase in the number of people fleeing conflicts in Syria, Afghanistan, and Iraq, with more than 911,000 migrants and refugees from these three countries migrating to EU nations. Over one year, the increase in migration led to tragic accidents and deaths, such as boats capsizing or people asphyxiating in trucks. This mass migration was quickly labeled the "European refugee crisis" by journalists and policymakers. Since then, the terms "refugee" and "crisis" have become fixed in relation to each other such that the collocation "refugee crisis" is assumed whenever the question of refugees or migrants is discussed. What marked this migration as a "crisis" different from the regular movement of thousands of people around the world between nations was that these individuals were willing to put themselves through daring journeys, including traveling the Mediterranean Sea on a raft or walking thousands of miles through Turkey, Serbia, and Hungary. Sadly, more than fourteen thousand people have drowned in the Mediterranean since 2014. Of the more heart-wrenching stories were those of Italian coastguards ignoring calls of distress and letting dozens of refugees drown. The desperation of these stories and geographic proximity to Europe suggest some reasons why the mass migration event caught the attention of Western audiences–the same audience who used the phrase "refugee crisis" to describe their perception of the phenomenon.

Yet, for those migrants fleeing conflict, *their* crisis began years earlier with either US-backed military interventions as part of the "War on Terror" or in the unfolding despotism of authoritarian leaders backed by Western[1] powers seeking to stifle local opposition and protest, as in Syria's case, or in global capitalist dispossessions facilitated by imperial and neocolonial superpowers. Often coproduced by Western military projects and mainstream media reports, the catch-all label of "crisis" was used to describe these migrants fleeing life-threatening conflicts in search of safety and security for themselves and their children. However, the "crisis" has not been met with mere curiosity or empathy. Instead, the borders on land and sea have become sites of heightened militarization, greater state control, and violence, with these states seeing the migration of racialized peoples as a "national security risk." The rhetoric of "crisis" and of the need to corral movement echoed across the Atlantic Ocean as asylum seekers from Honduras and other Central American states began to migrate toward the US through Mexico. For weeks, the US news media framed these asylum seekers as a "Central American caravan" that threatened to create a "border crisis."

In both European and US media discourses, the migration event is articulated as a crisis only when the borders of the white-Western state are breached by migrants seen as a large, undifferentiated brown mass threatening the "safety" of white-Western life. The "migration-as-crisis" discourse indexes a concentrated attention to policing immigration in Western states naturalized through laws that remain hidden from view. At the same time, the "migration-as-crisis" discourse also invisibilizes the economic precarity, wars, and tragic violence that migrating peoples have endured before embarking on such treacherous journeys (De Genova 2013). This attention to the migration-as-crisis, as opposed to understanding the war-as-crisis, has mobilized white nationalist movements across Europe, Canada, Australia, and America to police their national borders and prevent the "browning" of their societies (Bhattacharyya 2018). For example, according to the not-for-profit Transnational Institute, between 2014 and 2017 Europe went from five border walls—built following the 1985 Schengen agreement—to fifteen barriers along with a heavily patrolled maritime border. In 2015, Hungary's high-tech fence included thermal detection and cameras to monitor movement and speakers that blared warnings in five languages along its border with Serbia and Croatia. And yet, scholars have found that the surveillance and often violent border enforcement does not limit migration but only makes migration more dangerous (De Leon 2015).

As the "migration crisis" was framed as an epic phenomenon, images of the suffering subject, both the refugee and the migrant, began to propagate almost exponentially as "real evidence" of the emerging "crisis." De Genova (2013) argues that such images produce the Border Spectacle:

Spectacles of "illegal" passage and ever-increasingly militarized interdiction become emblematic precisely, in the haunting phrase of Joseph Nevins (2002: 144), as "landscapes of death," as well as zones that are inseparable from the accompanying experiences of rape, mutilation, disappearance and protracted irremediable trauma.

Yet, while those who are visibilized in such imagery are rendered inseparable from abject suffering, they are also rendered absolutely and radically separate from the audience. Strangely mimicking the physicalized borders between states, the image of the suffering migrant subject began to function as a *visualized border* separating the audience from the people and the experience captured in the static photograph. We offer the "image-as-border" metaphor to foreground the way that images themselves have, historically, reproduced processes of border and boundary creation. On the one hand, the metaphor mimics what scholars have described as the "dystopia" of physical borders (Abram et al. 2017), demarcations of nation-state territory that unnaturally prevent the movement of human beings. The physical borders that separate nation-states index virtual, imagined notions of identity and community, ossified by national and international law, that seek to separate people into those who "belong" inside versus outside (Anderson 1983). These imagined borders become materially consequential once they are reformulated into states of exception in which certain bodies, certain peoples, certain movements are caught within borders or between borders and even transform *into* borders (Agamben 1998; Balibar 2002; Abram et al. 2017). In this way, the image functions as an iconized border between the realities momentarily captured in the photograph and the context in which viewers see the image.

At the same time, conceptualizing the "image-as-border" also illuminates the layers of paradoxical meaning that are produced as a moment of movement is frozen in time, a frame that is then circulated to audiences ever further afield from the image's taking. As the Multiple Mobilities Research Cluster (2017: 24) writes:

> Images enact a mobility politics of their own, circulating with little or no citation, un-tethered in ways that often defy scholarly domestication, remaining ambiguous as to their origins and precise configuration. The lives and afterlives of such imagery expose the temporal depth of the aesthetics and politics of borders, the intersecting visual and political regimes.

Perhaps this is why Azoulay (2008: 89) argues in *Civil Contract of Photography* that the invention of the camera in the early nineteenth century was not merely a technological leap but an "invention of a new encounter." She explains how photographs gave people a chance to see places and peoples beyond their visual fields, a kind of "transit visa" for the viewer. Here, the image as border is further extended by the metaphor of the photograph as the "transit visa," resting upon an assumption of nation-based borders that filters how we see the image as a material artifact. The image-as-border foregrounds this viewing practice that imagines viewing an image to be akin to a literal border crossing or border encounter. This framework provides one foundation for how images become borders, particularly when the image is interpreted as providing the viewer with an "unmediated" lens into a visual field far removed from the viewer's own life.

In this vein, visual anthropologists have long shown how colonial photographers sought to "fix" racial types and bodies, believing that the photograph could be used as a kind of unmediated and authentic look at cultural Others (Pinney 1997; Rony 1996). The image of the Other—through staging, costume, static comportment—was intended to serve as the definitive representation of an entire "race." And yet, the problem remained that these typological racial imaginaries were challenged by those in the frame: the distinct individuals whose stories and humanity were conveyed through these images immediately subverted the kinds of bounded racialized cultural narratives that colonial photographers sought to tell. Colonial photographers were constantly beset by anxieties regarding the authenticity of their images precisely because they could not fix people into racial types as proof of the truths they intended (Shankar 2020). By investigating these colonialist anxieties, visual anthropologists have revealed the ways that humans grapple with the problem of "visual excess" in images—that is, the realization that the image always seems to spill beyond the intention of the photographer and whatever perceived explanatory power might be attached to it (Poole 2005). This dilemma of visual excess and the spilling beyond borders offers an apt metaphor for what is currently happening at physical borders, whose fixity continues to be questioned as real people travel across them in ways that do not fit into state-sanctioned categories and processes. Indeed, nation-state borders are constantly surveilled and safely guarded precisely because they are arbitrary constructions in the first place.

Within our theorizing of the image-as-border, images of children are an especially fraught terrain. Children's suffering has become iconic of the migrant and refugee "crisis." In fact, images of children seem to be the harshest and most heartless borders of them all, functioning within a de facto "savage slot" as perhaps the starkest reminder of the brutal violence rendered against migrant bodies as they travel across borders (Kromidas 2014). They seem to ossify passions, functioning as undeniable proof for whatever position a viewer of these images already might have about the crisis. This is partially because of how audiences view children: as agencyless, as victims, as innocent, and without their own subjectivities (Al-Ghazzi 2019). This process of perpetual dehumanization of children allows for viewers to see their bodies as "empty" signifiers. And yet, these images of suffering racialized children index the historical legacy of European colonization and savior discourses that justified efforts to dominate and maintain power, which included the ways that children of colonized subjects were racialized (Shankar 2014). Images of starving, destitute, and helpless children "somewhere" in Africa, Latin America, and South Asia were routinely mobilized in order to justify white-Western interventions and circulated across Western audiences as a means to garner empathy to the plight of the "Third World," in part as a means to pathologize previously colonized subjects who therefore needed Western powers to come save them (Chouliaraki 2012; Benton 2016; Spivak 1994). As such, images of migrant children mobilize this historical legacy and map it onto current geopolitical discourses that mix in hypernationalist sentiments with new processes of racialization to create a unique set of border discourses.

In making our claims about images-as-border and children as a central concern of these visual border constructions, we draw from four iconic images of movement that have become the source of media debates over the past five years. On 2 September 2015, three-year-old Aylan Kurdi tragically drowned in the Mediterranean Sea along with his mother and five-year-old brother. The photo of Aylan lying facedown in the sand as the waves lapped against his body produced headlines that finally seemed to "humanize" the over 16,500 migrant bodies that have drowned in the Mediterranean since January 2014. NPR reported that until the photo appeared, many Western audiences were not focused on the humanitarian crisis in Syria. Then in 2016, a photograph of a dust- and blood-covered young Syrian boy, Omran Daqneesh, spread quickly across the internet. The image of a frightened, pudgy-faced child again allowed Western audiences to recognize the plight of civilians besieged by government forces in Aleppo. Later, an image of seven-year-old Amal Hussain, a Yemeni girl suffering from severe acute malnutrition, was shared widely on social media, highlighting the suffering of Yemeni civilians amid a devastating war between Houthi rebels and a Saudi-led coalition aided by American-supplied bombs and intelligence. In late 2018, an image of a woman with her two children, running away from tear gas spread by the US border patrol at the Mexico-US border in California after she had undertaken a trek of over one thousand miles to seek refuge in the United States, reignited debates regarding white supremacy, authoritarianism, dehumanization, and militarization in the United States.

Our discussion focuses on the production and circulation of these four images of refugee and migrant children to interrogate the visual economy of racialized children's suffering. We argue that the photograph acquires value based on interlocking systems of violence—the violence endured at their homes of origin, the dangerous journey, and the violence encountered at land and maritime borders (Poole 1997; Combahee River Collective 1979). Specifically, we draw from theories in critical race studies, visual and semiotic anthropology, and critical media studies in order to show how the suffering child image mediates the conversations regarding the refugee crisis and functions as its own border.

For migrants for whom "home is the mouth of a shark," survival depends on the ability to migrate somewhere safer. In images of refugee/migrant children, we might instinctively think that the suffering of a child most immediately points to the forms of systemic violence found in their home of origin, whether that is war and extreme poverty created by local state or nonstate actors. However, the photograph itself becomes legible as an image of the suffering racialized child-subject to Western audiences based on responses by the white viewing subject, which is embedded in particular racialized and gendered ways of seeing. Drawing on Rosa and Flores's (2015) theorization of the "white listening subject" as one who "hears linguistic deficiency in racialized speaking subjects even when they engage in language practices that would be deemed normative were they produced by a white speaking subject," we posit that the "white viewing subject" sees the suffering of the racialized suffering child subject as a "crisis" produced elsewhere and by others. As such, the politics of image-making in the digital age necessitates an excavation of how racialized and gendered visual economies, in the form of *visual raciontologies*, function as a form of capitalist value creation.

Rosa and Diaz (2019) offer *raciontologies* as a theoretical framework that allows scholars to follow the "construction, circulation, surveillance, and, frequently, overdetermination of racialized models of personhood" (2019: 2). If the colonial gaze was structured to reproduce dominance over colonized subjects by colonial photographers, the racialized gaze is defined by the reformulation of the colonial gaze within modern, late-liberal capitalist media institutions. Echoing Rosa and Diaz (2019), we are interested in how media circulation of these images of children's suffering draws on raciontologies that reproduce white supremacist ideologies. This emphasis on how Western media reproduces white supremacy through the racialized gaze reveals the ways in which the media's ontological practices politicize the images of racialized children's suffering to shift attention away from the atrocities momentarily captured in the shot and, more importantly, the complicity of Western states in the ongoing violence. We question if the politicization of children's suffering in the migration "crisis" discourse has the potential to influence policies that recognize the humanity of the dispossessed, or if they allow Western audiences to momentarily consume racialized people's suffering before moving on with other concerns, leaving behind questions about how to alleviate the suffering of people "over there."

This chapter is divided into three parts, each of which captures one aspect of how images of suffering children "on the move" function as borders. In the first part, we investigate how these images force white-Western audiences to recognize the humanity of suffering migrants, even though they do so in, at best, a partial sense, only recognizing aspects of migrant humanity that fit into existing narratives of racialized Black and brown people's suffering. As such, one kind of border the image rests upon and seems to propagate is that between humanizing and dehumanizing migrant children. In the second part, we build upon the discussion of race and the suffering child by showing how these images are indexical of gendered and racialized ways of seeing, reinscribing narratives of deficiency *alongside* the experience of sympathizing with the suffering subject. That is to say, the way we interpret images of suffering children rests upon historically constituted racial boundaries as they are recontextualized in the present. In the third part, we emphasize the particular role of media institutions in creating these boundaries. Media portrayals seem to individualize suffering both in the atomizing of those depicted within the image frame *and* in the emotional responses assumed as appropriate responses to the consumption of suffering by white-Western audiences. These constructions support how the image both becomes a border for humanization and dehumanization of racialized subjects and an artifact to illustrate how neocolonial visual raciontologies continue into contemporary media institutions and their practices. Together these frames make clear how the production and circulation of these images constrain the kinds of redress that are possible, often focusing on helping individual children and their families rather than redressing the system of violence that begets their suffering.

Before we begin our analysis, we want to acknowledge that we do not hear the voices of subjects depicted in these images, nor have we conducted ethnographic fieldwork with the producers of such images. These areas of research are undoubtedly necessary. However, by focusing on the images of the suffering child and media engagement with these images, we begin to see how the refugee "crisis" is constructed visually. In other words, the "crisis" may lie in how we consume such images as much as it may be about the tragic events occurring all over the world. Without a more critical set of viewing practices, these images may never have the impact necessary to enact social or policy change.

Images as Humanizing, Images as Dehumanizing

Ever since Web 2.0 came into full bloom in the late 2000s, digital consumers have been saturated with images of suffering as they peruse their social media feeds and navigate mainstream online news media sources. If in the past images of suffering were heavily curated by journalists and mainstream media sources for consumption by their audiences, now images of suffering seem to come directly from a number of sources simultaneously and therefore from seemingly "no place" at all (Rafael 2003). Perhaps paradoxically, this lack of obvious sender can make images feel more "objective" as they circulate, compounded by the fact that an audience knows that a cameraman was there at the moment of an image's taking, providing the hint of proof or "truth" to the image itself. This feeling is only exacerbated when the images we see are so tragic: the image of a child lying face down, an emaciated girl, or a weeping mother seem to emotionally tie us to these events and make us feel as if we are experiencing these people's suffering as we voyeuristically gaze into a single moment of their lives. In this sense, the circulation of the refugee and migrant seems to do the work of humanizing these subjects, bringing their suffering to light in a way that forces us to see them and acknowledge the reality of what is happening to them.

Yet, the discourses regarding dehumanization have had a fraught history. They have been linked to human rights discourses that emerged as a "universal" claim in liberal democracies in the post–World War II period, primarily in light of the atrocities wrought during the Holocaust. The 1948 Universal Declaration of Human Rights, for example, "reaffirmed faith in fundamental human rights, and dignity and worth of the human person," the stripping away of which was considered an act of dehumanization (UDHR 1948). These types of human rights discourses have been hailed as the crowning achievements of liberal notions of justice even as the very idea of the "universal subject" imagined by the UDHR has been called into question. As early as 1947, the American Anthropological Association criticized the "universal" framing, asking: "How can the proposed Declaration be applicable to all human beings, and not be a statement of rights conceived only in terms of the values prevalent in the countries of Western Europe and America?" (The Executive Board, AAA 1947). In other words, our cultural vantage points dictate what constitutes universal humanity and what might not, when, and why. Moreover, by beginning with a post–World War II period for the production of the "universal human," histories of colonialism, imperialism, and slavery have been erased from conversations regarding how humans have been differentiated, hierarchized, and dehumanized (Johnson 2018).

Indeed, this same line of questioning permeates the decisions that audiences make when interpreting images of human suffering as dehumanizing or not. The momentary encounter with the reality of another's suffering brings the viewer to an ethical crossroads, forcing a reckoning with the extent to which we can or should consume the suffering of Others. Is it a dehumanizing act to consume someone else's suffering or not, and what visual raciontologies influence the answer? Oftentimes, the more devastating the image is–the more visceral the emotional response–the more likely it is for the image to be shared, retweeted, and further circulated across digital and print publications. The resharing of images on social media does not automatically transfer into political action or humanitarian aid, and yet this is the commonsense doctrine as to why these images are shared so widely. This begs the question: does the circulation of such images make Western audiences realize the extent of an unfolding tragedy and force them to put pressure on their political leaders to take action, or do these images become a kind of pornographic engagement, a voyeuristic pleasure in the suffering of Others?

Regarding the question of how audiences respond to images of pain and violence, Susan Sontag (2004) famously wondered about the extent to which people see images of pain and actually feel empathy for those within the image's frame. Speaking specifically of war photography, she writes:

> Photographs of the victims of war are themselves a species of rhetoric. They reiterate. They simplify. They agitate. They create the illusion of consensus. Invoking this hypothetical shared experience ("we are seeing with you the same dead bodies, the same ruined houses"), Woolf professes to believe that the shock of such pictures cannot fail to unite people of good will. Does it? (2004: 6)

Through this initial line of questioning, Sontag begins to focus the reader on the ideologies that situate how people see photographs of pain, remarking on just how much framing, mediation, and historical positioning is involved in whether or not we feel empathy, shame, or sadness at the suffering we view onscreen: are those within the frame people who we see as part of our community, or are they our enemies? In other words, are they one of "us" or are they one of "them"?

> To those who are sure that right is on one side, oppression and injustice on the other, and that the fighting must go on, what matters is precisely who is killed and by whom. To an Israeli Jew, a photograph of a child torn apart in the attack on the Sbarro pizzeria in downtown Jerusalem is first of all a photograph of a Jewish child killed by a Palestinian suicide-bomber. To a Palestinian, a photograph of a child torn apart by a tank round in Gaza is first of all a photograph of a Palestinian child killed by Israeli ordinance. To the militant, identity is everything. And all photographs wait to be explained or falsified by their captions. During the fighting between Serbs and Croats at the beginning of the recent Balkan wars, the same photographs of children killed in the shelling of a village were passed around at both Serb and Croat propaganda briefings. Alter the caption, and the children's deaths could be used and re-used. (2004: 10)

It is significant that Sontag uses an example of a photograph of a child to make her point about how images of death are more than likely political tools rather than obvious examples of tragedy. Even if we think that the pain of adults may be situated in our ideological worlds, surely the pain of children, at the very least, is above and beyond the vagaries of human difference. And yet, as Sontag points out, even when the figures in the frame are children, they do not seem to push beyond the ethnonationalist ideologies of those who are viewing. Instead, the figure of the child is *instrumentalized* as the best justification for further war, ossifying difference in how viewers make sense of the pain of the child being seen on screen.

When the photograph of the body of three-year-old Aylan Kurdi, who had drowned in the Mediterranean after his family had escaped the Syrian war, was catapulted into the global news cycles and became the iconic image of the "refugee crisis," it was accompanied by heated discussions as to whether it was morally and ethically appropriate to publish the image of a small child lying face down on a Turkish beach. A number of journalists and activists argued that such images are necessary in order for Western voters to understand the human toll of the war in Syria and the impact of European policies determined to limit migration into its borders (Mackey 2015). The question might be less about the circulation of images themselves and more about *how* they are circulated: what information is provided, what information is left out, and who is meant to consume these images. This is perhaps why visual and media studies scholars acknowledge that while journalists turn to images as a way to represent moments of crisis to public audiences, they remain reluctant to develop standards and practices that "account for the particularities of visual modes of knowing" (Zelizer 2010, cited in Ristovska and Price 2018). Without a critical analysis for how visual modes of knowing evoke raciontologies within the news media, it is unlikely that the media will change how racialized children's suffering is shown and circulated.

These circulations go far beyond the intentions of news media outlets, particularly given the proliferation of social media as a site for news-related information gathering and sharing. In her genre analysis of how the Kurdi image was appropriated across digital discourses, Mortensen (2017) found that *image recontextualization* is the most frequent mode by which audiences receive the Kurdi image. She follows the hashtag #humanitywashedashore to observe how the Kurdi image is decontextualized and recontextualized across social media through posts and likes. She excavates instances when the figure of the drowned child is isolated, and how the figure is inserted into new contexts such as nonrealistic drawings, photo collages, unaltered photos with text, and other photos. Ultimately, Mortensen concludes that the ubiquity of digitally circulating icons of crisis does not produce consensus as to what the humanitarian response should be. She remarks:

> While the visual icon swiftly became a standard reference in debates about the "refugee crisis," short hand for the humanitarian catastrophe and the missing political solutions, the appropriations point to diverging interpretive frameworks and local receptions. (2017: 1159)

In fact, Mortensen's study illuminates what one might expect: the iconic image is more likely to be recontextualized and instrumentalized to foment the anti-immigrant, anti-Muslim discourses echoed across the populist, white nationalist politics of twenty-first-century Europe.

At the very least, what Mortensen's study suggests is that when we get access to such images on our social media feeds, the individuals within the frame are "frozen" and become instrumentalized for the arguments made by those seeing and circulating these images. When we see images of suffering refugees and migrants, what is within the frame is always mediated by its path of circulation and the discourses that surround them. We might find ourselves seeing an image that was sent from a friend, directly from a photographer, from alternative news sites, or from the mainstream media, with each source providing textual context that reframes how these images and thus the stories of the people in the images are seen, consumed, and recontextualized. In other words, the information we glean and the political possibilities we assume *based* on these images are not so much about the image, per se, but the visual economies through which they circulate and are consumed. For example, when the Kurdi image inspired Ai Weiwei to reenact the pose on the beach of Lesbos in an effort to create a tribute to the child and other drowned refugees, the appropriation was met with criticism and skepticism about reenactment as an insensitive aestheticization of people's suffering (Jones 2017). Similarly, when *Charlie Hebdo* circulated a cartoon depicting a grown Kurdi as a sex attacker eager to grope European women in skirts, it was condemned for its racist rationalization of young Kurdi's death as a way to keep white European women safe from Muslim men.

Yet, photographs still seem to make self-evident truth claims. As visual studies scholars have described, the realism of documentary photography is "a core attribute that established its privileged claim on truth, facticity, and intelligibility" linked to the medium's evidentiary, typified, and mimetic dimensions (Feldman 1997: 24; Tagg 1993). Take, for example, another iconic image of the suffering child. In August 2016, the Aleppo Media Center posted an image of five-year-old Omran Daqneesh sitting expressionless, covered in ash and blood, in an ambulance after an airstrike destroyed his home where he lived with his parents and two siblings. Reading the Pictures, a web-based media organization, called attention to how major news publications such as NBC News and the *Washington Post* claimed that the image realistically portrayed how the Syrian war depicted the "horror" of children's suffering (Adelman 2017). Many commentaries focused on Daqneesh's impassivity indicating the ways that the photograph accrued value. While the child's face was emotionless, "observers read Daqneesh's blank face as an invitation to laminate their own feelings onto, and over, the photo" (Adelman 2017). What is implied, yet remains unsaid, is that this sentimentality relies on the visual raciontologies emplaced in the production, circulation, and reception of this image. When CNN reported on this story, the anchor began to tear up: "What strikes me is that we shed tears, but there are no tears here." Shortly after, a series of articles on CNN and other media sites cropped up with the headline "Story of Little Syrian Boy Moves CNN Anchor to Tears." For white Western audiences, the image of Daqneesh's suffering was seen as an unmediated truth, proven by the listlessness of the child's face—a listlessness that seemed to prove itself because of just how radically Other it seemed to those who were viewing the image because the child was not seen crying. This interpretative move was accompanied and overwritten by the story of white women journalists crying, an emotional reaction that resonated so completely with that of the expected audiences of CNN that these white women's tears became their own legitimate news headlines that also served as the *real proof* for why this child's suffering mattered. In other words, the child's suffering was not necessarily self-evident in and of itself, but it became so when accompanied by the white newscaster's emotional response.

Then, in June 2017, another image of Daqneesh was filmed by pro-Syrian government news agencies and circulated on global online news media platforms. This time he was all cleaned up, hair neatly combed, and with a smile on his face (McKirdy and Tawfeeq 2017). For viewers who had seen the original image of a dust-and-blood-covered, expressionless Daqneesh, the second image of him offered the viewer some comfort, a visible proof that things in Syria were not "that bad." But the second image also challenged the facticity of the original image, forcing viewers to wonder about the legitimacy of images of children's suffering. The second image was accompanied by an interview with Daqneesh's father, who accused rebel groups and the international media of using his son's image for anti–Syrian government propaganda. These tensions regarding the use of Daqneesh's image by media outlets—as an obvious example of atrocity in Syria, as a manipulation by Western news media or rebel groups, as lacking facticity—direct our attention to the unresolved signification of such images. The analysis of the two images of Daqneesh were instrumentalized for conflicting media narratives whether it is media coverage by CNN on their news shows and online, media coverage by the video news agency Ruptly (owned by a Kremlin-backed news channel), or coverage in the form of a YouTube video of a pro-opposition journalist Mousa Al Omar, who said Daqneesh's father was speaking as a hostage of the Syrian regime (Al Omar 2017).

As such, because of the way that images of migrant suffering reach our screens, images are recontextualized as borders unto themselves. We know that we are seeing people within the frame, but they and the violence in the image are "safely" behind the screen, flattened, distanced, and separated from us. This process of distancing also becomes the basis for a particular kind of dehumanizing: Yes, the people on screen are certainly "real" people, but the images make it clear that they are certainly *not* us. At the same time, because the people onscreen cannot speak, their images become a matter of debate and argument by those who consume these images. The images become blurred and contested borders, at once hardened against any counterbelief while also porous, allowing for significations and new meanings as they circulate This is how the images of Daqneesh suffering can be read as both positioning him as the "face of Aleppo" as well as propaganda against the Syrian regime. Similarly, the image of a smiling Daqneesh can be read as evidence of a child well cared for and as propaganda supporting the Syrian regime. How we interpret these images becomes its own kind of border creation or border crossing.

But this choice is not unmediated or random. Instead, this section has argued that the suffering racialized child-subject is constructed through a political economy of visual consumption that reproduces visualized raciontologies that influence how images of racialized "black and brown" suffering child-subjects are consumed. This visualized raciontology rests squarely on the historically entrenched notions of liberalism that already constitute racialized subjects along the axis of humanization/dehumanization, a situation that already presupposes their potential abjection. In this sense, Walter Johnson puts it best when he describes the way that discourses on dehumanization function in relation to discourses of black struggle and liberation, remarking:

> I continue to think that we have more to lose by employing the word "dehumanization" that we have to gain from it. First, because it is sucked too easily into the culturally dominant notion of redress through human rights. Second, because it is too sticky: it leaves a trace of abjection on those it (sincerely) seeks to celebrate, advance and protect ... it frames black history as a "never-ending audition" for humanity. (Johnson 2018)

Similarly, for those migrants racialized as they travel, the image seems to only reinscribe the humanizing/dehumanizing binary, functioning as the boundary condition for the "audition" that circumscribes migrants' life possibility. What this discussion tells us is that we must move away from simplistic "dehumanization" rhetoric to think more critically about the political and economic relations that historically situate how we determine migrants' humanity. We might ask: if their humanity is a border that is constantly encountered and must be crossed, then what possibility is there for redress of the political, economic, and material grievances that images are intended to be the conduit for?

In the next section, we further interrogate the history of image making that focused its colonial gaze on producing ideas of racialized pathology, ideas that continue to undergird how contemporary images of formerly colonized subjects' suffering accrue value.

The Colonial Gaze Becomes the Racialized Gaze

Anthropologists who focus on visual economies have argued extensively that modern circulation and consumption of images are based heavily on the history of colonial and imperial social relations. Anthropologist Deborah Poole, for example, draws on Edward Said's compulsory work on *Orientalism* in order to describe the "imperial condition" of photography. For her, questions regarding "image value"–that is to say, what kinds of images we think are important and should be produced and circulated–are entirely based on a long history of image production that largely overdetermines what kinds of images "sell." In her discussion, she notes that the "how" and "why" of white-Western audiences deriving pleasure from images are organized through a history of circulations focused on the "primitive" Black and brown Other, whose bodies were meant solely for white consumption (Poole 1997; Rony 1996; Lutz and Collins 1993). In many cases, this process of primitivizing through image making produced the perception of Black and brown peoples as "savage" and "barbaric," peoples whose "violent" tendencies justified colonial and imperial extermination or, at best, their need to be civilized by the white man. Based on this scholarship, maintaining the imagined border separating civilization from primitivity was a direct and deliberate purpose of colonial imagery. At the same time, colonial photographers related gender and age to race in order to position certain subjects as destitute, helpless, impoverished, and unhappy so as to justify their interventions. As Shankar (2022) has noted elsewhere, the boundary between the savior and those who are in need of saving continues to shape the discourse around suffering. Women and children were central to these early visual representations, with women sometimes being characterized as "ignorant children" and therefore justifying colonialist policies based on the idea that "white men are saving brown women from brown men" (Spivak 1994; see also: Khoja-Moolji 2020).

Colonial and imperial projects depended on the production and circulation of racialized pathology discourse and media that clearly indicated the lack of sophistication of the racialized subject. At the same time, the use of colonial visual depictions depended on media ideologies regarding viewers' raciontologies and therefore produced them: that the people in the photograph had consented to having their picture taken, that what was being depicted was "really" happening, and that the interpretation of seeing the racialized subject in the frame as threatening, or destitute, or exotic was a universal interpretation that necessitated a *particular* response by the civilized viewer and her compatriots. In the historical period that marked the independence of previous colonized peoples, these earlier colonial visual depictions found their footing in humanitarian and development imagery, which used the figure of the brown and Black child in order to justify continued interventions and produced what Teju Cole (2012) characterized as the "white savior industrial complex." In much of this imagery, women and children have stood for abject poverty in "Third World" countries (Manzo 2008), and these images are meant to produce an empathic, if distanced, stance toward the suffering of Others, facilitating philanthropic capital flows from the "First-to-Third" worlds. Images of children, functioning as images of the "uncivilized, uncared for, savage child," have been useful for both NGOs and governments to legitimate their interventions as well as to legitimate the larger project of outsider-led "development." Yet, these images are paradoxical in that they seem to justify intervention based on the same iconography and assumptions of earlier colonial imagery. As such, Manzo (2008) explains, the question for NGOs, and journalists as well, when using images of children experiencing abject suffering and violence is whether the accompanying texts or articles "can nullify the contradictory subliminal messages that emanate from the iconography of childhood" (2008: 632).

The suffering of racialized children, including in the case of racialized migrants and refugees, is consistently and constantly depicted across digital, analog, and print platforms. However, despite the fact that, as mentioned above, digital images may sometimes seem like they come from "no place," they are actually generated and disseminated by a group of mediators who have a disproportionate power to decide whether and how we should see the suffering of Others. These people, who Gursel (2016) calls "image brokers," make "the decisions behind the photographs we encounter in the news—and the organizations in which they work, whether agencies, publications, or visual content providers, [and] act as mediators for views of the world. Image brokers collectively frame our ways of seeing" (Gursel 2016: 2). Take, for example, the *New York Times* exposé about the young Yemeni child, Amal Hussain, whose emaciated body was depicted as part of the *Times*'s attempt to get American audiences to understand and care about the political situation in Yemen that has been produced by Saudi imperial interests in the region and facilitated by America's intimate relationship with the Saudis. The *New York Times*, in the aftermath of the exposé, acknowledged the difficult decision-making process that went into publishing the photographs of the emaciated girl who had been described by her doctor as such: "No meat. Only bones."

> *Times* editors don't decide lightly to publish pictures of the dead or the dying. The folders of photo editors bulge with powerful images that did not make the cut because they were considered too horrific, too invasive, or too gratuitous. ... The images we have now published out of Yemen may be as unsettling as anything we have used before. But there is a reason we made this decision. ... The story of Yemen and all its suffering is one that must be told, and as powerful as Declan's writing is, it cannot be told in words only. ... This is our job as journalists: to bear witness, to give voice to those who are otherwise abandoned,

victimized, and forgotten. And our correspondents and photographers will go to great lengths, often putting themselves in harm's way, to do so. (Nagourney and Slackman 2018)

Here, the *Times* editors are articulating a media ideology and their theory of the image in their justification for showing Amal Hussain's emaciated body, arguing to its audience that the story of Yemeni suffering *cannot* be told without seeing these images onscreen. It is the affective immediacy of this suffering that the *Times* editors seemed to suggest was the necessary contribution of the image without which (white) Americans cannot or will not reckon with the plight of the Yemeni people. This is why the "brutally honest" images of Yemeni suffering could not be "sanitized." At the same time, much of the justification for showing these images was the evocation of the heroic reporter who will "go into harm's way" to bear witness, a phrasing that obviated the agentic altruism of the journalist in opposition to the complete helplessness–"abandoned" and "forgotten"–of those who are depicted within the frame. We might say that this boundary is but one example of how image borders must function by maintaining racialized difference "that organizes bodies into victims and saviours" (Khoja-Moolji 2020: 5; see also: Shankar 2022).

David Furst, *New York Times International* picture editor, explained their decision further by stating: "But we felt it would be a disservice to the victims of this war to publish sanitized images that don't *fully* reflect their suffering" (quoted in Nagourney and Slackman 2018; our emphasis). In this justification, the modifier "fully" indexes that people's suffering cannot be felt unless the entirety of their suffering is revealed through the image. This ideology connects the devastation in the image to some notion of "service" being provided by the media as opposed to a critical discussion of how *New York Times* images and their circulation provide little to no "service" to the victims and their suffering. In other words, the *Times* editors are implicitly drawing from the racialized history of which it is a part, as a savioristic media source doing "good work." Indeed, there seems to be some pleasure in this voyeuristic look at racialized suffering, as the editors acknowledge that the images are "riveting." But riveting for whom? Would those experiencing this suffering find the images "riveting," or is this type of imagery "riveting" only for those audiences who sit and consume them from half a world away?

Of course, this is not the first time such justifications have been deployed. Nearly thirty years prior to the now ubiquitous circulation of digital images of racialized suffering, the photojournalist Kevin Carter set in motion an intensely debated conversation on whose suffering should be depicted and why after his photograph "Starving Sudanese Child Being Stalked by a Vulture" was published. Taken in 1993, Carter's photograph shows an extremely malnourished Sudanese girl keeled over as a vulture awaits her imminent death. Rather than help the child, Carter took a photograph, seeking to make Americans aware of the plight of the Sudanese in the wake of the Sudanese civil war but ultimately resulting in severe ethical debates regarding when and if photographers should intervene in the contexts in which they work. But most importantly, Carter's imagery forced a reckoning with the problematic of image immediacy itself. What was most shocking about the incident was how the potential for the image's immediacy when viewed—an unquestioned feeling that one is seeing a social ill that must be rectified—seemed to replace the demand for immediate need to help; that is to say, the image's immediacy replaced the need to reduce the suffering of the child, aestheticizing it and distancing Carter from the need to do anything other than bear witness and share the image with Western audiences. In the end, the case of the Yemeni child image seemed to suggest the very same thing: in the image's aftermath it was revealed that the child had died. Even as the image did nothing to rectify her suffering, she became iconized as a representation of violence, and her image was instrumentalized for the *Times*'s demonstration of how reporters go into "harm's way" to publish unsanitized images that "fully" reflect suffering and, therefore, provide the potential for redress.

The *New York Times* publication of Yemeni children's suffering and Carter's image of the starving Sudanese child highlight the ways in which such images draw on a particular kind of visual raciontology that fetishizes certain racialized subjects and hypervisibilizes Black, brown, and Muslim "suffering subjects" as justification for their need for help. As such, an analysis of visual raciontologies connected to the suffering subject could benefit from an attention to the depiction of suffering subjects perceived as white.

Depicting "white suffering" has traditionally been seen as gratuitous and insensitive, unnecessary given that audiences already understand that tragedy has occurred and that they must show solidarity with those who have been directly affected even if images of violence and suffering do not scroll across their media feeds. Overwhelmingly, the perceived suffering of white subjects has been focused on particular kinds of classed trauma: abject rural poverty, and in the last twenty years, drug overdoses, gendered domestic violence, and school/mass shootings. For example, in the 1930s and funded by the US agriculture department, the Farm Services Administration's visual project documented the lived experience of many rural, white farmers and families made destitute by the Great Depression. Solicited by the FSA, photographers and journalists collected a body of 250,000 images intended to popularize the case for the capitalist investments and bureaucratic restructuring of the New Deal. President Lyndon Johnson's 1964 declaration of the "war on poverty" is visually documented by an image of him visiting a family in rural Kentucky. Depictions of rural America, and specifically

Appalachia, have been critiqued for Othering the rural, white poor as in need of interventions, much like the development imagery discussed earlier. More recently, the circulation of images and video of people overdosing due to opioid addiction draw on an elitist gaze that sees certain persons as somehow deficient, abject, and in need of immediate help. However, cases of rural white drug addiction have been dealt with quite differently than earlier ones, which were associated with impoverished Black and brown peoples, with rehabilitation and incorporation being the primary strategies for redress.

In other cases, images of white-appearing people fleeing terrorist violence from the 1994 Oklahoma City bombings continue into the present era of mass shootings, where it is often white children fleeing, wounded, and distraught. Yet, the characterization of such violence has rarely been racialized when perpetrated by white criminals. Instead, white murderers are often considered "lone wolves," who have individuated pathologies that do not represent "all white people." Similarly gendered domestic violence of men abusing and killing their wives and children are seen as individual pathologies rather than as tokens of an endemic and systemic gender inequality and patriarchy in white society. Even if they are pathologized, they are depicted in humanizing ways as lonely, disturbed people who did not get the support they needed in order to deal with their mental illness. This problematic ableist framing further stigmatizes those who might actually be mentally unwell by linking mental illness to criminal and violent behavior. By contrast, attacks by nonwhite actors—whether in the public or private spheres—have been treated as examples of the pathology of entire cultural and racial groups, as in the now-ubiquitous anti-Muslim racist stereotypes that imply that all Muslims could be potential terrorists (Beydoun 2018; Durrani 2018; Kazi 2019). Images of Muslims as inherently violent consistently dehumanize these individuals, rendering them villainous and beyond resuscitation, similar to how *Charlie Hebdo* used Kurdi's image to imagine his future as a grown Muslim man who rapes white women.

Even images of white-passing refugees seem to follow this trope. Take, for example, the case of Bosnian refugees who migrated all over Europe in the early 1990s in the aftermath of the brutal violence of the Bosnian War. These refugees, like their contemporary counterparts, were fleeing violence and looking for stable homes in new contexts. Yet, unlike current refugee depictions, Bosnians were relatively well integrated into their new contexts, finding some economic opportunity and stable livelihoods. As Baker (2017) argues, this integration was largely due to the depictions of Bosnians that did not seem to fit normal stereotypes of Muslims because of their ability to pass as racialized white subjects. She writes:

> Throughout the 1970s and 1980s, news images of Palestinian hijackers and Libyan and Iranian state-sponsored terrorists, mediated further by the ste-

reotyped terrorist villains of Reagan- and post-Reagan-era Hollywood, had mapped the security threat of Islam on to brown, male, vigorous bodies of "Middle Eastern" appearance, and more specifically on to "Arabs." ... These Islamophobic representations catch today's refugees in their net but exempted Bosnians. Light-skinned Bosnians wearing Western clothes were not "visibly Muslim" in European symbolic politics, even when they were Muslim by religion and ethnic heritage and did not resemble the stock figure of the Islamic fundamentalist and militant.

That is to say, the figure of the Muslim was and is racialized as nonwhite, affecting the way that people can see their suffering and the possibility of redress of their suffering. When the image of the refugee crisis is a nonwhite Muslim person, the image often evokes questions about national safety and security, even when it is a three-year-old Syrian child lying facedown on a Turkish beach, as in the case of its subject's appropriation for the *Charlie Hebdo* cartoon.

These visual raciontologies have implications for how visual economies function: how images circulate, how bodies accrue value, and the differential possibilities for redress of migrant suffering, topics that we address in the next section.

Visual Economies and the Politics of Giving

In thinking about why and how certain racialized images gain social power in their circulation, we must also consider the visual economies of images, i.e., the asymmetries of capitalist power that determine which kinds of images circulate in greater numbers, over greater distances, for a longer period of time (Poole 2007). That is to say, not all images are created equally given their histories and given the regimes of production and consumption that structure how images circulate, influencing what audiences are intended to feel and how they respond. As Chouliaraki and Blaagard (2013) write, analyzing the production and circulation of migrant and refugee imagery reveals the

> social relations of power and the forms of moral–political action that the visual representations of such vulnerability call on us to perform and ... to the truth claims and modes of identification with those who suffer—what, that is, these visuals tell us about ourselves as moral actors and how they invite us to engage with them. (Chouliaraki and Blaagard 2013: 254)

As we have discussed, what we see in these images, including what is in the frame, what is not, and the context of circulation, interpellates the audience to respond. Particularly in the case of suffering children, the response can be immediate and personal. From a raciontologies perspective, we have discussed how a colonial gaze undergirds a contemporary racialized gaze that produces regimes of value and the responses that are deemed appropriate or not. This is why bodies that have been historically marginalized– based on class, caste, race, gender, sexuality, and ability (among others)– have a hard time accruing value beyond what is expected within dominant framings (Poole 1997). We might say that value begets value, and so to create surplus value almost necessarily involves the reproduction of hegemonic imagery.

This racialized hegemonic visual order facilitates a very particular form of giving aid while diverting attention away from the political and economic processes that produced such suffering in the first place. Instead, the images of suffering subjects facilitate an already ongoing circuit of capital–what some have termed "poverty capital" (Roy 2010) and others the "compassion economy" (James 2010)–which relies on images of suffering to promote the continued growth of the help economies by getting individuals to give funds (Shankar 2014). Indeed, current reports suggest that one in three people give to help organizations, and consumers assume that this is the best way of solving the problem of suffering they bear witness to in these images. This form of philanthropic giving functions paternalistically and is heavily gendered, assuming and reproducing the idea that those women and children cannot or no longer care for themselves and therefore need external forms of care in order to survive. Take, for example, the circulation and reception of the *New York Times* decision to publish the photograph of Yemeni child Amal Hussain. Although she died soon after the image was taken by the *Times*, viewers of the image "expressed heartbreak. They offered money for her family. They wrote in to ask if she was getting better." Each of these responses was individualized, concerned most directly with the fate of the child and less with the systemic causes for the malnourishment of Yemeni children caught in the violent conflict. In fact, what this form of response seemed to occlude was any awareness of how the United States was and is implicated in the Saudi-led strikes that resulted in the abject suffering and deaths of Yemenis like Hussain (Walsh and Schmitt 2018). Audiences of such images are not made aware of the arms and military training provided by the US government to the Saudis. Instead, those who read the exposé felt the need to give directly to Hussain's family, driven to solve their own feelings of helplessness and sympathy by offering money to help the suffering child, as if the relation between those on each side of the image-as-border was direct and immediate.

A similar situation unfolded in the aftermath of the circulation of an image of a Honduran woman, Maria Meza, taken on 25 November 2018 as she was seen running in fear holding the hands of her two children as tear gas was released by border patrol officers at the Mexican border. The US border patrol apparatus has become an iconic and physicalized symbol of the Trump regime's racist rhetoric and policies regarding migrants, viewing them as violent and pathological invaders who will cripple the "American" way of life. In April 2019, Trump doubled down on this anti-immigrant speech, claiming that the United States is "full" despite the fact that declining birth rates and increasing elderly populations have actually created a labor crisis for many of the towns and smaller cities in the United States.

There were several ways that Meza's image was deployed when it first began to circulate that bear special attention and point to the political economy of images of Central American asylum seekers at the US-Mexico border. First, the image of the mother and her two children was invoked by many as evidence of the Trump regime's anti-immigrant violence and to disprove the fearmongering rumors that he continues to stoke about the violent nature of those coming across the border as "rapists" and the like. This argument relied heavily on the fact that those on screen were women and children. How could it be, the argument went, that such helpless and vulnerable women and children could be the kinds of violent perpetrators that Trump claimed? In other words, it was the gendering of this particular visual raciontology and the ideologies associated with women and children that produced one of the fundamental axes of the image-as-border and, in turn, facilitated the particular form of empathy and outcry that ensued thereafter. On the other hand, the image was also used by some commentators to obviate the shortcomings of this mother, a different discursive path also premised on the gendered border image. A quick perusal on Twitter in the aftermath of the image's taking and circulation revealed a counternarrative to the seemingly obvious view that this image was a moment of suffering. Instead, this counternarrative justified what was seen within the image by arguing (1) that this kind of direct violence was the only way to keep these migrants from coming across the border and that the circulation of this image would "show" these migrants that they better stay away and (2) that the image proved the fact that this woman was unconcerned with the well-being of her children in pushing them to make such a treacherous journey.

These claims rest upon particular visual raciontologies that allow viewers to question whether or not images have been manipulated depending on what other racial ideologies they want a photograph to reinforce. *Even if* the viewer were to admit to the authenticity of the suffering they are seeing within the frame, they might still question the image by critiquing what "is not seen"; the fact that the photographer has intentionally taken this image at the expense of so many other images that might actually "reframe" the image of suffering they are seeing. Or the viewer might question the validity of the image not based on what is in the frame but instead on its networks of circulation. Indeed, in the example above, many of those who were dismissive of Meza's plight pointed to the fact that the photograph must have been manipulated, and that, even if it had not been manipulated, it was taken in order to manipulate the political leanings of those who view it by powerful media institutions like the *New York Times*. The photograph, therefore, became less about the suffering onscreen and more about the raciontologies of the photographer or the institutions who picked it up and circulated it.

The particularities of the aftermath of the image's circulation were also significant. Within one month of the incident, it was announced that the mother and her two children had been allowed into the United States, a circumstance that was hailed as a moment when political activism might actually beget the kinds of social change that we imagine. Indeed, the image seemed to play a key role in this activist possibility, the mother and child so obviously in need and at risk producing collective empathy that needed immediate recognition and redress. And yet, when we analyze just a bit deeper, we might question the "success" of this sort of image-focused, atomized activism. What seems apparent is that what such images do well is focus our gaze, not on a collective suffering or on the policies and practices that produce violent oppression for many but instead on the individuals who we see within the frame: whether we want to see them as victims or savages. That is to say, images like that of the mother with her children resonate because they function as a border, focusing on the specific horrors perpetrated on these individuals, therefore obscuring the historical, political, and economic processes at play and the systemic violence perpetrated by certain Western nations on racialized brown and Black migrants.

Conclusion

Images of children have become iconic of the migrant and refugee "crisis," functioning as perhaps the starkest reminder of the violence rendered against migrant children's bodies as they travel across borders. The images and stories of Aylan Kurdi, Omran Daqneesh, Amal Hussain, and Maria Meza holding her children have indexed both the intense suffering of migrants as well as the callous lack of empathy that various states have shown to those who are seeking to find better lives for themselves and their children. And yet, these images of suffering children also index the historical legacy of European colonization and savior discourses that justified efforts to dominate and maintain power. In the postcolonial moment, colonizer-colonized relationships were reproduced through the circuits of humanitarian and development aid, claiming that newly independent nation-states could not govern themselves because they could not take care of their own people, women and children in particular. Images of starving, destitute, and helpless children in Africa, Latin America, and South Asia were mobilized in order to justify white-Western interventions and circulated to white-Western audiences as a means to garner empathy to the plight of these "Third World" peoples (Benton 2016). The production of empathy that such images garner is distanced and separated, never implicating its audiences in the suffering of these children despite the fact that poverty in the Global South has and continues to be in large part a byproduct of colonization and imperialism. As such, images of migrant children mobilize this historical legacy overlaid by hypernationalist discourses, creating a unique set of border discourses. It is in this sense that the current chapter reframes the image-as-border through which these multiple narratives and discourses are contested.

In each of the cases provided, the images of women and children function as borders and render mute the larger discussions of policies and practices that caused the suffering of these and so many others. De Leon (2019) points to the way that this individualizing of suffering, framed within journalistic images, occludes as much as it produces. In the aftermath of yet another photo of a child at the US-Mexico border, this time a young girl Valeria Ramirez with her father, De Leon lamented the fact that this kind of photograph could never truly capture the extent of the epidemic, no matter how "riveting" the image. Perhaps, he suggests, we need a different kind of image, not one focusing the gaze on the bodies of already suffering individuals, whose historical racialization makes their suffering always visible yet produces no sustained change.

To illustrate this point, he posted a map on Facebook that showed the locations of each person found dead at the border, marked by a red dot, accompanied with the caption:

> Many people are outraged (sparked via a photo) about the death of Oscar Alberto Martinez Ramirez and his 23-month-old daughter Valeria. Please know that many migrants (including Oscar and Valeria) have lost their lives because of the US border policy known as "Prevention Through Deterrence." There aren't enough images in the world to convey the pain that this policy has caused but here is one that hints at the scale of this brutality. Each of these red dots is a person who has died because of America's federal border policies.

This quantitative rendering accompanied by a caption does something very different than the images of Maria Meza or Amal Hussain or Valeria Ramirez. Unlike the media ideologies espoused by the *New York Times*, which argued that the *only* way to rectify political violence was through "riveting" photographs "fully" depicting abject suffering, De Leon rightly points us to the fact that *no number of individual images of suffering* can ever capture the extent of the devastation that migrants and refugees experience because of policies and practices enforced by Western governments. Unlike images we have discussed thus far, his image seems to take the viewer in a different direction, one in which redress does not always necessitate the voyeuristic gaze into the suffering of Others. Instead, the image he provides highlights the scale of the crisis, rendering visible its systemic nature and the policies that have produced such brutal and violent death.

But the question is: can images like the map De Leon provides, when shared with people who have been gazing upon brown and Black suffering for nearing two hundred years, truly make an emotional impact, or are they, by the very intransigence of visual raciontologies, rendered mute before they ever reach our screens?

This question continues to challenge us. In the United States in 2021, as a new regime led by Joe Biden and the Democrats continued, and even increased, the number of deportations out of the United States, images of Haitian migrants fleeing border police began to circulate online. These images showed Haitian people running from border police who rode on horseback, evoking the figure of the white cowboy or Southern slave patroller ready to lasso the indigenous person or enslaved person in nineteenth-century America. In the aftermath, online discussions centered on the racialized brutality of American policies and the inhumanity of the techniques deployed by border patrol. Responding to the criticism of these images, Biden's regime promised that border police will no longer ride on horseback when seeking to capture and deport Haitian migrants (Hernandez 2021). In this absurd example of image-as-border ideology, the Biden regime's answer was to remove horses rather than remove the people riding the horses. This decision has ensured that US audiences would not have to be exposed to these specific kinds of violent images and would not have to acknowledge the very violence of militarized border regimes, ongoing deportations, and the urgency of these issues for migrants and their families. Yet again, the humanity of those refugees seeking a better life is rendered practically invisible, even as images of their suffering are made hypervisible for voyeuristic consumption by audiences who remain safely hidden behind a screen.

Mariam Durrani is a feminist anthropologist whose research brings together scholarship on transnational Pakistani Muslim youth, race and racisms, migration and mobility, empire, and the neoliberalization of higher education in the United States and Pakistan. She is an assistant professor of anthropology at Hamilton College.

Arjun Shankar is assistant professor of culture and politics at Georgetown University. His research draws from theories in globalization and development, digital and visual ethnography, critical race and postcolonial theory, and curiosity studies. In his current book project, *Brown Saviors and their Others*, he takes India's burgeoning help economy, specifically the education NGO sector, as a site from which to interrogate how colonial, racial, and caste capitalism undergird transnational and digitized NGO work in contemporary "global India."

Note

1. We use "West" in this chapter not as an actual physicalized location but as a colonial construction that conceptually separates colonizing nation-states from the "rest" (Trouillot 2003). The idea of the West finds a number of contemporary manifestations, including in the idea of the "Global North" and the "First World" and in the US imperial regimes.

References

Abram, Simone, Bela Feldman Bianco, Shahram Khosravi, Noel Salazar, and Nicholas de Genova. 2017. "The Free Movement of People around the World Would Be Utopian." *Identities: Global Studies in Culture and Power* 24(2): 123–55.
Adelman, Rebecca. 2017. "Overshadowed by His Photo: The Afterlives of Omran Daqneesh." *Reading the Pictures*. Retrieved 20 September 2021 from https://www.readingthepictures.org/2017/02/omran-daqneesh-visual-culture/.
Agamben, Giorgio. 1998. *Homo Sacer: Sovereign Power and Bare Life*. Palo Alto, CA: Stanford University Press.
Al-Ghazzi, Omar. 2019. "An Archetypal Digital Witness: The Child Figure and the Media Conflict Over Syria." *International Journal of Communication* 13: 3225–43.
Al Omar, Mousa. 2017. "About the Appearance of Imran's Father on the Regime's TV." Youtube, 5 June. Retrieved 20 September 2021 from https://www.youtube.com/watch?v=HaApaXPUdP8.
Anderson, Benedict. 1983. *Imagined Communities: Reflections on the Origins and Spread of Nationalism*. New York: Verso.
Azoulay, Ariella. 2008. *The Civil Contract of Photography*. Cambridge, MA: MIT Press.
Balibar, Etienne. 2002. *Politics and the Other Scene*. London: Verso.
Baker, Catherine. 2017. "Why Were Bosniaks Treated More Favourably Than Today's Muslim Refugees? On Differing Narratives of Identity, Religion and Security." *London School of Economics and Political Science* blog, 7 March. Retrieved 20 September 2021from https://blogs.lse.ac.uk/europpblog/2017/03/07/why-bosniaks-treated-more-favourably-than-todays-refugees/?fbclid=IwAR1MN4I-JuG3waSEuBhDNVbADncFlsZeuTiCrJv1zYaUggeDRKc2YoaRny-o.
Benton, Adia. 2016. "Risky Business: Race, Nonequivalence and the Humanitarian Politics of Life." *Visual Anthropology* 29(2): 187–203.
Beydoun, Khaled A. 2018. *American Islamophobia: Understanding the Roots and Rise of Fear*. Berkeley, CA: University of California Press.
Bhattacharyya, Gargi. 2018. *Rethinking Racial Capitalism: Questions of Reproduction and Survival*. London: Rowman & Littlefield.
Chouliaraki, Lilie. 2012. *The Ironic Spectator: Solidarity in the Age of Post-humanitarianism*. Cambridge: Polity Press.
Chouliaraki, Lilie, and Bolette Blaagaard. 2013. "The Ethics of Images." Special issue, *Visual Communication* 12(3): 253–59.
Cole, Teju. 2012. "The White Savior Industrial Complex." *The Atlantic*, 21 March. http://www.theatlantic.com/international/archive/2012/03/the-white-savior industrialcomplex/254843/2/.

Combahee River Collective. 1979. "A Black Feminist Statement." *Women's Studies Quarterly*, 42(3–4): 271–80.
De Genova, Nicholas. 2013. "Spectacles of Migrant 'Illegality': The Scene of Exclusion, the Obscene of Inclusion." *Ethnic and Racial Studies* 36(7): 1180–98.
De Leon, Jason. 2015. *The Land of Open Graves: Living and Dying on the Migrant Trail.* Berkeley: University of California Press.
———. 2019. "Many people are outraged …" Facebook, 26 June, 7:08 p.m. Retrieved 28 March from https://www.facebook.com/jason.deleon.988/posts/10219368187581615.
Durrani, Mariam. 2018. "Communicating and Contesting Islamophobia." In *Language and Social Justice: Case Studies on Communication and the Creation of Just Societies*, edited by Netta Avineri, Robin Conley Riner, Laura Graham, Eric Johnson, and Jonathan Rosa, 44–51. London: Routledge Press.
Entman, Robert. M. 2010. "Media Framing Biases and Political Power: Explaining Slant in News of Campaign 2008." *Journalism* 11(4): 389–408.
The Executive Board, American Anthropological Association (AAA). 1947. "Statement on Human Rights." *American Anthropologist* 49(4), part 1: 539–543.
Feldman, Allen. 1997. "Violence and Vision: The Prosthetics and Aesthetics of Terror." *Public Culture* 10(1): 24–60.
Gursel, Zeynep Devrim. 2016. *Image Brokers: Visualizing World News in the Age of Digital Circulation.* California: University of California Press.
Hariman, Robert, and John Lucaites. 2007. *No Caption Needed: Iconic Photographs, Public Culture, and Liberal Democracy.* Chicago: University of Chicago Press.
Hernandez, Joe. 2021. "The Biden Administration Will No Longer Use Horses at a Texas Border Crossing." NPR, 23 September. Retrieved 23 September 2021 from https://www.npr.org/2021/09/23/1040214077/the-biden-administration-will-no-longer-use-horses-at-a-texas-border-crossing.
James, Erica Caple. 2010. *Democratic Insecurities: Violence, Trauma, and Intervention in Haiti.* Cambridge, MA: MIT Press.
Johnson, Walter. 2018. "To Remake the World: Slavery, Racial Capitalism, and Justice." *Boston Review: A Political and Literary Forum*, 20 February. Retrieved 20 September 2021 from http://bostonreview.net/forum/walter-johnson-to-remake-the-world.
Jones, Jonathan. 2017. "Jake Chapman Is Right to Criticise Ai Weiwei's Drowned Boy Artwork." *The Guardian*, 13 January. Retrieved 20 September 2021 from https://www.theguardian.com/artanddesign/jonathanjonesblog/2017/jan/13/jake-chapman-ai-weiwei-refugee-crisis.
Kazi, Nazia. 2019. "Islamophobic Nationalism and Attitudinal Islamophilia." In *Beyond Populism: Angry Politics and the Twilight of Neoliberalism*, edited by Jeff Maskovsky and Sophie Bjork-James. Morgantown: West Virginia University Press.
Khoja-Moolji, Shenila. 2020. "Death by Benevolence: Third World Girls and the Contemporary Politics of Humanitarianism." *Feminist Theory* 21(1): 1–26.
Kromidas, Maria. 2014. "The 'Savage' Child and the Nature of Race: Posthuman Interventions from New York City." *Anthropological Theory* 14(4): 422–41.
Lutz, Catherine A., and Jane L. Collins. 1993. *Reading National Geographic.* Chicago: University of Chicago Press.
Mackey, Robert. 2015. "Brutal Images of Syrian Boy Drowned off Turkey Must Be Seen, Activists Say." *New York Times*, 2 September. https://www.nytimes.com/

2015/09/03/world/middleeast/brutal-images-of-syrian-boy-drowned-off-turkey-must-be-seen-activists-say.html.
Manzo, Kate. 2008. "Imagining Humanitarianism: NGO Identity and the Iconography of Childhood." *Antipode* 40(4): 632–57.
McKirdy, Euan, and Mohammed Tawfeeq. 2017. "Omran Daqneesh, Young Face of Aleppo Suffering, Seen on TV." CNN, 7 June. Retrieved 20 September 2021 from https://www.cnn.com/2017/06/07/middleeast/omran-daqneesh-syrian-tv-interview/index.html.
Mirzoeff, Nicholas. 2011. *The Right to Look: A Counter-history of Visuality*. Durham, NC: Duke University Press.
Mortensen, Mette. 2017. "Constructing, Confirming, and Contesting Icons: The Alan Kurdi Imagery Appropriated by #humanitywashedashore, Ai Weiwei, and Charlie Hebdo." *Media, Culture & Society* 39(8): 1142–61.
Multiple Mobilities Research Cluster, Miriam Ticktin, Radhika Subramaniam, Victoria Hattam, Laura Y. Liu, and Rafi Youatt. 2017. "Images Unwalled." *Anthropology Now* 9(3): 24–37
Nagourney, Eric, and Michael Slackman. 2018. "Why We Are Publishing Haunting Photos of Emaciated Yemeni Children." *New York Times*, 26 October. Retrieved 16 September 2021 from https://www.nytimes.com/2018/10/26/reader-center/yemen-photos-starvation.html.
Pinney, Christopher. 1997. *Camera Indica*. Chicago: University of Chicago Press.
Poole, Deborah. 1997. *Vision, Race, and Modernity: A Visual Economy of the Andean World*. Princeton, NJ: Princeton University Press.
———. 2005. "An Excess of Description: Ethnography, Race, and Visual Technologies." *Annual Review of Anthropology* 34: 159–79.
Rafael, Vincente L. 2003. "The Cell Phone and the Crowd: Messianic Politics in the Contemporary Philippines." *Public Culture* 15(3): 399–425.
Ristovska, Sandra, and Monroe Price. 2018. *Visual Imagery and Human Rights Practice*. New York: Palgrave Macmillan.
Rony, Fatimah Tobing. 1996. *The Third Eye: Race, Cinema, and Ethnographic Spectacle*. Durham, NC: Duke University Press.
Rosa, Jonathan, and Vanessa Diaz. 2019. "Raciontologies: Rethinking Anthropological Accounts of Institutional Racism and Enactments of White Supremacy in the United States." *American Anthropologist* 122(1): 120–32.
Rosa, Jonathan, and Nelson Flores. 2015. "The Raciolinguistics Catch-22." *Harvard Education Publishing Group*. https://www.hepg.org/blog/the-raciolinguistic-catch-22.
Roy, A. 2010. *Poverty Capital: Microfinance and the Making of Development*. London: Routledge.
Shankar, Arjun. 2014. "Towards a Critical Visual Pedagogy: A Response to the 'End of Poverty' Narrative." *Visual Communication* 13: 341–56.
———. 2020. "Primitivism and Race in Ethnographic Film: A Decolonial Re-visioning." In Oxford Bibliographies in Anthropology, edited by John Jackson. DOI: 10.1093/OBO/9780199766567-0245. New York: Oxford University Press.
———. 2022. "The Making of the Brown Savior: Race, Caste, Class and India's Global Help Economy. *Current Anthropology*, forthcoming.
Sontag, Susan. 2004. *Regarding the Pain of Others*. New York: Picador.

Spivak, Gayatri Chakravorty. 1994. "Can the Subaltern Speak?" In *Colonial Discourse and Post-colonial Theory: A Reader*, edited by Williams Patrick and Laura Chrisman, 6–11. Hertfordshire: Harvester Wheatsheaf.

Tagg, John. 1993. *Burden of Representation: Essays on Photographies and Histories*. Minneapolis: University of Minnesota Press.

Trouillot, Michel-Rolph. 2003. *Global Transformations: Anthropology and the Modern World*. New York: Palgrave Macmillan.

UDHR (Universal Declaration of Human Rights. 1948. United Nations General Assembly, 10 December, Paris. General Assembly resolution 217 A.

Walsh, Declan, and Eric Schmitt. 2018. "Arms Sales to Saudis Leave American Fingerprints on Yemen's Carnage." *New York Times*, 25 December. Retrieved 16 September 2021 from https://www.nytimes.com/2018/12/25/world/middleeast/yemen-us-saudi-civilian-war.html.

Weizman, Eyal. 2011. *The Least of All Possible Evils: Humanitarian Violence from Arendt to Gaza*. London: Verso

Zelizer, Barbie. 2010. *About to Die: How News Images Move the Public*. New York: Oxford University Press.

Part II

Host Country Economies and Attitudes

4

Why Do Employment and Socioeconomic Integration Have a Strained Relationship?

The International Protection Context and Syrians in Turkey

Saime Özçürümez and Deniz Yıldırım

Introduction

With no immediate end to the increasing number of displaced persons, the central concern for all stakeholders in the variety of receiving states has become how to facilitate the process and means by which they become self-reliant. While becoming self-reliant, the displaced persons are almost concurrently expected to progress in socioeconomic integration. There is scant evidence on whether self-reliance and socioeconomic integration affect each other positively. The rationale for conflating the two processes can be explained by focusing on various possibly consequential relationships. When gainfully employed, displaced persons may become financially independent of the humanitarian assistance schemes. In turn, host states are likely to circumvent the controversy over whether hosting refugees constitutes a financial burden. Scholars very recently have proposed that "combining objectives of labor migration and humanitarian protection" may facilitate redesigning policies for both purposes (Ruhs 2019). Through legal employment, refugees are likely to reinstitute their dignity, highlight their contributions to the host society, and engage in social connections in the workplace and beyond, which together are expected to foster their socioeconomic integration (Zetter and Ruaudel 2018). However, it is hard to identify such a causal path by analyzing the evidence from the experience of the refugee hosting countries. The evidence from a variety of cases reveals that while legal employment is a necessary condition for social inclusion of all vulnerable groups in a society (including refugees), it is not a sufficient condition for realizing socioeconomic integration and social cohesion (Zetter and Ruaudel 2018; OECD 2016; OECD and UNHCR 2018; Connor 2010). Such alarming evidence confirmed by several studies calls for the need for an even closer examination of the processes taking place in middle-income states hosting increasing numbers of displaced persons.

Displaced people's needs increase and diversify over time. States bordering protracted conflicts and receiving mass influx need to sustain institutional capacity prepared to remain resilient given such a challenge. These states also need to cope with the situation of wavering public approval about the presence of refugees and ever-expanding financial and administrative pressure on the national and local resources.

Aware of the multifaceted challenges of the larger set of refugee hosting countries in the low- to medium-income countries category, Betts and Collier (2017) argue that host countries may still transform refugees into economically productive actors. Their claim is that the low- to medium-income countries receiving displaced persons may introduce effective regulatory environments for employment, improve inclusive policies in the labor market, engage in skills development as well as qualification recognition of displaced persons, and promote entrepreneurial activities by refugees in order to enable them to access a variety of livelihood opportunities. These strategies, they expect, will lead to a "win-win" situation for refugees and the host states. While refugees will be relieved from the drama of victimhood, rising costs, and inhospitable public opinion, the host states will have more well-educated people and labor market supply to foster social and economic growth (Betts and Collier 2017). Different studies find that refugees also contribute to international trade and investment and increase entrepreneurship in host states (Bahar 2018). However, evidence from different cases and policy initiatives repeatedly prove that this approach is highly difficult to apply and even harder to sustain (Zetter and Ruaudel 2018; Ekren, 2018).

While not directly proposing a clear link between employment and socioeconomic integration of displaced persons, most studies assume that creating employment opportunities for refugees, even by undertaking strenuous structural transformations in the host economies, may result in overcoming most of the financial and social challenges attributed to hosting refugees. Most studies, then, brush over the complicated questions of whether, why, how, and to what extent being employed affects the likelihood of socioeconomic integration, instead focusing on the principle: legal employment is ipso facto necessary for social inclusion. However, principles need institutional paths to follow and social pillars to stand on. This study seeks answers to the questions: what are the institutional paths and pillars for deciphering the relationship between employment and socioeconomic integration, and under what conditions do they work and why? The research is based on a systematic review of existing reports and literature on the relationship between employment opportunities and socioeconomic integration prospects for displaced persons. By analyzing the relationship between the context of employment and socioeconomic integration prospects for Syrians in Turkey, the study suggests that gainful employment is a necessary but definitely not a sufficient condition for promoting socioeconomic integration of refugees. This is partly the case because employability policies aim to remove fundamental barriers of access to employment such as language, qualification recognition, and vocational training. However, such policies are not necessarily supported by practices that establish and promote positive social interaction among refugees and host communities in general and among refugees' coworkers in particular. The precarity inherent in refugee employment magnifies the scarcity of such policies and widens the gap between employability prospects and socioeconomic integration.

This study argues that both the existing international protection regime that aims to govern the employment prospects for refugees and asylum seekers and the *structural and agency* constraints in the economies of host countries constrain the attainment of policy objectives for employability of displaced persons in the host states. First, by reviewing evidence for those under international and temporary protection in Turkey, the study identifies the regulatory, structural, and agency-driven barriers to employability, which in turn affect socioeconomic integration. The point here is not that Turkey's case stands as unique or that policy initiatives in the country are flawed. The main argument is that the mass influx to Turkey (hosting up to four million Syrians and other displaced persons) magnifies the challenges associated with employability of displaced persons in host countries. Such a challenge is a consequence of how the international protection framework works in the national context in response to an unprecedented scale of demand on public resources. Therefore, the analysis of evidence from this case substantiates the need to facilitate employment policies with supportive practices for positive social interaction between refugees and host communities. Second, it discusses why the relationship between legal access to employment and prospects for socioeconomic integration through gainful employment in prolonged temporary protection conditions is strained. This study relies on historical institutionalism to explain the reasons for this continuous difficulty in overcoming this problem. The concept of "path dependence," this study argues, explains the reasons why policy innovations introduced for enhancing employability of refugees remain short of accomplishing their main objective: socioeconomic integration and self-reliance.

Research Design and Case Selection

The puzzle with Syrians in Turkey represents a significant case in relation to the research question on the nexus between employability and socioeconomic integration for several reasons. First, despite the huge scale of influx from 252 in 2011 to 3,691,333 by November 2019 (GIGM 2019) and high unemployment rates in the cities where refugees are concentrated, the country's economy remains relatively fragile (Özpınar, Çilingir, and Taşöz Düşündere 2016). Second, the country experiences the consequences of the Syrian humanitarian crisis with continuous fluctuating movements of forced migrants. Therefore, the data from this country reveals evidence that will account for understanding how a continuous and complex movement affects the causal relationship in question. Third, Turkey responded to the mass influx by introducing the Temporary Protection Regulation (TPR), which aimed to lead a favorable structural context for socioeconomic integration by removing the structural barriers to employability with national legal backing before the crisis peaked in 2015.

This study relies on a systematic review of scholarly articles and reports (from international organizations, public institutions, and nongovernmental organizations) published between 2011 and 2018, with a focus on how they discuss the link between employability and socioeconomic integration. The printed materials have been reviewed for their focus on the relationship between employability and socioeconomic integration of refugees. The study focuses on the changes in policies and discourse toward increasing access to labor markets, facilitating entrepreneurship opportunities and the development agenda, while referring to employability of refugees in Turkey.

"Path Dependence" in International Protection and Employability of Refugees

A narrow definition of path dependence helps explain the role of legal frameworks and regulatory approaches in shaping continuity and change in certain policy contexts such as those on international protection. Levi (1997: 28) explains that once a path is taken, costs of reversals increase in that the path chosen is usually followed until that path totally breaks down. Likewise, Arthur (1994: 112–13) stresses that paths are prone to create rigidity and inefficiency pointing out the costs of reversals. U-turns might push costs to *record levels* such that states might choose to proceed with the existing policies even though they may not be fully efficient. Hence, despite the changing nature and needs in this field, states might follow the existing frameworks to respond to emerging policy challenges as in the case of international protection policies implemented at the national level for many countries.

The 1951 Geneva Convention, the main legal document on international protection, has also produced reasons for ensuring its continuity and stalling global policy change. Continuity in the case of the Convention is not that its ratification provided a "lock-in" effect definitely for asylum governance at the global level and by the nation-states. However, the Convention created its own institutions[1] that led to the mobilization of certain actors, who were more interested in ensuring the continuity of the rules instead of pursuing change in those rules for a considerable period of time. North (1990) explains the insistence on continuity of the present management strategies, policies, and/or institutions through adaptation of individuals to the latter. In addition, the self-reinforcing trajectories of institutions persuade individuals to preserve the existing entities (North 1990) as well as processes pursued to attain them. Nevertheless, there is still some possibility of revision in the policies selected and paths taken by the institutions. Scholarly debates point to "critical junctures" that enable changes at certain points in time. The text of the 1951 Convention itself reflects the political compromises and struggles that depict the critical juncture that resulted in the embodiment of this legal framework. As the historical institutionalist approach would suggest, the Convention also constitutes particular interests crystallized in a certain historical moment, a critical juncture, whereby the international community aimed to produce a legal agreement on governing asylum internationally and putting in print legal commitments of nation-states in the event of persecution of individuals and human rights violations. One main standard operating practice that the Convention highlights is that nation-states decide on the extent to which they will comply with the principles outlined in the Convention and on the implementation of policies for meeting the needs of those seeking asylum and/or granted refugee status. One of those principles that states maintain is the principle of *nonrefoulement.* However, states introduced, for example, geographical limitations to the implementation of the Convention, and some, such as Turkey, have preserved this settlement to this day.

Recalling Mahoney's (2000) depiction of "path dependence" as referring to "historical sequences in which contingent events set into motion institutional patterns or event chains that have deterministic properties," this study asserts that the defining role of the 1951 Convention constraints on the relationship between refugee employability and socioeconomic integration prospects is critical. The 1951 Convention sets the formal rules for the global governance of international protection. It does so in a way that it also shapes the decades-long continuity in policies addressing employability of refugees in national contexts to be defined by nation-states' policies and preferences.

Tracing Path Dependence in Employability of Syrians in Turkey

Multiple articles of the 1951 Convention refer to gainful employment and labor market entry conditions for refugees in the host countries. Relying on Article 17 of the 1951 Convention, the signatory states are expected to provide refugees who lawfully reside on their soil with equal rights to join in wage-earning employment as other nationals of foreign countries. The same article regulates under which conditions a signatory state cannot impose restrictive measures on a refugee's entrance into the labor market.[2] Article 18, on the other hand, encourages the signatory states to treat refugees, who lawfully stay in their territory and are willing to set up their own businesses in primary, secondary, and/or tertiary sectors, "as favorable as possible" and "not less favorable" than other aliens who meet similar criteria. Likewise, Article 19 requires signatory states to approach refugees who lawfully reside on their soil and other aliens as equal as possible when they meet the necessary conditions to practice their profession (1951 Convention Relating to the Status of Refugees and 1967 Protocol). The spirit of the Convention, then, reminds nation-states that access to labor markets is one of the ways that eases the continuous survival of refugees and persons in need of international protection, who might otherwise remain dependent on social assistance schemes. However, signatory states interpret Article 17, which regulates providing refugees with equal rights to participate in wage-earning employment as favorably as other foreign residents, in ways that allow them to refer to the requirements of Article 17 as recommendations rather than obligations (MEDAM 2018). Furthermore, the 1951 Convention and its 1967 Protocol do not detail, nor do they endorse, what signatory states should do in order to promote and ease the entrance of refugees into their labor markets. Betts and Collier (2017) affirm this conclusion by indicating that the international legal framework does not prescribe, nor does it enforce, national regulations to be in place for labor market access or livelihood creation for refugees. In this context, signatory states mostly bestow national solutions that result in various responses apropos employment of refugees by distancing themselves from a universal solution (MEDAM 2018). Even efforts put into recent universal solutions, i.e., the New York Declaration for Refugees and Migrants (UN 2016) and the ILO's "Guiding principles on the access of refugees and other forcibly displaced persons to the labor market" (ILO 2016), maintain cautionary statements by prioritizing "needs of the existing labor force and employers" over refugees' needs.

Overall, the lack of international enforcement or sanctions for regulating labor market access to the benefit of displaced persons and integration of refugees, on the one hand, and the presence of a diverse repertoire of national policies, on the other hand, result in, even if inadvertently, reinforcing precarity of refugee employability. Refugees fall into the vicious cycle of having to sustain their lives either through humanitarian assistance schemes managed by international and/or national governmental and/or nongovernmental bodies for an indefinite period of time or remain vulnerable to the risk of working illegally and/or under poor conditions, and/or juggle for securing income from both. Such conditions are even more challenging in situations of protracted conflict.

The Settlement Law (1934) at the national level and the 1951 Convention at the international level defined Turkey's legal commitments in the field of international protection until the introduction of the Law on Foreigners and International Protection (LFIP) in 2014. The Settlement Law (1934) facilitated the support for those attached to Turkic and Muslim identity to migrate to Turkey from the former lands of the Ottoman Empire such as Bulgaria and Bosnia (Kirişçi 1996). Turkey has ratified the Convention with geographical limitation. Turkey does not allow those coming from outside Europe to be granted refugee status. The Settlement Law was consulted by governments for coping with the cases of mass influx of Iraqi Turks in the 1990s (Parla and Danış 2009) and while hosting them for a number of years. However, for those who come from outside of Europe and could not be received under the Settlement Law, Turkey has long remained as a country of temporary residence until moving toward other countries or returning to the country of origin.

Turkey's most extensive experience with mass influx coming from non-European origin countries resulted in Turkey receiving them in temporary accommodation centers and returning them to their country of origin within a short space of time. The lesson learned was that temporary refugee protection policies work in coping with forced migration, that there is no urgent need to prepare for labor market access for refugees (let alone socioeconomic integration), and that those who arrive either return or move on in a reasonable period of time. During the early 2000s, while the movement toward Turkey continued, the numbers hovered around a couple of hundred thousand, which were manageable by Turkish standards when considered as a percentage of the total population.

When Syrians started arriving in 2011, the earlier experience shaped the public and policymaker perceptions and, hence, the initial coping mechanisms and policy tools put to use. Policymakers and the public expected that the mass influx would end in a few years and the displaced persons would return to their countries of origin. In order to run temporary accommodation centers, set up for Syrians, the Disaster and Emergency Management Presidency (DEMP), whose portfolio consisted of attending to the needs of mostly natural disaster victims, had been in charge of managing the crisis. The emergency approach that pooled in multiple financial, technical, administrative, and human resources operated on the assumption that the situation was (and would remain) manageable by national means and actors, even with the increase in the arrival of displaced persons in the hundreds of thousands in the post-2013 period. The emergency approach to coping with the mass influx did not incorporate the social cohesion approach.

Drafted totally independent of the Syrian emergency, the LFIP helped set out the legal basis for (1) registration procedures, (2) the lawful stay of Syrians under Temporary Protection (SuTP) in the country until the conditions in Syria allow for safe return, (3) Temporary Protection identity cards, (4) free access to social services such as health and education as well as access to labor markets. The geographical limitation had a strong "continuity" in Turkey's asylum governance; therefore, while Turkey abided by the principle of *nonrefoulement*, the country limited the policies to the arriving Syrians in the framework of temporariness. As a result, Turkey, where geographical limitation is maintained, enacted the "Act No. 6735: International Labor Force Law" (ILFL) first as a secondary legislation in January 2016, then as a law in August 2016 (Uluslararası İşgücü Kanunu 2016) in order to facilitate Syrians' labor market access. The ILFL enabled beneficiaries of temporary protection to acquire work permits and access labor markets in Turkey. Despite the gradual transformation in policy principles easing the labor market entry of the Syrians under temporary protection, the increase in the number of full-time and legally employed lag behind any reasonable level to suggest that Syrians under Temporary Protection have become self-sufficient in general and/or legally employed in particular.

First, the ILFL regulated the conditions under which one might be eligible for work permits. Persons under temporary protection are primarily expected to sign fixed-term employment contracts with employers, with which the latter should apply for work permits. Once the work permit of a Syrian under temporary protection is approved by authorities, employers are required to pay a certain fee in order to finalize the procedure. Work permits are restricted to a position and an enterprise specified in fixed-term employment contracts. Hence, it provides limited access to the labor market and reinforces dependency on the preferences of the employer. With no sustainable incentives in sight for the employers, the legal employment prospects remain limited. Recruitment of Syrians under temporary protection is dependent on whether they meet the qualifications requested in the relevant regulations and/or no national qualifies for the position.

In the Turkish case, employers are not required to apply for work permits for the agricultural and livestock sectors, and there is no quota for employing Syrians under Temporary Protection in these sectors only. According to the World Bank statistics, the share of the agriculture sector was only 19.39 percent of the Turkish economy in 2017 (World Bank 2018). The low share of these sectors in the Turkish economy and the seasonal hiring trends maintain the precarity of employment prospects. In other sectors, the number of

Syrians under Temporary Protection cannot exceed 10 percent of the total Turkish workers in a given enterprise where there are more than ten workers. If there are less than ten Turkish employees in a given enterprise, then only one Syrian under Temporary Protection can be recruited. Implementation of quotas could be bypassed only when there is not a Turkish candidate who qualifies for the job that a Syrian under Temporary Protection has applied for. The major challenge that the ILFL does not overcome is those remaining in the informal sector. According to the Turkish Confederation of Employers' Associations (TCEA) report, well before being granted the right to work and access to labor markets in 2016, three hundred thousand Syrians had been working informally in various sectors (Erdoğan and Ünver 2015), and recent studies note that more than one million Syrians under Temporary Protection of working age (fifteen to sixty-five) work informally in Turkey (Del Carpio, Seker, and Yener 2018). Even two years after being granted the right to work and access to labor markets, only 19,925 Syrians reported working legally and most are working under poor conditions (İçduygu and Diker 2017).

The studies by the World Bank also point out that the younger the Syrians under Temporary Protection, the more they have opportunities of being hired by the employers (World Bank 2015). This stresses that employers prefer to hire children because they are able to learn the job and language rapidly and do not resist poor working conditions. As a result, Syrian children are employed in low-skilled jobs without regulated safety conditions in sectors such as textiles, construction, shoemaking, agriculture, and clothes shops (Caspani 2015). Especially in the southeastern part of Turkey, the number of children working in garbage collection is significantly high (Lordoğlu and Aslan 2016). Child Labor Report indicates that children work more than eight hours a day and six to seven days per week, going against international and national legal frameworks (Human Rights Watch 2015).

There are serious efforts to end child labor among Syrian refugees. UNICEF underlines that as of January 2016, more than six hundred children who were "at risk or engaged in child labor" were provided support services (UNICEF 2016). Similarly, the former Ministry of Family and Social Policies (current Ministry of Family, Labor and Social Services) provides parents with "conditional cash transfers" in exchange for children being enrolled in education (İçduygu 2016). Considering children compose almost 50 percent of the arriving displaced population (UNHCR 2018), implementing comprehensive child protection policies is indispensable for socioeconomic integration policies to work.

The employability of displaced persons is usually constrained by the incremental change that characterizes policy responses to transforming demands in most countries including Turkey. Despite several policy tools introduced to increase employability, their scope for impact is constrained by the structural conditions of the economy. A major gap resurfaces in this setting and in a more magnified way due to the scale of the problem, policies of employability address only barriers of employability. However, those policy tools remain in need of complementary policies to support socioeconomic integration.

From Employability to Socioeconomic Integration: Fixing the Broken Link

The link between employability and socioeconomic integration is complex. Studies identify that socioeconomic integration depends on the construction of social connections with the local level in the host state (Ager and Strang 2008). While employment presents a venue through which meaningful "two-way" social connections can be established, evidence proves that such a relationship is highly contingent. Neoclassical economics dictates that the reason why an individual is unemployed is strongly linked to his/her previous experience and/or skills that do not match the market's needs (Evans and Kelly 1991; Fugazza 2003). The findings of most research on displaced persons suggest that the ever-present difficulty for this group is more complex: it is the discrimination they endure by both the employers and coworkers in host state job searches and workplaces (Colic-Peisker and Tilbury 2007a). Studies confirm repeatedly that all displaced persons and those with refugee status continue to accept poor or unsatisfactory employment conditions in order to create their livelihoods and thus suffer through seriously debilitating job search processes (Ward and Masgoret 2007; Weiss, Sauer, and Gotlibovski 2001; Fugazza 2003; Colic-Peisker and Tilbury 2007b). Therefore, while accessibility of employment may suggest that the context meets one prerequisite for establishing social connections in the host state, the practices they encounter may still impede forming connections facilitating socioeconomic integration.

There is scant evidence to suggest that receiving states consistently take initiatives to remove structural barriers to labor market participation for displaced persons (MEDAM 2018; Del Carpio, Seker, and Yener 2018) and/or complement them with policies and practices for promoting social interaction among displaced persons and host communities in the workplace. There are sporadic efforts by employers in different countries, which upon closer examination are neither comprehensive nor sustainable (OECD and UNHCR 2016; Ekren 2018). Host states, in general, do not enforce policies penalizing employers for employing refugees without work permits (Degler and Liebig 2017) or introduce effective incentives for improving workplace conditions.

Some enterprises hire refugees on the basis of corporate social responsibility (OECD and UNHCR 2016). Such approaches, however, prove neither viable nor replicable, especially in the countries that have received the most refugees in the past decade (according to UNHCR statistics in the following order: Turkey, Pakistan and Uganda, Lebanon, and the Islamic Republic of Iran in 2018; UNHCR 2018). Many employers in the private sector prefer supporting refugees by offering them training and internships rather than hiring them for full-time jobs (OECD and UNHCR 2016). Additionally, while promoters of vocational training for refugees and displaced persons to increase their chances of employment are abundant, studies reveal that having gone through vocational training does not guarantee labor market participation by itself (Korkmaz 2017). The uncertainty around the labor market entry prospects of displaced persons and the lack of long-term employment opportunities for them result in double jeopardy for refugees' socioeconomic integration prospects. If they secure some form of employment (informal, part-time, or full-time), they attract the antagonism of fellow employees for having compromised the long-earned settlements about pay scale and working hours. They remain vulnerable to the discretion of employers due to lack of guarantees for securing long-term employment with long-term work permits and absence of effective enforcement mechanisms for formalizing work for them. The context, then, stalls prospects for establishing meaningful social connections with both the employees and coworkers.

Additional barriers persistently weaken the link between employment and socioeconomic integration of displaced persons. Research notes that obstacles faced by refugees are multifaceted and different from those faced by immigrants (Connor 2010; Bakker, Dagevos, and Engbersen 2017). When refugees arrive in the host state, most suffer from trauma and a variety of health problems, which become a barrier to even start planning for livelihood opportunities (Chiswick, Lee, and Miller 2008). They are uncertain about the duration as well as the conditions of their stay and highly unfamiliar with the new social, economic, and political context. Considering that most states immediately accommodate them in reception centers or camps, the prospect of self-reliance is further hampered by physical confinement for meeting humanitarian protection needs. Almost 60 percent of refugees live in cities instead of camps around the world (Park 2016). In time, displaced persons may move to the urban centers in large numbers.

Harmonized unemployment rates in Turkey are increasing, and the youth unemployment rate was 20.1 percent in 2018 (OECD 2019). The unemployment rates in the cities populated with displaced persons suggests that available positions may not suffice to meet the demand coming from job seekers, both Syrian and Turkish. Considering that the employment gap for disadvantaged groups including non-natives remained the highest in

Turkey compared to other OECD countries (OECD 2017), the likelihood of increasing the prospects of Syrians under Temporary Protection for access to the legal economy is low unless effective job creation policies are introduced. Statistics also reveal that of those employed, 18.3 percent are in the agricultural sector, 19.5 percent are in the industrial sector, 7.4 percent are in construction, and 54.8 percent are in the services sector. While most opportunities seem to be in the services sector for both locals and the Syrians under Temporary Protection, the language and qualification recognition barriers limit the likelihood of the latter being employed in this sector (Erdoğan and Ünver 2015; İçduygu 2016). Hence, even when effective job creation policies may be implemented, a lack of proficiency in the Turkish language severely impedes or holds back the Syrians under Temporary Protection from being recruited (Ortensi 2015).

In addition to the prevailing reluctance to hire refugees, employers in Turkey widely express their "pessimism" about the economic integration of the Syrians under Temporary Protection due to language and skill recognition barriers (Erdoğan and Ünver 2015). Having acknowledged that attitude and in order to ease the socioeconomic integration of displaced persons in Turkey, various public and private actors offer language training as well as vocational training. However, challenges of the variety of policy initiatives and interventions concerning training programs remain and are manifold. The most striking challenge is that all policies and practices are offered through short-term projects in need of monitoring, evaluation, and impact analysis. Almost eight years into the mass influx of Syrians and hundreds of thousands of people under international protection from different source countries, there is little data on either the cost of training programs and their returns or which actors would be more effective as suppliers for these skill enhancement policies; which sectors would have continuous demand for these peoples' labor; which vocations would need to be prioritized; and when, where, and why the trainings would need to be provided and for how long. Due to the lack of any reliable impact analysis, investing in the vocational training or financial literacy of those under international protection and temporary protection do not present a convincing case for a high priority policy objective. The initiatives require a complementary comprehensive approach to social integration supported by a concrete policy agenda as would be needed in all countries receiving refugees.

Policymakers expect that introducing opportunities for learning the language and increasing levels of education would increase chances of employment. However, researchers stress that there is not a definite positive correlation between the increase in the level of education and the probability of being recruited in well-paid jobs in formal sectors for refugees (İçduygu 2016). Yet the question of whether the currently employed Syrians under Temporary Protection have higher levels of education compared to those who are unemployed remains unanswered.

The recognition of academic degrees of immigrants in general and of refugees in particular (Frykman 2012; Liversage 2009; Dean and Wilson 2009; Dietz et al. 2015) is not straightforward and takes time. In addition, for those who have been subject to forced migration, providing proof of work experience in Syria and/or academic credentials and/or relevant education and skills when asked is extremely difficult. They usually lack credible documentation, and/or the available documents require translation and certification. In this context, accepting to work under poor conditions remains as a continuous challenge for the displaced persons and the policymakers. On the one hand, willingness to work under poor conditions facilitates access to a means of livelihood and establishes social networks. On the other hand, such a start usually seals the future prospects for employment as remaining precarious at best.

Syrians under Temporary Protection can also earn their livelihoods by setting up their own businesses in Turkey. Some reports quote that "there are 9.978 companies that are either owned or partnered by a Syrian in Turkey" (TEPAV 2018: 13). The report also notes that more than half of these companies employ less than five people, and the business owners note their lack of knowledge about how to seek subsidies to grow their companies (TEPAV 2018: 8). One of the striking findings of this report is that more than 70 percent of Syrian business owners would prefer to stay in Turkey even after the conflict is over (TEPAV 2018: 33) because they note by comparison that Turkey's business environment is better than Syria's. Srivastava (2016) had already claimed that Syrian entrepreneurs contribute positively to Turkey's economy. Further studies are also needed regarding the financial and social context for promoting Syrian-operated businesses in Turkey in order to analyze their effects on socioeconomic integration in detail.

Conclusion

Coping with the influx of displaced persons fleeing a humanitarian crisis unearths multiple policy dilemmas and challenges for countries receiving and hosting these persons. These challenges are partly due to the structure of the existing labor markets in receiving countries and partly due to the characteristics of the foreign workforce, which is expected to become economically active in a given period of time. In the case of Turkey coping with mass influx, current legal instruments and policy tools point out the incentives for national policymakers to sustain continuity of existing policies and resort to only incremental change for employability of refugees. While Turkey pursues a combination of policies to facilitate labor market access for refugees, such as formalizing temporary protection as well as facilitating work permit acquisition through renewing regulations, these policies still might not include all employable SuTP in formal sectors and might not prevent them from remaining in precarious work conditions. There is also limited evidence that complementary policy initiatives could address the challenges of SuTP employment in particular. Even though a combination of policies has been introduced to ease the entrance of SuTP into Turkey's legal economy, the present circumstances resonate the call for the exigency to shift to a development agenda with more urgency than ever because the existing policy toolkits for employment can surmount the myriad of challenges only for so long with no end date for the Syrian crisis in sight.

A whole host of studies on employability of refugees and how this would benefit both refugees and host countries around the world does exist. Most of them overemphasize the role of employment for facilitating socioeconomic integration. This chapter has major implications for current debates that rely on employability as clearing the path to enhance socioeconomic integration of displaced persons in host states. First, the national policy instruments promoting employment with objectives compatible with the international framework have limited impact on socioeconomic integration. Second, national-level structural and agency-related challenges to increase employability need national-level solutions. Third, further research is needed to design employment policies and pursue enabling conditions for facilitating socioeconomic integration for the benefit of both host states and refugees.

Saime Özçürümez is director of the Human Mobility Processes and Interactions Research Lab (HMPI-Bilkent) and associate professor in the Department of Political Science and Public Administration at Bilkent University. She conducts research and publishes on migration and asylum governance in the European Union, Turkey, and Canada. She also focuses on health and diversity, gender and forced migration processes, and social cohesion.

Deniz Yıldırım is a PhD candidate in the Department of Political Science and Public Administration at Bilkent University. Her dissertation explores how the recent institutional change has taken place in the areas of asylum and international protection in Turkey in the 2000s. She is particularly interested in the institutional contexts within which the policy and institutional entrepreneurs emerge, function, and create change. She carried out research at Harvard FXB Center for Health and Human Rights in 2018–19. She has coauthored a book chapter on Syrians under Temporary Protection (SuTP), health services, and NGOs in Turkey, and has worked on various national and cross-national collaborative research projects on migration.

Notes

1. Thelen and Streeck (2005: 9) define institutions as "collectively enforced expectations with respect to the behavior of specific categories of actors to the

performance of certain activities." Hall emphasizes the institutions as also being constituted of "formal rules, compliance procedures, and standard operating procedures" (Thelen and Steinmo 1992).
2. A refugee could not be constrained to enter the labor market if s/he has been living in the receiving country more than three years and/or has a spouse or a child who holds citizenship in the country of residence. However, Article 17 paradoxically and legally renders possible the preventing of a refugee from entering national labor markets of signatory states for his/her first three years of residence if s/he is not married to a national or has a child holding the citizenship of the receiving country.

References

Ager, Alastair, and Alison Strang. 2008. "Understanding Integration: A Conceptual Framework." *Journal of Refugee Studies* 2(1): 166–91. https://doi.org/10.1093/jrs/fen016.
Arthur, W. Brian. 1994. *Increasing Returns and Path Dependence in the Economy*. Ann Arbor: University of Michigan Press.
Bahar, Dany. 2018. "Why Accepting Refugees Is a Win-win Formula." Brookings, 19 June. Retrieved 5 October 2021 from https://www.brookings.edu/blog/up-front/2018/06/19/refugees-are-a-win-win-win-formula-for-economic-development/.
Bakker, Linda, Jaco Dagevos, and Godfried Engbersen. 2016. "Explaining the Refugee Gap: A Longitudinal Study on Labor Market Participation of Refugees in the Netherlands." *Journal of Ethnic and Migration Studies* 43(11): 1775–91. https://doi.org/10.1080/1369183x.2016.1251835.
Betts, Alexander, and Paul Collier. 2017. *Refuge: Rethinking Refugee Reform Policy in a Changing World*. Oxford: Oxford University Press.
Carpio, Ximena V Del, Sirma V Del Seker, and Ahmet Levent V Del Yener. 2018. "Integrating Refugees into the Turkish Labor Market." *Forced Migration Review*, no. 58 (June): 10–13. https://www.fmreview.org/economies/delcarpio-seker-yener.
Caspani, Maria. 2015. "Child Labor on the Rise among Syrian Children as Crisis Spirals: Agencies." *Reuters*, 2 July. Retrieved 7 September 2021 from https://www.reuters.com/article/us-syria-children-labour/child-labor-on-the-rise-among-syrian-children-as-crisis-spirals-agencies-idUSKCN0PB6C920150701.
Chiswick, Barry R., Yew Liang Lee, and Paul W. Miller. 2008. "Immigrant Selection Systems and Immigrant Health." *Contemporary Economic Policy* 26(4): 555–78. https://doi.org/10.1111/j.1465-7287.2008.00099.x.
Colic-Peisker, Val, and Farida Tilbury. 2007a. "Integration into the Australian Labor Market: The Experience of Three 'Visibly Different' Groups of Recently Arrived Refugees." *International Migration* 45(1): 59–85. https://doi.org/10.1111/j.1468-2435.2007.00396.x.
———. 2007b. "Refugees and Employment: The Effect of Visible Difference on Discrimination." Murdoch University Centre for Social and Community Research. Retrieved 7 September 2021 from http://researchrepository.murdoch.edu.au/10991/1/refugeesandemployment.pdf.

Connor, Phillip. 2010. "Explaining the Refugee Gap: Economic Outcomes of Refugees versus Other Immigrants." *Journal of Refugee Studies* 23(3): 377–97. https://doi.org/10.1093/jrs/feq025.

Dean, Jennifer Asanin, and Kathi Wilson. 2009. "Education? It Is Irrelevant to My Job Now. It Makes Me Very Depressed…: Exploring the Health Impacts of Under/Unemployment among Highly Skilled Recent Immigrants in Canada." *Ethnicity & Health* 14(2): 185–204. https://doi.org/10.1080/13557850802227049.

Degler, Eva, and Thomas Liebig. 2017. "Finding Their Way: Labor Market Integration of Refugees in Germany." OECD. Retrieved 7 September 2021 from https://www.oecd.org/els/mig/Finding-their-Way-Germany.pdf.

Del Carpio, Ximena V., Sirma Demir Seker, and Ahmet Levent Yener. 2018. "Integrating Refugees into the Turkish Labour Market." *Forced Migration Review* 58. Retrieved 20 September 2021 from https://www.fmreview.org/economies/delcarpio-seker-yener.

Dietz, Joerg, Chetan Joshi, Victoria M. Esses, Leah K. Hamilton, and Fabrice Gabarrot. 2015. "The Skill Paradox: Explaining and Reducing Employment Discrimination against Skilled Immigrants." *International Journal of Human Resource Management* 26(10): 1318–34. https://doi.org/10.1080/09585192.2014.990398.

Ekren, Elizabeth. 2018. "Obstacles to Refugees' Self-Reliance in Germany." *Forced Migration Review* 58: 30–32. https://www.fmreview.org/sites/fmr/files/FMRdownloads/en/ekren.pdf.

Erdoğan, M. Murat, and Can Ünver. 2015. "Türk İş Dünyasının Türkiye'deki Suriyeliler Konusundaki Görüş, Beklenti Ve Önerileri [Opinions, prospects and recommendations of Turkish business world on Syrians residing in Turkey]." TİSK. Retrieved 7 September 2021 from https://www.tisk.org.tr/tr/e-yayinlar/353-goc/353-goc.pdf.

Evans, M. D. R., and Jonathan Kelley. 1991. "Prejudice, Discrimination, and the Labor Market: Attainments of Immigrants in Australia." *American Journal of Sociology* 97(3): 721–59. https://doi.org/10.1086/229818.

Frykman, Maja Povrzanović. 2012. "Struggle for Recognition: Bosnian Refugees Employment Experiences in Sweden." *Refugee Survey Quarterly* 31(1): 54–79. https://doi.org/10.1093/rsq/hdr017.

Fugazza, Marco. 2003. "Racial Discrimination: Theories, Facts and Policy." *International Labor Review* 142(4): 507–41. https://doi.org/10.1111/j.1564-913x.2003.tb00542.x.

GIGM (Göç İdaresi Genel Müdürlüğü). 2019. *Geçici Koruma* [Temporary protection]. November. Retrieved 7 September 2021 from https://www.goc.gov.tr/gecici-koruma5638.

Güven, Sibel, Murat Kenanoğlu, Omar Kadkoy, and Taylan Kurt. 2018. "Syrian Entrepreneurship and Refugee Startups in Turkey: Leveraging the Turkish Experience." TEPAV, Ankara.

Human Rights Watch. 2015. "Turkey: 400,000 Syrian Children Not in School." 8 November. Retrieved 7 September 2021 from https://www.hrw.org/news/2015/11/08/turkey-400000-syrian-children-not-school.

İçduygu Ahmet. 2016. *Turkey: Labor Market Integration and Social Inclusion of Refugees*. European Parliament, Directorate-General for Internal Policies, Policy Department, Economic and Scientific Policy, Study for the EMPL Committee.

İçduygu, Ahmet, and Eleni Diker. 2017. "Labor Market Integration of Syrian Refugees in Turkey: From Refugees to Settlers." *Göç Araştırmaları Dergisi* 3(1): 12–35. http://www.gam.gov.tr/files/5-2.pdf.

ILO (International Labour Organization). 2016. "Guiding Principles on the Access of Refugees and Other Forcibly Displaced Persons to the Labor Market." Retrieved 7 September 2021 from https://www.ilo.org/wcmsp5/groups/public/—ed_pro tect/—protrav/—migrant/documents/publication/wcms_536440.pdf.

Kirişçi, Kemal. 1996. "Refugees of Turkish Origin: 'Coerced Immigrants' to Turkey since 1945." *International Migration* 34(3): 385–412. https://doi.org/10.1111/j.1468-2435.1996.tb00534.x.

Korkmaz, Emre Eren. 2017. "How Do Syrian Refugee Workers Challenge Supply Chain Management in the Turkish Garment Industry?" *How Do Syrian Refugee Workers Challenge Supply Chain Management in the Turkish Garment Industry?* International Migration Institute (IMI). Retrieved 7 September 2021 from https://www.migrationinstitute.org/publications/how-do-syrian-refugee-workers-challenge-supply-chain-management-in-the-turkish-garment-industry.

Levi, Margaret. 1997. "A Model, A Method, and A Map: Rational Choice in Comparative and Historical Analysis." In *Comparative Politics: Rationality, Culture, and Structure*, edited by Mark Irving Lichbach and Alan S. Zuckerman, 19–41. Cambridge: Cambridge University Press.

Liversage, Anika. 2009. "Finding a Path: Investigating the Labor Market Trajectories of High-Skilled Immigrants in Denmark." *Journal of Ethnic and Migration Studies* 35(2): 203–26. https://doi.org/10.1080/13691830802586195.

Lordoğlu, Kuvvet, and Mustafa Aslan. 2016. "En Fazla Suriyeli Göçmen Alan Beş Kentin Emek Piyasalarında Değişimi: 2011–2014." *Çalışma ve Toplum* 49(2): 789–808. http://www.calismatoplum.org/sayi49/lordoglu.pdf.

Mahoney, James. 2000. "Path Dependence in Historical Sociology." *Theory and Society* 29(4): 507–48. www.jstor.org/stable/3108585.

MEDAM (Mercator Dialogue on Asylum and Migration). 2018. *2018 MEDAM Assessment Report on Asylum and Migration Policies in Europe*. Kiel: IfW

North, Douglass C. 1990. *Institutions, Institutional Change and Economic Performance*. Cambridge: Cambridge University Press.

OECD (Organisation for Economic Co-operation and Development). 2016. *Making Integration Work: Refugees and Others in Need of Protection*. Paris: OECD Publishing.

———. 2017. *International Migration Outlook 2017*. Paris: OECD Publishing.

———. 2019. *Harmonized Unemployment Rate (HUR) (indicator)*. doi: 10.1787/52570002-en.

OECD and UNHCR. 2016. "Hiring Refugees: What Are the Opportunities and Challenges for Employers?" *Migration Policy Debates*, no: 10.

———. 2018. *Engaging with Employers in the Hiring of Refugees: A 10-Point Multi-stakeholder Action Plan for Employers, Refugees, Governments and Civil Society*. Retrieved 5 October 2021 from https://www.unhcr.org/protection/livelihoods/5adde9904/engaging-employers-hiring-refugees-10-point-multi-stakeholder-action-plan.html.

Ortensi, Livia Elisa. 2015. "The Integration of Forced Migrants into the Italian Labor Market." *Journal of Immigrant & Refugee Studies* 13(2): 179–99. https://doi.org/10.1080/15562948.2014.907952.

Özpınar Esra, Yasemin S. Çilingir, and Ayşegül Taşöz Düşündere. 2016. "Syrians in Turkey: Unemployment and Social Cohesion." Ankara: TEPAV.

Park, Hans. 2016. "The Power of Cities." UNHCR Innovation. 25 November. Retrieved 7 September 2021 from https://www.unhcr.org/innovation/the-power-of-cities/.

Parla, Ayşe, and Didem Danış. 2009. "Irak ve Bulgaristan Türkleri Örneğinde Göçmen, Dernek ve Devlet" [Useless kinship: Immigrants, association and state, the cases of Iraqi and Bulgarian Turks]. *Toplum ve Bilim* 114: 131–58. http://research.sabanciuniv.edu/26757/1/NafileSoydaslik.pdf.

Ruhs, Martin. 2019. "Can Labor Immigration Work for Refugees." *Current History*: 22–28. https://cadmus.eui.eu/bitstream/handle/1814/60384/Ruhs-CH-Jan2019.pdf?sequence=2&isAllowed=y.

Srivastava, M. 2016. "Syrian Refugee Entrepreneurs Boost Turkey's Economy." *Financial Times*. Retrieved 27 July 2020 from https://www.ft.com/content/93e3d794-1826-11e6-b197-a4af20d5575e.

Steinmo, Sven, and Kathleen Ann. Thelen. 1992. "Historical Institutionalism in Comparative Politics." In *Structuring Politics: Historical Institutionalism in Comparative Analysis*, edited by Sven Steinmo, Kathleen Thelen, and Frank Longstreth, 1–32. Cambridge: Cambridge University Press.

Thelen, Kathleen, and Wolfgang Streeck. 2005. "Introduction: Institutional Change in Advanced Political Economies." In *Beyond Continuity: Institutional Change in Advanced Political Economies*, edited by Kathleen Thelen and Streeck Wolfgang, 1–39. Oxford: Oxford University Press.

Uluslararası İşgücü Kanunu [Law on international labor]. 2016. Retrieved 7 September 2021 from http://www.mevzuat.gov.tr/MevzuatMetin/1.5.6735.pdf.

UN (United Nations). 2016. "Resolution Adopted by the General Assembly on 19 September 2016: 71/1 New York Declaration for Refugees and Migrants." Retrieved 5 October 2021 from http://www.unhcr.org/57e39d987.

UNHCR (United Nations High Commissioner for Refugees). 2018. "Syria Regional Refugee Response." Retrieved 7 September 2021 from https://data2.unhcr.org/en/situations/syria/.

UNICEF (United Nations International Children's Emergency Fund). 2016. "Children of Syria in Turkey." http://www.unicef.org.tr/files/bilgimerkezi/doc/Childrenpercent20ofpercent20Syriapercent20inpercent20Turkey_Infopercent20Sheet_ percent20February percent202016_3.pdf.

Ward, Colleen, and Anne-Marie Masgoret. 2007. "Immigrant Entry into the Workforce: A Research Note from New Zealand." *International Journal of Intercultural Relations* 31(4): 525–30. https://doi.org/10.1016/j.ijintrel.2007.03.001.

Weiss, Yoram, Robert M. Sauer, and Menachem Gotlibovski. 2001. "Immigration, Search and Loss of Skill." *SSRN Electronic Journal*. https://doi.org/10.2139/ssrn.301554.

World Bank. 2015. "The Impact of Syrians on the Turkish Labor Market." Working Paper. Retrieved 7 September 2021 from https://data2.unhcr.org/en/documents/download/54522.

———. 2018. "Employment in Agriculture (Percent of Total Employment) (Modeled ILO Estimate)." https://data.worldbank.org/indicator/SL.AGR.EMPL.ZS.

Zetter, Roger, and Héloïse Ruaudel. 2018. "Refugees' Right to Work and Access to Labor Markets: Constraints, Challenges and Ways Forward." *Forced Migration Review* 58: 4–7. https://www.fmreview.org/sites/fmr/files/FMRdownloads/en/zetter-ruaudel.pdf.

5
Welfare Nationalism and Rising Prejudice against Migrants in Central and Eastern Europe

Anıl Duman

Introduction

Even though Central and Eastern European (CEE)[1] countries have not traditionally been the prime destinations for immigrants and refugees, the significance of migration has been increasing in the political debates as well as in academic research. In the past, the focus has been on the demographic challenge posed by the mass outflow of CEE citizens after accession to the European Union (EU). Since the arrival of a massive number of asylum seekers in 2015, the debate shifted toward the containment of refugee flows and non-European immigrants. At the EU level, CEE governments in general, and the Hungarian government in particular, opposed the mandatory scheme for the relocation of asylum applications and pushed for anti-immigrant policies. This scheme involved mandatory quotas for accepting refugees with the goal of a more equal geographical distribution; however, it was abandoned in 2018 after the strong opposition by CEE countries. Currently, the member states are allowed to receive refugees on a voluntary basis in designated areas within their territories and to screen migrants for their eligibility in applying for asylum prior to reaching the EU (Sarnyai 2018). These changes at the EU level are taken as a signal of CEE countries becoming policymakers and shapers after 2015, as the domestic responses to the refugee crisis and more broadly to international migration were influential in shaping the migration regimes and views across European countries (Geddes and Scholten 2016).

There are three main arguments in this chapter with regards to the relationship between public attitude toward refugees and migrants and policy outcomes. First, we claim that the recent explosion of anti-immigrant sentiments in the CEE region can only be partially explained by the rise in the number of refugees and asylum seekers. While the salience of immigration peaked during the massive refugee flows to Europe, it considerably declined, with the exception of Hungary, immediately afterward. We also show that while a majority of the people in the CEE region believe that foreigners working and living in their nation do not improve the economy, there is less concern about foreigners undermining the cultural life. Over the years there has been a higher proportion of people who deem immigration as harmful for the economy; however, there is no uniform trend with regards to the opinions about the effect of immigration on the country in general, even after the refugee influx. Hence, we propose that the economic fears are relatively stable and are vastly crucial in shaping the public attitudes against migrants and refugees across CEE countries.

Secondly, we argue that welfare nationalism in the region is particularly high and resilient, which can explain a large part of the anti-immigrant sentiments among citizens. We assert that the already existing prejudices against migrants are further elevated by the political discourse in the CEE region through the instrumental usage by politicians and feed into welfare nationalism. Similar to many other European countries, also in all CEE nations, immigration is overwhelmingly portrayed as a security problem by the politicians and as a potential threat to the homogeneity of the nation. Nonetheless, the symbolic threats in the region are often packed tightly together with economic losses, especially in terms of reductions in welfare benefits for the local citizens. Especially, with the imminent and visible flow of a huge number of refugees and asylum seekers, politicians are able to enmesh the deeply rooted economic fears and cultural sensitivities, leading to strong public opinions about who should receive welfare benefits in general and under what conditions the immigrants should be given the same rights and services. We show that all countries, but particularly Hungary and Czechia, saw large increases in welfare nationalism after the refugee crisis, which is not the general trend in Europe. A very significant part of the public affirmed that immigrants should never obtain social benefits and services even if they contribute to the labor market and pay taxes or become citizens.

Finally, we suggest that welfare nationalism and the perceptions about the immigrants' deservingness of social rights are not primarily determined by the individuals' socioeconomic position. Although income, education, and labor market status can be undeniably significant in explaining welfare attitudes, sociotropic concerns about the overall health of the system, and a sense of shared identity, might dominate self-interest motives. On the one hand, people who might have either nothing to lose or something to gain from immigrants' inclusion into the welfare system could have very restrictive attitudes. On the other hand, people who might typically be exposed to greater economic competition might be more supportive. As discussed previously, economic anxieties with respect to immigration have always been more prevalent in the CEE region and remain so in the aftermath of the refugee crisis. However, our findings indicate that perceived economic threats are not necessarily driven by individuals' socioeconomic positions, and a significantly higher percentage of the citizens in the CEE countries deem ethnic identity or belonging to a nation as the main basis for welfare entitlements and social assistance. Hence, as outsiders, the immigrants are denied social benefits after they work and are perceived to generate a burden for public resources. In all CEE countries, the percentage of people who view immigrants as not deserving of the same rights, even when they obtain citizenship, is notably higher than in the rest of the EU member countries, which clearly implies that ethnic or other common identities together with more economic anxieties are fundamental to understand the anti-immigrant sentiment in the regions.

In the next section, we summarize a number of theories about the determinants of migration attitudes, how these are shaping welfare nationalism and leading to exclusionary preferences. The third section discusses public opinion and salience of migration in the CEE region between 2002 and 2018. In the fourth section, we look into the development of welfare nationalism in these countries and possible determinants. The final section offers a few concluding remarks on the further impact of selective solidarity for migration policies in the CEE region.

Migration and Welfare Nationalism

In the literature, economic and cultural anxieties are discussed as the two most important sources of anti-immigration prejudices. The most widely discussed effects of migration on the recipient country's economy occur through labor market adjustments. When a large number of foreigners enter, labor supply expands and, depending on the skill composition of the newcomers, the relative returns in the labor market change. For example, the low-skilled immigrants would hurt low-skilled natives primarily due to reduced wages, which in turn increases the possibility that the latter group would oppose migration-friendly policies (Scheve and Slaughter 2001). Despite their intuition, labor market competition theories usually fall short of explaining the public opinion on migration. There is little evidence indicating whether skills, unemployment rate, or GDP per capita is significant in capturing the variance of attitudes toward immigrants and refugees either at the country level or across countries. It has been shown that immigration does not decrease wages or generate unemployment (Card 2005). Yet, the beliefs about economic competition and perceptions about immigrants lowering wages mean job opportunities and welfare benefits can have major effects on the formation of attitudes (Hainmueller, Hiscox, and Margalit 2015). Hence, the more recent work focuses on the perceptions rather than objective threats in the labor market, and it has been confirmed that perceptions about competition rather than actual competition is explanatory for public opinion on migration across nations (Hainmueller et al. 2015; Schneider 2008).

Cultural anxieties that are related to migration include a fear of the unknown and an aversion to becoming exposed to new beliefs and customs. If the members of a particular ethnic or cultural group perceive differences in values, norms, and beliefs with the immigrants, they are more likely to have prejudices and favor anti-immigration policies (Sidanius and Pratto 1999; Stephan, Ybarra, and Bachman 1999). These symbolic threats would be more pronounced if the sensed social distance from the immigrant groups was higher. The existence of outsiders could serve to raise the cohesion within the group and hence could be used as a tool by politicians and people controlling the social and cultural practices. The realistic and symbolic threats might not be related to self-interest, and arrival of immigrants could be viewed as detrimental to the overall institutional setup or the way of life of all citizens in a nation. In other words, sociotropic concerns might be as important as self-interest in shaping people's opinions about migration and their policy preferences. Nonetheless, there is scarce empirical testing of sociotropic considerations both economically and culturally. The difficulty of operationalization and lack of cross-country data make it hard to distinguish the impact of perceived collective threats on immigration attitudes. However, in the existing studies it has been found that there are substantial differences between societies, and while in some nations the sociotropic economic issues are found to be more prevalent, in other nations the cultural conflicts are key to the determination of the public views on refugees and migrants (Hainmueller and Hopkins 2014).

Beliefs about economic losses that are usually associated with an influx of migrants also include reduction of welfare benefits, and even though these could be subjective, they are still realistic threats concerning material interests of the citizens of the nation. Additionally, ideas about welfare benefits can be closely linked to group identity and belonging. All welfare states are based on a complex web of relations among the recipients and providers who perceive themselves as belonging to a particular state. National identity, social rights, and obligations intersect and form strict divisions in terms of deservingness. Immigration adds further complications to welfare state relations as there is no straightforward answer to the question of what the responsibilities of the states should be in delivering welfare benefits to non-citizens (Bommes and Geddes 2000). Welfare nationalism is offered as a bridge between citizens' opinions about who should be receiving social transfers, public assistance, and immigration preferences. Even though the term "welfare nationalism" has different meanings for different researchers, it can broadly be understood as the restriction of welfare state access to the native citizen population and denial of entitlements to new members that do not share common ancestry within that state (Heizmann, Jedinger, and Perry 2018). People who have restrictive preferences for welfare state entitlements are more likely to resist open migration policies and demand exclusion of migrants having access to social rights. Contrarily, people who are more generous toward others with regards to social benefits and services are expected to also be more welcoming to refugees and immigrants.

Although the literature on welfare nationalism is growing, it is a difficult subject to examine fully at a cross-country level. For example, considering the basis of national identity, the perceived distance between the immigrants from national identity criteria and the deservingness of immigrants on nonidentity criteria, such as need or work ethic, have to be defined (Kootstra 2016; Reeskens and van Oorschot 2012). While any one of these dimensions is difficult to conceptualize, the overall lack of solidarity with the migrants appears to be the most crucial aspect of welfare nationalism. When the individuals believe that immigrants are free riders and do not contribute their fair share, it is highly unlikely that there will be support for their access to social benefits. However, it should be noted that assessment of the non-natives' deservingness is not binary, and across countries, on average, people support conditional inclusion (Reeskens and van Oorschot 2012). Once immigrants begin working and paying taxes they are regarded as being worthy of entitlement and can be granted similar welfare advances as the natives. (Reeskens and van Oorschot 2012). On the other hand, there are welfare nationalists who would like to exclude the migrants from social benefits and services all together, and we observe that the share of welfare nationalists is exceptionally high in the CEE region.

Borrowing from the realistic and symbolic threat theories, welfare nationalism at the individual level can also be explained by the perceived competition between natives and immigrants. The social benefits are scarce, and the distributional conflicts are zero-sum games in which one group wins at the expense of the others (Kootstra 2016; Reeskens and van Oorschot 2012). A direct implication of these models is a higher welfare nationalism among individuals who have more to lose if the immigrants are given the same access to welfare provisions. For example, the unskilled employees, the unemployed, and the people who are dependent on transfer payments would be more opposed to the inclusion of migrants. In contrast, the socioeconomically advantaged groups who might not fear competition and do not typically receive welfare benefits can be more open to inclusion and granting social rights to immigrants. In the limited number of studies, it has been found that strict forms of welfare nationalism are associated with low education, income, occupational status, and perceived economic insecurity (Mewes and Mau 2013; Larsen, Frederiksen, and Nielsen 2018). Besides the individual level factors, welfare nationalism can be related to the sociotropic concerns people hold about the well-being of the society they live in rather than their own self-interest. The group identity, which can be based on class, ethnicity, industry, or nation as a whole, could have a larger impact on opinions about immigration (Ford 2011; Dancygier and Donnelly 2013). While some of the characteristics that form the group identity will overlap with the personal characteristics, there can also be mismatches between them. A highly educated and well-employed individual could have higher degrees of welfare nationalism and restrictive attitudes toward immigration, despite the potential gains from cheaper and complementary labor, if the collective concerns are overwhelming.

There is considerable divergence between the extent of welfare nationalism across Europe as well as within countries. In the empirical studies, it has been shown that the majority of Europeans ask for conditional inclusion either based on work and tax payments or on becoming citizens (Mewes and Mau 2013). There is also a significant portion of respondents, around 16 percent, who favor unconditional access, and another 9 percent who demand to be completely exclusive and prefer denying immigrants the same rights to social benefits and services. The inclusionist and exclusionist views are highly concentrated in Scandinavian regions where support for unconditional access is, on average, more widespread, and support for unconditional restriction is most common in the CEE region and the Baltics (Kulin, Eger, and Hjerm 2016). Yet socioeconomic positions are argued to be insignificant to account for favoring skilled migrants over unskilled ones across countries (Valentino et al. 2019). While this finding is interpreted as verification for lack of welfare nationalism, it only suggests that individual factors are not crucial. Besides, the low-skilled migrants usually are perceived to have higher dependency on welfare benefits and social assistance, which might be the reason for disfavoring them as a group. Research has also shown that during the latest refugee flows, asylum seekers have been treated with more generosity, and welfare nationalism went down on average in Europe but not in CEE countries (Heizmann et al. 2018).

We focus on the role of welfare state attitudes and argue that they represent both economic and social fears people hold about immigrants, which do not always correspond to the individual's labor market and social status.

As will be shown later, the CEE region continues to be the exception with no clear decline in welfare nationalism and even substantial increases in Hungary and Czechia after the refugee crisis. Hence, examining welfare state attitudes can potentially inform us about the sociotropic concerns of the natives with regards to protection of the ethnic identity and how these translate into migration preferences. To this end, we investigate the developments in welfare nationalism and reasons for observing high and resilient levels of welfare nationalism in some CEE countries. Additionally, a number of individual characteristics such as education, labor market status, and income are considered to understand whether welfare nationalism is self-interest driven. Before moving to the analysis of welfare nationalism, the following section looks into the public opinion on migration and its political salience over time in the CEE region.

Public Opinion on Migration and Its Salience in the CEE

The majority of the studies in migration literature pay attention to public opinion and how this influences policy. Even though there would not be a perfect correspondence between the individual-level preferences and policy outcomes, it is hardly conceivable that the elected politicians would disregard public opinion. Moreover, politicians might find it beneficial to instrumentally use the anxieties people have over migration to steer the policy platform in a specific direction. Hence, studying public opinion is very relevant in the context of migration, and there are many studies looking at the perceived economic, social, and cultural threats influencing people's views on the issue. A number of empirical regularities have been established in the literature despite huge cross-country differences. For example, not the actual but rather the perceived economic competition and overall macroeconomic conditions are found to be significant. Although prejudice and ethnocentrism are generally associated with restrictive immigration attitudes, there are crucial differences with regards to the immigrant groups. Also, at the individual level, education is argued to be consistently and positively related to more positive attitudes toward immigration, and not merely due to the lower labor market competition (Hainmueller and Hopkins 2014).

The literature on individual preferences with regards to migration almost exclusively concentrates on the determinants and does not necessarily explore the changes in opinions over time. Besides, the overwhelming majority of the studies does not focus on the CEE region but looks at all EU member states, which overlook the significant variation across regions. In the few studies that consider evolution of migration attitudes, it has been established that antimigrant sentiments go up with the size of non-EU populations. However, the changes in GDP per capita are found to be not explanatory for attitudes suggesting the secondary role of economic variables (Semyonov, Raijman, and Gorodzeisky 2006). The later works investigating the changes over time also support these results, as the share of foreign-born populations repeatedly emerge as an important predictor. However, higher unemployment and proportion of social benefit expenditures in GDP are also documented as factors that are increasing antimigrant preferences (Hatton 2016). We first try to examine the impact of a sudden rise in the number of asylum seekers and refugees over the last five years on public opinion about migration and the political salience of the issue. One of the immediate effects of migration is raising the possibility of interaction, hence making the issue more salient for the general public. Also, if the flow is rapid, as it was in the case of refugee arrivals in 2015, the visibility of immigrant groups would go up, fueling the numerous types of anxieties evident in mainstream society.

Historically, CEE countries are not key destinations for migration, and, as can be seen from table 5.1, the total number of immigrants in the region is extremely low compared to some Western European countries. Migrants from both the EU and countries outside it remain limited, which raises doubts about the possibility of economic competition. In Czechia and Slovenia, the stock of foreign-born populations is around 4.9 percent and 5.9 percent respectively, but in the rest of the countries, it is well below 1 percent and has not increased over time. A similar picture arises when the number of asylum seekers is taken into account, since, with the exception of Hungary, there was no abrupt rise in applications. Hungary, on the other hand, had 177,135 asylum applications in 2015 alone, which is larger than the total number of asylum seekers in the rest of the CEE countries. Nonetheless, this number dropped to 671 in 2018, primarily due to the harsh policies implemented by the government. It should also be noted that more than 60 percent of the applications were from Syrian and Afghan refugees. In other parts of the region, the asylum applications were at 12,815 in Poland and 1,515 in Czechia even during the peak of refugee flows. As can be understood from these figures, Hungary appears to be the only country that received a sizable number of refugees, and we argue that political salience of immigration in Hungary increased due to both the negative media coverage and the relatively large number of asylum seekers in the aftermath of 2015 events.

In order to understand how the refugee flows have altered the public opinion about immigration, we examine people's views about foreigners' impact on economic and sociocultural conditions. We argue that economic concerns in the region are more persistent than social and cultural threats today and that the increase in the recent arrival of refugees has raised the economic fears even further. To measure each, we use two questions from the European Social Survey that have been continually asked since 2002.

Table 5.1. Population and Stock of Immigrants in CEE–2018.

	Population	EU-28	Non-EU
Czechia	10,649,800	219,400	296,100
Hungary	9,778,371	78,000	83,400
Poland	37,879,862	30,100	208,600
Slovakia	5,457,526	19,500	102,300
Slovenia	2,078,768	55,900	15,400

Source: Eurostat.

The same wording of the questions and the repeated nature enable us to understand the evolution of economic and social fears related to migration at the national level. Although both questions are very broad and vague, they provide a measure of the average opinion in all EU member states. Table 5.2 presents the share of people who reported that immigration is bad for the country's economy in the first column for each country and the share of people who asserted that immigrants make the country a worse place to live in the second column.[2] As can be seen from the data, with the exception of Poland, immigrants were increasingly recognized as harmful for the economy over the years. The largest rise was observed in Hungary where more than 21 percent of the respondents claimed that having immigrants would be bad for the economy. Also, in Czechia, the share of people who are concerned about the nation's economy has nearly doubled since 2002. Contrarily, in Western European countries, the views about immigrants harming the economy only slightly increased from 5.8 percent to 6.5 percent, on average. Also, unlike the CEE nations, there is no persistent increase as economies that received the largest number of refugees such as Germany and Greece experienced declines in the negative opinions.

When we look at the portion of surveyors affirming that immigration makes a country a worse place to live, the bias influences movement in the region. Besides Poland, in all CEE countries in 2016, more people agreed with the statement, and the ratios are comparative with 12 percent in Czechia and 14 percent in Hungary. Once again, Hungary stands out for having the least pro-migration attitudes. Nevertheless, it should be noted that economic fears are still much higher than social fears, and this is true for all cases excluding the 2016 results in Czechia. In all of the CEE countries, respondents have always been more worried about the perceived economic costs of migration at the national level than perceived social costs. This is in stark contrast to the anxieties respondents declared in the old EU member states, which display much lower ratios for immigrants being viewed as bad for the economy, and the rise over the years is much less substantial.

Table 5.2. Social versus Economic Fears in the CEE.

	Czechia		Hungary		Poland		Slovenia	
	Bad for Economy	Bad for Country	Bad for Economy	Bad for Country	Bad for Economy	Bad for Country	Bad for Economy	Bad for Country
2002	5.9	4.2	8.8	9.5	6.1	2.4	7.5	4.5
2004	9.1	7.8	11.6	7.6	8	3.7	7.5	3.6
2006			17.1	12.8	4.3	1.6	8.9	5.4
2008	7	5.2	12.9	10.6	2.7	0.9	7	5.3
2010	7.3	5.4	10.4	7.1	3.7	1.2	6.4	4.6
2012	9.6	7.8	10.6	7.4	4.9	2.1	8.6	5.1
2014	10.6	7.6	12.1	7.6	5.9	1.9	11.8	6.4
2016	10.3	12	21.5	14	5.3	1.2	12.3	7.9

Source: Author's calculations based on the European Social Survey (ESS).[3]

However, with respect to two cultural fears, the differences between the two regions are not equally high. For example, in Italy and Austria, there have been comparable increases in the share of people asserting that immigrants make the country a worse place to live. This ratio is 15.6 percent in Italy and 10.5 percent in Austria, but the average share of respondents remained at 6 percent in 2016 for Western Europe. Hence, economic concerns in the CEE region remain particularly relevant and need further investigation, especially for grasping the reasons why these fears instead of worries about culture and social life have become more widespread after the refugee crisis in 2015.

In addition to public opinion on migration, salience has the potential to affect policy and shape the migration regime in a country. Salience of an issue can be effective on policymaking as politicians cannot fully ignore the matters that are viewed as highly important by the voters. For example, several studies demonstrate that media coverage of politics indicates the salience of an issue and raises political accountability through informing voters (Snyder and Stromberg 2010). A positive association between the salience and effect of public opinion on policy has been found in the literature over a range of different issues. Yet with regards to migration, it has been suggested that there is loose correspondence between public opinion and policy (Lax and Phillips 2012). Even the restrictive migration systems are not meeting the demands of the public, and there is a large deviation between the rules governing the migratory flows and what citizens prefer. A number of potential reasons, such as low salience, lack of mobilization among anti-immigrant individuals, and relative autonomy of governing

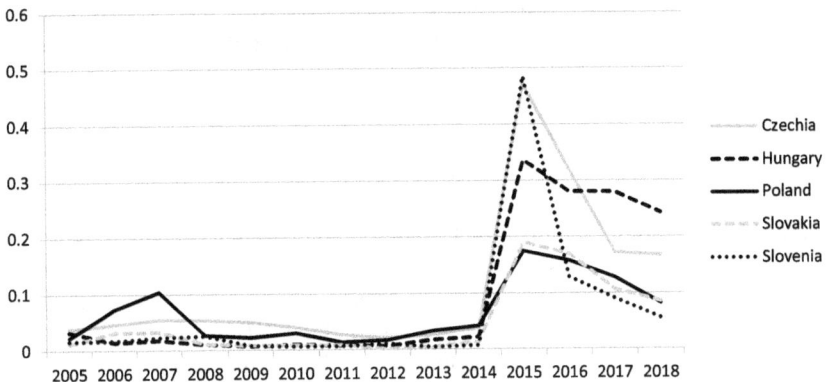

Figure 5.1. Salience of Immigration in CEE. © Anıl Duman.

elites, have been offered to explain the divergence between the immigration attitudes and policy results (Hatton 2017). In recent studies, it has been proposed that the rise in the salience of migration and higher share of negative sentiments obliged governments to change the policies in various European countries (Ford, Jennings, and Somerville 2015).

As mentioned in the introduction of this chapter, migration has always been an important component of the political debates in the region, but these are mostly focused on the within-EU labor flows and integration of CEE nationals in the Western European countries. However, the onset of the civil war that began in 2011 in Syria and the following displacement of people transformed the contours of public debate in the region, and migration became one of the most politicized topics. This development can also be seen from the sudden rise in people's opinion about the significance of immigration as an issue, which is taken to be the core measure of salience in this chapter. We use a question in the Eurobarometer survey that has been repeated over the years in which the surveyors are asked to pick the two most important issues facing their country at the moment. Immigration is among the fourteen political issues[4] that are listed, and, as can be seen from figure 5.1, it was hardly selected by the respondents as the most important issue. Only after 2015 did the citizens of CEE countries begin to express their concerns about migration, yet in 2015 nearly 50 percent of the surveyors cited it as the most significant matter in Czechia and Slovenia, In Poland and Slovenia, the salience was below 20 percent even during the refugee crisis period. Hungary, however, ranked in the middle with almost 34 percent of the respondents stating migration as the most important issue in 2015. Nevertheless, Hungary deviates from the other countries in the region as the salience continued to be high, and it was recorded to be around 25 percent in 2018. The only other country where migration was seen as a significant matter is Czechia, with slightly more than 16 percent of its respondents indicating the issue. After 2015, immigration lost its weight in the eyes of citizens in Poland, Slovakia, and Slovenia and became much less of a concern.

One of the factors that affects the salience of an issue is the press coverage. It is no surprise that the media's portrayal of immigration-related controversies and events increases people's awareness. The refugees and migrants' arrival to Europe was framed as a crisis by the press, and the newcomers were primarily characterized as outsiders. Hate speech and hostility toward refugees and migrants was systematically presented in the media and was much more widespread in the CEE countries, especially Hungary. Another distinguishing feature of the Hungarian media was the heavy emphasis on economic reasons for migration along with narratives of security (Georgiou and Zaborowski 2017). Additionally, Prime Minister Orban launched a "National Consultation campaign on immigration and terrorism"[5] in early 2015, explaining that migrants needed to be stopped as they were all illegally crossing the borders and seeking to exploit welfare systems and employment opportunities. The press coverage together with the political discourse adopted by the governing party, Fidesz, and main opposition party, Jobbik, has elevated the salience of immigration since 2015 and supported it to remain the most important concern in Hungary even after the refugee crisis subsided. Contrarily, in Poland migration was not picked by the mainstream media, although there were various verbal attacks and negative portrayals in the right-wing press. For example, one of the most prominent newspapers, *Gazeta Wyborcza*, published with several other outlets an informative campaign on refugees in Poland with the goal of lowering fears through knowledge (Narkowicz 2018). Yet, it should be also noted that various state officials, church representatives, and civil society organizations continue to emphasize the Otherness of the refugees and tend to criminalize these groups in Poland.

Economic developments influenced the relative salience of migration, particularly the global financial crisis that put economic concerns at the top. Indeed, nearly 50 percent of the respondents picked economic issues as the most important in the CEE region during the 2009 and 2010 era with the exception of Poland. And in all of the countries, the salience of the economy declined gradually afterward, falling to less than 10 percent in Czechia yet remaining relatively high, around 23 percent, only in Slovenia by 2018. However, it should be noted as well that the economy continues to be seen as a problem regularly in these countries, and even though there has been a decline in recent years, it remains to be the top-ranking issue after the refugee flows in Poland, Slovakia, and Slovenia. Only in Czechia and Hungary can immigration be seen as a bigger concern than the economy over the recent years. In contrast, among the Western European countries, economy is

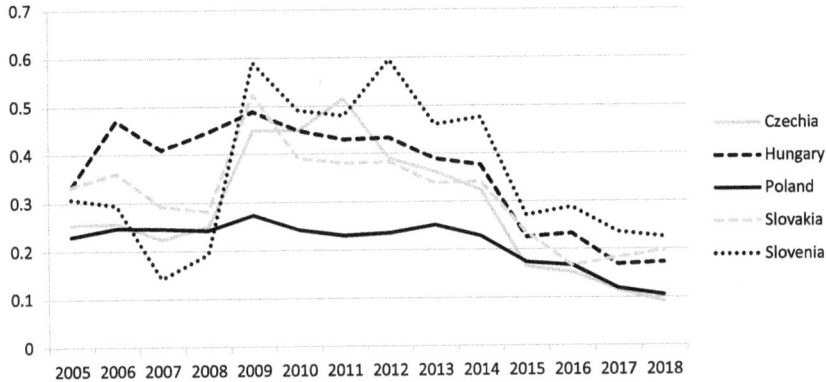

Figure 5.2. Salience of Economy in CEE. © Anıl Duman.

ranked above immigration with the exception of Greece. The latest refugee influx to this country caused migration to be viewed as the greatest problem. These examples suggest that in the CEE region, the arrival of asylum seekers turns out to be an important factor behind the growing political salience of immigration. In the next section, we try to establish the links between the resilient economic fears and negative attitudes toward refugees and migrants through welfare nationalism, and we propose that welfare nationalism based partially on economic fears and partially on sociocultural identities is explanatory for the rising anti-immigrant sentiments.

Resilience of Welfare Nationalism and Anti-Immigration Sentiments in the CEE

As mentioned earlier in this chapter, the migration attitudes in the region shifted dramatically, and people became much more concerned about foreigners living in their countries. We suggest that the rise of the antimigration sentiments in the CEE region can be attributed to the growing welfare nationalism. Table 5.3 presents the share of respondents opposed to granting the same rights to immigrants with citizens between 2008 and 2016.[6] There are five options that surveyors can choose from: immediately upon arrival; after a year, whether or not they have worked; after working and paying taxes for at least a year; once they have become a citizen; and the last option, they should never get the same rights. While people who ask for immigrants having the same rights upon arrival can be denoted as inclusionary, people who are in favor of never giving the same rights are accepted as welfare nationalists. As can be seen in table 5.3, there is an increase in welfare nation-

Table 5.3. Welfare Nationalism in the CEE Region.

2008	Immediately on arrival	After a year, whether or not have worked	After worked and paid taxes at least a year	Once they have become a citizen	They should never get the same rights
Czechia	2.5	5.3	35.4	41.3	15.4
Hungary	1.5	3	29.4	52.1	14.1
Poland	5.6	7.2	39.4	45.5	2.3
Slovenia	4.1	4.9	32.7	51.4	6.8
2016	Immediately on arrival	After a year, whether or not have worked	After worked and paid taxes at least a year	Once they have become a citizen	They should never get the same rights
Czechia	5.2	3.7	31.9	34.1	25.1
Hungary	2	3.2	37	28.7	29.1
Poland	4.1	5.2	40.9	41.8	7.9
Slovenia	4.3	7.9	34.3	46	7.6

Source: Author's calculations based on the ESS.

alism in all CEE countries. Given that the survey data was collected before and after the refugee crisis in Europe, part of the surge can be ascribed to the events that took place in 2015. However, with the exception of Hungary, none of these countries had a significant migrant flow, and yet welfare nationalism went up significantly, which is not the case for the rest of the EU member states. On average, welfare nationalism rose from 8.4 percent to 9.1 percent in Europe between 2008 and 2016. Contrarily, Hungary and Czechia, which already had much higher levels of welfare nationalism–14.1 percent and 15.4 percent in 2008–also experienced the biggest changes and represent the highest degrees within Europe, 29.1 percent and 25.1 percent. Poland and Slovenia had lower support for welfare nationalism, and despite the increase, they are still below the EU average.

It should also be noted that the share of respondents willing to grant rights immediately after the migrants arrive in the CEE region is well below the European means in all nations including Poland and Slovenia. For example, in 2008, the share of people who agreed that immigrants should be given the same benefits once they enter the country ranges from 19.5 percent in Sweden to 10.1 percent in Portugal. After the refugee inflow in 2015, these ratios did not go down at all and remained at approximately 18.2 percent in Sweden and rose to 18.8 percent in Portugal. Thus, welfare nationalism cannot be said to have increased everywhere in Europe, and even in countries that received a high number of refugees and asylum seekers public opinion became more inclusionary. In contrast, the views about immigrants obtain-

Table 5.4. Welfare Nationalism in the CEE Region across Education.

	Lowest Education	Highest Education
Czechia	30.6	17.2
Hungary	32.4	27.2
Poland	12.1	5.4
Slovenia	9.6	4.1

Source: Author's calculations based on ESS-2016.

ing the same social rights deteriorated over time: migrants are accepted to be welfare-deserving only after they contribute to the economy by working and paying taxes.

Self-interest could be the driving force behind welfare state attitudes, and as discussed previously in this chapter, individuals with lower socioeconomic positions are expected to be less favorable of sharing scarce welfare benefits with immigrants. Hence, low education, low income, and unemployment would raise welfare nationalism, as these groups will be the recipients of social assistance. Tables 5.4 and 5.5 show the distribution of welfare nationalism across education and income categories. There is a clear inverse relation between education and welfare nationalism in Czechia, Poland, and Slovenia, where respondents having lower degrees of education are significantly more in favor of excluding migrants from social rights and welfare benefits. Yet in Czechia, 17.2 percent of the highest-educated people tend to be welfare nationalists. In Hungary, education only slightly influences respondents since even the highly educated are opposed to granting the same social benefits and services. The welfare systems in the CEE countries display commonalities in terms of the nature of the groups receiving transfers, and there is no evidence that the Hungarian welfare state is more favorable to the skilled people.

Comparable results are obtained for the relationship between income and welfare nationalism in the CEE region. As can be seen from Table 5.5, in Czechia, Poland, and Slovenia, surveyors from the bottom decile have greater inclination for exclusion, whereas their top decile counterparts are more favorable toward immigrants. However, it should be noted that like the case of education in Czechia, still 18.3 percent of the individuals with high incomes are welfare nationalists, and this ratio is well above Western European countries. Once again, Hungary exemplifies an interesting case where the relatively wealthier group, tenth decile, has more welfare nationalistic tendencies than the relatively poorer group, first decile, with 29.2 percent and 26.2 percent respectively. We also looked into the association between labor market status, employed, unemployed, and retired; we

Table 5.5. Welfare Nationalism in the CEE Region across Income.

	1st decile	10th decile
Czechia	33.5	18.3
Hungary	26.2	29.2
Poland	14.6	4.8
Slovenia	14.1	0

Source: Author's calculations based on ESS-2016.

found no links, with the exception being a retiree in Czechia and Hungary. However, the number of respondents in each category is too low to reach any meaningful conclusions. Overall, our preliminary empirical investigation points out that the self-interest motives are not accountable for the high levels of welfare nationalism in all CEE countries, particularly in Hungary. In the remaining section we consider the role of ethnic identity and how it is instrumentalized by political parties for understanding the rise in welfare nationalism and more generally anti-immigrant prejudices in the region.

Welfare nationalism, described as a unique combination of egalitarianism and social exclusion, has been growing across most European countries, and it has been shown that "welfare for our own kind" gained prominence in the political discussions among right-wing parties (Eger and Valdez 2014). In Western societies, the emphasis on deservingness and need for social protection for only the legitimate part of the nation has been generally explained by the large influx of immigrants throughout the 1990s, increasing diversity. Nonetheless, the CEE region has not experienced any major migrant inflows, and most of the immigrants traditionally have come from neighboring countries. In some cases, in this instance Hungary, often ethnic Hungarians were returning to their nation, so the ethnic composition did not change much (Juhasz 2003). Yet table 5.5 reveals that some CEE countries have much higher degrees of welfare nationalism and have experienced increases over time. The success of right-wing parties in exploiting and shaping welfare attitudes proves to be one of the main factors as to why exclusion of migrants is more widely preferred in the region. The frames of us versus them and arguing that only the true citizens should receive public help are highly common in the political debates, as is blaming the imagined outsiders (Lugosi 2018). Immigrants, especially outside of Europe, become easy targets, and the perceived social distance between them and natives has been manipulated by right-wing parties to consolidate power domestically. These rhetorical tools have been frequently employed by leaders like Orban, who claims to be the defender of European borders and European values that are betrayed by the EU and politicians in Brussels.

Cultural conflicts have been at the core of party politics in many of these countries since the transition, and these conflicts have provided space for political polarization along ethnic and religious lines (Enyedi 2016; Pytlas 2015). From the very beginning of democratization, a significant divide has existed between the cosmopolitan liberals and nationalists in Hungary, and although the cultural battles are less pronounced in the rest of the CEE countries, they maintain a key position in the right-wing party rhetoric. For example, similar discursive tools are utilized for non-European immigrants in comparison to the ethnic and religious minorities, such as Roma and Jews being identified as foreign elements and criminals. By not being members of the imagined communities, these groups are claimed to have no legitimacy for enjoying the same rights and benefits as the natives. Given the significance of ethnic homogeneity in the national discourses, debates on minority rights, and the radical right's ability to capitalize on the movement against non-European immigrants, cultural anxieties are undoubtedly explanatory for the public opinion on migration (Korkut 2014; Bustikova 2018). However, it should be noted that in all CEE countries, right-wing parties bundle the cultural fears together with economic losses, particularly migrants draining welfare benefits. Not only is this group portrayed as culturally distant and dangerous for the ethnically defined communities but migrants are criticized and held accountable for taking away social assistance and economic opportunities from the truly deserving members of the nation. This kind of propaganda obviously has the capability not only to affect the opinions of right-wing voters but also to steer the views of the general public in the direction of welfare nationalism.

Conclusion

CEE nations occupy an interesting position with regards to immigration attitudes and policies in contemporary Europe given both a low share of a foreign-born population and a very common share of negative attitudes. This chapter highlights welfare nationalism as an explanation for the high and persistent antimigrant sentiments. Welfare nationalism provides a link between the cultural and economic fears citizens hold about outsiders, yet these fears do not always overlap with the individuals' socioeconomic status. First, we show that migration attitudes in the region became more negative since the beginning of 2000s, and although this has been the case for both economic and cultural dimensions, perceived economic losses were larger. Additionally, the salience of the issue peaked in 2015 but fell significantly afterward, with the exception of Hungary, while the salience of economic concerns was mostly maintained and surpassed the worries about immigration. The right-wing political parties and the associated media outlets were instrumental in stimulating the existing anxieties in these societies and successfully combined the perceived economic threats with sociocultural ones. Hence, immigrants became the center of political attention, and the political discourse managed to affect public opinion negatively by playing into the economic fears.

Our findings also reveal that welfare nationalism in the CEE region increased significantly and remained high, particularly in Hungary and Czechia. Economic anxieties with respect to immigration have always been more prevalent in the region and they remain so in the aftermath of the refugee crisis. Nevertheless, a major share of the citizens in CEE countries regards ethnic or other social identities as the main basis for welfare entitlements and social assistance, rather than economic bases, and refute the same rights and services for the immigrants. While welfare nationalism is not unique to the region, the degree of exclusion in these countries is particularly high and even rose higher with the inflow of refugees and political campaigns. Notions of deservingness have been repeatedly used by the right-wing political parties to emphasize the social divides between insiders and outsiders. Due to the historical peculiarities of the region, such as the magnitude of cultural conflicts, disputes over the existing minority groups and lack of experience with integration made it easier to politicize immigration and consolidate support for exclusionary policies.

We show that a big part of the welfare nationalism in the CEE region cannot be fully captured by the individual-level factors, such as education, income, and labor market status. Although socioeconomic position is relevant and, as expected, poorer and less-educated individuals are more opposed to immigrants' social rights, still a large number of relatively better off individuals share the same opinion. This suggests that ethnic or other social identities are taken to be the main basis for welfare entitlements and social assistance in the CEE countries. The immigrants who are perceived to be outsiders are easily viewed as undeserving of receiving social benefits even after they participate in the labor market and become citizens. "Welfare for our own kind" plays an important role in the political discourse of these nations, and right-wing parties are able to defend and foster restrictive policies on the grounds of deservingness and need for social protection. The public supports exclusionary rhetoric, given the persistent and highly salient economic concerns and abrupt exposure to the refugee flows.

Welfare nationalism and its role in raising prejudices against migrants has become the center of many political studies and policy analyses in recent years. The vast cross-country differences in terms of citizens' willingness to share welfare benefits with the immigrants versus favoring restrictions could hint at the future direction of policymaking. The CEE region and several countries, especially Hungary and Czechia, display significantly higher welfare nationalistic attitudes, which already have a negative impact on the debates about migration policies across Europe. This might imply that sustainability of welfare systems that are based on solidarity and inclusion can be shaken even in societies where there is no visible change in the ethnic composition. Given that perceptions about "us versus them" and seeing migrants as outsiders are sufficient to fuel welfare nationalism in regions like the CEE where the foreign-born population is not sizable, social policy could still be based on identity. At the moment, both the significance of immigration as an issue and how this issue is discussed are very much determined by the right-wing political parties. The mainstream parties could be forced to accept even more restrictive agendas in the future if welfare nationalism and associated discourse in the CEE region are not strategically challenged.

Anıl Duman is currently associate professor at Central European University, Budapest. Her broad research interests include political economy, industrial relations, welfare state policies, and redistribution. In her recent research, she has been specializing on the interrelations between labor market status and socioeconomic inequalities. Her previous research focuses on analysis of skill formation, skill distribution, and their relation to individual policy preferences across countries and over time. She is also involved in research projects examining the transformation of social protection regimes in several transition countries.

Notes

1. We include Hungary, Poland, Czechia, Slovakia, and Slovenia in the sample of Central and Eastern European countries throughout the analyses in the chapter.
2. The exact wording of the questions is as follows: "Would you say it is generally bad or good for [country]'s economy that people come to live here from other countries?" "Is [country] made a worse or a better place to live by people coming to live here from other countries?" The respondents have a scale from zero to ten, zero being bad/worse and ten being good/better.
3. The ESS is a face-to-face conducted survey that started in 2002, and it has been held every two years in a number of European countries with a list of standard questions and special modules in each wave.
4. The fourteen issues are crime, the economic situation, energy-related issues, rising prices/inflation, taxation, unemployment, terrorism, defense/foreign affairs, housing, immigration, the healthcare system, the education system, pensions, and environmental protection; "other" and "do not know" are additional choices.
5. The questionnaire was criticized by many researchers and policymakers for ignoring any professional and ethical standards. It was argued to not be suitable for any in-merit consultation, and it was found to fuel already high xenopho-

bia and intolerance toward immigrants (see European Commission documents among others for the details of the questionnaire).

6. The question in the ESS reads as follows: "Thinking of people coming to live in [country] from other countries, when do you think they should obtain the same rights to social benefits and services as citizens already living here? Please choose the option on this card that comes closest to your view."

References

Bommes, Michael, and Andrew Geddes. 2000. *Immigration and Welfare: Challenging the Borders of the Welfare State.* London: Routledge.

Bustikova, Lenka. 2018. "Radical Right in Eastern Europe." In *The Oxford Handbook of the Radical Right*, edited by J. Rydgren, 565–82. Oxford: Oxford University Press.

Card, David. 2005. "Is the New Immigration Really So Bad?" *Economic Journal* 115(507): 300–323.

Dancygier, Rafaela M., and Michael J. Donnelly. 2013. "Sectoral Economies, Economic Contexts, and Attitudes toward Immigration." *Journal of Politics* 75: 17–35.

Eger, Maureen A., and Sarah Valdez. 2014. "Neo-nationalism in Western Europe." *European Sociological Review* 31(1): 115–130.

Enyedi, Zsolt. 2016. "Populist Polarization and Party System Institutionalization." *Problems of Post-Communism* 63(4): 201–20.

Eurobarometer. 2019. "Public Opinion." Retrieved 1 January 2019 from http://ec.europa.eu/COMMFrontOffice/publicopinion/index.cfm/Chart/getChart/chartType/gridChart/themeKy/42/groupKy/208/savFile/54.

European Commission. 2015. "Hungary: Government's National Consultation on Immigration and Terrorism Creates Widespread Debate." Retrieved 12 November 2018 from https://ec.europa.eu/migrant-integration/news/hungary-governments-national-consultation-on-immigration-and-terrorism-creates-widespread-debate.

European Social Survey. 2019. "Data and Documentation." Retrieved 1 January 2019 from https://www.europeansocialsurvey.org/data/round-index.html.

Eurostat. 2019. "Migration and Migrant Population Statistics." Retrieved 1 January 2019 from https://ec.europa.eu/eurostat/statistics-explained/index.php/Migration_and_migrant_population_statistics.

Ford Robert. 2011. "Acceptable and Unacceptable Immigrants: How Opposition to Immigration in Britain is Affected by Migrants' Region of Origin." *Journal of Ethnic Migration Studies*, 37: 1017–37.

Ford, Robert, Will Jennings, and Will Somerville. 2015. "Public Opinion, Responsiveness and Constraint: Britain's Three Immigration Policy Regimes." *Journal of Ethnic and Migration Studies* 41: 1391–411.

Geddes, Andrew, and Peter Scholten. 2016. *The Politics of Migration and Immigration in Europe.* 2nd edn. London: Sage.

Georgiou, Myria, and Rafal Zaborowski. 2017. "Media Coverage of the 'Refugee Crisis': A Cross-European Perspective." Retrieved 12 November 2018 from https://rm.coe.int/1680706b00.

Hainmueller, Jens, and Daniel J. Hopkins. 2014. "Public Attitudes toward Immigration." *Annual Review of Political Science* 17: 225–49.

Hainmueller, Jens, Michael J. Hiscox, and Yotam Margalit. 2015. "Do Concerns about Labour Market Competition Shape Attitudes toward Immigration? New Evidence." *Journal of International Economics* 97(1): 193–207.

Hatton, Timothy J. 2016. "Immigration, Public Opinion and the Recession in Europe." *Economic Policy* 86: 205–46.

———. 2017. "Public Opinion on Immigration in Europe: Preference versus Salience." *IZA Discussion Paper Series*, no. 10838.

Heizmann, Boris, Alexander Jedinger, and Anja Perry. 2018. "Welfare Chauvinism, Economic Insecurity and the Asylum Seeker 'Crisis.'" *Societies* 8(83): 1–17.

Juhasz, Judit. (2003). "Hungary: Transit Country Between East and West." Retrieved 21 December 2018 from https://www.migrationpolicy.org/article/hungary-transit-country-between-east-and-west.

Kootstra, Anouk. 2016. "Deserving and Undeserving Welfare Claimants in Britain and the Netherlands: Examining the Role of Ethnicity and Migration Status Using a Vignette Experiment." *European Sociological Review* 32: 325–38.

Korkut, Umut. 2014. "The Migration Myth in the Absence of Immigrants: How Does the Conservative Right in Hungary and Turkey Grapple with Immigration?" *Comparative European Politics* 12(6): 620–36.

Kulin, Joakim, Maureen A. Eger, and Mikael Hjerm. 2016. "Immigration or Welfare? The Progressive's Dilemma Revisited." *Socius: Sociological Research for a Dynamic World* 2: 1–15.

Larsen, C. A., M. Frederiksen, and M. H. Nielsen. 2018. "European Welfare Nationalism: A Democratic Forum Study in Five Countries." In *Attitudes, Aspirations and Welfare: Social Policy Directions in Uncertain Times*, edited by P. Taylor-Gooby and B. Leruth London, 63–91. New York: Palgrave Macmillan.

Lugosi, Nicole. 2018. "Radical Right Framing of Social Policy in Hungary: Between Nationalism and Populism." *Journal of International and Comparative Social Policy* 34(3): 210–33

Lax, Jeffrey R., and Justin H. Phillips. 2012. "The Democratic Deficit in the States." *American Journal of Political Science* 56: 148–66.

Mewes, Jan, and Steffen Mau. 2013. "Globalization, Socio-economic Status and Welfare Chauvinism: European Perspectives on Attitudes toward the Exclusion of Immigrants." *International Journal of Comparative Sociology* 54: 228–45.

Narkowicz, Kasia. 2018. "'Refugees Not Welcome Here': State, Church and Civil Society Responses to the Refugee Crisis in Poland." *International Journal of Politics, Culture, and Society* 31(4): 357–73.

Pytlas, Bartek. 2015. *Radical Right Parties in Central and Eastern Europe: Mainstream Party Competition and Electoral Fortune*. London: Routledge.

Reeskens, Tim, and Wim van Oorschot. 2012. "Disentangling the 'New Liberal Dilemma': On the Relation between General Welfare Redistribution Preferences and Welfare Chauvinism." *International Journal of Comparative Sociology* 53: 120–39.

Sarnyai, Gabor. 2018. "European Leaders Agree to End Mandatory Refugee Quota Scheme. Hungary Today." *Hungary Today*, 29 June. Retrieved 4 September 2019 from https://hungarytoday.hu/european-leaders-agree-to-end-mandatory-refugee-quota-scheme/.

Scheve, Kenneth F., and Matthew J. Slaughter. 2001. "Labor Market Competition and Individual Preferences over Immigration Policy." *Review of Economics and Statistics* 83(1): 133–45.

Schneider, Silke L. 2008. "Anti-immigrant Attitudes in Europe: Outgroup Size and Perceived Ethnic Threat." *European Sociological Review* 24(1): 53–67.

Semyonov, Moshe, Rebeca Raijman, and Anastasia Gorodzeisky. 2006. "The Rise of Anti-foreigner Sentiment in European Societies, 1988–2000." *American Sociological Review* 71(3): 426–449.

Sidanius, Jim, and Felicia Pratto. 1999. *Social Dominance: An Intergroup Theory of Social Hierarchy.* Cambridge: Cambridge University Press.

Snyder, James M., and David Stromberg. 2010. "Press Coverage and Political Accountability." *Journal of Political Economy* 118: 355–408.

Stephan, Walter G., Oscar Ybarra, and Guy Bachman. 1999. "Prejudice toward Immigrants." *Journal of Applied Social Psychology* 29(11): 2221–37.

Valentino, Nicholas A., Stuart N. Soroka, Shanto Iyengar, Toril Aalberg, Raymond Duch, Marta Fraile, and Kyu S. Hahn et al. 2019. "Economic and Cultural Drivers of Immigrant Support Worldwide." *British Journal of Political Science* 49(4): 1–26.

6

Vulnerable Permanency in Mass Influx

The Case of Syrians in Turkey

Ahmet İçduygu and Damla B. Aksel

Introduction

Periods of civil war and political turmoil frequently initiate population dislocations and mass refugee flows across national boundaries (Keely 2001; Huysmans, Dobson, and Prokhovnik 2006; Salehyan 2008). Naturally, neighboring countries are the ones primarily affected by these movements, as people leave their homes in search of safety elsewhere. In recent history, millions of people escaping from the conflicts in Afghanistan, Somalia, Sudan, Iraq, Congo, and Syria have crossed their borders and moved into neighboring countries. The most recent example of this has been the Syrian civil war, which generated a massive influx of refugees who are currently residing in five nearby countries; as of late 2019, they number as follows: 3.7 million in Turkey, 924,000 in Lebanon, 657,000 in Jordan, 228,000 in Iraq, and 130,000 in Egypt, adding up to a total of more than 5.6 million Syrian refugees residing in the Middle East and North Africa (UNHCR 2019b). In addition to these huge numbers, there is also a sizable number of Syrian refugees who are settled in other countries beyond the Middle East as a spillover effect of the mass displacement in the region. For instance, the number of Syrians arriving in the twenty-eight member states of the European Union (EU) seeking international protection reached nearly one million as of 2018 (EUROSTAT 2018).

As far as the mass flows of refugees are concerned, there are huge gray areas, particularly regarding the acceptance, protections, and settlements of refugees by their targeted asylum countries (Koser and Black 1999; Lippert 1999; Nyers 2013). Although the international and national legal arrangements on the protection of refugees, based on the 1951 Geneva Convention and the 1967 Additional Protocol, are well established and working robustly in the case of individual arrivals of refugees, they are not functioning with the same efficiency in the case of mass flows of refugees. Given the difficulties associated with accommodating large numbers of refugees that arrive in a short time span, states are circumspect about the mass movement of refugees. In particular, the questions of how long refugees will remain, and the conditions and legal arrangements of their stay, pose several challenges to the receiving states. Moreover, in several countries that have adopted the international legal arrangements within certain limits, or who have not adopted them at all, the management of asylum seekers and refugee settlements remains a blurry policy area. Finally, some countries are not part of this international protection system; hence, they could avoid taking certain responsibilities for asylum seekers and refugees.

When a country experiences a mass movement of incoming refugees, one of the initial questions that is inevitably on the public agenda is, "How do we provide protection to these vulnerable people?" (Fitzpatrick 2000; Durieux and McAdam 2004). The second most frequently asked question, often from a politically sensitive point of view, is, "Will this movement lead to a permanent settlement or not?" (Fitzpatrick 2000; Ashrafi and Moghissi 2002; Kronenfeld 2008). The answers to these questions are inevitably dependent on context and inherently require a comparative perspective. It is within this context that this chapter, drawing lessons from the historical case of Afghan refugees in Iran and Pakistan, elaborates the nature of mass flows and settlement of Syrian refugees in Turkey, debates the characteristics of protection provided to these refugees by the Turkish state, and questions the likelihood of the permanent settlement of these refugees in the country. Presently addressing the question of whether the Syrian refugees in Turkey are likely to settle permanently is very timely, since there exists a growing debate on the likelihood of the repatriation programs in the near future (İçduygu and Nimer 2019). It is also timely since the resettlement in the third countries, particularly in the developed countries of the West, still cause a high level of controversy in public and policy agendas of those countries.

After these introductory comments, the second part of the chapter engages in an analytical and theoretical framework and elaborates the literature on the determinants of permanent settlement of immigrant populations, identifying three main determinants: home country structures, host country structures, and individual factors. It will also suggest a fourth one particularly relevant for refugee populations, existence, and type of protection. The third part of the chapter applies this framework to the case of Afghan refugees in Iran and Pakistan over the last three decades as a point of comparison for the Syrian refugees in Turkey today. Focusing on the case of Syrians in Turkey, the fourth part of this chapter, in essence, argues that even in the case of Afghanistan, where the four determinants were not particularly favorable to long-term settlement of refugees, a substantial number of Afghans have become permanent settlers in the countries of refuge, Iran and Pakistan. It is argued that, given that the four determinants are more potent in the case of Syrians in Turkey, it should therefore be expected that the likelihood of permanent settlement is very high. The chapter also implicitly makes the claim that while refugees continuously live in a state of "permanent temporariness," mainly because of the nature of mass influxes to the neighboring countries of first asylum, the tendency toward becoming permanent settlers does not mean moving away from vulnerability but rather settling in a state of "vulnerable permanency." The issue of permanency versus temporariness, which is widely debated in the context of temporary labor migration, is central to the debates that cover the whole chapter, as the issue of permanency also seems to be fundamental to settlement and integration questions of refugees.

Determinants of Permanent Settlement: Implications for Refugees

The question of permanency versus temporariness has been a point of concern in various migratory settings. For instance, one of the most important features of mass labor migration is the fact that a significant proportion of temporary migrants become permanent settlers over time. Although temporary migrants becoming permanent settlers has drawn attention from students of international migration that focused on temporary labor migration (Massey and Liang 1989; İçduygu 1993; Castles 2006; Khoo, Hugo, and McDonald 2008), there has been limited research on the process in which refugees turn into permanent settlers. In this section, we first examine discussions on permanency and temporariness in the general literature on migration and then focus on the questions within the framework of mass influx of refugees.

The long-term consequences of temporary migration have been an issue of concern for policymakers and academics on migration alike, especially as a result of the temporary recruitment programs in the postwar era (Castles 2006; Massey and Liang 1989). Fashioned as strictly systematized programs for recruiting temporary migrants, the European guestworker system and the American bracero program sought to exclude migrants from much of the societal, economic, and political life in their host countries. Seeing integration as the primary promoter of permanency of persons in the host countries, host governments introduced structural impediments to integration. Such measures included limiting migrants' period of stay, allowing them restricted social and labor rights, and minimizing opportunities for family reunification (Massey and Liang 1989: 202). However, despite these initial arrangements by the governments, many temporary migrants settled in the receiving countries.

Arguing that "there [was] no such thing as a temporary worker program," Massey and Liang (1989: 223) emphasized that structural conditions mattered because as temporary migration promoted structural economic changes in host countries, the demand for foreign workers became self-perpetuating. More importantly, scholars suggested that the process of migration changed migrants' motivations and aspirations. Those who experienced migration had a higher probability of making additional trips, spreading migratory behavior through family and friendship networks, and settling in the host country. For Castles (2006: 743), who analyzed European guest worker programs of the postwar era, migrant workers became permanent settlers due to changes in their life intentions with longer stays and family reunifications as well as economic incentives in host countries. Migrants' partial integration into host country welfare systems and the emergence of rights-based discourse also made it possible for migrants to secure residence status.

Analytically, the discussions on the transformation of temporary migration into permanent settlement highlights three main processes: (1) the motivations and aspirations of migrants' changes over time; (2) despite the initial structural configurations, the process of migration itself alters the conditions related to permanency in the host countries; and (3) the socioeconomic conditions in the home country matter. Contrary to the cases of economic migration, mass influxes of refugees can be rather sudden and spontaneous, forcing host governments and the international protection institutions to make quick policy choices (Stein 1986; Jacobsen 1996: 657). While focusing on the case of refugees, this chapter introduces the fourth process that the existence and the type of protection regime matters for the possibility and conditions of permanency. As a determinant of host states' approach toward refugees, protection status has a direct effect on the opportunities that refugees might have regarding permanency or temporariness, as well as the intervening role that international organizations play between the countries and refugees. Moreover, in countries where a reliable protection regime does not exist, or the cooperation between the international regime and the sovereign state is limited, the politicization of displacement may intensify the susceptibility of the refugees.

Notwithstanding the substantial attention paid by migration literature to the conditions of permanency in cases of economic migration, the focus on refugees remains limited, especially in cases of mass influx (Stein 1986; Jacobsen 1996; Albert 2010). As a result of the 1951 Refugee Convention

Relating to the Status of Refugees and the Additional Protocol of 1967, conventional refugee regulation is based largely on a case-by-case eligibility and status determination for those who apply as asylum seekers. Attaining refugee status is a step on the road to permanency where alternative routes depend on factors related to the national and international processes. Following the granting of refugee status, three durable solutions become available for the individuals as viewed in various policy documents of the United Nations High Commissioner for Refugees (UNHCR) and related academic research (Stein 1986; Chimni 1998, 2004; Frelick 2007): (1) voluntary repatriation, (2) local settlement, and (3) third-country resettlement. Traditionally, only a small percentage of refugees have been resettled to third countries. Hence, Stein (1986) argued that only the first two aforementioned solutions were the realistic options for the refugees from developing countries, mainly because UN donor countries enforced durable solutions of local settlement or voluntary repatriation. Moreover, the refugee status and the right to remain in the asylum country can be revoked if conditions in the country of origin change and if the individual is no longer qualified as a refugee. The path to permanency in the host country depends on procedures related to the settlement and naturalization regime in the country of asylum.

At the present time, two conducts of refugee status determination, which are often confused with one another, exist in the refugee governance regime that is applied during times of mass influx (Albert 2010). The first type of refugee status determination (RSD) is prima facie, which is based on the UNHCR and the UN protocols of 1951 and 1967, even though the term does not appear in any international legal instruments on refugees (Albert 2010: 62). The prima facie status is granted to a group of individuals immediately following the event that causes the mobility. Since the state does not exhaust its funds for administering RSD processes, more time and resources can be utilized by the state to provide material assistance, including health services, food, or other privileges (Albert 2010: 68). The second type of RSD is temporary protection, which was codified by the European Union's Temporary Protection Directive during the Yugoslavian refugee crisis in the 1990s. Similar to the prima facie protection status, temporary protection is not a case-by-case status and is usually operationalized as a response to a mass influx. While the prima facie status is not limited to a certain period, temporary protection is limited by time—although it can be reviewable after a prescribed period of time. Different from the prima facie status where refugees can participate in one of the durable solution programs of the UNHCR cited, individuals under the temporary protection cannot locally integrate and are expected to repatriate (Albert 2010: 77–80). Initially recognized as a short-term solution to the need for protection of vulnerable populations, temporary protection also made it possible for host states to restrict asylum and impede the long-term integration of migrant populations. However, the historical case of Bosnians illustrates that refugees may in fact become permanent residents despite the emphasis on temporariness in this protection regime (Koser and Black 1999).

There is no doubt that the way in which initial refugee status determination operates is very crucial for the consecutive stages of protection, settlement, and integration possibilities in the hosting states. The questions of how much the policies and practices of the individual hosting states are aligned with the frameworks of the international refugee regime and how much the national policies and practices of these states are open to the options of protection, settlement, and integration are also crucial to the whole process. In addition to these legal and administrative frameworks and their applications, as noted earlier, so many various factors operating through the agency of refugees themselves and the settings of the host and origin states determine the outcomes concerning the settlement and integration possibilities. It is within this context that to elaborate the cases of the Syrian refugees in Turkey in a comparative perspective with the cases of Afghan refugees in Pakistan and Iran, this chapter benefits from the fourfold framework presented above, emphasizing the determinants of settlement in cases of mass influx (see table 6.1). The first determinants are the home country structures, which establish the measures for refugees' repatriation and reintegration, depending primarily on the duration and the magnitude of the conflict. Refugees' accessibility to housing or private property, to labor market and public services in the event of their return, are crucial determinants at the sublevel (Harild and Christensen 2010; Sert 2010; Schmeidl 2011). The second source consists of the existence and type of protection regime. The protection regime is indicated by how migrants or refugees are defined by the state-led regime, what it covers (i.e., the duration of the protection regime and the public services provided), and whether it is also safeguarded by an international protection regime that allows for burden/responsibility sharing between several states (Jacobsen 1996; Koser and Black 1999; Harild and Christensen 2010; Scalettaris 2010). The third determinant incorporates host-related factors. These include socioeconomic conditions, provision of basic needs, and the existence of a secure status in the host country, which create a hospitable environment for the longer stay of refugees. Yet as in the case of temporary labor migration, the process of migration may alter the conditions in the host countries as a result of various factors, including the politicization of the displacement or the exhaustion of resources provided by the host country (Kunz 1981; Stein 1986; Jacobsen 1996). The fourth and final determinant is the refugees' individual motives and incentives, which are subject to change over time (Castles 2006). In addition to the initial motives for flight, factors including sociodemographic characteristics of the household, ethnic and religious ties with the host community, and the conditions of socialization (participation in the labor market, welfare system, and education system) determine refugees' motives for permanency in the host country.

Table 6.1. Determinants of Permanent Settlement in Mass Influx.

Determinant	Sublevel determinants
Home country structures	*Measures for repatriation and reintegration* Housing *or* existence of private property Economy and employment Security and intensity of conflict Public services Accountable and responsive governance
Existence and type of protection	*Which type of status?* Status determination Coverage Safeguard by the international protection regime
Host country structures	*Measures for integration* Legal grounds for participation in the labor market Legal grounds for participation in the welfare system *and/or* access to aid and services Access to citizenship Politicization of the displacement Public opinion and public perception
Individual factors	*Motives and incentives* Reason for flight Duration of displacement and stay Sociodemographic characteristics of the household Ethnic and religious ties with the host community and previous history of migration Participation in the labor market Participation in the welfare system Participation in the education system Country of birth

Table constructed by the authors with the use of following studies: Kunz 1981; Jacobsen 1996; Koser and Black 1999; Castles 2006; Sert 2010; Harild and Christensen 2010; Schmeidl 2011; Scalettaris 2010.

A Historical Case, Mass Influx of Afghans to Pakistan and Iran, and Their Settlement: What We Already Know?

This chapter focuses on the case of Afghan refugees in Pakistan and Iran as a comparison with the current Syrian refugees' crisis in Turkey. The Afghan case provides a comparable background due to several characteristics of the exodus: (1) a large-scale displacement, especially during the peak years when it reached a magnitude of 6.2 million; (2) the protracted conflict, which includes numerous players, necessitating a long-term displacement; (3) the arrivals of millions of refugees immensely affecting the two neighboring countries, Iran and Pakistan; (4) intense international interest (then and now) from regional and international actors. In the following sections, we will elaborate on the ways in which these four characteristics resemble the current Syrian mass influx.

The Afghan refugee influx occurred in several waves, following a recurrent pattern of outward migration and repatriation campaigns. The process first began in April 1978 with the overthrow of the government, which was followed by the Soviet invasion of the country. In the early 1990s, the withdrawal of the Soviet Union led to a massive repatriation campaign by the UNHCR along with international assistance, eventually reaching a scale of 1.5 million Afghans returning in less than a year in 1992 (Schmeidl 2002: 10; Margesson 2007: 2). The subsequent Islamic regime introduced by Taliban after 1996 further eroded human rights in the country, causing a new outward displacement and a substantial population of internally displaced refugees. Another return movement began after the US-led invasion in October 2001, reaching 2.15 million by 2002 (Margesson 2007: 2–3), and a further phase of Afghan displacement began in 2004, with the deterioration of the security situation in Afghanistan. In the years 2002–12, nearly 3.8 million people from Pakistan and nearly 1 million people from Iran returned to Afghanistan (Human Rights Watch 2013). Some of these returns have been due to voluntary repatriation, while others were the result of mass deportations and deterrence by the host governments, forcing many long-term inhabitants to repatriate. The final phase of migration from Afghanistan took place following the United States' withdrawal in 2021, which led to the fall of the Afghan government and the rise of Taliban, creating a new wave of migration towards the neighboring countries and beyond.

Today Afghanistan remains the second largest source country of refugees worldwide, with more than 2.7 million refugees residing in 82 countries. It also has one of the highest levels of Internally Displaced Persons (IDPs), with a population of nearly 950,000 people displaced within the borders of the country. Since the outset of the conflict, Afghanistan's two neighboring countries, Pakistan and Iran, have been the main host countries, harboring as many as 6 million in the 1990s. Despite massive returns, as of 2019 there were 1.4 million registered Afghan refugees in Pakistan and 3 million in Iran (of which nearly 1 million are registered) (UNHCR 2019a).

The history of protracted conflict in Afghanistan and the further waves of migration toward Pakistan and Iran since the 1970s illustrate how the conditions in the homeland had a significant role in Afghan refugees' longer stay and permanent settlement in the new host countries. According to Harild and Christensen (2011), four issues continue to create barriers to durable solutions for returned refugees in Afghanistan: (1) the lack of rights to land, property, and houses; (2) the disruptions of livelihoods or dependence on humanitarian aid; (3) inadequate or absent delivery of services; and (4) the limitations regarding accountable and responsive governance in the homeland. As discussed by Kronenfeld (2011: 6) tens of thousands of Afghans still "daily cross back and forth into Pakistan and Iran in search of work, education, health care, and other needs." This cyclical mobility across borders and the high population of IDPs within the country reveal the government's inability to provide basic services for its population (Kronenfeld 2011; Schmeidl 2011: 8).

In terms of the type and existence of protection, the conditions of stay for the Afghan refugees have been drastically altered over a period of forty years. Pakistan, on the one hand, is not a signatory of the 1951 Convention or the 1967 Protocol and therefore has no national legal mechanism for asylum or refugee status determination (Zieck 2008: 254). Iran, on the other hand, ratified the 1951 Convention and the 1967 Protocol; however, these agreements were never incorporated into domestic law (Koepke 2011). Initially, both countries developed a nearly open-door policy with a certain degree of toleration toward refugees, with the support of international assistance (Schmeidl, 2011:10). The open-door approach became exhausted in the 1990s as Iran and Pakistan became reluctant to provide protection to newly arriving refugees. Since 2001, repatriation programs were buttressed by registration campaigns in the two countries in an attempt to monitor the existing population. Refugee identity cards were issued in the mid-2000s, which allowed Afghans only temporary stay and either no rights or restricted rights to work and move about freely (Margessen 2007). Along with the difficulties of reintegrating into Afghan society, the politicization of displacement by the host governments and the recurrent gap in the refugee and security regimes created tensions between the national and international actors (Schmeidl 2011). Since 2010, conditions have deteriorated for Afghan refugees: Iran has actively pursued mass deportations despite criticism from the international community (Koepke 2011), and the Pakistani government has been making declarations about mass deportation and closing down refugee camps since 2012.

In terms of the conditions in the host country, the mass influx of Afghan refugees since the 1980s led to drastic demographic transformations, especially in terms of the ethnic balance in regions in Pakistan and Iran largely populated with refugees. In Pakistan, Pashto has become the dominant language spoken in provincial capitals of Peshawar, Karachi, and Quetta, and the ethnic recomposition has often been coupled with ethnic tensions between indigenous and Afghan communities (Borthakur 2017). In Iran, the majority of the Afghans are Hazara Shias, who fled their home country due to extreme ethnic and religious persecution (Tober 2007). In both cases, although neither country favored or encouraged it, local integration has been in practice. However, refugee return has been favored for a durable solution rather than a systematic local integration (Schmeidl 2011: 11). Both Iran and Pakistan adopted restrictive policies for naturalization, permanent settlement, and accessibility to legal employment or social integration. The policies restricting accessibility to the economic, social, or cultural rights in the host countries pushed many Afghans to return to their home country, although many stayed on.

In Pakistan, the Citizenship Act restricts migrants who arrived after 1951 from obtaining citizenship. The government has tightened its control in recent years in response to rising public and state concern over economic privileges and security. The conditions of stay for Afghans in Pakistan are currently tenuous, as the national assembly decided to allow 1.6 million registered Afghans, many of whom have been living in the country for over 30 years, to stay "at least until the end of 2015" (Craig 2014). Although more than 450,000 people voluntarily repatriated by the UNHCR's facilitation since 2016, the returns are taking place at a slower pace due to the ongoing security situation in Afghanistan (UNHCR 2019a). In Iran, the nationality law does not allow Afghans to gain citizenship or permanent residency and has severe restrictions against marriage rights. The law bans Afghan men married to Iranian women from applying for Iranian citizenship, and even the children of such marriages face barriers to citizenship (Human Rights Watch 2013). Although Afghan refugees have been permitted to work in both countries, they are limited in their employment prospects to jobs not easily filled by the native population, such as the construction industry, and often work without any legal documentation (Koepke 2011). As these examples on different policy areas illustrate, the lack of a permanent and secure status results in a situation of vulnerability for the Afghan refugees, who are often stigmatized as the source of security, drug, or health problems in their host countries (Borthakur 2017; Tober 2007).

The analyses of Afghan refugees in Iran and Pakistan illustrate that a fourth determinant factor, a set of individual factors, also influenced the conditions of permanency or temporariness. Schmeidl (2011: 1) argues that local integration has been practiced in Iranian and Pakistani even though governments implemented no policies favoring or encouraging it. One of the main reasons for the choice of migration to these two countries is the existence of former temporary migration patterns from Afghanistan. Even before the period of instability, Afghans had a tradition of traveling to Iran and Pakistan as pilgrims, students, merchants, or temporary workers (Koepke 2011: 1; Kronenfeld 2008: 50). Such patterns accounted for an already established population in Pakistan and Iran, making it easier for subsequent migrants from Afghanistan to settle (Kronenfeld 2008: 51). A pertinent debate in academia questions the correlation between settlement in camps and permanency. It has been argued that the return rate for non–camp residents would be higher, as they would not receive the basic needs available in camps provisioned by governmental or international humanitarian aid organizations. However, scholars such as Kronenfeld (2008) argued that, especially in cases with a long history of displacement, settlement in the urban areas created greater possibilities for integration into the social and economic environment of the host country. Life in the cities changed the livelihood patterns and self-conceptions of refugees, making it harder for the UNHCR and the host government to keep track of them and their further repatriation (Kronenfeld, 2008: 52–54).

The case of Afghan refugees provides insights on the potential permanency or temporariness of Syrian refugees in Turkey. In Afghanistan, the lack of a reliable government and ongoing environment of security reduced the chances of a durable return by refugees. The challenges regarding the alignment of a solid international protection regime, together with the host governments' immigration systems, pushed Afghans toward vulnerability despite their long-term stay. The previous section illustrated that notwithstanding the structural restrictions, many refugees opted for alternative and often irregular outlets of stay in their host countries. This phenomenon underscores the implications of individual-level factors such as ethnic ties, socialization, and previous experiences of migration to the host country. Based on the reading of the thirty-year-old experience of displacement from Afghanistan, the next section discusses the likelihood that and the extent to which Syrian refugees' temporariness may lead to permanency in Turkey.

The Syrian Refugees in Turkey: An Overview

As of 2019, the Syrian civil war had caused the displacement of an estimated around 12 million Syrians, which is equal to half of Syria's total population. This population had fled their homes and taken refuge in neighboring countries or within Syria itself. According to the UNHCR, about 5.6 million fled to Syria's close neighbors of Turkey, Lebanon, Jordan, and Iraq, and almost 6.2 million were internally displaced within Syria. During this time, while the flow of Syrians from their home continued, there were also some returns, particularly from 2017 to 2019, to relatively secured areas of the country (Bulur 2018; Ghazal 2018). Since the beginning of the Syrian crisis, Turkey has become home to an enlarging Syrian community. While the Syrian refugees are now the world's largest refugee population, Turkey has become the world's largest refugee-hosting nation, hosting 65 percent of Syrian refugees according to the UNHCR Syria Regional Refugee Response website in late 2019 (UNHCR 2019b).

The earliest flows of Syrians to Turkey began in April 2011, when the Syrian government started using lethal force to crack down on antigovernment protests. In fact, during the first phase of the Syrian civil war in 2011, the pace of the refugee flows was relatively slow, with some even returning. After Kofi Annan failed to broker a ceasefire in the second half of 2012, clashes

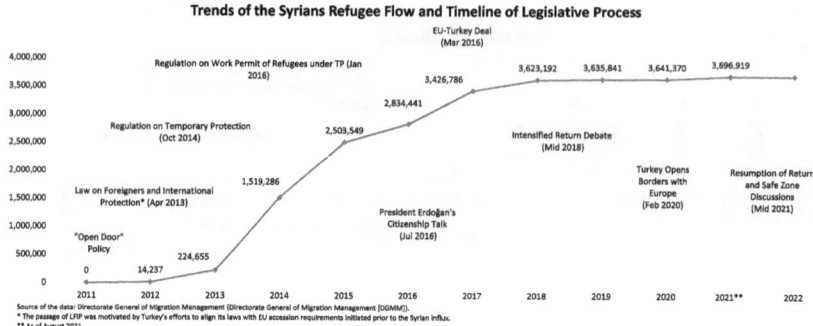

Figure 6.1. Syrian Refugees and Policy Responses in Turkey. © Ahmet İçduygu and Damla B. Aksel.

in Syria escalated, and arrivals in Turkey increased to 20,000[1] refugees per month: by the end of the year, there were over 170,000 registered refugees in Turkey. In 2013, the average monthly number of refugees arriving in the country reached 40,000. The figures related to the migration stock, and flows of Syrians in Turkey soared in the period between June 2014 and January 2015, as a result of both the significant increase in the number of refugees reaching Turkey's borders and the mass registration process by the Turkish state as it attempted to control the incoming populations. The number of registered Syrian refugees in the country reached 1.5 million in 2014 and rose to 2.5 million in 2015. As of late 2019, 3.6 million Syrian citizens live in Turkey, with only 63,000, or only 1.7 percent, of them living in the camps, and the remaining population residing in urban areas throughout the country (DGMM 2019).

From the first day of the Syrian crisis, Turkey has had an open-door policy. Syrians escaping from the civil war and entering Turkey were called "guests," not "refugees," and generously welcomed to the country. First, they were called as guests because the Turkish authorities were noticeably cautious about any possibility of their long-term or permanent stay. Second, Turkey was viciously involved in the Syrian crisis and nakedly anti-Assad in its stance: the Turkish authorities openly accused Bashar al-Assad's regime of being a dictatorship and harming its citizens while greeting refugees fleeing into the country. The country's proactive position toward the Syrian civil war was conceivably due to its direct concerns for the future of Syria, particularly related to the prospects of Kurdish and Turkmen populations there. Third, Turkey tended to substantiate its "soft power" by actively contributing to the solution for the refugee crisis of the Syrian civil war, positioning itself as an important–and highly visible–player in the region (İçduygu

2015). While Turkey has been reinforcing its involvement in Syria through military operations since 2016, it publicly declared that two operations since 2018, Operation Olive Branch and Operation Euphrates Shield, were aimed at repatriating a part of the Syrian refugees residing in its territories.

The Syrian Refugees in Turkey: Toward a Vulnerable Permanency

In situations of influx, return to the country of origin, local integration in the country of first asylum, and third-country resettlement are generally considered to resolve the precariousness of refugees. In the case of the Syrian influx to Turkey, no durable solution has been implemented, and the short-term solution has been limited to local integration in Turkey rather than full return or resettlement to a third country. In this section, we discuss the issue of permanency for Syrian refugees in Turkey by elaborating on the four aspects: (1) conditions in Syria, (2) type of protection and available outlets for permanency, (3) conditions of integration in Turkey, and (4) the motives and incentives of Syrians in Turkey.

Conditions in Syria

Before the start of the unrest in 2011, Syria was a fast-growing, lower-middle-income country. It was, however, suffering from the lack of broader economic and political inclusion and further transparency and civil liberties (Hınnebusch 2008; Perthes 2011). The country was also suffering from high levels of perceived corruption and low trust in public institutions. Added to these enabling conditions were the external factors that contributed to the onset of the conflict in the climate, the Arab Spring and a sudden shift in the regional context (Gause III 2011). In the last eight years, the conflict has caused extensive damage to Syria's physical infrastructure, including provision of water, electricity, and sanitation. Additionally, social infrastructure such as schools and healthcare centers have been severely damaged or destroyed altogether. In a World Bank (2017) study, it is estimated that, for instance, the war damaged or destroyed about a third of the housing stock and about half of medical and education facilities, which led to significant economic loss. It is also estimated that the losses in GDP between 2011 and 2016 sum to about four times the size of the Syrian GDP in 2010. The destruction of physical infrastructure and the financial losses, nevertheless, do not demonstrate the full toll of the war. Syria has become the largest forced displacement crisis in the world since World War II; as noted earlier, over half of the country's preconflict population has been forcibly displaced. Remaining civilians in the country have experienced increasingly vulnerable living conditions in affected communities; ongoing casualties have imposed insufferable distress and psychological impacts on individuals and their families in the country. As the conflict continues, socioeconomic outcomes further deteriorate, and more Syrians tend to emigrate. And one can easily claim that the longer the conflict continues, the slower the postconflict recovery will be.

In late 2019, the situation in Syria was characterized by principally three factors: first, ISIS was substantially but not completely defeated; second, the Assad regime seemed to have won its war to stay in power and controls more than half of Syria's territory and its population; and third, while some peace talks took place in a fragile setting, serious clashes persistently continued among the stakeholders, including the Assad regime, local opposition groups, and foreign powers. Although some cautiously claim that there was a de-escalation deal that seems to mark a step toward the final phase of the Syrian civil war and crisis, many others argue that the country entered a dangerous and much more volatile phase that was going to be characterized by the key stakeholders seeking to hold on the ground and ensure their interests are protected (UK Parliament 2018; Araabi and Hilal 2016).

In short, presently, Syria is a war-torn country that is heading toward "failed state" status. Despite some major changes in the dynamics of the clashes and violence in the country, which occasionally give a positive signal toward a de-escalation process, a peaceful resolution still remains elusive, suppressing the opportunities for refugees to return. In general, the conditions for return are in line with the balance of power among actors on the ground, affected by violent clashes, the deterioration of property, and looting in Syria. Over the last eight years, although there have been reports in the media of limited instances of repatriations following temporary procurements of local security, many of these were short-lived by new and more populous entries to Turkey (Hürriyet Daily News 2015). However, since 2018 there have been increasing joint efforts by Russia and Turkey to put forward a plan to return some large numbers of Syrian refugees in neighboring countries back to their homeland, particularly to the so-called "safe zones" created by these two countries. The creation of safe zones took place in mid-2019, as a result of an agreement between Turkey and Russia following the Turkish offensive in Northern Syria. Collating information on returns remains a challenge due to different patterns of mobility of Syrians (1) within Turkey, (2) across Turkey and the neighboring countries, and (3) from Turkey to third countries (especially Europe), as well as (4) cyclical mobility to Syria as participants in the armed conflict. Against this background, Turkey's minister of interior declared that some 354,000 out of 3.6 million Syrians had returned to their homeland by 2019, and the Turkish president announced that some 371,000 Syrian refugees returned to Northern Syria from the beginning of Turkey's military operation in November

2019 to December 2019 (Al Jazeera 2019). One should note that there is a strong established view stressing that although the governments and aid agencies are already beginning to consider the repatriation of the millions of Syrian refugees, the Syrian conflict shows little or no sign of coming to end in the near future (Crisp 2018). Yet Syria today is still a divided country where conflicts are caused by different clashing domestic and international forces: Syrian government and allied Russian military, Turkish troops and allied Syrian rebels, Kurdish armed groups backed by the United States, groups supported by Iran, and ISIS. As can be deduced from the Afghan case, in the absence of a politically and economically stable environment, the repatriation programs will not be able to support the principles of voluntariness, security, and sustainability, which are necessary to build a legitimate ground for repatriation (İçduygu and Ayaşlı 2019).

Type of Protection and Available Outlets for Permanency

Turkey's policy reactions to the Syrian refugee issues have been complicated both by its expectation that the political crisis in Syria would be short-lived. The influx of Syrian refugees unexpectedly emerged as Turkey was in the midst of a major migration policy reform taking place in the context of Turkey's EU-ization process (İçduygu 2015), and consequently, the dynamics and mechanisms of these reforms have been affected by this crisis. As a result, Syrian refugees have been subject to a transitioning asylum and protection regime as policymakers try to implement broad legislative overhauls while simultaneously responding to the protracted humanitarian crisis on the ground.

Turkey is a signatory of the 1951 Geneva Convention and the 1967 Additional Protocol, albeit with a geographical limitation that only grants asylum rights to Europeans. As such, a significant portion of "non-Turkish or non-Muslim" migrants arriving to Turkey since the 1980s has been irregular and defined by Turkish law as "illegal." Furthermore, almost all non-European asylum seekers are not entitled to stay in Turkey, even after gaining recognized refugee status. Rather they are provided with a temporary protection scheme during their refugee status determination period (Kiris̗çi 2003). In an attempt to take the necessary steps toward allowing immigrants into the country and treating asylum seekers and irregular migrants in accordance with the international norms, the Parliament in 2013 adopted the Law on Foreigners and International Protection (LFIP), which has only been in force since April 2014. The new law established the Directorate General of Migration Management (DGMM), which became the central authority in the governance of asylum and migration in the country (İçduygu and Aksel 2013).

Although the Turkish asylum system is geographically restricted, there have been prior instances of more or less permanent acceptance of refugees under conditions of mass influx, such as those following the exodus from Bulgaria in 1989 and from Iraq in 1991. Turkish policies toward Syrians escaping the civil war were initially welcoming. The open-door policy has been accompanied by three policy elements based on a directive adopted in March 2012 to determine the conditions of management of Syrians in Turkey: (1) temporary protection, (2) nonrefoulement, and (3) optimal humanitarian assistance (Kirişçi 2014). The implementation of the LFIP further clarified the protected status of Syrians in Turkey. The law also clarified the conditions under which the temporary protection could be rescinded by the Turkish state, including the normalization of conditions in the home country, the voluntary return of refugees to their homeland, and the endangerment of Turkey's national security by individuals (Eksi 2014: 167). Following the LFIP, a new Temporary Protection (TP) Regulation came into effect in October 2014, setting out specific provisions on registration and documentation procedures in Turkey. The TP also provided refugees with the right to a lawful stay in the country until the conditions for safe return were established in Syria, regulated the TP Identification Document containing the foreigners' ID number, and granted access to social benefits and services such as health, education, and entry to the labor market.

Over the last eight years, the government's policies and discourses on the Syrian refugees in Turkey have dramatically changed (Memişoğlu and Ilgit 2017). Indeed, amendments to national immigration and asylum policies gained momentum with the arrival of Syrian refugees. Although, it had been drafted long before the arrival of Syrian refugees to the country, the Law on Foreigners and International Protection brought about major changes and provided a legal ground for Syrians to be classified as "persons under temporary protection" who were continuously and preferably referred to as "guests" (İçduygu 2015). Later, in October 2014, a clear definition of the rights and obligations of temporary protection beneficiaries was set out with the introduction of the Temporary Protection Regulation. In the early years of the conflict, the policies of the Turkish government asserted the temporariness of the refugees based on the presumption that the crisis would end and the refugees would return home.

In the summer and fall of 2015, when over one million people mostly from Syria landed on Europe's shores, fleeing war and persecution, seeking a better life for their families, and as Turkey functioned as a transit country for many of these people, the issues related to Syrian refugees in Turkey were placed high at the top of the international agenda, particularly in Europe. As this process resulted in the signing of the EU-Turkey statement, which aims at stopping the transit flows from Turkey, some policy changes toward the Syrians in Turkey were enacted. In early 2016, the government began to shift its approach toward long-term planning, implementing policies such as the introduction of the Work Permit Regulation for Syrians, the decision to gradually phase out Temporary Education Centers with Syrian curriculums to integrate Syrian children in Turkish schools, and the establishment of Migrant Health Centers staffed by Syrian medical professionals. Again, in mid-2016, Turkish president Erdoğan unexpectedly declared that Syrian refugees living in Turkey could eventually be granted citizenship. Consequently, since early 2017, there has been a new policy concerning the naturalization of Syrians with "high qualifications" who can contribute to Turkey. It appears that as of December 2019 there were around 110,000 Syrians who have been naturalized as Turkish citizens. It also appears that although there would be further moves in this direction, mostly due to high social reactions from native communities, this would not be a policy of mass naturalization but rather one with more exceptional measures—such as providing only some selected groups of Syrians, such as highly skilled or those with high incomes, with this opportunity (Erdoğan 2017; Akçapar and Şimşek 2018). Nevertheless, the policies toward naturalizations indicate that the Turkish authorities will circuitously accept the likelihood of the process in which the protracted displacement of Syrians turns into their long-term, and even permanent, settlement, at least for some portion of these displaced populations.

In late 2017 and early 2018, another contradictory shift in policy-related discourses occurred in Turkey. Possibly again being affected by the rising public reactions against Syrians in the country, President Erdoğan made the following statement: "We want our refugee brothers and sisters to return to their own land, their own homes; we cannot keep 3.5 million people here forever" (İçduygu and Nimer 2018). Later, the Turkish officials repeatedly announced that the government had a commitment to create the necessary humanitarian conditions, complete with infrastructure and superstructure facilities, in Syria so that all Syrians could return to their homes. Undoubtedly, this revealed a major change in Turkey's policy toward its massive population of displaced Syrians.

Conditions of Integration in Turkey

Turkey's long-established immigration regime remains a stringent impediment to legal integration of Syrian refugees in Turkey. The regime is based on the 1934 Law on Settlement (Kirişci 2003), which established two divergent statuses by (1) facilitating the migration and integration of those of "Turkish origin and culture" either as migrants or as refugees and (2) preventing and impeding the entry as migrants or refugees of those who did not meet this criterion. Although the new Settlement Law of November 2006 has made changes toward the liberalization of migration policies, it continues to limit formal immigration to Turkey to individuals and groups of "Turkish descent and culture." The identifying features of "Turkishness" are not solely related to Turkish ethnicity but the ability and willingness to adopt the Turkish language and membership of the Muslim Sunni ethnic group often associated with past Ottoman rule. In this context, it appears that many Syrians, from Kurds and Arabs to Assyrians and Yezidis, are likely to face difficulties in settling and integrating themselves in Turkey despite claiming historically established community links to the country. Moreover, even though only Turkmen of Syria can be formally incorporated and naturalized into the Turkish nation according to the Settlement Law, the political interest of the Turkish state in keeping Turkish-origin populations in the neighboring countries (as was the case in Iraq during the 1990s) might hinder their settlement and naturalization process in Turkey. Consequently, as far as the future of integration of Syrian refugees is considered, from the official perspective, the presence of a large number of Syrians in Turkey not only requires a long-term solution but also a recognition of the long-term economic, social, and political responsibility of supporting the refugee communities in the country. Against this background, the most recent government position toward Syrian refugees has two main dimensions: on the one hand, it aims at halting the flow of refugees and reversing their movement; on the other hand, it intends to provide them, at least some of the selected groups of Syrians (highly skilled or high-income groups), with better settlement and integration opportunities.

What we know from the deep-rooted literature on migrant and refugee integration is that well-established, comprehensive integration policies are needed to cater to migrants and refugees, firstly to provide for their immediate need for housing, education, employment, and health. In the area of housing, the state pursues a policy of self-financed accommodation for the majority of the Syrian population. Although the temporary accommodation centers were provided as the initial response by the state for the early comers, there is an ongoing practice of reducing the number of camp populations and closing down the camps. Since the early days of the refugee influx, Syrian refugees have been provided with free healthcare services at Migrant Health Centers established in highly populated areas and public hospitals through referrals. In the area of education, Syrian and other refugee children are supported to have access to education via Temporary Education Centers or through the state schools under national curriculum. According to UNICEF, for the 2018–19 education year, 616,000 Syrian and other refugee children were registered to receive formal education in Turkey; however, more than 430,000 children were out of school (UNICEF 2018). In the area of labor force participation, the Turkish parliament has amended a law in 2016 for those under temporary protection on access to the formal labor market in Turkey. With this law, those under temporary protection could obtain work permits six months after they had received their TP identities; however, the applications for the permits had to be initiated by their employers. Despite this legal setting, the number of Syrians who participated in the formal labor market remained low at 31,000 people in 2019, due to its limited added benefits, in comparison to informal labor force participation.

As refugees become more permanent, mostly due to both the refugees' own spontaneous integration into communities and the continuing deterioration of the situation in Syria, public opinion has grown less hospitable and, at times, hostile. Complaints about the strain that refugees place on the local economy and their competition for jobs is a widely voiced complaint in Turkey's public discourse (Erdoğan 2015; Orhan and Gündoğan 2015; Öztürkler and Göksel 2015). Especially in the bordering cities such as Gaziantep, Hatay, Kahramanmaraş, and Mersin, protests and clashes have occurred in parallel with growing competitiveness in the job market and soaring inflation. Furthermore, economic argument did not emerge in isolation from concerns about culture, security, and the social system (Özden 2013; Dinçer et al. 2013; Kirişci 2014). Even though these concerns have not mainly been voiced though reactionary behavior, there is a rising discontent and xenophobia among the public opinion that alarms the policymakers (Erdoğan 2018).

Motives and Incentives of Syrians

Along with the structural factors, the motives and incentives of refugees are subject to change over the course of this protracted conflict. The existence of continuous passages across the Syrian-Turkish borders reveals that a certain group of Syrian refugees is still actively involved in the conflict. Repatriation is expected for this group in the event of a political restructuring in Syria. For the remaining majority of the population, their longer stay in Turkey leads to a certain permanency. There is a significantly higher population of younger Syrians in Turkey: according to the DGMM (2019), 47 percent of the Syrian population is under eighteen, and based on the Ministry of Interior, as of November 2018, 405,500 Syrians were born in Turkey. Under current conditions, Syrians born in Turkey receive no citizenship rights. Still, especially in the camps, the Turkish state has been proactive in socializing the young Syrians into Turkish society and culture through schooling–this has been reflected in the curriculum used in the camps, which includes the Turkish national anthem. The socialization through education or participation in professional and social life may act as a pull factor for Syrians to stay in Turkey.

Existing empirical research on Syrians provides limited knowledge on the changing motivations of the Syrians living in Turkey. According to a survey conducted by Turkey's Disaster and Emergency Management Authority (AFAD) in 2013, some 2 percent of the respondents reported thinking of returning as early as possible, and 88 percent thought of returning in case of a change in the conditions in Syria, their hometown, or regime change. Only 7.7 percent reported that they never thought of returning (AFAD 2013). In a follow-up survey in 2017, 71 percent of the respondents reported thinking of returning, and 16 percent reported never thinking of returning to Syria. A similar result was obtained in another survey conducted in 2017, where 16 percent of the participants reported that they never thought of returning to Syria (Erdoğan 2018). This change in the self-projection of Syrians illustrates that their longer stay in Turkey increases their likelihood of not returning in the future.

Conclusion

The challenge of human displacement from Syria is large and growing in scale. A great deal of qualitative and quantitative evidence suggests that the situation of Syria's displaced people is becoming increasingly problematic. On the one hand, those who succeed in escaping from their country are struggling to find a safe refuge in other states; on the other, those who have found safe refuge in other states are trying to integrate their lives into the receiving communities over time.

The central problem of this chapter is how, in what ways, and to what extent the long-term or permanent settlement of Syrian refugees in Turkey has occurred over the last five years. In that respect, assuming a dialogical interplay between individual characteristics of refugees and local/national and global/international processes and structures, this analysis reexamines and problematizes the settlement prospects of Syrian refugees in Turkey. A comparative perspective, referring to the cases of Afghan refugees in Pakistan and Iran, has also been provided.

Consequently, it is possible to draw the following conclusions. The early notion of Syrian refugees as temporary "guests" in Turkey has been increasingly questioned, as a protracted displacement seems increasingly inevitable along with the likelihood that permanent settlement in the country will be an option for a significant proportion of the refugee population (Kirişçi and Karaca 2014). Based on the existing literature on the determinants of settlement and the case of the Afghan refugees in Pakistan and Iran, time and other factors imbue a "vulnerable permanency" for this population.

First and foremost, despite the attempts for a safe zone on the Turkish-Syrian border that is expected to host voluntary repatriations, the current conditions in Syria provide an environment for refugees in the short and medium term that is far from secure. As in the case with Afghanistan, the restructuring of the country after its protracted conflict and the establishment of accountable and responsive governance is a long-term process. This is especially critical considering the former failed examples of safe zones in

Bosnia and Rwanda that provided far from secure shelters for refugees. Furthermore, the history of Afghan refugees has illustrated that, even though the repatriation may become a possible scenario during the periods of relative security, its sustainability depends on a number of factors, including the existence of property rights, accountable and responsive governance, and adequate delivery of services. In the case of Syria, the prospects for return remain limited in an environment rent by internal and international conflict. If returning home is not an option, two other choices exist for refugees in Turkey: either staying in their current country or moving on to other countries—but in doing so they often become subject to temporary protection status. One can expect that, as happened in the case of the Afghan refugees, there will be spillover effects of Syrian refugee flows beyond the immediate region, not only to relatively close regions such as Europe but also to more distant lands such as North America and Australia over the coming decades.

Second, despite providing a rapid protection under the conditions of mass influx, temporary protection does not easily facilitate a status of integration into the receiving communities in Turkey or elsewhere. Under the current international refugee regime, the long-term solutions for refugees in the cases of mass influx depend on the decisions of the sovereign states and the political confrontations in the international realm. Europe's response to Bosnian refugees with temporary protection and the less systematic protection schemes offered by Pakistani and Iranian governments to Afghan refugees are illustrative of the ultimate authority of each case. In Iran and Pakistan, the restrictive policies for naturalization, permanent settlement, and access to legal employment and social integration continue to be the main impediments against Afghans' legal integration in these countries, despite having lived there for many years. For the Syrian case, there are certain legal and administrative measures that have already been taken to provide some comfort to the temporarily protected Syrian refugees: the changes to Turkey's labor laws and the provisions toward limited inclusion in the welfare state facilitate Syrians' socialization and integration to the Turkish society. Still, even though the refugees have been subject to a transitioning asylum and protection regime in Turkey, their secure status will be limited unless the geographical limitation and the Settlement Law are revised by the Turkish state.

Third, the natural process of migration and settlement itself, and the changes in the actions and perceptions of refugees, may alter the conditions of permanency in Turkey. For instance, in the case of many Afghan refugees who were born or spent their childhood in Iran, Afghanistan is an "unknown" they have never seen, making it more difficult to decide on repatriation (Tober 2007). For the Syrians in Turkey, the changes in the self may be reinforced through spontaneous integration of Syrians via the emergence of new generations, processes of schooling, employment, or intermarriages into the receiving communities.

Ahmet İçduygu currently holds a dual appointment as full professor at Koç in the Department of International Relations and the Department of Sociology. He is also the director of the Migration Research Center at Koç (MiReKoç). In addition to his numerous articles in scholarly journals such as *Ethnic and Racial Studies, Citizenship Studies,* and *International Migration*, his most recent books include *Critical Reflections in Migration Research: Views from the South and the East*, coedited with Ayşem Biriz Karaçay (Koç University Press, 2014), *Forced Migration and Social Cohesion*, in Turkish, coauthored with Saime Özçürümez (Bilgi University Press, 2020), and *Migrants and Cities*, coedited by Jan Ruth (Edward Elgar, forthcoming).

Damla B. Aksel is assistant professor at the Department of Political Science and International Relations at Bahçeşehir University (İstanbul) and a research associate at Migration Research Center at Koç University (MiReKoç). Her research focuses on migration governance, transnationalism, diasporas, irregular migration, and migration in the context of Turkey-EU relations. She is the author of *Home States and Homeland Politics: Interactions between the Turkish State and Its Emigrants in France and the United States* (Routledge, 2019).

Note

1. For the figures cited in this paragraph, see the UNHCR Syria Regional Refugee Response website: https://data2.unhcr.org/en/situations/syria.

References

AFAD (Republic of Turkey Prime Ministry Disaster and Emergency Management Presidency). 2013. *Syrian Refugees in Turkey, 2013: Field Survey Results*. Ankara: Republic of Turkey Prime Ministry Disaster and Emergency Management Presidency.

Akçapar, Şebnem K., and Doğuş Şimşek. 2018. "The Politics of Syrian Refugees in Turkey: A Question of Inclusion and Exclusion through Citizenship." *Social Inclusion* 6(1).

Albert, Matthew. 2010. "Governance and Prima Facie Refugee Status Determination: Clarifying the Boundaries of Temporary Protection, Group Determination, and Mass Influx." *Refugee Survey Quarterly* 29(1): 61–91.

Al Jazeera. 2019. "UN Chief Urges World to Share Refugee Burden More Equitably." 17 December. Retrieved 19 December 2020 from https://www.aljazeera.com/news/2019/12/chief-urges-world-share-refugee-burden-equitably-191217104720889.html.

Araabi, Samer, and Leila Hilal. 2016. *Reconciliation, Reward and Revenge: Analyzing Syrian De-escalation Dynamics through Local Cease Fire Negotiations*. Berlin: Berghof Foundation.

Ashrafi, Afsaneh, and Haideh Moghissi. 2002. "Afghans in Iran: Asylum Fatigue Overshadows Islamic Brotherhood." *Global Dialogue* 4(4): 89.
BBC Türkçe. 2019. "Türkiye'de Kaç Suriyeli Var? En çok Suriyeli Nüfusu Hangi Şehirde Yaşıyor?" [How many Syrians are there in Turkey? In which city do most Syrians live?] 20 August. Retrieved 19 December 2020 from https://www.bbc.com/turkce/haberler-turkiye-49150143.
Borthakur, Anchita. 2017. "Afghan Refugees: The Impact on Pakistan." *Asian Affairs* 48(3): 488–509.
Bulur, Sertaç. 2018. "190,000 Syrians Return to Liberated Hometowns." Anadolu Agency, 31 July. Retrieved 19 December 2020 from https://www.aa.com.tr/en/middle-east/190-000-syrians-return-to-liberatedhometowns/1218961.
Castles, Stephen. 2006. "Guestworkers in Europe: A Resurrection?" *International Migration Review* 40(4): 741–66.
Chimni, Bhupinder Singh. 1998. "The Geopolitics of Refugee Studies: A View from the South." *Journal of Refugee Studies* 11(4): 350–374.
———. 2004. "From Resettlement to Involuntary Repatriation: towards a Critical History of Durable Solutions to Refugee Problems." *Refugee Survey Quarterly* 23(3): 55–73.
Craig, Tim. 2014. "Pakistan Cracks Down on Afghan Immigrants, Fearing an Influx as U.S. Leaves Afghanistan." *Washington Post*, 12 May. Retrieved 19 December 2020 from https://www.washingtonpost.com/world/pakistan-cracks-down-on-afghan-immigrants-fearing-an-influx-as-us-leaves-afghanistan/2014/05/12/74057f62-cfa9-11e3-b812-0c92213941f4_story.html.
Crisp, Jeff. 2018. "It's Far Too Early to Talk of Return for Syrian Refugees." Chatham House, 10 August. Retrieved 19 December 2020 from https://www.chathamhouse.org//node/31020.
DGMM. 2019. "Geçici Koruma" [Temporary protection]. Retrieved 19 December 2020 from https://www.goc.gov.tr/gecici-koruma5638.
Dinçer, Osman Bahadır, and Vittoria Federici, Elizabeth Ferris, Sema Karaca, Kemal Kirişci, and Elif Özmenek Çarmıklı. 2013. *Turkey and Syrian Refugees: The Limits of Hospitality*. Ankara: Uluslararası Stratejik Araştırmalar Kurumu and the Brookings Institution.
Durieux, Jean-François, and Jane McAdam. 2004. "Non-refoulement through Time: The Case for a Derogation Clause to the Refugee Convention in Mass Influx Emergencies." *International Journal of Refugee Law* 16(1): 4–24.
Ekşi, Nuray. 2014. *Yabancılar ve Uluslararası Koruma Hukuku* [Foreigners and international protection law]. Istanbul: Beta Basım Yayın.
Erdoğan, Murat. 2015. *Türkiye'deki Suriyeliler: Toplumsal Kabul ve Uyum Araştırması* [Syrians in Turkey: Research on social acceptance and adaptability]. Istanbul: Bilgi Üniversitesi Yayınları.
EUROSTAT. 2018. "Asylum Decisions in the EU." News release. Retrieved 19 December 2020 from https://ec.europa.eu/eurostat/documents/2995521/9747530/3-25042019-BP-EN.pdf/22635b8a-4b9c-4ba9-a5c8-934ca02de496.
Fitzpatrick, Joan. 2000. "Temporary Protection of Refugees: Elements of a Formalized Regime." *American Journal of International Law* 4(2): 279–306.
Frelick, Bill. 2007. "Paradigm Shifts in the International Responses to Refugees". In *Fear of Persecution: Global Human Rights, International Law, and Human Well-Being*, edited by James Daniel White, Anthony J. Marsella, 33–57. Lanham, MD: Lexington Books.

Gause, Gregory F., III. 2011. "Why Middle East Studies Missed the Arab Spring: The Myth of Authoritarian Stability." *Foreign Affairs* 90(4): 81–84, 85–90.

Ghazal, Mohammad. 2018. "Around 8,000 Syrian Refugees Return Home in 2017." *Jordan Times*, 7 February. Retrieved 19 December 2020 from http://www.jordan times.com/news/local/around-8000-syrianrefugees-return-home-2017.

Harild, Niels, and Asger Christensen. 2010. "The Development Challenge of Finding Durable Solutions for Refugees and Internally Displaced People." Washington, DC: World Bank Group.

Hinnebusch, Raymond. 2008. *What Does Syria Want? A Presentation by Raymond Hinnebusch for the Center for Naval Analyses and the Forum du Futur (France)*. Alexandria, VA: Center for Naval Analyses. Retrieved 19 December 2020 https://apps.dtic.mil/sti/citations/ADA488351.

Human Rights Watch. 2013. "Unwelcome Guests: Iran's Violation of Afghan Refugee and Migrant Rights." Retrieved 19 December 2020 from http://www.hrw.org/reports/2013/11/20/unwelcome-guests-0i.

Hürriyet. 2019. "Son Dakika: Bakan Soylu Geri Dönen Suriyeli Sayısını Açıkladı" [Last minute: Minister Soylu announced the number of returning Syrians]. 19 October. Retrieved 19 December 2020 from http://www.hurriyet.com.tr/gundem/son-dakika-bakan-soylu-turkiyedeki-suriyeli-sayisini-acikladi-41333583.

Hürriyet Daily News. 2015. "Syrian Refugees Return to Bordertown After ISIL Defeat." 17 June. Retrieved 19 December 2020 from http://www.hurriyet dailynews.com/syria-refugees-return-to-border-town-after-isil-defeat--.aspx?pageID=238&nID=84135&NewsCatID=352

Huysmans, Jef, Andrew Dobson, and Raia Prokhovnik (eds). 2006. *The Politics of Protection: Sites of Insecurity and Political Agency*. New York: Routledge.

İçduygu, Ahmet. 1993. *Temporariness versus Permanence: Changing Nature of the Turkish Immigrant Settlements in Australia and Sweden*. International Population Conference, Montreal, vols. 1–4: 71–84.

———. 2015. *Syrian Refugees in Turkey: The Long Road Ahead*. Washington, DC: Migration Policy Institute.

İçduygu, Ahmet, and Damla B. Aksel. 2013. "Turkish Migration Policies: A Critical Historical Retrospective." *Perceptions* 18(3): 167–90.

İçduygu, Ahmet, and Enes Ayaşlı. 2019. "Geri Dönüş Siyaseti: Suriyeli Mültecilerin Dönüş Göçü İhtimali ve Gelecek Senaryoları" [The politics of return: The probability of the return migration of Syrian refugees, and scenarios for the future]. *MiReKoc Çalışma Notları*. April. Retrieved 19 December 2020 from https://mirekoc.ku.edu.tr/wp-content/uploads/2019/05/Mirekoc_Rapor_GeriDonusSi yaseti.pdf.

İçduygu, Ahmet, and Maissam Nimer. 2019. "The Politics of Return: Exploring the Future of Refugees in Jordan, Lebanon and Turkey." *Third World Quarterly*. https://doi.org/10.1080/01436597.2019.1675503.

İçduygu, Ahmet, and Deniz Yükseker. 2012. "Rethinking Transit Migration in Turkey: Reality and Re-presentation in the Creation of a Migratory Phenomenon." *Population, Space and Place* 18(4): 441–56.

Jacobsen, Karen. 1996. "Factors Influencing the Policy Responses of Host Governments to Mass Refugee Influxes." *International Migration Review* 30(3): 655–78.

Keely, Charles, B. 2001. "The International Refugee Regime(s): The End of the Cold War Matters." *International Migration Review* 35(1): 303–14.
Khoo, Siew-Ean, Graeme Hugo, and Peter McDonald. 2008. "Which Skilled Temporary Migrants Become Permanent Residents and Why?" *International Migration Review* 42(1): 193–226.
Kirişci, Kemal. 2003. "The Question of Asylum and Illegal Migration in European Union-Turkish Relations." *Turkish Studies* 4(1): 79–106.
———. 2014. *Misafirliğin Ötesine Geçerken: Türkiye'nin "Suriyeli Mülteciler" Sınavı* [Beyond being guests: Turkey's "Syrian refugee" test]. Ankara: Uluslararası Stratejik Araştırmalar Kurumu and Brookings Enstitüsü.
Kirişci, Kemal, and Sema Karaca. 2014. *Türkiye'de Suriyeli Mülteciler: Uzun Döneme Hazırlanmak* [Syrian refugees in Turkey: Getting prepared for the long-term]. Uluslararası Stratejik Araştırmalar Kurumu, 4 March.
Koepke, Bruce. 2011. "The Situation of Afghans in the Islamic Republic of Iran Nine Years After the Overthrow of the Taliban Regime in Afghanistan." Washington, DC: Middle East Institute, MEI-FRS(c).
Koser, Khalid, and Richard Black. 1999. "Limits to Harmonization: The 'Temporary Protection' of Refugees in the European Union." *International Migration* 37(3): 521–43.
Kronenfeld, Daniel. 2008. "Afghan Refugees in Pakistan: Not All Refugees, Not Always in Pakistan, Not Necessarily Afghan?" *Journal of Refugee Studies* 21(1): 43–63.
———. 2011. "Can Afghanistan Cope with Returnees? Can Returnees Cope in Afghanistan? A Look at Some New Data." Washington, DC: Middle East Institute, MEI-FRS(c)
Kunz, Egon F. 1981. "Exile and Resettlement: Refugee Theory." *International Migration Review* 15(1/2): 42–51.
Lippert, Randy. 1999. "Governing Refugees: The Relevance of Governmentality to Understanding the International Refugee Regime." *Alternatives* 24: 295–328.
Margesson, Rhoda. 2007. *CRS Report for Congress: Afghan Refugees; Current Status and Future Prospects*. Washington, DC: Congressional Research Service.
Massey, Douglas S., and Zai Liang. 1989. "The Long-Term Consequences of a Temporary Worker Program: The US Bracero Experience." *Population Research and Policy Review* 8(3): 199–226.
Memişoğlu, Fulya, and Aslı Ilgit. 2017. "Syrian Refugees in Turkey: Multifaceted Challenges, Diverse Players and Ambiguous Policies." *Mediterranean Politics* 22(3) (3 July): 317–38.
Nyers, Peter. 2013. *Rethinking Refugees: Beyond State of Emergency*. New York: Routledge.
Orhan, Oytun, and Sabiha S. Gündoğar. 2015. *Suriyeli Sığınmacıların Türkiye'ye Etkileri* [The impact of Syrian asylum seekers on Turkey]. Ankara: ORSAM and TESEV.
Özden, Senay. 2013. *Syrian Refugees in Turkey*. MPC Research Reports, May 2013. San Domenico di Fiesole (FI): Robert Schuman Centre for Advanced Studies, European University Institute
Öztürkler, Harun, and Türkmen Göksel. 2015. *Suriyeli Mültecilerin Turkiye'ye Ekonomik Etkileri: Sentetik Bir Modelleme* [The economic impact on Turkey of Syrian refugees: A synthetic model]. Ankara: ORSAM.

Perthes, Volker. 2011. "Europe and the Arab Spring." *Survival* 53(6): 73–84.
Salehyan, Idean. 2008. "The Externalities of Civil Strife: Refugees as a Source of International Conflict." *American Journal of Political Science* 52(4): 787–801.
Scalletaris, Giulia. 2010. "Refugees or Migrants? The UNHCR's Comprehensive Approach to Afghan Mobility into Iran and Pakistan." In *The Politics of International Migration Management*, edited by Martin Geiger and Antoine Pécoud, 252–271. New York: Palgrave Macmillan.
Schmeidl, Susanne. 2002. "(Human) Security Dilemmas: Long-Term Implications of the Afghan Refugee Crisis." *Third World Quarterly* 23(1): 7–29.
———. 2011. "Protracted Displacement in Afghanistan: Will History Be Repeated." *Middle East Institute*. Washington, DC: Middle East Institute, MEI-FRS(c).
Sert, Deniz S. 2010. "Internal Displacement: Return, Property, Economy." *International Migration* 52(5): 227–44.
Stein, Barry N. 1986. "Durable Solutions for Developing Country Refugees." *International Migration Review* 20(2): 264–82.
T.C. İçişleri Bakanlığı Göç İdaresi Genel Müdürlüğü. 2019. *Geçici Koruma* [Temporary protection]. https://www.goc.gov.tr/gecici-koruma5638.
Tober, Diane. 2007. "My Body Is Broken like My Country: Identity, Nation, and Repatriation among Afghan Refugees in Iran." *Iranian Studies* 40(2): 263–85.
UK Parliament. 2018. "Syria: De-escalation Zones." House of Common Hansard, vol. 636, 26 February. Retrieved 19 December 2020 from https://hansard.parliament.uk/commons/2018-02-26/debates/2159AE6A-DDF9-4345-BD7B-180EE4840C9A/SyriaDe-EscalationZones.
UNHCR (United Nations High Commissioner for Refugees). 2019a. "Pakistan: Voluntary Repatriation of Afghans from Pakistan Update." Retrieved 19 December 2020 from https://reliefweb.int/sites/reliefweb.int/files/resources/69624.pdf.
———. 2019b. "Syria Regional Refugee Response." Retrieved 19 December 2020 from https://data2.unhcr.org/en/situations/syria.
UNICEF (United Nations International Children's Emergency Fund). 2018. *Turkey 2018 Humanitarian Situation Report*. Retrieved 19 December 2020 from https://www.uniceturk.org/public/uploads/files/UNICEFpercent20Turkeypercent20Humanitarianpercent20Situationpercent20Reportpercent20No.percent2025 percent20-percent20September percent202018.pdf.
Zieck, Marjoleine. 2008. "The Legal Status of Afghan Refugees in Pakistan, as Story of Eight Agreements and Two Suppressed Premises." *International Journal of Refugee Law* 20(2): 253–72.

Part III
Europe and Migration

Past and Present

7

Legal Topography of the 2015 European Refugee "Crisis"

Everita Silina

During the summer of 2015, the Greek island of Kos in the eastern Aegean Sea was one of the main crossing points from Turkey for Syrian refugees hoping to reach Europe. The main squares and parks were full of exhausted men, women, and children who had transformed these spaces into temporary living areas. Every morning, a line of people formed outside the local police station along the waterfront, sharing the sidewalk with the passing tourists on summer holiday, while just a few yards away in the harbor more migrants and refugees were disembarking from the Greek Coast Guard vessels back from the morning surveillance rounds. Similar scenes played out all along the Aegean coast and further along the Balkan route.

By the summer of 2016, everything had changed. On 20 March 20, the EU-Turkey Deal took effect, and by June the street in front of the Kos police station was empty. There were no refugees and barely any tourists either. Scared off by the images of desperate people arriving on the beaches, vacationers had decided to avoid the islands altogether. The busy water promenade and lively squares were empty. Restaurants were open, large TV screens transmitted games from the UEFA European Championship, yet customers were lacking.

In the summer of 2017, the life on Kos had returned to its usual vibrancy. The harbor front and restaurants were once again full of tourists. Refugees and migrants were still crossing the Aegean, but once on Greek soil they were moved to camps set up as official Reception and Processing Centers farther away from city centers and the public gaze. In Kos, the camps were so well hidden in the hilly countryside that even many locals had no clear idea where it was. The restaurant owners too no longer talked about refugees to their customers. The "refugee crisis" was over. All that was left behind was a new European topography dotted with various structures of permanence.

* * *

The European refugee crisis of 2015 is commonly depicted as a circumscribed event with clear start and end dates. The successive changes on the Greek islands, such as those detailed above, from 2015 to 2017, reinforce the view that timely policy innovations effectively managed the situation that was spiraling out of control. In response to what was seen as an unprecedented humanitarian challenge, the EU and various member states undertook actions to contain the movement of the refugees and migrants by a mixture of spatial controls and economic deals with regional countries, most notably Turkey and Jordan. This has resulted in a complex and confusing patchwork of policies and legal frameworks implemented in the core countries along the route and an ever-multiplying presence of actors and EU agencies with seemingly overlapping authorities. The immediate response, as well as the longer-term measures, in the form of the European Agenda on Migration, have focused on the frontier states, Greece and Italy, as the epicenter of the migration crisis and as the weak spots in the EU's migration management system. In turn, this geographic perspective has had direct consequences on the spatial management of the refugee crisis, including decisions regarding the location of refugee camps and Reception and Identification Centers (RICs), and the legal exemptions that would apply to each. Specifically, the five "hotspot" islands of the east Aegean–Chios, Kos, Leros, Lesvos, and Samos–have become the "anomalous zones" (Neuman 1996: 1197–234) of Europe, where the new policies can be tested and variously defined groups of migrants compete for legal rights.

The EU's asylum system is governed by the Dublin Regulations, which impose geographic limits on migrant mobility to the first country of entry. The aim is to ensure that a specific member state is responsible for processing the asylum claim and to discourage secondary movement within EU territory. The new emergency measures that saw the creation of the "hotspot approach" and the signing of the EU-Turkey Agreement gave the EU a stronger role in border enforcement that it had been seeking.

The "hotspot approach" was developed by the European Commission and proposed in the initial document of the European Agenda for Migration in May of 2015. It aimed to offer better-coordinated assistance to the frontline member states dealing with the increase in irregular migration and to provide greater uniformity in immigration procedures across all states. The assistance would "focus on registration, identification, fingerprinting and debriefing of asylum seekers" (European Commission 2015). According to the document, this would create a much more efficient and expedited set of procedures. However, it is a mistake to reduce the role that the islands have played in migration management to their geographical location on the edge of Europe. As major tourism hubs, they are pivotal in the EU's economic development plan for Greece and the broader EU economic agenda. Hence, the speed with which the refugee crisis was able to endanger the livelihoods and economic security of the island residents reveals a deeper contradiction at the heart of the European integration model. The contradiction is driven, on the one hand, by the increasing economic insecurity that has been generated by the EU's neoliberal policies and, on the other hand, by the lack of democratic space to contest these policies. It is this contradiction that is responsible for the rise of right-wing politics across the continent and that constitutes the EU's *crisis of governance.* In response, the "hotspot approach," the EU-Turkey Agreement, and the European Agenda on Migration represent yet another set of technocratic solutions that uses the emergency narrative to remove the issue of migration from the sphere of democratic control. The deeper contradictions are for the time being displaced by simply removing migrants and refugees from public view and Europe. In this chapter, I will argue that the response to the 2015 refugee crisis must be understood in this broader context of the EU crisis of governance.

To this end, the next section opens with an overview of the various crisis narratives that have populated the EU public domain over the last decade. In contrast to the typical segmented framing of each episode as sui generis, I suggest that these crises are interlinked through a larger crisis of EU governance. In the section that follows, I sketch out this argument by offering a brief history of the European integration process with particular focus on its ideological foundations and the broader international financial context of which it is a part. The theoretical framework I develop here reveals European Union's economic logic and the tradeoff between efficiency (technical expertise) and democracy that it demands and that undergirds the integration project to this day. Paradoxically, it is the failure of *this* economic logic that has revealed the weakness of the tradeoff and resulted in the crisis of governance. In the second part of this chapter, I use the refugee situation of 2015 to draw out the manifestations of the governance crisis in everyday policymaking. A critical reading of the evolving spatial and legal nexus allows me to link the emergency measures instituted to deal with the immediate situation in the Aegean Islands to the broader externalization strategy for migration management. Hence, while the analysis here focuses extensively on one case study, the EU-Turkey Statement, specifically its implications in the eastern Aegean, I draw on insights from the Jordanian Compact to show patterns of convergence and to capture the essence of the EU's migration agenda and the contradictions inherent to it. In this way, the chapter combines elements of critical international political economy and comparative policy studies. As I note in the conclusion, the EU's response to the 2015 refugee situation bears all the characteristics of the crisis of governance. On the one hand, technocratic responses to deeply political issues have not assuaged the public discontent generated by the contradictions inherent in the EU's model of integration. The elaborate spatial control of the migration flow has not dampened the appeal of right-wing parties in Europe. On the other hand, the more overtly political gestures embrace a shift to the right in an attempt to co-opt the right-wing voters. Paradoxically, such moves legitimize the very phenomenon they seek to eradicate.

Competing Crisis Narratives?

On 4 March 2019, French president Emmanuel Macron called on his fellow European citizens to "renew" their commitment to the European project in the face of a growing danger from "nationalist retrenchment." Cautioning that time was short, he proposed a new renaissance for Europe, one anchored in the ambitious pursuit of freedom, protection, and progress. His appeal was grounded in the recognition that Europe was in the midst of a crisis generated by its failure "to respond to its peoples' needs for protection from the major shocks of the modern world" (Macron 2019). To many, he noted, Europe had become "a soulless market." He warned that this popular disillusionment opened the way for nationalist forces that were capitalizing on people's anger. But "business as usual" and resignation were equally dangerous attitudes as they would deny the fears of the people and undermine the value of democracies. Instead, he announced, it was time for people to take back control of the European project and their future.

For a couple of days, Macron's letter generated considerable attention in the European media. It seemed to offer a new broader definition of the European crisis, its sources, and its consequences, one that treated Brexit and the rise of nationalism as its symptoms rather than causes and declined to reduce either to a backlash against migration. The EU is no stranger to discussions about crises, including the crises on the nature of its overall project. Recently the term has been bandied about with some frequency–during the run-up to the Constitutional Treaty, Europe was said to be facing the crisis of democratic deficit and public alienation. At the same time, multiple successive enlargements eastward had brought about a form of crisis described as "enlargement fatigue." Then in 2008, the global financial meltdown caused the Eurozone crisis accompanied by the Greek government-debt crisis, which still lingers today. While 2015 was defined by the refugee crisis, from

2016 onward the Brexit crisis has dominated the EU agenda. Most recently, the rise of right-wing and nationalist forces is said to be threatening the EU with an existential crisis.

The tendency has been to view these episodes as independent phenomena. Hence, the 2008 Eurozone crisis and the Greek debt crisis that grew out of it have only rarely been linked to the earlier democratic deficit debate or to the more recent political crisis associated with the 2015 refugee influx and the divisions it has produced among the member states. For most observers, the former was the result of economic variables alone, technical failures rather than political decisions. Only the most critical voices are willing to point out that the European economic model itself is implicated in the production of these crises. Specifically, the imbalance between export-driven economies, like Germany, and major importers, like Greece, creates a dangerous and unsustainable situation. The neoliberal turn with the adoption of the Maastricht Treaty has enshrined such market contradictions at the very heart of the EU (EuroMemo Group 2010; Streeck 2012: 63–71; Patomäki 2013). The dominance of the competition policy above all other values, especially the protections enshrined in the European Social Model, has indeed reduced the EU to a "soulless market."

I want to extend this critique and suggest that the crisis the EU is facing is more fundamental than the economic contradictions highlighted above. It is not defined by the economic crisis, though much of the source of concern stems from the economic ideology that defines the EU project. It is also more than institutional overreach, democratic deficit, or right-wing backlash, as many would describe it. In a sense, what I sketch here is a crisis that emanates from the core logic that underpins the design of the European Union. This is a *governance crisis*, and as such it once again raises the question as to which foundational values (efficiency, technocracy, democracy, social justice, solidarity, etc.) should be chosen and how they should be ordered in this new polity. Hence, it speaks to the legitimate source of authority and its limits, its fiduciary obligations, and its claims to expertise and truth making. It determines how the refugee crisis of 2015 is framed, how the causes are identified and linked (or failed to be linked), and what solutions are offered.

EU Governance Crisis

At the core of the EU's governance crisis is a contradiction between democratic principles (popular legitimacy) and market principles enshrined in the founding treaties of the European Union (then Community). Of course, most international organizations can be said to suffer from some form of democratic deficit (Dahl 1999: 19–36). This typically means that there is a gap between the authoritative decisions and policies they produce and the principle of popular sovereignty or the assumed equality of all those affected by the decisions of the governing authority. Yet, in the EU context, this deficit has much more contentious history, and its challenge to the legitimacy of the European Union has much more severe and far-reaching implications for both the EU and the member states.

From the very outset, the design of the new entity was predicated on a nondemocratic, highly technocratic model that focused on economic growth and efficiency as the founding values of the integration project. This framework was justified by appeals to the broadly utilitarian (and paternalistic) argument that by pooling sovereignties and establishing expert-driven authority, the new community would be able to guarantee better management of sensitive natural assets (coal and steel), which would lead to greater prosperity and utility for all. The assumption behind the argument was that there was a technically (in economic terms) correct solution for how best to guarantee progress, and its implementation had to be isolated from both the narrow and self-interested actions of nation-states and the influence of interest-based politics. In other words, the common management of coal and steel was not about party politics or sectional interests, it was an issue that could be settled and managed scientifically. It was presented as a problem-driven and pragmatic response to the violence of the two world wars and interwar protectionism. The liberal economic arguments that trade and integration lead to peace were accepted as fact. As Jean Monnet had argued during the war, the only way forward for Europe was through a common market. An overall belief in economic integration was coupled with a belief in economic efficiency to form the scientific creed of the European Union. Since the very beginning, then, the character of the European Union was marked by the belief (or at least a claim) that economic issues that drive European integration are nonideological and nonpolitical. Hence, they do not require much oversight by elected officials. The job should be left to experts or technicians, who will apply the best scientific knowledge and respond *pragmatically* to any problems that arise to help move the European Union forward. It is worth pointing out that the view that economic policy is simply a technical matter persists among many who argue that the EU does not suffer from a democratic deficit because the issues it oversees are economic (and therefore technical).[1] More recently, the EU's response to the 2008 Eurozone crisis and the Greek debt crisis has shown the same commitment to shield economic policies from the democratic sphere. Caretaker governments were installed in both Italy and Greece led by economic-technocrats—Mario Monti, the former EU commissioner for competition in Italy, and Lucas Papademo, the former president of the Greek Central Bank in Greece. Even the Greek referendum of 25 June 2015 could not persuade the EU technocrats that its economic formulas should be subject to public scrutiny.

European integration has progressed a long way from the early days of the European Coal and Steel Community. Today the EU is a complex and multifaceted entity with considerable influence in the member states' domestic affairs; it also has a strong international presence. Its policy reach now extends far beyond the Single Market and single currency, the euro, which can be considered the major policy accomplishments of the EU. Yet, despite the many changes in the character of the EU, the masterstrokes of integration remain economic, specifically, liberal economic. This is due in part to the dominant economic nature of the early days of the European project and the persistent liberalization of European policymaking. The dominance of economic thinking in European integration has meant that all other social spheres and issues are viewed through the lens of economic logic and are subject to evaluation based on their compatibility with market principles. But partly, the economic character remains, as we can see in the case of the Lisbon Treaty, because economics is still the main focus of the European Union's self-conception. Therefore, even the most recent attempts at recasting the EU have been clothed in primarily economic language. Economic principles and goals are still accorded higher significance than social or political aims, and little is said about how to reconcile these principles when they come into conflict.

By emphasizing the economic logic behind integration, I do not mean to suggest that other concerns and interests were not equally compelling and significant in motivating the decision-makers at different points in EU history. Instead, I argue that economic considerations have been *the most consistent and enduring* element in the building of today's European Union. Economic policy has been the staple of European decision-making even where the ultimate goal might have been peace and security.[2] The same linking of security and economic interests is now revealed in the steps taken to manage irregular migration and the refugee crisis. For example, both the Africa Trust Fund and the Jordanian Compact, are market-oriented economic solutions to perceived security challenges posed by migration. The rhetoric and principles that accompany them make a distinction between security and economic goals almost impossible. Put more succinctly, economic reasoning and efficiency play the role of a metanarrative of the integration process and, therefore, drive policy innovations.

The 2015 European "Refugee Crisis"

The Syrian refugee crisis of 2015 seemed to catch the leaders in the national capitals and Brussels off guard. Migration from the Middle East and sub-Saharan Africa, mostly via Libya to Italy and other parts of the Mediterranean, had been an issue of concern for EU decision-makers for years. It had prompted emergency meetings and had justified new security operations, temporary border closures, the building of fences, and an expanded role for FRONTEX (the EU border management agency) (European Council 2015). But images of columns of desperate people crossing Europe on foot during the summer and fall of 2015 evoked deeper reactions and brought to the fore unpleasant historic associations. The seeming lack of a unified response challenged Europe's self-image as a prosperous and advanced region able to deal with humanitarian disasters in an organized manner and in accordance with the principles of human rights. As Spanish prime minister Mariano Rajoy had said a few months earlier, "As Europeans we are gambling with our credibility ..." (Yardley 2015). It highlighted the political stalemate in Brussels over refugee quotas as well as the absence of solidarity and burden sharing among the EU members. And, to many, it confirmed the anxieties and insecurities associated with the Schengen Area, the disappearance of internal borders and the porous nature of the external ones. A public backlash against various proposed measures to tackle the crisis and the growing strength of the right-wing parties across the continent threatened social instability. The daily scenes unfolding along the tourist beaches of the eastern Aegean Islands and at the border crossings between EU and non-EU Balkan states encapsulated all these fears about the political, economic, and social state of the European Union and dominated the framing and the sense of the crisis. The EU's formal documents and press briefings portrayed the crisis as the greatest humanitarian challenge to face the continent since World War II. Such framing justified emergency measures that were adopted and still operate today (European Commission 2019). At the core of these emergency measures are policies of spatial control and legal innovations that accompany them. In the second part of this chapter, I take a closer look at two cases that represent this new spatial ordering. The first case concerns the eastern Aegean islands, which were the focus of two crucial policy decisions—the "hotspot approach" and the EU-Turkey Agreement—that together transformed them into *extra*legal spaces where normal EU asylum procedures do not apply. The second case, concerning the Jordan Compact, looks in more detail at the EU's rapidly evolving externalization policy and the economic logic that accompanies it.

The Aegean islands nearest to the coast of Turkey have been a preferred crossing point for irregular migrants for years. After Greece joined the Schengen Area in 2000, the former Ottoman territories became the external border of the EU, and the rocky islands acquired new strategic significance. Their location only a few nautical miles from a long Turkish Aegean coast provides ample opportunities for crossing the international waters in small dinghies and light crafts that can avoid detection by the Turkish and the Greek coast guards and navies. The Aegean route became the focal point when the much safer land route across Turkey's western border with Bulgaria and Greece was sealed by the neighboring states.

As a result, the islands had seen a continuous increase in arrivals by sea in the years leading up to the 2015 crisis. Local police departments with limited capacities for housing, services, and processing arrivals had nevertheless been engaged in the task of serving as frontline humanitarian and immigration offices. They were assisted in this task by the Hellenic Coast Guard and FRONTEX, which has been deployed in the area as part of the EU's Operation Poseidon since 2011 (Bacas 2014: 173). Jutta Lauth Bacas has chronicled the evolution of procedural and administrative changes on the island of Lesvos, now the most targeted crossing point, since 2004. She notes that the spike in arrivals in 2013 prompted the local Hellenic Coast Guard to set up the first improvised detention center in the Mytilini port area (Bacas 2014: 164). And, by the end of September, the now notorious Moria detention center was also operational. Far from the public gaze, Aegean islands were already spaces where the overlapping and complex authority structures allowed for an ambiguous application of immigration law (Bacas 2014: 175). More importantly, the islands, and the Mediterranean more broadly, played a crucial role in the EU's economic model. As argued previously, it is this very model of neoliberal development, the contradictions between the economic character of the European Union, and the social and democratic expectations of the public that created the governance crisis for the EU in the first place. The legal and spatial response to the 2015 refugee influx in the Aegean Islands must be understood in the context of this crisis of EU governance.

Crisis on the Islands

The EU's response to the refugee presence in the islands cannot be understood without considering the role that the islands play in the broader EU economic agenda. As discussed, the European integration project has been dominated by particular economic reasoning that emphasizes economic efficiency and competition as drivers of economic growth. Entry into the European Union requires each candidate state to submit their economy to deep restructuring to be able to join the Single Market without bringing with it too much volatility. As Costas Passas and George Labrinidis point out, this restructuring involves adapting to "a peculiar kind of EU division of labor" and specialization. In the restructuring of the Greek economy that followed the country's accession to the EEC in 1981, Greece came to play the role of "the front door and the hallway of the EU to the East" (Passas and Labrinidis 2016). Its ports provided a crucial link with regional and international trade routes, and soon other large infrastructure projects followed. The structural reorganization meant that the agricultural sector, which had accounted for a large part of the Greek economy and employment, would be reduced, and the trade in agricultural products went from surplus to deficit in a short time. This was done to serve the interests of large food monopolies in the north (France and Germany). Hence, Greece integrated into the common market by specializing "(a) as [the] outsourced management, banking, transportation, and logistics hub of north European manufacturing capital in South Eastern Europe and (b) as [the] tourism heaven for north European (mainly British and German) workers" (Passas and Labrinidis, 2016). Islands became crucial in restyling Greece as a competitive tourism destination.

Indeed, the entire Mediterranean has increasingly been defined in economic terms. The process has accelerated since the 1990s and the signing of the Maastricht Treaty with an increased neoliberal reimagining of space everywhere. According to Beste İşleyen "The Mediterranean island, whether Greek or Italian, has for the last decades been constituted as an economic space—a space of private investment, capital accumulation as well as the exchange of services, capital and goods relating to its production as a tourism attraction." Specifically, both the Euro-Mediterranean Partnership and the European Neighborhood Policy have promoted the Mediterranean as a space to be created and fostered for increasing transnational interactions, exchange of goods, and opportunities for investment (İşleyen 2016: 328).

Island economies would feel this shift in specialization very directly. For the last three decades, it has defined the economic and much of the social life on the islands (Spilanis and Vayanni 2004). On some islands, like Kos, the dependence on tourism constitutes 95 percent of economic activity. Hotel construction and restaurant businesses account for a large part of the increased performance of the service sector (Passas and Labrinidis 2016). Even during the heights of the refugee crisis when occupancy rates for holiday bungalows were dismally low, new holiday accommodations were being built on the island of Chios. To my puzzled inquiry, a local hotel owner responded that there is always money in hotels. Similar building activity was taking place along the north shore of the nearby island of Lesvos even as the neighboring hotel owner complained that migrants and refugees had driven off all the tourists.

The arrival of thousands of refugees to the Aegean Islands revealed the dangers inherent in the EU's economic model based on such mono-specialization. Throughout the summer and fall seasons of 2015, stories quickly circulated in the international media showing perplexed tourists witnessing panicked and often traumatized people disembark on the beaches. The full effect of the mass arrival of refugees manifested during the 2016 tourism season. During the summer of 2016, business on the islands seemed to have ground to a halt. Streets, shops, and restaurants were mostly empty save for the few elderly locals. The severity of the impact varied from island to island and provided a quick sense of the extent of local dependence on tourism. The island of Kos was perhaps most affected as it is oriented almost entirely toward the tourism industry, including mass package tours at larger resort hotels. Local shop and restaurant owners were desperate and angry. The little island of Leros was equally affected. When I spoke to one local restaurant owner in early June, he was considering closing his beachfront establishment and moving to Athens. The impact on Chios and Lesvos seemed less noticeable in part because both island economies are more diversified. Yet, even as late as January 2017, the deputy mayor of Chios reported that the number of chartered flights for the coming summer had declined by 100 percent.[3]

It was clear that the mass arrival of refugees had put enormous pressure on island economies. Economic specialization imposed by accession into the EEC had rendered islands dependent on mass tourism and vulnerable to sudden drops in supply. Since the flow of refugees could be expected to continue, the response would need to ensure that their presence on the islands, however temporary, would not compromise the tourist industry. The "hotspot approach" drafted in 2014 had already identified the islands as useful emergency sites for restricting the movement of migrants and refugees until their status could be assessed. Their location at a safe distance from the Greek and European mainland made them a perfect choice in the EU's attempt to control the flow of migrants by adopting a set of externalization programs. The signing of the EU-Turkey Agreement in the spring of 2016 turned the five "hotspot islands" into extraterritorial spaces where spatial and legal innovations were meant to overcome the contradictions inherent in the European integration project.

New Spatial and Legal Topography

The 2016 EU-Turkey deal is seen by most commentators, government officials, and NGO staff as a crucial moment of change in the management of the refugee situation in Europe. The agreement was a continuation of an earlier Joint Action Plan signed on 15 October 2015 and part of a new European Agenda on Migration inaugurated by the Juncker Commission in June of 2014. The Joint Action Plan was an agreement between the European Commission and the Republic of Turkey and was endorsed by all twenty-eight heads of state and government. It identified "a series of collaborative actions to be implemented as a matter of urgency by the European Union and the Republic of Turkey with the aim of confronting common challenges in a concerted manner and supplementing Turkey's efforts in managing a large number of people in need of protection in Turkey" (European Commission 2016). Under the provision of the Action Plan, the European Commission undertook to set up the Facility for Refugees in Turkey, providing a sum of €3 billion for the next two years to be allocated toward "humanitarian aid, education, labor market integration, health care access, social inclusion and infrastructure projects." This assistance was to be provided in return for Turkey's efforts in preventing irregular departures and smuggling from its territory along with more effective and full implementation of preexisting Readmission Agreements with Greece and the EU (European Commission 2016). The preexisting agreements provided the legal basis for the return of irregular migrants and refugees laid out in the EU-Turkey deal.

The EU-Turkey Statement was issued on 18 March 2016 and, like the previous Joint Action Plan, was presented in large part as an attempt to alleviate the pressures caused to Greece by irregular migration from Turkey. Its geographical focus on the Greek Aegean islands inaugurated a new bifurcated asylum procedure effectively splitting the legal domain in Greece into two distinct spheres. From a legal perspective, the islands became what Gerald L. Neuman has described as "'anomalous zones,' a geographical area in which certain legal rules, otherwise regarded as embodying fundamental policies of the larger legal system, are locally suspended" (Neuman 1996: 1201). He observes that such suspension is typically justified on the basis of perceived necessity and conceives of border areas as uniquely vulnerable.

The EU-Turkey Statement reconstituted the islands into just such "anomalous zones" through two additional points that were not part of the original Joint Action Plan. The first point announced that starting on 20 March 2016, all irregular migrants crossing from Turkey to Greek islands would be returned to Turkey. The statement stipulated that the returns would be done in compliance with the relevant international law and the principle of non-refoulement. The procedure was recognized as a "temporary and extraordinary measure" necessitated by the desire "to end the human suffering and restore public order" (European Council 2016). The second point stipulated that for every Syrian returned through this procedure to Turkey another Syrian from Turkey would be resettled in the EU with specific attention to UN vulnerability criteria (European Council 2016). Though the statement itself does not reference a separate set of procedures for those entering the asylum system on the mainland versus those doing so on one of the islands, in practice the clear geographical restrictions of the first two points mandated such a delineation. This spatial ordering is further buttressed by the "hotspot approach."

The current "hotspot approach" is focused on five Aegean islands seen as frontline locations in mass migration from Turkey. The policy establishing the hotspots is very much an exceptional measure presented as temporary. Yet, if successful, the approach could be replicated elsewhere in Europe. The Moria "hotspot" on the island of Lesvos was already operational in summer of 2015. Following the March 2016 EU-Turkey agreement, four more "hotspots" were opened at different intervals on the islands of Chios, Kos, Leros, and Samos. All five islands had already been part of the irregular migrant crossings. A "hotspot" meant that a confined Reception and Identification Center was set up on each island to process the irregular migrants and asylum seekers and to adjudicate the appeals before people would be allowed to proceed to the mainland or be returned to Turkey or their country of origin.

The practical requirements of the EU-Turkey Statement hence create several layers of legal and spatial anomalies. As noted before, the islands are conveniently distanced from mainland Greece to remove the issue from public attention. At the same time, islanders feel that camps are a permanent blight on their livelihoods and lifestyles and that the presence of "hotspots" speaks to the neglect and indifference by the government and the EU toward local interests. In February 2016 Kos residents clashed with local police over the planned opening of the Reception and Processing Center. In Lesvos and Chios, attempts to expand the facilities in light of overcrowding have met with staunch local opposition. Local administrators feel caught between the demands created by the presence of the "hotspots" and those of local residents. When the municipality of Chios decided to pay for the heat generators in Souda camp, a local resident sued the mayor's office for the misuse of public funds.

At the same time, the need to restore the viability of the tourism industry has meant that where possible the camps could not be placed near major tourist sites, hotels, and other recreational spaces. In Kos, the camp and the refugees are so well hidden it would be hard to know that arrivals continue. In Chios, the centrally located Souda camp has been closed. All detentions and processing now take place at Vial camp further inland, and there is no public transport access from there to the town of Chios. In an interesting commentary on the changing international climate, since the end of the Cold War half of the camps in Greece are housed on the grounds of decommissioned military bases. No doubt these were selected for their availability, yet they are all located at a distance from major urban centers. Even where the local public transport is readily provided, the location of the camps removes most asylum seekers from daily interactions with local populations.

The EU-Turkey deal effectively creates two parallel but separate legal spheres for processing asylum cases. Those passing through the islands are subjected to new legal and procedural measures meant to identify migrants without sufficient claim to asylum and expedite their removal from EU territory. Those who apply for asylum on the mainland follow the usual immigration procedures. Inside the camps on the islands, the EU-Turkey deal has created an additional legal ordering in which Syrian refugees are seen as more genuine and deserving of asylum, followed by Afghans and Iraqis, leaving everyone else in a gray category of potentially illegal migrants. This legal segregation is enforced by various spatial measures. Before the initial registration and processing are completed, all migrants are confined to a restricted area inside the Registration and Identification Center. The so-called *ausweis* cards issued to all migrants who have completed the initial intake interview further reinforce legal categorization. The card acts as a geographical gatekeeper. Those with a red stamp on the card are required to remain on the island until their case is processed. If caught traveling to the mainland, they can be arrested and returned to Lesvos where they are further segregated in the pre-removal detention center.

The EU-Turkey deal and the use of "hotspots" are roundly seen by the critics as being responsible for the deplorable conditions and overcrowding in camps on Lesvos and Samos. Anecdotal accounts claim that even Turkish smugglers are aware of the hierarchies of misery that distinguish one camp from another, and the journeys to islands with better situations now cost more than those to Lesvos and Samos. The peculiar legal character imposed on the islands by the "hotspot approach" and the EU-Turkey Agreement has turned them into "anomalous zones" simultaneously inside yet functionally outside the EU territory. This aspect links the "hotspot" islands to the EU's broader policy evolution that uses externalization to third countries as a preferred migration management strategy.

2015 Emergency and New Externalization Measures

The focus on the EU-Turkey Statement often serves to remove attention from a broader policy shift toward externalization of migration controls and third-country partnerships that have become the core of the European migration management in the face of growing domestic backlash (Lavenex 2002: 164). Since the 1990s, various types of trade-related Association Agreements have granted non-EU countries "highly preferential access to the EU's internal market" and have allowed the EU to demand that partner states implement specific immigration controls aimed at their own citizens as well as the third country nationals. The perceived crisis of the 2015 population movement led to a host of new emergency measures. In all of them externalization of migration played a key role. By claiming at the November 2015 Malta conference that it was responding to emergencies in several African countries, the EU created one of the largest migration funds, the EU Emergency Trust Fund for Africa: Trust Fund for Stability and Addressing Root Causes of Irregular Migration and Displaced Persons in Africa (EUTF). Incredibly, it covers twenty-six different African states considered to be in crisis situations, including Ghana, Kenya, and Senegal, and allocates a €4.6 billion budget to address these emergencies (Vermeulen et al. 2019). According to the EU's own documents, migration control constitutes the EUTF's major policy concern (European Commission 2018). In a parallel step, the EU signed development-based contracts with individual countries of Jordan and Lebanon as part of the attempt to reduce onward movement of Syrians.

Of all such externalization projects, the Jordan Compact is seen as the most innovative and the most successful. This valuation reflects the fact that it represents a paradigmatic case of the new development-based migration model that has been gaining traction at the international level, which is reflected in the 2018 UN Global Compact for Migration. Sometimes referred to as "the Compact approach," the new perspective sees refugees as an economic boon to the host countries (Temprano-Arroyo 2018). By building refugees' self-reliance and resiliency through access to job markets and local public services, such as education and healthcare, the approach reconceptualized refugees as economic assets rather than humanitarian burdens. It is a win-win formula that is seen to restore dignity to refugee populations and to reignite the economic vitality of host countries. The approach emphasizes the crucial role of the private sector, and it is often linked to preferential trade agreements and special economic zones (SEZs). This enhances its appeal to actors like the EU and the World Bank, whose policies toward migration are situated in broader commitment to liberal economic agenda.

At a February 2016 London Conference, Jordan, Lebanon and Turkey agreed to improve the conditions for Syrian refugees residing in their territories. The "Jordan Compact," announced at the end of the conference, envisaged the most proactive agenda of all three. Donors pledged €1.7 billion, with at least €700 million earmarked for infrastructure and municipal services (Howden et al. 2017). Within the terms of agreement, Jordan undertook the issuance of 200,000 work permits for Syrians in coming years and the removal of some of the hurdles that prevented Syrian refugees from entering the job market. It aimed to turn "the Syrian refugee crisis into a development opportunity that attracts new investments." As part of this economic agenda, the Jordanian government agreed to "designate five development zones and provide these with maximum incentives under the new investment law" in order to generate much-needed jobs. The special economic zones were envisaged as incubators of change (Lenner and Turner 2018). "It was expected that stakeholders would be able to encourage investment in SEZs, particularly in manufacturing, and thereby provide employment for Syrians and Jordanians alike." The backbone of the agreement was renegotiated terms of trade between Jordan and the EU similar to the 1990s trade association agreements. The special customs union would grant "preferential access to European markets for firms based in particular zones and employing Syrian refugees as a minimum proportion of their workforce" (Lenner and Turner 2018).

Unlike the "hotspot" approach, the Jordan Compact has been hailed as a welcome and an innovative step in global refugee management by international donors, the UN, and many humanitarian actors. Turning the refugee crisis into a development opportunity for host communities while promoting self-reliance and resilience among refugees seems like a winning formula to many and one that is quickly gaining attention around the world. Julia Morris, however, finds little to justify their optimism. On all indicators, the compact has failed to deliver the expected benefits. By the spring of 2018, only six Jordanian companies "were approved by the Ministry of Industry, Trade, and Supply to export to Europe under the new EU-Jordan Association Agreement. Only three businesses had exported to the EU with net earnings of just 1.5 million euros" (Morris 2018: 8). In reality, Jordanian businesses do not have the training and necessary business development skills to be able to export to the European market and compete in it as the compact envisaged.

The job growth envisioned by the contract has also been limited. Of the target two hundred thousand work permits for Syrians, just over eighty thousand had been issued by January of 2018. But even this figure is not a good indicator of how many jobs had been created, as many of these were renewals of expiring work permits and "several thousand permits issued to the same people upon switching jobs" (Lenner and Turner 2018). The majority of available jobs were in agriculture and construction, areas that have a high level of informal employment. The government expected that all these workers would wish to formalize their employment by obtaining work permits, but staying informal has its advantages. In construction, where many Syrians are already employed, informal jobs pay better, and nobody is expected to make the social security payments (Howden et al. 2017). For seasonal agricultural workers, work permits are even less attractive. Instead of being a job-creation engine, the compact, by prioritizing the Syrian refugees, has pushed the costs of adapting to the new development agenda onto Egyptian, Bangladeshi, and other "irregular" migrants who are now losing their jobs to Syrians as businesses aim to fulfill the donor requirements and put off hiring non-Syrian migrants due to increased fees (Howden et al. 2017).

Yet, despite much negative evidence that the intended effects on refugees and benefits for Jordanian firms were not materializing, the agreement was renewed again in 2018. Its imputed success has generated interest further afield in places like Afghanistan, Malaysia, and Niger. A jobs contract in Ethiopia prompted Werner Hoyer, the president of the European Investment Bank, to observe that such agreements can be win-win tools for preventing migrants from traveling to Europe, allowing them to stay closer to home while providing the economic boost to the local community (Howden et al. 2017).

Like all other externalization measures, such as the EUTF, Lebanon Compact, and Khartoum Process, the Jordan Compact conceives of migration management through an economic metric. Given the EU's economic identity, this is hardly surprising. As Sandra Lavenex notes, the EU uses its economic weight as an instrument in the pursuit of goals other than purely economic ones through its external trade policy" (Lavenex 2002: 162). In the attempt to stem the flow of Syrian refugees toward Europe, the economic development approach provides the EU with the cover of a win-win justification for what is, in reality, a highly coercive policy that restricts individual mobility through an exercise of remote control. The SEZs in Jordan, like those on the Aegean islands, function as "anomalous zones" where the EU can pursue "innovative" measures as part of its refugee crisis management policy.

Technocracy versus Democracy

The failure of the Jordan Compact to live up to its lofty economic expectations has much to do with its top-down technocratic character. The drafters of the compact were much more interested in fulfilling the market-based metrics and demonstrating the economic gains to be had from refugee management than generating locally viable policies. Most refugees did not have input into the programs that were designed to impact their lives and contribute to their self-sufficiency and resilience. Likewise, the drafters of the compact failed to consult local NGOs or experts and have consequently largely overestimated Jordan's ability to become a competitive and globalized member of the MENA region. Instead of offering some "training or development for local businesses in how to improve or be meaningful competitors in the European marketplace," the compact emphasizes the importance of work permit quotas as the measure of its ability to foster a more dynamic economic environment (Morris 2018: 8).

The European Agenda for Migration explicitly aims to use the refugee crisis to impose common standards for border management and immigration procedures and to centralize the migration management under EU control. The EU Commission sees this as an opportunity to bypass what it refers to as national idiosyncrasies and exceptions that are the result of local politics. The EU-Turkey deal and the "hotspot" approach are technocratic solutions that remove decision-making from the national democratic and legal arena. Greece was not a party to the EU-Turkey agreement, yet it bears the responsibility for its implementation. The drafters of the "hotspot" approach, which turns the islands into semipermanent prisons for migrants and refugees, did not consult with the local mayors, much less, the populations. The islanders, who were celebrated for their assistance to refugees in the initial months of the crisis, now feel their voices and interests are ignored and their communities are used as dumping grounds for Europe's unwanted. Island governments often find themselves caught between the policies coming from the EU and the demands of local citizens. As has been the practice for decades, the EU's economic policies are not subject to democratic control. With the adoption of the European Agenda on Migration, border and migration management will further limit the oversight from national democratic and legal processes.

In this respect, these developments are entirely consistent with the EU's decades-long practice of exerting its dominance in international trade to advance the European Union's migration goals. Since the early 1990s, the EU has been increasingly using bilateral trade and association agreements to externalize its migration controls to third countries. As is the case with the Jordan Compact and the EUTF, the agreements make trade and aid conditional on the implementation of a wide set of social and economic policies that aim to reduce push factors and that restrict the mobility of migrants from outside the state (Lavenex 2002: 161). As a matter of trade policy, the agreements have been exempt from democratic review in both contracting parties. In fact, the inclusion of conditionalities subverts the democratic process in the partner countries. Paradoxically, many of the agreements, especially those signed with African states, stipulated that democratic improvements must also accompany the implementation of the trade agreement.

The externalization of migration through such agreements has a direct effect on the quality and function of democracy in the EU as well. In the case of the Trust Fund for Africa, by declaring that the twenty-six partner countries are in a state of crisis, the EU has been able to sidestep its own public procurement procedures and the democratic oversight and transparency that they provide. An investigation by legal scholars Thomas Spijkerboer and Elies Steyger revealed that the EUTF's project proposal process is closed off and opaque. There is a dizzying variety of projects, from migration management and border control to food aid and awareness campaigns, yet how projects are chosen for funding remains unclear. The fund is run directly by the EU Commission, and 65 percent of the funding ends up in the hands of just five major actors: IOM, UNHCR, German development agency GIZ, the Italian government, and French organization Civipol. The EU parliament has no oversight function, and its calls for "more democratic handling of EUTF's project choices" have gone unheeded (Vermeulen et al. 2016), nor are African countries allowed to vote on the projects. They can sit in and observe the meetings but otherwise have little say in the selection process.

Conclusion

From the vantage point of 2017, the legal and geographic innovations marshaled in response to the 2015 "refugee crisis" appeared to deliver instantaneous results. The change on the Aegean Islands, highlighted in the opening vignette, was immediate and palpable. Most actors on the ground agreed that the EU-Turkey deal had drastically decreased the number of people arriving on the islands from Turkey. The introduction of "hotspots" with specially designed Reception and Identification Centers effectively cut off the flow of refugees out of Greece and prevented the accumulation of people at the border with North Macedonia. Together with the newly built border fences along the Balkan route, the policies put an end to the mass flow of people through the Balkans toward Western Europe.

However, by the summer of 2018, the number of asylum seekers was starting to increase just enough to overtax the system and the facilities. The RICs in Lesvos and Samos have become overcrowded and poorly equipped, and they lack many of the basic services. Instead of the efficiency and standardization of processing envisioned by the "hotspot approach," the islands have become detention centers where people languish in legal limbo for months and years. The "European refugee crisis" has been solved with its relocation to the periphery of Europe.

Even these "solutions" are only temporary. As an emergency response to a perceived crisis, the EU's Agenda on Migration is under constant pressure from the changing political landscape in the partner countries and the regions of which they are a part. The protracted nature of the Syrian conflict means that the negotiated externalization agreements might any day lose their appeal to the partner countries. In the meantime, such spatial controls require that the EU is sanguine about many human rights violations its policies generate and condone.[4]

The changes that might strain the EU's innovative migration management are gathering. On 7 July 2019, the general election in Greece swept away the ruling Syriza Party and ushered in a center-right government dominated by the New Democracy Party (Smith 2019). Prime Minister Kyriakos Mitsotakis had campaigned on a broadly anti-immigration platform. Upon assuming the office, he immediately shut down the Ministry for Migration Policy. Henceforth, the issues related to migration would be housed within the Ministry of Citizen Protection, which deals with public order and security. As the outgoing minister observed, the move signals that the government intends to deal with the issue of migration as a matter of delinquency rather than one of humanitarian concern (Keep Talking Greece 2019).

In November 2019, members of the Greek parliament approved a government bill aimed at improving the situation on the Aegean Islands by speeding up the asylum process and the return to Turkey. In a heated debate that preceded the passage of the bill, the prime minister echoed the commitments outlined in the EU Agenda for Migration and the "hotspot approach" when he argued that the new legislature would unclog the overburdened asylum process by separating bogus refugees from real ones. In line with the emphasis on speed and improving efficiency, the bill also envisions a shorter and more restricted appeals process for those whose asylum claims are rejected. To further reduce the applicant numbers, the area of the eastern Aegean would receive additional patrols and thermal cameras to help with the interception of boats before they leave Turkish waters (Kokkinidis 2019). As a harbinger of things to come, in late July of 2019 a zeppelin appeared above the hotspot island of Samos(Kokkinidis 2019). The airship was a gift from FRONTEX. It is equipped with a radar thermal camera and an automatic identification system that can monitor the area twenty-four hours a day (*Tornos News* 2019*)*. While Greece is the first EU member state to deploy a zeppelin for coastal surveillance purposes, this pilot project is part of the Joint Operation Poseidon and the larger pan-European maritime and cross-border surveillance agenda.

While the new conservative government in Athens might bring to the EU's Migration Agenda a blunt interpretation the EU might find distasteful, the developments across the Aegean in Turkey and Syria threaten to unravel the entire policy of externalization agreements as an emergency measure for mass population movement. Throughout 2019, Assad's forces, backed by Russian airpower, were advancing against the remaining rebel-held areas in the country's northwest, uprooting thousands of people in the process. Between 12 and 25 December, 235,000 people were forced to flee, many for the second time in the year (OCHA 2019). The vast majority were heading toward the Turkish border for the promise of safety that lies beyond. Yet, in Turkey itself, the mood of the population and the leadership has been turning against the refugees.

Following the government party's (AKP) electoral defeat in the March 2019 municipal elections in Istanbul and Ankara, Erdoğan has become increasingly vocal about the burden that Turkey is carrying for Europe by hosting more than three million Syrian refugees. The large presence of Syrians, especially in Istanbul, is seen as part of the reason for the voter backlash. Several reports in 2019 indicated that Turkish authorities had illegally deported several hundred Syrians back to Syria. Since spring, police had been stepping up random document checks on streets and in other public places to apprehend "illegal migrants." Yet the Human Rights Watch claims that even some Syrians with legal permission to stay in Turkey had been forcefully returned to Syria. The organization spoke to several Syrians, all of whom recounted being held in detention until they agreed to sign a document stating that they had wanted to return voluntarily. Afterward, they were bused to the border and released on the Syrian side (Human Rights Watch 2019). The forced returns are in clear violation of Turkish law, EU law, and the international principle of nonrefoulement. They raise uncomfortable moral questions about the continuation of the EU-Turkey deal but also potentially signal its demise.

The attack on Idlib prompted Erdoğan to issue the most direct threat yet against Europe's apparent inaction. At an award banquet in Istanbul on 22 December, Erdoğan warned the EU that Turkey would not shelter the new group of migrants. He noted that instead of criticizing Turkey's plan to establish "safe zones" inside Syria, the EU should focus on preventing the exodus of affected civilians in the first place. He promised that unless the European states took measures to stop the violence in Idlib, they would see a repeat of the 2015 refugee crisis, with Greece feeling the most direct effect (BBC News 2019).

The EU has not yet altered its policy in light of these growing challenges. Instead, in September 2019, Ursula von der Leyen, the newly elected president of the EU Commission, announced her team of top EU executives. Among the established commissioners was a new supercommissioner with oversight for migration, security, employment, social rights, youth, and education whose new job title was to be commissioner for "protecting our European way of life." The title was roundly ridiculed and criticized for being an embarrassment and out of touch with reality. Liberal and left-leaning politicians accused van der Leyen of pandering to the nationalist and far-right forces (Rankin 2019). Van der Leyen responded by altering the final title to "promoting our European way of life." In face of the mounting problems associated with the EU's responses to the migration "crisis," the leadership has internalized the view that co-opting some of the more hackneyed phrases from the populist right might buy them public sympathy and support.

The technocratic solutions offered by the new migration agenda and the externalization agreements show that the EU elites either do not care or do not understand the source of public unease in Europe that such migration control measures are meant to assuage. As a consequence, they are likely to inflame the sentiments that drive the appeal of the far-right parties rather than dampen them. First, treating the refugee and migration issue as a purely technical problem that can be resolved outside the democratic sphere has depoliticized what is an essentially highly political matter. By removing it from the public arena, the EU denies that people have a direct interest in how the issue is managed and that the costs for its implementation are likely to be unequally distributed among the member states and communities. Under the "hotspot approach," the eastern Aegean islands bear the brunt of the new migration agenda. The emergency measure that was ostensibly adopted to assist Greece (and Italy) with the influx of refugees has turned the islands into open prisons. While local communities resent being forced to serve as an experiment for population control, they have no effective way to impact the EU policymaking. This speaks to the second problem with the technocratic governance approach. The EU's paternalistic attitude to voter concerns generates the kind of anti-EU attitude that contributes to the appeal of the far right and nationalist forces. The EU claims that its emergency measures aim to relieve the pressure created by the mass influx of refugees into the "frontier" states of Greece and Italy. Yet, the measures have not removed the refugees from these states. Greece and the islands specifically still carry the higher burden of hosting most of the arrivals. Under these conditions, the EU's technocratic form of governance leaves people feeling increasingly disempowered and ignored. In Greece, the sense of resentment is compounded by years of austerity measures and the EU's refusal to subject them to any form of democratic control. In the islands, the EU's own economic development agenda is very much implicated in the way the crisis is experienced by the local population. With the tourism industry accounting for as much as 95 percent of economic activity on some islands, the arrival of refugees and decline in tourism has meant that people experience the crisis as a direct impact on their personal well-being and economic security. Finally, the technocratic response to the crisis is typical of the EU's failure to engage with the deeper causes of public discontent. The primary aim of the "hotspot approach" and various externalization measures seems to be to remove the migrants and refugees from the public site. Such a short-term response, one conceived as an emergency measure, acts as a divergence from the deeper crisis of governance that remains unacknowledged.

Everita Silina is an assistant professor of international affairs at the Julien J. Studley Graduate Program of International Affairs (SGPIA) at the New School. She is the MA chair of the graduate program and chairs the conflict and security governance and rights concentrations. Her research focuses on the nexus between identity, interests, and security. She is the chair of the Migration Studio: Topography of the Refugee "Crisis" and International Field Program (IFP) in the Balkans. She has chaired the Hong Kong IFP for many years and also an IFP in Turkey. Everita is a faculty fellow at Zolberg Institute on Migration and Mobility.

Notes

1. Moravscik is among the most prominent advocates of this view. He argues that economic issues are of little interest to voters who find them tedious and complicated. It is acceptable therefore to entrust them to the economic elite of the EU without a concomitant fear of having compromised the values of democracy (Moravcsik 2002: 603–24).
2. Until more recently, the only notable attempt at furthering the integration through security policy was the ultimately doomed plan for the European Defense Community, which in 1954 was rejected by the National Assembly of France. If European states wanted to form a military alliance, they would have to do so outside the structures of the ECSC, specifically, the West European

Union. It is perhaps important to note that almost every attempt at creating a more robust security policy for the EU has been met with rather destabilizing and acrimonious debates that expose more than any other issues deep-seated national differences that exist among the member states. Participation in external wars (often a unifying theme in popular politics) has also not produced a coherent voice or strategy vis-à-vis security policy. Intervention in the Yugoslav wars exposed the EU's unpreparedness to deal with such complex emergencies. The agonizing decision on the Iraq war was responsible for driving sharp cleavages between the "old" and the "new" Europeans that still linger in public consciousness.

3. Interview with George Karamanis, deputy mayor, Chios, January 2017.
4. Several reports indicate that money from the EUTF has indirectly been used to fund Sudan's Rapid Support Forces—a government-sponsored paramilitary group, which includes former Janjaweed fighters who were implicated in the genocidal violence in Darfur (Chandler 2018).

References

Bacas, Jutta Lauth. 2014. "Grey Zones of Illegality: Inhuman Conditions in Receiving Irregular Migrants in Greece." In *The Anthropology of Security: Perspectives from the Frontlines of Policing, Counterterrorism and Border Control*, edited by Mark Maguire et al., 158–82. London: Pluto Press.

BBC News. 2019. "Syria War: Turkey Can't Handle New 'Refugee Wave' Says Erdoğan." 23 December. Retrieved 23 December 2019 from https://www.bbc.com/news/world-europe-50886120.

Chandler, Caitlin L. 2018. "How Far Will the EU Go to Seal Its Borders?" *Dissent*, summer. Retrieved 14 September 2018 from https://www.dissentmagazine.org/article/how-far-eu-seal-borders-khartoum-process-central mediterranean-migration.

Dahl, Robert. 1999. "Can International Organizations Be Democratic? A Skeptic's View." In *Democracy's Edges*, edited by Ian Shapiro and Casiano Hacker-Cordon, 19–36. Cambridge: Cambridge University Press.

EuroMemo Group. 2010. "Europe in Crisis: A Critique of the EU's Failure to Respond." *EuroMemorandum 2009/2010*. Retrieved 3 July 2010 from http://www.euromemo.eu/euromemorandum/earlier_euromemoranda/euromemorandum_2009/index.html.

European Commission. 2015. *Hotspot Approach*. Migration and Home Affairs. 11 September. Retrieved 5 March 2019 from https://ec.europa.eu/home-affairs/content/hotspot-approach_en.

———. 2016 *Managing the Refugee Crisis: Commission Reports on Implementation of EU–Turkey Joint Action Plan*. Press release. 10 February. Retrieved 15 March 2019 from http://europa.eu/rapid/press-release_IP-16-268_en.htm.

———. 2018. *EU Emergency Trust Fund for Africa: Trust Fund for Stability and Addressing Root Causes of Irregular Migration and Displaced Persons in Africa*. 20 December. Retrieved 4 April 2019 from https://ec.europa.eu/europeaid/sites/devco/files/eu-emergency-trust-fund-for-africa-20181220_en.pdf.

———. 2019. *The European Agenda on Migration: EU Needs to Sustain Progress Made over the Past 4 Years*. Press release. 6 March. Retrieved 5 March 2019 from http://europa.eu/rapid/press-release_IP-19-1496_en.htm.

European Council. 2015. *Special Meeting of the European Council, 23 April*. Retrieved 5 March 2019 from https://www.consilium.europa.eu/en/meetings/european-council/2015/04/23/.

———. 2016. *EU–Turkey Statement, 18 March*. Press release. Retrieved 4 April 2019 from https://www.consilium.europa.eu/en/press/press-releases/2016/03/18/eu-turkey-statement/.

Howden, Daniel, et al. 2017. "The Compact Experiment: Push for Refugee Jobs Confronts Reality of Jordan and Lebanon." *Refugees Deeply*, December. Retrieved 23 December 2019 from http://issues.newsdeeply.com/the-compact-experiment.

Human Rights Watch. 2019. *Turkey: Syrians Being Deported to Danger; Authorities Use Violence, Threats, Detention to Coerce Returns*. 24 October. Retrieved 23 December 2019 from https://www.hrw.org/news/2019/10/24/turkey-syrians-being-deported-danger?fbclid=IwAR2RmgutdpOFNR_gvmoKtgAP0fCPu9PXq9SoD1mrORQMCA6ItbYsIbCCaJk.

İşleyen, Beste. 2016. "Rendering Space and People Economic: Naguib Sawiris' Refugee 'Country.'" *Mediterranean Politics* 21(2): 326–30.

Keep Talking Greece. 2019. "Citizen Protection Ministry Absorbs Greece's Migration Ministry." 9 July. Retrieved 23 December 2019 from https://www.keeptalkinggreece.com/2019/07/09/migration-ministry-citizen-protection-greece/.

Kokkinidis, Tassos. 2019. "Greek Parliament Approves Stricter Asylum Law." *Greek Reporter*, 1 November. Retrieved 23 December 2019 from https://greece.greekreporter.com/2019/11/01/greek-parliament-approves-stricter-asylum-law/.

Lavenex, Sandra. 2002. "EU Trade Policy and Immigration Control." In *Migration and the Externalities of European Integration*, edited by Sandra Lavenex and Emek M. Uçarer, 161–77. Lanham, MD: Lexington Books.

Lenner, Katharina, and Lewis Turner. 2018. "Learning from the Jordan Compact." *Forced Migration Review* 57. Retrieved 5 March 2019 from https://web.archive.org/web/20180425233737.

Leys, Colin. 2001. *Market-Driven Politics: Neoliberal Democracy and the Public Interest*. London: Verso.

Macron, Emmanuel. 2019. "Renewing Europe." *Project Syndicate*, 4 March. Retrieved 5 March 2019 from https://www.project-syndicate.org/commentary/three-goals-to-guide-european-union-renewal-by-emmanuel-macron-2019-03.

Moravcsik, Andrew. 2002. "In Defence of the "Democratic Deficit": Reassessing Legitimacy in the European Union." *Journal of Common Market Studies* 40: 603–24.

Morris, Julia. 2018. "Manufacturing Landscapes: The Politics and Practices of the Jordan Refugee Compact." Draft. Zolberg Institute on Migration and Mobility, New York: The New School.

Neuman, Gerald L. 1996. "Anomalous Zones." *Stanford Law Review* 48(5): 1197–234.

OCHA (Office for the Coordination of Humanitarian Affairs). 2019. *Syrian Arab Republic: Recent Developments in Northwest Syria; Situation Report No.2–As of 26 December*. Retrieved 30 December 2019 from https://reliefweb.int/sites/reliefweb.int/files/resources/nw_syria_sitrep2_20191226_final.pdf.

Passas, Costas, and George Labrinidis. 2016. "EU and the Structure of the Greek Economy." *Voice of the People,* Working Papers no 2. 1 June. Retrieved 3 July 2017 from http://www.voiceofpeople.eu/index.php/en/sources/working-papers/16-wp2-eu-and-the-structure-of-the-greek-economy.

Patomäki, Heikki. 2013. *The Great Eurozone Disaster: From Crisis to Global New Deal.* London: Zed Books.

Psaropoulos, John. 2019. "Human Rights Community Decries New Greek Asylum law." *Al Jazeera,* 1 November. Retrieved 30 December 2019 from https://www.aljazeera.com/news/2019/11/human-rights-community-decries-greek-asylum-law-191101114606304.html.

Rankin, Jennifer. 2019. "MEPs Damn 'Protecting European Way of Life' Job Title." *The Guardian,* 11 September. Retrieved 23 December 2019 from https://www.theguardian.com/world/2019/sep/11/meps-damn-insulting-protecting-our-european-way-of-life-job-title.

Schedler, Andreas. 1997. *The End of Politics? Exploration into Modern Antipolitics.* London: Macmillan Press.

Smith, Helena. 2019. "Greek Elections: Landslide Victory for Center Right New Democracy Party." *The Guardian,* 7 July. Retrieved 23 December 2019 from https://www.theguardian.com/world/2019/jul/07/greeks-choose-between-beach-and-ballot-in-first-post-debt-bailout-poll.

Spilanis, Ioannis, and Helen Vayanni. 2004. "Sustainable Tourism: Utopia or Necessity? The Role of New Forms of Tourism in the Aegean Islands." In *Coastal Mass Tourism: Diversification and Sustainable Development in Southern Europe,* edited by Bill Bramwell, 269–91. Bristol: Channel View Publications.

Streeck, Wolfgang. 2012. "Markets and People: Democratic Capitalism and European Integration." *New Left Review* 73 (January–February): 63–71.

Temprano-Arroyo, Heliodoro. 2018. "Promoting Labor Market Integration of Refugees with Trade Preferences: Beyond the EU-Jordan Compact." Kiel Working Paper, no. 2018, Kiel Institute for the World Economy.

Tornos News. 2019. "Frontex Surveillance Zeppelin Deployed Over Samos Maritime Area in Greece." 30 July. Retrieved 29 September 2021 from https://www.tornosnews.gr/en/greek-news/society/36379-frontex-s-surveillance-zeppelin-deployed-over-samos-maritime-area-in-greece.html.

Vermeulen, Maite, et al. 2019. "How the EU Created a Crisis in Africa–and Started a Migration Carte." *The Correspondent,* 11 December. Retrieved 30 December 2019 from https://thecorrespondent.com/166/how-the-eu-created-a-crisis-in-africa-and-started-a-migration-cartel/18654631468-bbae5ced.

Yardley, Jim. 2015. "Hundreds of Migrants Are Feared Dead as Ship Capsizes off Libyan Coast." *New York Times,* 19 April. Retrieved 5 March 2019 from https://www.nytimes.com/2015/04/20/world/europe/italy-migrants-capsized-boat-off-libya.html.

8

"The Preparation of Living Corpses"

Immigration Detention and the Production of the Non-person

David Herd

Introduction

The premise of this chapter is twofold. First, it takes the view that the period through which we are living can be defined by the existence or, rather, the production of the non-person. Non-personhood, as will be explained, amounts to a legal category, or at least, a category that describes a person's relation to the law. To understand non-personhood, the chapter contends, it is necessary to understand the spaces in which it is produced—the spaces in which non-persons are compelled to operate. Detention, and especially the alarmingly increased use of extrajudicial and extraterritorial indefinite detention, is key to understanding such spaces, critical as it is to the way non-personhood is made.

The fact that we are living through a period in which, as a matter of legal and political routine, people find themselves rendered non-persons through the process of detention indicates that something in our understanding, or our language, has been lost. We have lost sight of what it means to the individuals concerned, but also to the societies in which we operate, to permit the construction of spaces in which non-personhood is conventionally at stake. From which it follows; the chapter's second working supposition contends that we need to recover the history of such spaces. In part, this is because we need to understand the legal and political decision-making that has historically permitted the production of non-persons. Crucially however, we need to capture the arguments by which such decision-making has been challenged. What we currently lack, or have failed to reconstruct, is a language by which to gauge the meaning of contemporary modes of expulsion. The larger project of which this chapter is a fragment is an attempt to help address that deficit.[1]

Starting with an account of the function of detention in the United Kingdom's "hostile environment" for people seeking asylum and comparing that use of detention to other practices in the Anglophone world, the chapter proceeds to address two historical junctures. The first is the moment, at the turn of the twentieth century, when emergent liberal democracies granted themselves the power to detain under immigration law. The second is the period from 1948 to 1958: a decade that can be said to have started with the promulgation of the *Universal Declaration of Human Rights* and to have ended with the publication of Hannah Arendt's *The Human Condition*, and through which one sees the emergence of geopolitical dynamics that continue to inform the politics of non-personhood in the present period. The basic processes of arbitrary detention, historical inquiry confirms, remain largely constant. What we must recover, as a matter of urgency, are discursive resources that can enable us to counter such detention and its devastating human and political costs.

Indefinite Detention and the Hostile Environment

In 2012 the British home secretary, and now former British prime minister, Theresa May announced her intention with forthcoming legislation (the immigration bills of 2014 and 2016) to produce "a really hostile environment for illegal migration." In itself this did not signify an exception. There are, of course, many national settings in which human movement is treated with hostility, just as the UK itself, under the previous New Labor administration, had increasingly demonstrated scant regard for migrant rights. What distinguished Theresa May's announcement was the deliberateness with which she both named and set out to shape an antimigration regime. I have written elsewhere about the scale and intensity of that regime, of the multiple ways in which it assaults personhood, and a full account of its procedures and effects is beyond the scope of this chapter.[2] It is crucial to register, however, that behind the aggressively delineated everyday spaces of the hostile environment, giving meaning and force to their negative architectonics, is the institutional fact and spatial reality of indefinite detention.

Such detention is, in theory, an administrative provision, reserved for people whose removal or deportation (either to a "first safe country" or to their "country of origin") is imminent, or at least pending. In practice, it is a deeply arbitrary and frequently protracted experience. Since 2007, one trigger for such detention has been sentencing.[3] In the event that a non-citizen commits a crime—whether they are an asylum seeker, a failed asylum seeker, or a person with limited leave to remain—and where the crime attracts a sentence of twelve months or more, then they automatically become liable for deportation and are therefore detained the moment their sentence ends. There are many ways one might contextualize this practice, by observing, for instance, that the precarity of the asylum process tends to criminalize the individual, with typical offences being illegal working or the use of false papers. Either way, for the non-citizen caught in this context, the sentence served for an offence is not the end of the matter but a trigger for further, and this time indefinite, incarceration.

Equally likely, however, as Teresa Hayter observed in *Open Borders: The Case against Immigration Controls*, is that "people may be picked up in the street, on the underground or at work, or their houses may be raided in the early hours" (Hayter 2000: xvii). Such methods of detention have been documented by the Refugee Tales project, with numerous accounts confirming both the systemic nature of the practice, in that the patterns are clearly discernible, and also its arbitrariness, in that the individual is neither warned nor charged.[4] Frequently, at the point of detention, the detained person will only be allowed to take with them the clothes they are wearing and not, for instance, any medication they might be using or any evidence that might help secure their release. More fundamentally, given that immigration detention is indefinite, they will not know when they will be released.

Periods of detention can be short, a matter of days or perhaps weeks, but equally a person can be detained for months and years. The longest period of indefinite immigration detention the Refugee Tales project is aware of is nine years, in the case of a Somali man "found" by Her Majesty's Chief Inspector of Prisons, Nick Hardwick, in Lincoln Prison, having been abandoned to the paralegal processes of the asylum system.[5] Of all of those detained, in a statistic that has remained stubbornly static over several years, 50 percent are released back into "the community." What "the community" refers to, in this context, is a fundamentally negative spatial reality in which people are subjected to profound and protracted prohibition: unable to work, unable to circulate freely, permanently vulnerable to detention and re-detention. Even so, and the euphemism notwithstanding, the fact of their release plainly begs the question why such people were detained in the first place.

That detention constitutes a defining feature of the period through which we are living is, however, best indicated by the scale on which the practice is increasingly used. In 1973, 95 people were indefinitely detained under immigration rules in the UK. By 1988, that number stood at 2,166. In June 2019, according to Home Office statistics, over 24,052 people were detained across a detention estate that includes 10 immigration removal centers and has recourse to various prisons. Shocking as this number is, it nonetheless represents a decrease since the historic high of 2015, when 32,053 people were indefinitely detained in the UK.[6] That the number has begun to fall is unquestionably due to political pressure, and in particular due to the extra parliamentary campaigning of a range of antidetention groups. At the same time, since detention is arbitrary and re-detention is common, tens of thousands of people in the UK are currently, which is to say at any one moment, vulnerable to detention and re-detention.

Such general growth in the detention population is mirrored elsewhere in the Anglophone world. In the United States, for example, as the Global Detention Project reports, "the number of people placed in detention annually increased from some 85,000 people in 1995 to a record 477,523 during fiscal year 2012" (Global Detention Project, n.d.). As in the UK, the US figure has fallen from that historic high, standing at 323,591 in 2017. One explanation for that decrease, as the Global Detention Project reports US officials as claiming, is the reduction in "unauthorized arrivals," a measure in itself of an increasingly aggressive border regime.[7] A comparable graph can be drawn in the case of Australia, which, as has been well reported, externalizes the process by the practice of offshoring detention and where (unlike in the United States and United Kingdom) detention is mandatory for all non-citizens without a valid visa. It is partly, then, in the sheer scale of contemporary detention estates that the periodizing claim arises.

What is at issue also, however, is the definitive quality of the practice, the fact that, as I have indicated, indefinite detention produces, and stands behind the further production, of non-persons. Still the most concerted theoretical expression of such non-personhood is given by Giorgio Agamben in *State of Exception*. As Agamben observes, "The state of exception is not a special kind of law (like the law of war): rather, insofar as it is a suspension of the juridical order itself, it defines law's threshold or limit concept." It is a juridical zone, in other words, "in which application is suspended, but the law (*la legge*), as such, remains in force" (Agamben 2005: 4). The purpose of this chapter (and of the larger project of which it is a part) is to understand how such non-personhood is a function equally of how the individual perceives their spatial reality, how non-personhood is produced through the spaces in which non-persons are compelled to operate, and how, therefore, any attempt to address contemporary non-personhood must reckon with questions of space. Thus, for the person detained the space of detention (the Immigration Removal Centre in the UK) is determined by the fact that they do not know when they will be released. A corollary of such a loss of basic recognition is that the institution itself comes invariably to dehumanize them, with the effect that violence against the detainee is a matter of common report. When, for instance, the BBC program *Panorama* reported on the Brook House Immigration Removal Centre in 2018 using undercover cameras, such violence was abundantly clear, the defining moment being when, having found a detainee after his failed self-strangulation, a detention center officer tried to complete the attempt.[8] The space of the removal center, in other words, simultaneously defines and produces non-personhood.

So too, however, do institutionally adjacent spaces, notably the tribunals in which the individuals' appeals are heard. At the bail hearing, for instance, whereby an individual might be released from detention, the appellant is rarely present but is instead relayed by video link from the detention center. This has two effects: firstly, it makes the incarcerated individual seem, in their appearance, like a criminal; secondly, it displaces the quality of human presence that might otherwise bear on the proceedings of the court. More strikingly, the bail hearing itself is not a court of record. While the judge will issue a determination, in which some account of the proceedings is given, there is no full transcript, and therefore the words of the appellant are not on record. This is true also of the deportation appeal hearing, on which occasion the individual's future security is at stake. In such settings, in other words, the exclusion is linguistic; there is no account of the situation that registers the appellant's contribution to the proceedings. This should put us on notice, that the spatial production of non-personhood is intrinsically linguistic. A person's movement can be compromised or prevented because their access to the language is prevented, because their externality to the language makes it possible to dismiss them from space.

That detention informs and stands behind the negative spaces that constitute the non-person's environment flows directly from the fact that at any point the asylum seeker can be re-detained. At any point, in other words, and in any setting, the individual might be returned to that defining space of nonrecognition, where their vulnerability to the processes of the state is immediate and absolute. Hannah Arendt provides an account of such vulnerability when she observes that her concern is with "the arbitrariness by which victims are chosen, and for this it is decisive that they are objectively innocent, that they are chosen regardless of what they may or may not have done" (Arendt 1979: 6). At times, Arendt's value as a writer is to be found in the quality of her descriptive analysis rather than in her categorical structures, and what she is aiming to define, as she articulates the effect of arbitrariness, is terror. Which is not to argue, of course, that the UK is in any sense analogous to the regimes Arendt describes in *Origins of Totalitarianism*. It is to argue, however, that some people living here, in the present period, experience a kind and degree of anxiety that answers to Arendt's term.

The Entry Fiction

The history of the spaces in which non-personhood has been produced is not easy to tell, but one place we might start is the border. As we recognize it all too clearly today, with its brutally enforced regime of categorization, the border is a relatively recent invention. There has always been a border, as Thomas Nail eloquently lays out, but as a setting for the suspension of an individual's personhood, the border is a late-nineteenth-century or early twentieth-century configuration.[9] As Daniel Wilsher notes, prior to the latter part of the nineteenth century, migration, which chiefly meant "labor migration," was embraced by the logic of free trade. There were many kinds of check, as Nail's history of passport documentation records, but the border, broadly speaking, retained a permeability until that point. This is to present a historical reality, or rather, of course, multiple historical realities, in highly abstract terms. What justifies the level of abstraction is the fact that, with the turn of the twentieth century, the reality of the border was fundamentally altered. What resulted at that historical moment was a conceptual shift.

Where that shift occurred was in a series of acts of legislation, notably in the United States and the United Kingdom. In the American context the pivotal document was the Immigration Act of 1891, legislation that introduced a provision known as the "entry fiction." According to the terms of this provision, an individual at the point of entry could be removed to shore for examination, subject as migrants were to rigorous health checks, but would not be "considered as landing during the period of examination" (Wilsher 2012: 13). To reinforce this provision, the 1891 Act was the first legislation in the American juridical tradition to mention "detention," with the first "large-scale exclusion and detention" being directed at Chinese immigrants on the West Coast and including, as Wilsher points out, "many longstanding and lawful Chinese residents" (Wilsher 2012: 20). The first comparable UK legislation was the 1905 Immigration Act, which, following the recommendations of the 1903 Royal Commission on Immigration, enacted the power to inspect and exclude immigrants, authorizing also that, pending a hearing, "the immigrant may have been placed under suitable charge" (Wilsher 2012: 37). As Wilsher records it, this was "the first official mention of a system of administrative detention in UK law" (Wilsher 2012: 37).

In neither context were the numbers of detentions high, and, given the relatively low initial impact of the change, a historian might choose to record these acts of legislation as simply formalizing administrative convenience. It is there, though, in the difference between administrative convenience and fundamental juridical change, that a principal question of the modern border opens up. As contemporary commentators recognized, such legislative authorization of detention constituted a breach of principle. As the constitutional theorist A. V. Dicey observed, it represented an "indifference to that respect for the personal freedom, even of the alien, which may be called the natural individualism of the common law" (Wilsher 2012: 37). Winston Churchill was more direct, objecting that it made detention "a matter of administration and not justice" (Wilsher 2012: 39). For N. W. Sibley and A. Elias, on the other hand, writing in their 1906 study *The Aliens Act and the Right of Asylum*, the introduction of immigration detention clearly infringed "the principles of the common law and Magna Carta that a person could be liable to be sent to prison without committing a crime" (Wilsher 2012: 40). As Wilsher argues, what such infringements of the Magna Carta tradition flowed from was an elision, in the UK and US juridical contexts, of the power of expulsion and the power of detention. Detention, in other words, was allowed to fall under immigration policy, whereas in other jurisdictions, notably France, detention has historically been understood as a matter of policing. What is at issue, then, historically, is not a matter of administrative convenience but a conceptual consideration.

To detain in the manner described was to breach both Magna Carta and habeas corpus, where what both documents articulated was the imperative that incarceration could only legitimately follow what the Fifth Amendment of the American Constitution would term "due process." As Chapter 39 of Magna Carta had it:

> No free man is to be arrested, or imprisoned, or disseized, or outlawed, or exiled, or in any way destroyed, nor will we go against him, nor will we send against him, save by the lawful judgement of his peers or by the law of the land.

The purpose of this provision was to defend the individual against tyranny, or as it would imply in subsequent historical incarnations, against the unfettered authority of the state. To authorize detention in the name of immigration legislation was not, therefore, simply to adjust policy to changing reality; it was to alter the conception of the border such that an individual might no longer be deemed entitled to fundamental legal recognition. The implications of this were grave, as critics realized. The most immediate consequence, however, was the construction of an impossible kind of space. Thus, the person held in immigration detention was "deemed not to have been landed, even if conditionally disembarked" (Wilsher 2012: 42). Such are the contradictions by which the law enforces the juridical non-person's experience of space.

Articulating the Non-place in the *Universal Declaration of Human Rights*

Insufficiently documented and difficult to record as it is, for certain reasons that will be immediately apparent and for others that will become clear, the history of the juridical non-place gained focus in the period following

World War II, a period during which both the non-spaces of detention and the non-persons those spaces were intended to produce became subject to extensive, cross-disciplinary commentary. One source of such commentary was the period's defining document, the *Universal Declaration of Human Rights*. Intended to articulate principles of juridical consistency in the face of the segregations of fascism, the declaration also outlined the non-place whose existence it was formulated to prevent. Insofar, that is, as the authors of the declaration collectively imagined a new kind of polity, so several of its articles combine to bring the dynamics of that non-place into view. Consider:

> Article 5. No one shall be subjected to torture or to cruel, inhuman or degrading treatment or punishment.
>
> Article 6. Everyone has the right to recognition everywhere as a person before the law.
>
> Article 9. No one shall be subjected to arbitrary arrest, detention or exile.
>
> Article 12. No one shall be subjected to arbitrary interference with his privacy, family, home or correspondence, nor to attacks upon his honor and reputation. Everyone has the right to the protection of the law against such interference or attacks.
>
> Article 14. (1) Everyone has the right to seek and to enjoy in other countries asylum from persecution.
>
> Article 15. (1) Everyone has the right to a nationality. (2) No one shall be arbitrarily deprived of his nationality nor denied the right to change his nationality.

It could be argued that all the articles of the *Universal Declaration* contribute, in negative at least, to an outline of the juridical non-place. By describing rights, and therefore a preferred polity, the declaration's articles by definition articulate those elements the non-place lacks. Of the articles identified here, as speaking directly to the dynamics of the non-place itself, Article 6 is included because it specifies a defining absence: the absence of "recognition before the law." In all the other examples, what is specified is a concrete reality of the non-place, a defining element of its topography and fabric: torture, cruel, inhuman, or degrading treatment; arbitrary arrest, detention, or exile; arbitrary interference with privacy; persecution; arbitrary deprivation of nationality. What this list constitutes is the *Universal Declaration*'s internal description of the non-place, a working sketch against which future political practice should be formed. To properly understand that description, however, and the values that underpin it, one needs to perform a kind of textual archeology, the aim being to draw out the discussions that informed key articles.

The discussions that informed the formulation of two articles, Articles 6 and 9, indicate the nature of the debates. What Article 6 means to establish is what John P. Humphrey, the *Declaration*'s principal early drafter, termed "legal personality," the point being to assert that no person might at any point, in any context, fall outside of legal consideration. The force of this point was not immediately felt, with the United Kingdom, the United States, and India each at some point proposing to vote against the article on the grounds that the concept underpinning it was either too legally technical or too vague (Morsink 1999: 44). It was in the Third Committee that the underlying issue became apparent, when the Canadian delegate H. H. Carter drew on recent historical experience to clarify the issue. It was, he said, "important to keep in mind ... the possibility that certain persons might be deprived of their juridical personality by an arbitrary act of their government. Nazi Germany offered a recent example" (Morsink 1999: xx). To deprive a person or group of their juridical personality was, in effect, the necessary preliminary to the other mistreatments that shaped the non-place. Only after that deprivation had been affected could the state justify such actions to itself.

The discussions informing Article 9, framed to prevent "arbitrary arrest, detention or exile," were less skeptical, since it was clearly understood that some such provision was necessary. The question, in this case, was how the right should be formulated. Early versions of the statement referred to the existing legal context as a guarantee against the kind of deprivation entailed. The limitation of any such formulation was pointed out by Dr. Franz Bienenfeld, representative of the World Jewish Congress. As he observed, "Under the Nazi regime thousands of people had been deprived of their liberty under laws which were perfectly valid" (Morsink 1999: 50). The question was, therefore, if, as recent history demonstrated, reference to the law did not, in and of itself, guarantee protection against the kind of deprivation of liberty envisaged, how was such a protection to be formulated? The term taken to catch that meaning was "arbitrary," signaling that form of treatment that might, in extreme circumstances, be permissible within a given legal framework but which nonetheless fundamentally offended against the principles enshrined in a declaration of rights. As the Lebanese delegate, Charles Malik, observed, the word "arbitrary" carried a great deal of weight in the article, as elsewhere in the declaration, becoming, in fact, the document's key qualifier. "Arbitrary" conduct, as in Articles 12 and 15, was taken to constitute the opposite of a practice that gave due recognition to rights.

How we are to understand the term "arbitrary" as it appears in the context of the declaration is thus a matter of some importance, it being the term against which a contemporary articulation of rights was poised. What it specified in the moment of the declaration's composition was a defining dynamic of fascism, whereby people rendered beyond juridical recognition were subject to treatment for which no account was deemed due. As a descriptor in a high-level legal-political document, the term "arbitrary" is at a considerable remove from historical reality, from the appalling brutality it intends to reference but does not catch. Its value, at that remove, is partly that it places us on the alert, that at the point at which we discern the arbitrary in politics then at some level of administration a practice traceable to authoritarianism has started to emerge.

Picturing the Non-place in the Postwar World

The value of tracing the implications of detention and its production of non-personhood through intersecting postwar discourses is that we come to an understanding of what, politically and ethically, is at stake. And crucially the setting in which the structural circumstances of the non-place reemerged in the immediate aftermath of the war was the environment to which the obligations of human rights should most clearly have been extended. As Hannah Arendt observed of what she termed the "internment camp":

> Human rights ... are enjoyed only by citizens of the most prosperous and civilized countries. ... The situation of the rightless themselves ... has deteriorated just as stubbornly, until the internment camp—prior to the Second World War the exception rather than the rule for the stateless—has become the routine solution for the problem of the "displaced persons." (Arendt 1979: 279)

Writing in 1957, with the "number of stateless people ... larger than ever" (with "one million 'recognized' stateless" and more than "ten million so-called 'de facto' stateless"), Arendt observed the paradox that "the moment human beings ... had to fall back upon their minimum rights, no authority was left to protect them and no institution willing to guarantee them" (Arendt 1979: 292). Abandoned to "the barbed-wire labyrinth into which events had driven them," what the postwar stateless demonstrated, in the non-places they were compelled to occupy, was that "no one seems able to define with any assurance what the general human rights, as distinguished from the rights of the citizen, really are" (Arendt 1979: 293).

Arendt's account of the pathology of the postwar internment environment remains critical to our understanding of the human reality of the non-place. Arendt, this is to say, understood as well as anybody what non-personhood entailed, and the degree to which the non-places that produced it were structural to the contemporary environment. Where she erred, I will come to suggest, is in the way she assessed the implications of human rights. Rather, arguably, than a lack of clarity on the question of general human rights, what the procedures governing the non-place demonstrate is a certainty about the principles and entitlements that are being breached. Where one finds this, immediately after the war, is in the way the question of rights was handled in a European context, or more precisely, the way Europe allowed itself to be defined by the stance it adopted on the question of the extension of rights. One way to observe this, in the postwar environment, is in relation to two texts relating to the question of qualification, the first in the context of the displacement camp, the second bearing on the European colony.

The context in which the logic of the non-place most quickly became visible in the postwar environment was, as Arendt observed, the displaced persons camp. As Gerard Daniel Cohen has documented, the American term "displaced person" was applicable to great numbers of people across the globe in the immediate aftermath of the war: between twenty-four and forty million people in China could be said to be displaced; up to twelve million people in Japan (Cohen 2011: 14). What the term principally came to refer to, however, under the auspices of the United Nations, was those displaced in Europe, with approximately eight million so-called DPs occupying Germany at the end of the war. Of those, some six to seven million people were quickly repatriated, often, as Cohen reports, with tragic consequences. Where policy came to settle and develop was in relation to those still displaced at the beginning of 1946, the so-called "last million," whose future was understood to predict the postwar international environment. As a *New York Times* editorial of 2 February 1946 put it, "The fate and status of hundreds of thousands of human beings" was "clearly an international issue," a sense of obligation that triggered far-reaching pronouncements– witness Emanuel Mounier's declaration that France was "a country where an exiled, desolate, and desperate man will always find a hand stretched out to him with no questions asked" (Cohen 2011: 14, 16). The hand stretched out was the rhetorical equivalent of the implied scope and extent of the *Universal Declaration.* In practice, the interrogation, and all the forms of suspension that followed, quickly became the norm of the displaced person's environment.

Where the interrogation occurred was at the point of definition. The key task in the context of the DP camp, as an International Refugee Organization (IRO) handbook outlined, was to determine "who is a genuine, bona fide and deserving refugee" (Cohen 2011: 35). Inscribing administrative practice that would inform much subsequent policy toward human movement, the *Manual for Eligibility Officers* issued detailed advice to IRO staff on how to identify the nongenuine claimant. First published in 1948 and running to 160 pages, the manual constituted the formalization of a policy the IRO inherited from its predecessor organization the United Nations Relief and Rehabilitation Organization. As Cohen documents, under the auspices of the UNRRA, "Allied screenings" of displaced persons "borrowed from denazification proceedings" conducted under the auspices of the Nuremberg Trials. Thus:

> Just as German citizens filled out much-despised questionnaires designed by Allied occupiers to uncover active supporters of Nazism, their DP neighbors

were handed "eligibility questionnaires" issued by UNRRA to verify nationalities, dates of displacement, and wartime personal histories. (Cohen 2011: 37)

The rationale for the guidelines set out in the IRO manual was that they would shield staff from "improvisation and arbitrariness," ensuring, so it was argued, "uniform jurisprudence" (Cohen 2011: 43).

This did not obscure the fact that the purpose of such "uniform jurisprudence" was to determine the question of jurisdiction itself, to establish who, having been genuinely displaced, was permitted then to be relocated–genuine displacement during the war entailing the obligation to ensure that the person in question was granted a new home. It was here, in the face of this obligation, that the questions were put. To answer satisfactorily was to be granted juridical standing, recognition somewhere before the law. Not to answer satisfactorily was to have such recognition thrown into doubt, to be held in the suspense of what Arendt termed "internment," in the quasi-juridical process determining jurisdiction. What this meant in reality was prolonged deprivation, not least because residency in the camps invariably entailed the incapacity to work. Reporting on the situation of the DP camps in 1953, the Council of Europe confirmed Arendt's view:

> The conscience of the peoples of Europe should revolt at the fact that among them are living millions of persons bearing the label of "surplus." ... What of the mental outlook of these beings cast out by society? What of the young people, whose earliest impressions are of the wretchedness of refugee camps or of permanent unemployment? (Cohen 2011: 123)

The fact that such institutionally sponsored suspension of personhood–"wretchedness" as the Council of Europe termed it–occurred at the point at which the obligations entailed by rights ought to have properly been invoked is what prompted Arendt to diagnose an indefinability at the heart of the discourse. In fact, what institutional practice demonstrated was something like the reverse, the process of interrogation regarding eligibility disclosing a sure understanding of the entitlements and commitments the recognition of rights entailed. The state's task, or the task of their international representatives, was to limit such eligibility as far as they could, hence the proliferation of questions and guidelines concerning the individual's claim. As the British-based Refugee Defence Committee report (titled *Is It Nothing to You?*) put it 1949, "It does not need a complicated system of legal jurisdiction such as that set up by IRO to discover the fact that a person is a Refugee" (Cohen 2011: 41).

What the processes of sifting and interrogation that shaped the postwar environment of the displaced person can be taken to demonstrate is not the weakness and incoherence but instead the substance of the concept of general rights. Such was the force of the implied claim that a whole new jurisprudence had to be created, the express purpose of which was to establish that a recognizable entitlement did not apply. To observe the non-place at work, this is to suggest, is to register a setting generated by an identifiable act of institutional denial. Where this was writ largest in the postwar moment, as Marie-Benedicte Dembour has brilliantly documented, was in the institution of Europe itself, which is to say in the formulation of the European Convention of Human Rights.

Drafted in the two years following the *Universal Declaration* and adopted in 1950, the ECHR, as Dembour describes, was intended

> to defend citizens–not any human being–against arbitrariness by the state. The hope was that the revolutionary mechanism put in place, with complaints by mere individuals allowed for the first time in history to be adjudicated by an international court, would make it possible to avoid another European descent into anything resembling Nazism or Fascism ... (Dembour 2015: 1)

Where the convention differed from the *Universal Declaration* was in its intended usability, the purpose of the document being to effect protection rather than simply outline what such protection should consist of. From which it followed that the question of scope and of extent was more sharply drawn, focusing in particular on whether the articulation of rights inscribed by the document carried as far as the colonial setting.

Dembour describes in detail the arguments that shaped the drafting process, noting that in its first iteration the understanding was that a convention that did not apply in the colonies was "politically unfeasible" (Cohen 2011: 71). For the Belgians, who held to this basic view, the object with respect to the overseas territories was to secure an acknowledgment of what was termed "local needs and the standards of civilization of the native population" (Dembour 2015: 67–68). For the British, repeating arguments they had made during the drafting of the *Universal Declaration*, what was required was an acknowledgment of the "autonomy which its dependent territories constitutionally enjoyed," and therefore the inapplicability, via British endorsement of the final document, of the extension of rights to its colonial regimes (Dembour 2015: 68). What resulted, despite arguments to the contrary that clearly spelled out the contradictions, was a clause (Article 63) that accommodated the colonial position. Thus:

1. Any State may at the time of its ratification or at any time thereafter declare by notification addressed to the Secretary General of the Council of Europe that the present Convention shall, subject to paragraph 4 of this Article, extend to all or any of the territories for whose international relations it is responsible.

2. [Provides for a one-month delay before this declaration comes into force.]

3. The provisions of this Convention shall be applied in such territories with due regard, however, to local requirements.

4. Any State which has made a declaration in accordance with paragraph 1 of this article may at any time thereafter declare on behalf of one or more of the territories to which the declaration relates that it accepts the competence of the Court to receive applications from individuals, non-governmental organizations or groups of individuals as provided by Article 56 (now 34) of the Convention.

Clause 1 and Clause 4 entitle the signatory power, should it so wish, to extend the convention to territories for which it is "responsible," not declaring explicitly, because the document doesn't like to, that such an extension need not apply. Clause 3, on the other hand, allows for "due regard ... to local requirements," a phrase that cuts irremediably across the spatial consistency to which the *Universal Declaration* aspired. What Article 63 enters is a qualification, just as the IRO handbook sought a qualification, generating a circumstance, a non-place, in which the protections entailed by a general concept of rights do not apply. The document, in other words, and the institution for which it stands, is compelled to enter into a contradiction, producing a non-place, a space in which the principles in question are suspended, at precisely the juncture at which the extension of rights ought properly to obtain.

What needs to be pictured, of course, is what in reality the qualifications of Article 63 referred to, what really were the local requirements that a curtailment of the convention's geographical extent was intended to meet. To which end one might consider a footnote in *The Wretched of the Earth*, in which the non-place delineated by the qualifying article is shown to be brutally maintained. As Fanon (1965) puts it, quoting his own article in *Résistance Algérienne* 4, dated 28 March 1957:

> It was then agreed (in the Assembly) that savage and iniquitous repression verging on genocide ought at all costs to be opposed by the authorities: but Lacoste replies, "Let us systematize the repression and organize the Algerian man-hunt." And, symbolically, he entrusts the military with civil powers, and gives military powers to civilians. The ring is closed. In the middle, the Algerian, disarmed, famished, tracked down, jostled, struck, lynched, will soon be slaughtered as a suspect. Today, in Algeria, there is not a single Frenchman who is not authorized and even invited to use his weapons. There is not a single Frenchman, in Algeria, one month after the appeal for calm by the UNO, who is not permitted, and obliged to search out, investigate and pursue suspects.
>
> One month after the vote on the final motion of the General Assembly of the United Nations, there is not a European in Algeria who is not party to the most frightful work of extermination of modern times. A democratic solution?

> Right, Lacoste concedes; let's begin by exterminating the Algerians, and to do that, let's arm the civilians and give them *carte blanche*. The Paris Press, on the whole, has welcomed the creation of these armed groups with reserve. Fascist militias, they've been called. Yes; but on the individual level, on the plane of human rights, what is fascism if not colonialism when rooted in a traditionally colonialist country? (Fanon 1965: 71)

Fanon's footnote draws *The Wretched of the Earth* into deep connection with the discourse of the non-place outlined in this chapter. In the image of the ring closed around the Algerian resistance, in flagrant breach of the United Nations' assertion of minimal human rights, Fanon identifies an inevitable concentration of the colonial topography the basic contours of which he delineates in the introduction to his text. "The colonial world," as he puts it, outlining the basis of all subsequent actions, "is a world cut in two. The dividing line, the frontiers are shown by barracks and police stations" (Fanon 1965: 29). What the line divides are different juridical zones, the settler zone where the law applies and the native zone where it is arbitrarily enforced. Thus:

> All that the native has seen in his country is that they can freely arrest him, beat him, starve him: and no professor of ethics, no priest has ever come to be beaten in his place. (Fanon 1965: 34)

Recovering a Language for the Meaning of Non-personhood

The purpose of this chapter has been, in part, to show how the juridical non-place effected by detention has been historically constructed. Crucially also, however, its aim is to outline how such arbitrary situations have been understood to affect persons themselves. The importance of the former is that it allows us to discern the outline of the non-place as it comes into view, and therefore to recognize that structures underpinning forms of fascism are being revisited. The importance of the latter, of assessing how the realities of the non-place have affected persons, is that in the present moment we find ourselves devoid of a language for what non-personhood entails.

There are many texts in which one might find versions of such a language, but it is Arendt who gives the overview, who made it her intention to articulate what might be called the phenomenology of the non-person. Her work in this area dates principally to the mid-1950s, to the additional material included in the revised edition of *Origins of Totalitarianism* and to *Human Condition*. Writing about the origins, the effects, but also the legacy (in internment and statelessness) of totalitarianism, Arendt identifies as her object of study "groups of people to whom suddenly the rules of the world around them had ceased to apply" (Arendt 1979: 267). Her intention in considering such status is to diagnose what in practice it means, how it feels, in reality, for humans to be held outside.

In arriving at such a diagnosis, Arendt identifies a series of effects and symptoms that bear directly on our contemporary situation. Significant among these is criminalization, Arendt's straightforward observation being that to hold a person outside the law is, in effect, to compel them toward illegality, if not, simply, to render them illegal. Thus: "The stateless person, without right to residence and without the right to work, had of course consistently to transgress the law" (Arendt 1979: 269). For Arendt, there was to be no ambiguity: to render a person rightless and therefore outside the law was to cause them to transgress it. This practical reality had two very significant aspects. The first, perversely, was that criminality afforded a degree of protection. Thus:

> The same man who was in jail yesterday because of his mere presence in the world, who had no rights whatever and lived under threat of deportation, or who was dispatched without sentence and without trial to some kind of internment because he had tried to work and make a living, may become almost a full-fledged citizen because of a little theft. (Arendt 1979: 286)

Such an improvement of circumstance should not be overstated, not least since the commitment of a crime, for all that it invokes certain due processes, frequently results, in the present moment at least, in the penalty of deportation. The juridical personhood afforded by criminality, in other words, is short-lived.

The second consequence of compelling people to live outside the rules that apply to the world around them is the power it accords those who enforce the law. Again, Arendt is unambiguous: "This was the first time the police in Western Europe had received authority to act on its own, to rule directly over people" (Arendt 1979: 287). From which it followed that "the greater the ratio of statelessness ... the greater the danger of a gradual transformation into a police state" (Arendt 1979: 287–88). Extending the argument to the European colony, Fanon makes the same point:

> In the colonies it is the policeman and the soldier who are the official, instituted go-betweens, the spokesmen of the settler and his rule of oppression. ... In the capitalist countries a multitude of moral teachers, counselors and "bewilders" separate the exploited from those in power. In the colonial countries, on the contrary, the policeman and the soldier, by their immediate presence and their frequent and direct action maintain contact with the native and advise him by means of rifle-buts and napalm not to budge. The intermediary does not lighten the oppression, nor seek to hide the domination ... he is the bringer of violence into the home and into the mind of the native. (Fanon 1965: 29)

It can be argued of Arendt's discussion of non-personhood in *Origins of Totalitarianism* that at times she shifts between categories, conflating circumstances of different degrees and intensity. Similarly, it could be argued here that to shift from Arendt to Fanon, and therefore from statelessness to colonization, is to equate situations whose differences are critical. Arendt's point, however, like mine, is to draw out the structural qualities of juridical non-personhood. What one sees here, then, in the combined commentaries, is a form of mutual re-enforcement. To set a person outside the law, to designate them as illegal, is both to render them permanently vulnerable to the intrusions of the police and, at the same time, to greatly enhance police power. What that leads to is increasing levels of violence against the individual—witness such treatment as *Panorama* reported of detainees in the detention system in the United Kingdom. Such are the consequences, as Arendt anticipated, of a "greater ... extension of rule by police decree" (Arendt 1979: 290).

It is not sufficient, however, as both Arendt and Fanon observe, to describe the structural effects of juridical non-personhood. What has to be understood also is the pathology of such a circumstance, the way it feels to the individual whose status is in suspense. What has to be grasped accordingly is that the segregated space takes its character from the fact that legality is not consequential on action but on status. Thus, as opposed to a framework "where one is judged by one's actions and opinions," the juridical non-place entails

> the loss of the relevance of speech (and man, since Aristotle, has been defined as a being commanding the power of speech and thought) and the loss of all human relationship (and man, again since Aristotle has been thought of as the "political animal," that is one who by definition lives in a community), the loss, in other words, of some of the most essential characteristics of human life. (Arendt 1979: 297)

That such essential characteristics are lost is due to the fact that the individual's status is unrelated to their actions. Nothing they have done or said, nor anything they can do or say, determines their situation.

It is a situation that has its reverse in what Arendt calls "the space of appearance"—her account of a polis, in *Human Condition*, grounded in her determination to outline a situation in which non-personhood would not apply. There again, as she describes what is at stake, what she points to is the absence of consequence. Thus: "A life without speech and without action ... is literally dead to the world; it has ceased to be a human life because it is no longer lived among men" (Arendt 1958: 176). What a life lived among men amounts to, as Arendt details at length, is the occupation of what she terms the "space of appearance," to be deprived of which, as she observes, is to be "deprived of reality" (Arendt 1958: 199).

The point here, to repeat, is that we find in Arendt a language for the meaning of non-personhood that either we have forgotten or we are choosing not to recollect. Such deprivations are entirely characteristic of the person who occupies the contemporary non-place, the person who is either detained or detainable, the person whose capacity to act is profoundly inhibited by restrictions on movement and on work, and in which the capacity to speak meaningfully is fundamentally impeded by official processes in which the default setting is one of disbelief. The value of Arendt, then, is partly that she gives us a way of understanding what such a fundamental assault on personhood entails for the individual, "a life without speech and without action" being "literally dead to the world."

We have to hear this for what it is, for what it means in the present of an individual's existence, for the degree of abjection that lived juridical non-personhood entails. As Arendt wants to observe also, however, we must understand what such civic death can become preparatory to, or at least has historically prepared for, by way of political action. Thus, as she goes on to observe in her consideration of what she terms "Total Domination":

> In comparison with the insane end-result–concentration camp society–the process by which men are prepared for this end, and the methods by which individuals are adapted to these conditions, are transparent and logical. The insane mass manufacture of corpses is preceded by the historically and politically intelligible preparation of living corpses. (Arendt 1979: 447)

Or as she puts it in terms of the law, and in terms the law can understand, "The first essential step on the road to total domination is to kill the juridical person in man" (Arendt 1979: 447).

Twenty-First-Century Detention

To view the present political moment through the optic of detention is to find ourselves precariously poised. Where we are, in fact, is where Agamben warned us we were in 2005 when he investigated what he termed the "state of exception." "From this perspective," as he wrote, "the state of exception appears as a threshold of indeterminacy between democracy and absolutism" (Agamben 2005: 3). The principal form of that threshold, as he explained, was "indefinite detention," a practice conspicuously reinstituted in the US context in the form of the Patriot Act that followed the 11 September 2001 attack on the World Trade Center. As Agamben put it:

> The immediately biopolitical significance of the state of exception as the original structure in which law encompasses living beings by means of its own suspension emerges clearly in the "military order" issued by the president

of the United States on November 13, 2001, which authorized the "indefinite detention" and trial by "military commissions" (not to be confused with the military tribunals provided for by the law of war) of noncitizens suspected of involvement in terrorist activities. (Agamben 2005: 3)

There had already been a Patriot Act in response to 9/11, "issued by the U.S. Senate on October 26, 2001" (Agamben 2005: 3). What was new about President Bush's order was that "it radically erases any legal status of the individual, thus producing a legally unnamable and unclassifiable being" (Agamben 2005: 3).

As this chapter has documented, and as Agamben understood when he wrote *State of Exception*, the US executive's response to 9/11 did not inaugurate such a "legally unnamable and unclassifiable being." The history of such a non-person can be traced to the turn of the twentieth century, and their full emergence as a figure in modern geopolitics can be located in the decade that followed World War II. From this point of view, 9/11 was not so much a turning point as an intensification of existing legal and political procedures. By invoking "indefinite detention," the US administration reinstituted a procedure that has since become integral to the apparatus by which various governments have also responded to crises of forced displacement, some of which have followed the wars that the United States and Britain prosecuted under the pretext of the 9/11 attacks. The 2001 Patriot Act, in other words, did not initiate arbitrary detention but made it once again politically normal. From which, broadly speaking, it has followed, as Agamben warned it would, that we have slipped into an age of detention; an age in which detaining people arbitrarily and for indefinite periods has become acceptable as a response to various forms of geopolitical pressure, including to the requests for asylum of unprecedented numbers of refugees.

Moral and political outrage has been slow to catch up, but the fact that the campaign to end indefinite detention in the United Kingdom is now politically mature, that it has gained strength and profile over the past decade, is positive. This ongoing call for a change of law recently culminated in the formulation of an amendment to the proposed 2019 immigration bill. Through the hard work of numerous NGOs and pressure groups, that amendment secured the support of MPs across all parties, including sufficient government MPs that, had the amendment come to a vote, a change of law would very likely have resulted. In the event, the immigration bill was suspended, in part, no doubt, because of this cross-party support, and will now be redrafted and represented in the new parliament. A great deal has been achieved, and it is very possible that campaigning progress can be built on, but, with a new parliamentary arithmetic, the battle for a change of law starts again.

At the same time, as the campaign to end indefinite detention in the United Kingdom teeters on the brink, so detention practices in the United States intensify and harden. Following the caging of people seeking asylum at the US-Mexico border, and the separation across the detention estate of children and families, a new rule introduced by the Trump administration replaces the Flores settlement—which previously placed a limit on detention—thus allowing for children and adults to be indefinitely detained. What this regressive rule change reminds us, as all such changes should always remind us, is that it is through the practice of detention that the incipient authoritarian state defines its power. Whenever we discern an increase in the use of detention, in other words, we are observing an authoritarian logic at work, one that must be identified, called out, and opposed as such.

How to do this, how to oppose the use of arbitrary immigration detention, is both an urgent and, given the power dynamics at work, a most demanding political question. The argument here is that for such opposition to be effectively staged, it is necessary to recover and reconstruct existing discursive resources. To revisit such resources, in particular those developed in the immediate aftermath of World War II, is to achieve three interconnected objectives. In the first place, it is to recover a language that allows us to understand what is at stake in detention, the degree to which it damages both individuals and the polity at large. In the second place, it is to better understand what detention implies as practice, how it revives and replicates earlier forms of institutionalized racism, most notably, in the UK context, the practices of colonialism. Finally, what the recovery of existing resources clarifies is the force, in all situations of detention, of the language of human rights. This is both an obvious fact and one to which it is necessary to draw constant attention given the lengths to which the state and its apparatuses will go to prevent that fact coming to the fore. What one sees as one investigates the intersecting postwar discourses of detention and non-personhood is a constant effort to limit the extension of the framework of human rights. To which one could respond, as Arendt appeared to, by calling the validity of that framework into doubt. But Arendt was wrong on this, or at least she came to the wrong conclusion. The right conclusion, as Jacques Rancière has argued, is to observe in the state's challenge to the language of rights the enduring force of that language disclosed.

Where Rancière is in dispute with Arendt is on the question of how individuals or groups relate to human rights. Thus, whereas Arendt finds the *Universal Declaration* to be fundamentally flawed in its seeming implication that rights are inherent, or intrinsic, or otherwise automatically guaranteed, Rancière understands rights much more actively as that which must be fought for, claimed, or won. As he puts it in his decisive contribution to the discourse, "Who Is the Subject of the Rights of Man?":

The strength of these rights lies in the back-and-forth movement between the first inscription of the right and the dissensual stage on which it is put to test. ... This is ... why today the citizens of states ruled by religious law or by the mere arbitrariness of their governments, and even the clandestine immigrants in the zones of our countries or the populations in the camps of refugees, can invoke them. These rights are theirs when they can do something with them to construct a dissensus against the denial of rights they suffer. And there are always people among them who do it. It is only if you presuppose that the rights *belong* to definite or permanent subjects that you must state, as Arendt did, that the only real rights are the rights given to the citizens of a nation by their belonging to that nation, and guaranteed by the protection of their state. If you do this, of course, you must deny the reality of the struggles led outside of the frame of the national constitutional state and assume that the situation of the "merely" human person deprived of national rights is the implementation of the abstractedness of those rights. (Rancière 2004: 305–6)

Rancière construes rights as a site of permanent struggle in which the motivating claim is permanently underwritten by the universality in whose name it is made. They exist as that which whose denial is the basis of the claim they give rise to, the act of dissensus through which the struggle of greater universality is achieved. Fundamental to any such expression of rights is the statement given by Article 9 of the *Universal Declaration* that "no one shall be subjected to arbitrary arrest, detention or exile." The urgent task of anybody seeking to oppose immigration detention and the escalation of such detention is to animate the right articulated in Article 9. It is to help forge the conditions in which those rendered detainable can resist such a status, conditions in which their rights are established through being won. To say so is not to suppose, for one moment, that any such progress is easily achieved. It is to contend that the nature of our polity tilts on the question of detention, that now, more than ever, we must understand that question as central to our political definition.

David Herd is a co-organizer of the project Refugee Tales and professor of modern literature at the University of Kent. His collections of poetry include *All Just* (Carcanet, 2012), *Outwith* (Bookthug, 2012), *Through* (Carcanet, 2016), and *Walk Song* (Equipage, 2018). He has given readings and lectures in many countries, and his poems, essays, and reviews have been widely published. As a critic, he is the author of *John Ashbery and American Poetry* (2000), *Enthusiast! Essays on Modern American Literature* (2007), and the editor of *Contemporary Olson* (2015). His writings on the politics of human movement have appeared in *Detention Unlocked, Los Angeles Review of Books, Parallax*, and the *TLS*, and he is currently completing a book titled *Making Space for the Human: Writing against Expulsion in the Postwar World*.

Notes

1. For a more comprehensive consideration of the questions raised by this chapter, see my forthcoming monograph *Making Space for the Human: Persons, Non-persons, Movement in the Postwar World*.
2. See, for instance, the "Afterwords" to *Refugee Tales*, *Refugee Tales II*, and *Refugee Tales III*, published by Comma Press in 2016, 2017, and 2019.
3. See UK Borders Act 2007, Section 32, retrieved 3 May 2018 from https://www.legislation.gov.uk/ukpga/2007/30/section/32.
4. Founded in 2014 by Gatwick Detainees Welfare Group, Refugee Tales is a civil society project that calls attention to the fact that the United Kingdom is the only country in Europe that detains people indefinitely under immigration rules; as such, the project calls for that policy to end. The way the project makes its call is by sharing the stories of people who have experienced detention, and the way it shares those stories is in the context of a public walk. For more information about the project, see www.refugeetales.org
5. In August 2012, "prisons inspector Nick Hardwick discovered a Somali man in Lincoln prison who had been in immigration detention for nine years beyond the end of his sentence, because he had been 'forgotten.'" See Webber (2012).
6. For UK immigration detention statistics up to June 2017, see UK Government 2017.
7. For an overview of US immigration detention statistics, see Global Detention Project (n.d.).
8. For the full broadcast of the *Panorama* program "Undercover–Britain's Immigration Secrets" see https://www.youtube.com/watch?v=_fp0QLDKgME (retrieved 10 October 2021).
9. For Thomas Nail's account of the history of border formation, see his interconnecting texts (Nail 2016, 2015).

References

Agamben, Giorgio. 2005. *State of Exception*. Translated by Kevin Attell. Chicago: University of Chicago Press.
Arendt, Hannah. 1958. *The Human Condition*. Chicago: The University of Chicago Press.
———. 1979. *Origins of Totalitarianism*. 1st edn., 1950. New York: Harcourt Brace Jovanovich Publishers.
Cohen, Gerard Daniel. 2011. *In War's Wake: Europe's Displaced Persons in the Postwar Order*. Oxford: Oxford University Press.
Dembour, Marie-Benedicte. 2015. *When Humans Become Migrants: Study of the European Court of Human Rights with an Inter-American Counterpoint*. Oxford: Oxford University Press.
Fanon, Frantz. 1965. *The Wretched of the Earth*. Translated by Constance Farrington. London: Penguin Books.

Global Detention Project. n.d. 'United States'. Retrieved 10 October 2021. https://www.globaldetentionproject.org/countries/americas/united-states.
Hayter, Theresa. 2000. *Open Borders: The Case against Immigration Controls.* London: Pluto Press.
Morsink, Johannes. 1999. *The Universal Declaration of Human Rights: Origins, Drafting and Intent.* Philadelphia: University of Pennsylvania Press.
Nail, Thomas. 2015. *The Figure of the Migrant.* Stanford, CA: Stanford University Press.
———. 2016. *Theory of the Border.* Oxford: Oxford University Press.
Rancière, Jacques. 2004. "Who Is the Subject of the Rights of Man?" *South Atlantic Quarterly* 103 (Spring/Summer): 297–310.
UK Government. 2017. "National statistics: How Many People Are Detained or Returned?" 24 August. Retrieved 2 January 2020 from https://www.gov.uk/government/publications/immigration-statistics-april-to-june-2017/how-many-people-are-detained-or-returned.
Webber, Frances. 2012. "Revealing the Impact of Immigration Detention." Institute of Race Relations, 21 December. Retrieved 2 January 2020 from http://www.irr.org.uk/news/revealing-the-impact-of-immigration-detention/.
Wilsher, Daniel. 2012. *Immigration Detention: Law, History, Politics.* Cambridge: Cambridge University Press.

9

The Germans' "Refugee"

Concepts and Images of the "Refugee" in Germany's Twisted History between Acceptance and Denial as a Country of Immigration and Refuge

Marion Detjen

The "Refugee" of the "Summer of Welcome" 2015

"We can tear down the walls!" It was a plain and often-heard message that Angela Merkel offered her American audience in her commencement speech at Harvard University in June 2019, asking the graduates not to lose their belief in the openness of the future; a message so plain that many Germans were a bit embarrassed, considering the speech to be a "wall" in itself–"walled into stereotypes," as one newspaper put it (Reents 2019). But messages do not need to be sophisticated to teach us complicated lessons. While alluding to famous quotes by US presidents ("Tear down this wall"; "Don't ask what your country can do for you"; "Yes, we can") in order to argue for the ability to change, for multilateralism, and for getting rid of barriers of all sorts, Merkel not only challenged Trump, she also presented a historical narrative, one in which she and the country she represents, Germany, having been the model students of US democratization and liberalization efforts, were now taking the lead, drawing confidence and strength from exactly the biographical and historical experiences of wars, walls, and limitations that motivated these US efforts toward Germany in the first place.

Of course, everyone in the audience knew that the specific and real "walls" that Merkel's metaphorical speech alluded to—Trump's wall and the Berlin Wall—serve or served completely different purposes in the migration and refugee histories of the two countries: Trump's wall tried to shut people out, and the Berlin Wall tried to shut people in. While the right to emigrate and to leave a country is protected by international law, the laws to regulate immigration are mostly left to the nation-states. Merkel in 1989/90 left behind her the Berlin Wall that limited her personal prospects and her freedom to travel. But as the head of the German government, she actively participated in the securitization and fortification of the EU border, a border not less costly and inhumane than the US border with Mexico. Under Merkel's leadership in Germany and Germany's leadership in the EU, more than twenty thousand migrants and refugees have drowned in the Mediterranean since 2014 alone ("Geschätzte Anzahl der im Mittelmeer ertrunkenen Flüchtlinge" 2012). Under Merkel's leadership, the EU made a deal with Turkey that shifted the main migration routes across the Mediterranean from Turkey to Libya. And it supported Turkey building a wall on the Syrian border, thereby causing the Syrian refugees and deportees to be trapped in Idlib, where they are now (as of fall 2019) being bombed and sieged and left to die at the hands of Assad's and Russia's troops. Merkel's interior minister Horst Seehofer has been incessantly churning out anti-asylum laws since the formation of the new grand coalition in March 2018, and it is fair to say that her party's migration politics have been at least partly driven by the xenophobic agenda of the far right already since fall 2015, if not long before.

There are two reasons why Merkel in spite of all this can still claim the moral authority to challenge Trump's wall, and these are the same reasons why she is still hated by the far right for allegedly being the "refugees' chancellor" (*Flüchtlingskanzlerin*), allegedly not representing German interests and replacing the German population with a migrant one. Firstly, she realized in 2015, albeit rather late, that policies towards migration need to be multilateral and coordinated with the European partners and also with non-European partners. While up to 2015 Germany relied on being surrounded by so-called safe countries and left it mainly to Italy and Greece to deal with the migrants that were washed upon their shores, Merkel attempted to show solidarity and a human face when in August/September 2015 Hungary shook off all responsibility and left the migrants and protection seekers who had arrived in large numbers over the "Balkan route" altogether to themselves. Confronted with these unregistered people marching by foot toward the Austrian and the German border, Merkel decided to exercise the so-called sovereignty clause of the Dublin Regulation and let them in to Germany in order to prevent a humanitarian catastrophe and also to take pressure from the struggling European partners. Ever since, Merkel has been extremely reluctant toward unilateral solutions.

The second reason for her lasting good reputation in matters of "tearing down walls" is her stubborn insistence that Germany was perfectly able to cope with the so-called refugee crisis in 2015/16. Her claim "Wir schaffen das" (we can manage) did not only reflect adequately the economic and administrative resources of one of the strongest and wealthiest countries in the world. Germany took a small percentage of the number of refugees that much poorer countries like Turkey could take in. It also showed a total absence of racism and Islamophobia: she never utilized culture and religion as arguments, and that earned her the particular hostility of the entire right spectrum as much as the sympathy of the transnationally oriented liberals and leftists around the globe.

The "Summer of Welcome" 2015 has left a deep and dividing mark in German collective memory. The government's decision not to close the borders, to accept the protection seekers, and, thereby, to stop the chain reaction that had been sparked by Hungary and the Southern and Southeastern European border states went along with a huge wave of volunteer activity among the German population. For a short time, it seemed as if, simply put, the forces of good–solidarity, kindness, hospitality, readiness to help–had revealed themselves in our dark historical reality, against all odds. I was in my hometown in Bavaria at the German-Austrian border at that time and will never forget the invigorated atmosphere of those days, the insurgence of civil society in the name of humanity, in this surprising coalition with the chancellor. More than 10 percent of the population actively engaged in one way or another in the "welcome culture," more than fifteen thousand projects and initiatives emerged to help the protection seekers and support the strained administrative structures (Schiffauer, Eilert, and Rudloff. 2017). Years later, one of my Syrian students at Bard College Berlin told me that after months of suffering and being on the run, chased by police and security forces in every country he passed through, he arrived in my hometown, Rosenheim, in August 2015, and could not believe his ears when a German policeman actually told him upon registration, "Welcome to Germany!"

Certainly, such words from a German policeman came unexpectedly in a traditionally Catholic-conservative Bavarian border town. But they also need to be seen as part of a development that, in the years before 2015, had led to some fundamental changes in Germany's approach toward immigration. Since 1998, when the conservative and anti-immigrationist government of Helmut Kohl had given way to a social democratic–green, halfway pro-immigrationist government, a series of reforms have been undertaken, slowly turning Germany into an almost self-acknowledged immigration country. In 2000, a new citizenship law attributed citizenship not only to those of German ancestry, i.e., having German parents, but also to those born in Germany whose parents are non-German legal residents. The dominant attitudes toward non-German immigrants changed from exclusion to "integration," from treating them as a temporary phenomenon and wanting to send them home as soon as the immediate reasons for their coming to Germany were not valid anymore (be it labor market needs, a war, or political crisis) to accepting them and trying to meld them into the German populace. In 2005 a new residency and immigration law was introduced that replaced what used to be called the "foreigner's law," eased residency, formulated some legal pathways into Germany, and generally improved the status of legally residing foreigners. This development culminated in another reform of citizenship law in 2014 when German citizenship gave up its claim to be exclusive even for non-EU citizens. Since then, children of non-German legal residents who are born and brought up in Germany do not have to opt anymore between German citizenship and the citizenship of their parents once they turn eighteen: dual citizenship has become a legally accepted, although still-contested, reality. At the same time, in those formative years between 1998 and 2014, the numbers of newly arriving, and especially legally arriving, migrants were relatively low, and neither did these meet the needs of the labor market nor did they seem adequate in the face of the migration crisis unfolding in the Global South and around the Mediterranean. Therefore, the large numbers of "illegally" arriving migrants in 2014–15 were received by many even moderately pro-immigrationist Germans with almost a sense of closure. Finally, all these people, whom we had ourselves prepared for and whom we could now "integrate," arrived, taking our share of responsibility and simultaneously solving our demographic problems.

In hindsight, the enthusiastic state of mind of the German "welcome culture" in 2015 does seem naïve, but it was not a dream or an illusion. Even the usually staunch right-wing and xenophobic yellow press newspapers, like *Bild* and *BZ*, participated in it, publishing an edition in Arabic and titling it "BILD is welcoming refugees!"[1] Since then, in less than four years, the public mood has shifted to the extreme opposite, again headed by *Bild*, now not missing one day to agitate against refugees with the most appalling xenophobic and Islamophobic stereotypes. And nevertheless, many of the initiatives and volunteer efforts that sprang up in 2015 have been continuing their work. Up to this day, most villages and small towns in West Germany, but also some in the East, have a so-called "helpers circle" (*Helferkreis*) or other such associations that take care of the local refugees and try to protect them against obstructionist politics.[2]

The ambivalent situation today can be described in simple and general terms of political backlash and reaction and put into the context of a massive global shift toward right-wing populism. But there are also German peculiarities to it. In the following sections, I want to show some of the historical strands of development, reaching far back into the twentieth and nineteenth centuries, that have converged and helped create the present ambivalent attitudes. They can be called specifically German inasmuch as they are connected to German nation building, German statehood, and the German public sphere, but of course the problems that they responded to always had a global dimension, appeared in other countries too, and cannot be understood without inter- and transnational analysis and contextualization.[3] I want to inquire about the specifically German understandings of what a refugee (*Flüchtling*) is, what a migrant is, and how these topoi evolved historically and are still evolving today, in certain discourses, in relation to the German nation-state.

The "German Refugee" up until 1945 and Beyond

Since the French Revolution, concepts of the refugee have always been connected to concepts of what it means to be German. Up until the Nazis' seizure of power in 1933, and again since 1945, German nation building and German state building formed on the concept of Germany being a nation of ancestry (*Abstammungsnation*) with uncertain external and internal borders and a decentralized, federalist state organization. The German people were, in the again untranslatable word *Volk*, imagined "in their tribes" (*Abstammung* means literally "from the tribe"). This tribal thinking was then cast into state citizenship laws that up to 1913—more than forty years after Germany's unification—made someone a German citizen only through holding citizenship of one of the German countries (*Länder*). That created a couple of conceptual contradictions, especially in relation to the Jews (Schneider 2017). French, Polish, Danish, and other origins tended to be ignored. Ancestry was ethnisized and essentialized. Immigration officially did not exist, and non-German refugees did not have any positive rights and could face deportation at any time (Heizmann 2012: 48–82).

A refugee, in the sense of someone having a legitimate claim to be given protection and to settle down permanently, used to be first and foremost a *German* refugee—a German who, as part of the German colonization movements to the Eastern empires, had lived in German communities outside of Germany sometimes for centuries and was forced to go "back" because of other nation-states' ethnic-cultural homogenization projects or revolutions; or a German who suddenly found themselves outside of Germany because of shifting borders. These refugees were made to be "German" in a political sense, by the fact that they were given safety, civic belonging, and often material compensations for their losses. After World War I, when Germany lost parts of Prussia and its colonies, Germans were included in larger numbers in the demographic engineering projects of drawing new borders and exchanging populations (Gatrell and Zhvanko 2017).

This experience, of Germans being displaced or becoming refugees, became a widely shared mass experience at the end of and after World War II, when more than twelve million Germans were expelled from the formerly German regions in the East and from countries that had German minorities and sought to dispel them, also because of their support for the Nazi occupation during the war. In addition, the Soviet occupation of the eastern part of what was left of Germany, and the subsequent partition of Germany into two countries, produced another three to four million refugees fleeing from Soviet and communist rule to West Germany (Beer 2011).

Those numbers, on the backdrop of wartime destruction, misery, and the refusal to face questions of guilt and responsibility, made it hard to acknowledge the suffering of the up to eleven million non-Germans, mostly victims of Nazi Germany, who found themselves on German territory at the end of the war—concentration camp survivors, former forced laborers, and prisoners-of-war, who did not want to go home or had nowhere to go, and new non-German refugees from the East. They were categorized as "displaced persons" by the UN and as "homeless foreigners" by the German authorities, to be repatriated or resettled, and fell under the jurisdiction and care of the Occupation Forces and the United Nations while the German local communities had to pay for their accommodations.

Recent historiographies of forced migration have successfully and meritoriously managed to integrate all the mass movements in the aftermath of World War II into one story, on a European or even on a global scale (Gatrell 2013; Ahonen et al. 2008). But the emerging international order after World War II sharply distinguished between German and non-German forced migrants. Since the end of the war, the United Nations and the Geneva Refugee Convention 1950/51 denied the German expellees and refugees the status of refugee. The UNRRA (United Nations Relief and Rehabilitation Administration) and the UNHCR (since 1951) were not organizations intended to support displaced members of the nations that had started and lost the war. On the other hand, the United States especially took a strong interest in getting Germany back on its feet and insisted on the German state's continuing existence. In the frame of the international nation-state system, there was a widely agreed division of labor that the nation-states that had caused the war should take care of their "own" displaced population, and be made able to do so, while the UN would take care of the members of the nation-states that had been victims and those who had become stateless altogether.

The two competing German states founded in 1949 did not protest against this international arrangement and accepted responsibility for the German expellees and refugees, bowing to the occupation powers but also functioning in accordance with the old ethnic-cultural concept of the *Volk*. The West German constitution considered all Germans—German by culture and language—living outside German territory as *Volksdeutsche* who automatically became members of the nation-state once they entered German territory.⁴ Also, both German states, in spite of not talking to each other, clung to a common German citizenship, constitutionally treating each other's inhabitants not as foreigners but as citizens. Only in 1968 did the GDR depart from this principle and establish a GDR citizenship, consequently aggravating its legitimacy problems as a German state. The Federal Republic, bound by its Constitutional Court to a common citizenship, never gave up the constitutional claim for reunification. And only in 1990, when that was the price to be paid to achieve reunification, did it let go of its right under international law for a Germany within the borders of 1937–i.e., the restitution of the Eastern territories lost to Poland and Russia in 1945.

This irredentism, mitigated by the overwhelmingly accepted obligation never to go to war again, no matter the national grievances, deeply affected Germany's attitudes toward non-German refugees. Too busy with their "German question" and having to integrate all the Germans, the governments and the majority society were unable to feel responsibility for non-Germans, including those whose displacement had been caused by Germany in the first place.

The Constitutional Right for Asylum

Therefore, it seems ever more astonishing how the right for asylum, as an objective, individual right for non-Germans, could enter the German Constitution in 1948/49. In international law, the right of asylum was traditionally the right of a state to grant asylum to a political refugee, even if other states object to it. In national law, not many nation states have a right *for* asylum, a civic right, a right to be claimed by an individual.[5] But the meeting of the constitutionalists and legal scholars in Herrenchiemsee in 1948 to draft a provisional constitution for West Germany was a historically unique moment: it was also the time of the *Universal Declaration of Human Rights*, and the German constitutionalists wanted to live up to it, also for the sake of Germany gaining back sovereignty and eventually being accepted into the United Nations.[6] The constitution's section of civil and human rights read like a model student's work on the *Universal Declaration*, and Article 16 was its masterpiece: "Politically persecuted get Asylum," a statement that stood until 1993 with no limitations. While the *Universal Declaration of Human Rights* is not legally binding, the German constitution transposed the human right for asylum into constitutional law, anticipating legislations at the national level of the member states of the UN that the Geneva Refugee Convention in 1950/51 could and should have initiated but did not, because in the 1950s that special moment had already passed.

The progressiveness of the constitutional right for asylum should not deceive us to overestimate the transnationalist and humanitarian motives of its inventors. For sure, they wanted to learn from the past, but their lessons differed from those that were projected onto them later. Pro-Western but conservative Hermann von Mangoldt had up until 1945 agreed with the National Socialist, racist, and antisemitic Nuremberg Laws.[7] An ethnically, culturally, and probably also racially homogeneous German nation-state was what they most certainly all still believed in. Taking in large numbers of "foreigners"–no matter how severely these were persecuted and threatened–would have gone completely against the grain. The right for asylum that they had in mind would not have helped the Jews or any other group that had been persecuted by the Nazis. It was meant for politicians and people like themselves: to enable the political and administrative elites in the emerging international order of nation-states to engage politically and democratically and to take risks for their political convictions, with a pathway out, into the safety of another country, if things turned wrong, the way things had turned wrong in Germany after 1933. The principle of "Politically persecuted get Asylum" was conceived as an individual right, not as a right for large groups, for the sake of the functioning of democracies and was and is also practiced as one, with recognition rates below 2 percent up until today (Poutrus 2019).

The right for asylum remains, though, in spite of these limitations, of fundamental importance for the whole constitutional structure. It opens German statehood to non-Germans, giving non-Germans and non-residents an unalienable right, which is a rare thing in the closed world of nation-states. And it secures a procedural security for the applicants toward the police, the administrations, and courts, which not only works in favor of the 1 to 2 percent of the applicants whose entitlement for asylum according to Article 16 of the constitution is recognized but also helps all those who then obtain refugee status according to the Geneva Convention or other statuses of protection, or even only a short-term permit or a suspension of deportation. Furthermore, the general appreciation and respect for the constitution among the German public and politics eventually rubbed off on the general perception of refugee rights, by the widespread misidentification of the constitutional right for asylum with the rights for refugees granted by the Geneva Convention.

The "Integration" of German Expellees and Refugees after World War II

The fifteen million German expellees were excluded from the Geneva Convention and also exempt from going through the German asylum procedures. They were, according to Article 116.1 of the constitution, *Volks-Germans* who received German citizenship once they entered German territory or, if coming from the GDR, already had German citizenship. Exclusion on the international level resulted in a privileged status on the national level, even though, in social reality, the expellees still experienced manifold discriminations and xenophobia (Holler 1993; Beer 2011: 99–126).

Legal "refugees," on the other hand, were those who came from the GDR to the territory of the Federal Republic after the founding of the two states, sometimes in the dead of night over the inner-German border, sometimes via Berlin, the loophole until the Berlin Wall was built in 1961. A specific procedure, the so-called emergency admission procedure, determined who a refugee was and restricted their freedom of movement if they wanted to be registered for social benefits. A separate "Refugee Permit C" was intended for those who were recognized as political refugees in the strict sense (Limbach 2011).

Despite difficulties, the displaced Germans, whether refugees or expellees, eventually were able to successfully integrate over the years and decades after the war due to the massive state support programs, the interlocking of the national discourse of solidarity with the anticommunist discourse against the Soviet Union and the GDR, and the favorable conditions of West Germany's so-called economic miracle. Frequent intermarriages over generations ensured that the minority status of the expellees and refugees eventually faded out. Today, probably around half of all Germans have a "migration background" of some sort, as many have parents, grandparents, or great-grandparents who migrated or fled from somewhere.[8] And even though the expellees served as a conservative factor in German politics, allowing political powers to foster nationalism and revanchism, the individual and family experiences often told another story, one about the cruelty of the disruption of the old multiethnic and multicultural societies. Research has shown that the expellees in general cultivated rather unpolitical memories of their *Heimat* in order to deal with the trauma (Demshuk 2012). The revanchist and nationalist impact of this group primarily manifested in their special interest organization, the Bund der Vertriebenen (League of the expellees), and the position it claimed in German politics to grant compensations and privileges.

The "Refugee" and Human Rights

With the shift of power and discourse through the generational change in the 1960s, specifically the 1968 protest and student movement, a new understanding of the "refugee" was established that lost its anticommunist thrust and eventually adopted more of a humanitarian, human rights, and anti-dictatorship argument. The refugees from Chile arriving in West Germany after the 1973 coup, though not in large numbers, were the first non-German refugees who profited from this new paradigm (Poutrus 2019: 65–70; Dufner 2013). Interestingly, the shift toward human rights then also affected the perception and the strategies of the East Germans who sought to overcome the wall and leave the GDR. In their struggle for legal exit possibilities, they invoked human rights obligations to obtain their national right, as Germans, to resettle in West Germany, according to the West German constitution (Wolff 2019: 651–719). This occurred at a time when public opinion and politics were almost at a point of recognizing the GDR citizenship law, and only a ruling of the constitutional court prevented the national framework of the "German refugee" from breaking off altogether.

Even more paradoxically, in the 1980s the constitutional provisions that considered the refugee or migrant from the GDR a "German" who enjoyed all rights that West Germans had turned into a vehicle that also made it easier for non-German refugees and migrants to enter the territory of the Federal Republic. As long as the GDR government did not object, it was relatively easy to smuggle someone who would otherwise have needed a visa across the Berlin Wall through the GDR's inspection points. It is one of the ironies of the history of the Berlin Wall that it became a loophole for extra-European migration into Germany when mass migration from the Global South gained momentum due to the decline of the Soviet Empire and the rise of neoliberalism (Göktürk, Gramling, and Kaes 2007: 69).

The "Guest Worker" and "Asylant"

While the emergency humanitarian situation of non-German refugees became increasingly accepted, work migration for a permanent stay remained in place without systematic legal provisions and was excluded from the nation-state's conception until the year 2000. In the style of the nineteenth century, industry's and agriculture's need for labor was supposed to be covered by temporary workers, ideally through formal agreements with the laborers' countries of origin. Although permanent residency and naturalization after fifteen years were possible on an individual basis, the decision was left entirely up to local German authorities and the governments.

Large parts of certain sectors of the German economy have always depended on illegal, irregular migrants. Regular temporary labor migration was often by no means more human. An extreme case, based on exclusion and racialization, had been the forced labor under National Socialist rule, where so-called "alien workers" were mostly forcibly transported to Germany and there completely disenfranchised and virtually enslaved, all in accordance with National Socialist laws.[9] The Federal Republic of Germany obviously had to mark the discontinuity with the Nazi past when in 1955, and in the following decade, it made recruitment agreements first with Italy and then with Spain, Greece, Turkey, Morocco, Portugal, Tunisia, Yugoslavia, and others. The foreign laborers had social rights that were more or less equal to those of their German fellow workers, and they were called "guest workers," a term that both trivialized their position and emphasized their supposedly temporary stay (Herbert 1990; Göktürk et al. 2007: 21–64). For the Europeans, the bilateral agreements were, in the course of European integration, replaced by the multilateral agreements and the supranational framework of the Treaty of Rome and following regulations. Within the EEC and since 1993 the European Union, the fundamental right of free movement effectively channeled cheap labor from the South to the economies of Northwest Europe, with Germany profiting most from it (Comte 2018). For the extra-European workers, European integration led to a two-class system that not only underprivileged them and denied them the political rights that were eventually granted to Europeans but also created a hypervisibility for them as "migrants." The public understanding of what constitutes a migrant attached itself especially to the Turkish and then to the Muslim migrant, racially and culturally fixed as the "Other."[10] While in 2016 only 6 percent of the population had a Muslim background, the population estimated their share at 20 percent, a misperception that reveals more than anything else the structural failures of German politics and society to come to terms with the fact that Germany is an immigration country.[11]

Europeanization and internationalization also had paradoxical effects on the development of the institutions and perceptions of the non-German refugees. Due to the exemption of Germans from the refugee provisions defined by the United Nations and the exceptionality and alleged generosity of the right of asylum in the German constitution, until 2005 there was not much public or political awareness of the international system designed to protect refugees under the Geneva convention. Topics of asylum were often discussed as if Germany did not have to respect international obligations, also due to the lack of presence of the UNHCR in Germany and to the decision-making residing in the hands of a national authority. In the absence of work immigration provisions following the 1973 decision of the federal government under Willy Brandt to stop the "guest worker" programs altogether, the right for asylum became the only legal entrance for foreigners into the German job market and social security systems. But the separation between work migration and flight/displacement is not as clear in practice as it is in theory: persecuted groups impoverish more easily and then also have economic reasons to leave their country, while, conversely, poor people are more often victimized politically. The growing numbers of persons seeking protection, security, and livelihood since the 1980s did not often have much in common with the "political refugee" projected in the constitution. Since the 1980s, in the confusion of terminologies and categories, a "refugee" in everyday language has become a stigmatized figure, also called an "asylant," someone asking for protection while really "just" looking for a better life and allegedly straining, or even threatening, state and society, no matter their real status.

Exclusion and "Integration"

After reunification, the economies in Eastern Europe and other parts of the world collapsed, and the Yugoslav wars and other conflicts produced mass-migration movements on an unprecedented scale. While the consolidation of the democratic German nation-state meant that the "German refugee" became altogether extinct, Germany developed into one of the main destination countries for both political and economic migration, both within and outside Europe. This would have been a good time to reconceptualize Germany as a country of immigration and to look for fair and adequate European solutions—for example, working with quotas. But instead of seizing the moment, the German government under Chancellor Helmut Kohl took the congested and overstrained asylum procedures as an opportunity to reinscribe the racialized fears of the foreign "Other" into a nation that bases itself on ancestry. As a consequence, massive racist attacks in the 1990s cost the lives of dozens of innocent people.[12] The government created procedures at airports that made coming to Germany by plane without a visa granted by a German embassy virtually impossible. Then it introduced the concept of safe third countries, hoping that Germany's geographical position would prevent protection seekers from reaching German territory on the ground. The Dublin Regulation established a fragile and, for the protection of refugees or a fair burden-sharing in Europe, totally inadequate system. To do all of this, the German constitution had to be amended; in 1993, the Right for Asylum in the constitution was mutilated, with the help of the Social Democrats, without the government keeping its promise to introduce an immigration law in turn. The progressing European integration was accompanied by the expansion of "Fortress Europe." Since 2001, the fight against migration, the fight against smuggling, and the fight against terrorism have more or less merged into a single fight. The protection of the European borders is being increasingly exterritorialized: deserts and seas have turned into mass graves.

While the numbers of asylum applicants indeed fell drastically in the year 2000, and even while they have increased again since 2011, the moral and political implications of these policies were practically absent from public discourse. Only one left-wing newspaper, the *Taz*, regularly published reports on the desperate situation at the European borders in Italy and in Greece. The public knew that people were dying but didn't really take notice. Since the change of government in 1998 and the Greens' accession in power, however, Germany finally made major steps to recognize itself as an immigration country. A new citizenship law in 2000 fundamentally changed the understanding of what it means to be German. With the introduction of elements of citizenship by birthplace (jus soli), it became possible to be born as a German to non-German parents. Finally, in 2005, after long and tedious struggles, an immigration law was put into place that, despite bearing in its name that its purpose was to control and curb rather than to open up and enable, acknowledged for the first time that immigration is a reality.[13]

Again 2015: The "Refugee" as a Challenge and the Topos of the State's "Loss of Control"

By the end of 2014, when the so-called "refugee crisis" set in, considerable parts of the German society were ready to show solidarity. Sports centers had to be closed to the public in order to serve as shelters for a large number of asylum seekers, and hardly anyone complained; on the contrary, families from the neighborhood lined up to donate clothes, offer help, and deliver home-baked cakes. In September 2015, thousands of Syrians, stranded and stuck in the Budapest area following Hungary's announcement that it would no longer register protection seekers, started walking toward Austria on the motorway with the aim of reaching Germany. In response, Chancellor Angela Merkel made use of the "sovereignty clause" in the Dublin Regulation and temporarily took them, all while having to coordinate with the Hungarian and the Austrian governments and other members of her own government, along with German authorities, through extremely difficult communications. Her actions throughout this situation displayed tremendous symbolic power.[14] In almost all villages and towns, "helpers circles" volunteered. Local administrations worked around the clock. Many were up to the challenge, some failed, and some became openly cynical. A countless number of Germans took "refugees" into their homes.

In those months, many Germans who volunteered and engaged in pro-refugee activism developed an awareness of the term *Flüchtling* being problematic in itself. They preferred to call them "newcomers," "forced migrants," or *Geflüchtete*, which is a participle construction like "refugee," arguing that the ending "-ling" in *Flüchtling* could be interpreted as belittling and condescending. The wording and the choice of language became one of the manifestations of the divide between a persistent pro-immigration and pro-asylum minority and a majority that was only supportive in the "summer of welcome" or indifferent, reluctant, hostile from the beginning. The ambiguous semantics of the word, tainted by the multilayered interpretations of the "German" and the "foreign refugee" and the racist traditions connected to them, compromised even the most benevolent references, while it was almost impossible to find a language that completely satisfied the need for accuracy and justice.

Meanwhile, members of the government itself employed images and forms of speech when talking about "refugees" that pulled the rug out from under Angela Merkel's proclaimed culture of welcome. Her minister of finance, Wolfgang Schäuble, warned in November 2015 that the movement of refugees might escalate into an "avalanche": "An avalanche can be set off, if just any a little bit imprudent skier enters a slope and moves a little bit of snow."[15] Here Schäuble insinuates that Merkel's policies are careless, and he dehumanizes "refugees" with one of the many weather metaphors that were used to incite fear and create the impression of a loss of control.

Apparently taking fright at their own courage, the originally pro-refugee public tide turned first against the "welcome culture" and then against the refugees themselves. The infamous "Kölner Sylvesternacht"–New Year's Eve 2015/16 in Cologne, where the police could not prevent a large number of sexual assaults by men who were collectively and inaccurately perceived as refugees–became a turning point. German politicians from all parties, even the Greens, suddenly deemed it necessary to show consideration and understanding for the "worries" of the white German majority, whereas political support for the refugees and the "refugee helpers" steadily declined. The civil society initiatives that still to this day, in almost every village and town, take care of the real challenges of getting the newcomers into apartments, schools, trainings, German courses, social services, and, eventually, jobs found themselves increasingly frustrated and overburdened, in unfavorable environments.

In the face of all the difficulties, homegrown or imported, the "refugee" was given again a new shade of meaning: one who is granted rights, initially receives help and goodwill, but then proves to be disappointing, "ungrateful," unwilling to integrate, and finally deserving of people turning their backs to them. Those Germans who actively participated in the civil society initiatives and entered relationships with real persons could deal with intercultural challenges more or less successfully in a nonideological way, using psychological, cultural, and/or political interpretations depending on their beliefs and experiences. But the media discourse, following its own dynamics, got bored of integration stories quickly and struggled–is still struggling–to address the many questions posed by Germany's new identity as a country of immigration. The large majority of Germans adopted the role of a bystander, watching warily how Merkel's "experiment" of "opening the doors" unfolded and how the *Gutmenschen*, the allegedly unrealistic Left-Greens and idealists, toiled for it. The atmosphere of distrust and resentment unleashed in xenophobic outbursts whenever something happened, every failure, every crime, and also every made-up scandal was put into the "refugee's" account.

And it was not only the ever-rising extremist right-wing party AfD, the yellow press, the populists, and conspiracist social media who fed this dynamic. Liberal conservative voices, social democratic voices, left wing, right wing, moderates and centrists, intellectuals and academics, serious and respected people started to share narratives that made the acceptance and inclusion of refugees seem to be something bad, something that should be avoided, at best a burdensome duty, at worst a stupid mistake, a divisive, unreasonable, or unlawful action, or even a betrayal against the nation. An unholy alliance of conservative law experts, journalists, and politicians spread the theory of the "breach of law" allegedly committed by Merkel when she opened the borders, allowing "illegal entrance" and thereby hurting the nation-state's sovereignty and integrity (Steinbeis and Detjen 2019). Even though this theory was rebuked by an overwhelming majority of constitutional law professors, the notion of Merkel having done something wrongful and stupid stuck with the public. Another even more successful theory was the one of "loss of control": if letting the "refugees" in could not be considered illegal, it was seen as a fundamental weakness, a blackout, a collapse of the state and the rule of law and order, a moment of chaos and extreme danger.[16]

Over weeks and months, Merkel stubbornly insisted that her policy had been right. But as all attempts to reform the Dublin system and to reach a redistribution mechanism within the European Union failed, and pressure domestically and externally increased, she resorted to a measure that she herself must have felt to be a "pact with the devil."[17] Under Merkel's leadership, the EU in the winter of 2015/16 negotiated an agreement with Turkish prime minister and authoritarian ruler Recep Tayyip Erdoğan that, on paper, committed the EU to take in official, registered refugees from Turkey in the same numbers that migrants who had crossed the Mediterranean to Greece and entered the EU "illegally" were sent back to Turkey. Erdoğan promised to block "illegal" migration from Turkey to Europe in return for €6 billion to support provisions for refugees in Turkey, plus visa-free travel for Turkish citizens and accelerated accession talks with the EU. It is still today contested which elements of this agreement worked, and to what result. The number of migrants reaching the EU has indeed dropped drastically—not only because of Turkish efforts but also because Eastern European countries have secured their borders. Turkey, too, closed its borders with Syria. As a consequence, almost four million Syrians in Northwestern Syria, around Idlib, were caught, left without support to face the genocidal actions of Assad and his allies, many of whom had fled or been deported to Idlib from Assad-occupied Syria before. The principle of nonrefoulement, cornerstone of the Geneva Convention, has since become a sheer hypocrisy. Even the knowledge of the founders of the German constitution, that all political, democratic, civic activity depends on being able to save oneself from persecution, to emigrate, if things turn wrong, and find protection elsewhere, is now willfully being ignored.

Effectively having sealed off Syria, Germany, showing superficial respect to international law while acting in the sole interest of the nation-state, can now on its territory afford to follow through with a migration policy that has three basic goals: rejection and deportation of anyone who is considered "illegal"; economic but also cultural "integration" of those one cannot get rid of without turning "illegal" oneself; and proactive recruitment of workers and professionals who are directly needed for the German economy, preferably in their home countries, in agreement with their governments.[18]

Furthermore, the government and state intensively continue to work toward a European migration management system in the countries beyond the EU's external borders. Such management is intended to take care of the labor market interests of the member states as well as achieve readmission agreements with the unwanted migrants' countries of origin, to research current migration movements, and to prevent "illegal" migration altogether and house and immobilize migrants in camps (Buckel 2013: 186–225). Meanwhile, sea rescue in the Mediterranean has been dramatically reduced: the naval EU Operation Sophia withdrew altogether, leaving the job to the unwilling coast guards of the mostly undemocratic or failing states like Libya bordering the Mediterranean Sea. Private rescue organizations have stopped working or are pressed to do so under the constant threat of being criminalized as supporting the "smugglers" and being denied access to Italy's, France's, or Spain's harbors. Commitments to resettle UNHCR refugees in Germany are easy to talk about, reluctantly promised, and hardly ever fully met. Additional complementary pathways that would be legally possible and politically feasible remain largely unused.[19]

At least rhetorically but probably also subjectively, the German government and all political parties except the AfD remain obliged to the general idea of refugee protection, to a fair share of the burdens, as well as to international law. But effective measures in that direction appear to be impossible. The constant assurances that bringing down the numbers and fighting "illegal" migration is a political priority, the framing of migration in terms of terrorism and crime, the lack of practiced solidarity with other European countries, Islamophobia and the ignorance about own entanglements in colonial history, and, more than anything else, the prerogative of the sovereign nation-state in thinking and practice form an amalgam that obviously prevents a rational and humane approach toward the displaced and forcibly exiled.

The "Refugee" as the Alleged Cause for Growing Right-Wing Extremism

The longer these disputes go on, the more a threatening question comes to the fore: Would it be possible that the hostility against migrants in general and "illegal" migrants specifically might one day lead to the return of fascism to Germany, to a nationalistic, antisemitic, and racist government, a replay even of Nazi rule? These questions loom over the non-white minorities living in Germany; however, they also loom over the white Germans themselves and have a great deal of influence on perceptions and attitudes.

We have to go back a few steps again. The principle of ancestry that still dominates German citizenship, even though in 2000 it was significantly restrained, is ambivalent in itself. On the one hand, it perpetuates the ethnic foundation of the "Germans" as a nation. On the other hand, it negates racism by including everyone who becomes naturalized, and their descendants, irrevocably into that nation. Not every German is expected to be ethnically German, but every nonethnic German is expected to be selected carefully and "integrated" into an ethnically based nation. The Nazis indeed violated this principal of ancestry, without abolishing it altogether. They created a two-class system of citizenship and deprived German Jews and German Sinti and Roma from all their rights, deported them to the occupied eastern territories outside of Germany, disowned them, and murdered them in the Holocaust, where citizenship did not make a difference anymore. But, bureaucratically, the semblance of legal procedures and legal continuity was even maintained in Auschwitz (Neander 2008).

In the decades after the war, both politics and the public in the Federal Republic of Germany eventually learned to acknowledge guilt and responsibility for the National Socialist crimes. The slogan "Never again!" has a broad consensus in the German society. Not even the AfD, not even the right wing of the AfD, propagates a return to National Socialism the way Germany had it under Hitler.[20] There is even an argument that the relativizations and trivializations of National Socialism undertaken by some of the AfD politicians have limited the party's attraction for ultraconservative and nationalist Germans, who otherwise agree with them.

But what if it is exactly this "Never again!" in memory culture that paradoxically adds to the German apprehensions against the migrant? National Socialism had antisemitism as its core ideology; antisemitism in turn, at least until 1948 when the state of Israel was founded, had a strong antimigrant current. The phantasmagoria of a handful of Jews secretly ruling the world in the West went along with the phantasmagoria of their countless poor and ragged relatives from the East flooding into the country and eventually replacing the native population. These delusions made any attempt by the "emancipated" German Jews to integrate and assimilate in order to solve the equally delusional Jewish question futile. The antisemitism controversy between the two liberal historians Theodor Mommsen and Heinrich von Treitschke in 1880 revolved around these questions: while Treischke conjured up the image of the young, industrious Jewish man coming to Germany to "sell trousers," who would beget children and grandchildren and would pull others after him "from the inexhaustible cradle" of the East, Mommsen countered that Germany needed the Jewish "cultural ferment" and that the "Jewish question" would eventually be resolved by Christianization, assimilation, and modernization (Treitschke 1879; Mommsen 1880).

In historical reality, indeed, due to the pogroms, the violence, and the destruction in the crumbling empires of the East, especially in the Russian Empire and after World War I in Poland and the Soviet Union, Jewish immigration to Germany constantly added to the already existing Jewish population. The so-called "Eastern Jews" were mostly on their way to the United States, but some of them became stranded in Germany and tried to get asylum and a residency to settle down. Staying in Germany became an option especially since 1924, when the Immigration Act of the United States drastically reduced the possibilities to relocate there. The parallels between the "Eastern Jews" and the "refugees" of our days are striking.[21] Impoverished, victims of failed revolutions, of violent homogenization processes and "nation building" in the East, often stateless, they had witnessed the darkest side of the modern nation-state paradigm. In the Weimar Republic, the state of Prussia granted asylum to some of them, but only in the form of "toleration," which could be revoked at any time. The authorities' efforts to deport them often failed because Poland and the Soviet Union refused to take them back. The rise of antisemitism in Germany in the 1920s was decisively linked to the influx of the Eastern European Jews, who were regarded as altogether foreign, too foreign to be assimilated, giving fuel to the antisemitic idea of an "international Jewry" allegedly undermining the nation-states.[22] Even after the Nazi seizure of power in 1933, seventy-two thousand Polish Jews were stuck in the German Reich. In the Polenaktion (Poland action), seventeen thousand of them were forcibly deported to Poland in October 1938, among them the parents of Herschel Grynszpan, a seventeen-year-old man who had made it to Paris. In his grief and rage, Grynszpan killed a German diplomat in the German embassy in Paris, an event that was then taken as a pretext in Germany to unleash the so-called Reichspogromnacht on 9 November 1938, destroying more than a thousand synagogues and thousands of shops and businesses, killing more than thirteen hundred people and arresting more than thirty thousand (Benz 2001: 56–58).

The interrelation between antimigrant sentiments and antisemitism in the interwar period and its significance for the rise and the rule of National Socialism has not been reflected sufficiently in historiography and is widely ignored in German memory culture. The German "Never again!" relates to the Holocaust, the war, and the disenfranchisement and exclusion of the mostly assimilated German Jews from the German citizenry. It does not relate to events like the Poland Action and the deportation of Herschel Grynszpan's parents; it does not relate to the treatment of Jews of the 1920s and 1930s as illegal or unwanted immigrants and refugees; and it does not relate to the German bureaucracies' efforts to legitimize even the Holocaust as "legal migration" on paper and in the eyes of many contemporaries.

This blind spot in German memory culture contributes to a specifically German link that exists between the perception of the foreign refugee and the perception of the threat of growing right-wing extremism. Since World War II, there has been a strong fear among social and cultural elites both in the Federal Republic and in the GDR that the German *Volk* might again freak out and turn Nazi. The *Volk* is seen as the ultimate source of the state's sovereignty, but also as a highly unreliable, potentially dangerous variable. The liberal spectrum specifically imagines that the *Volk*, overwhelmed and overstrained by the impositions of modernity, is potentially disconnected, declassed, predisposed to demagogy, and prone to envy the profiteers of modernization and globalization. In this frame of thought, the genocidal drive against the Jews and their educated, successful, geographically and socially mobile modern existence finds an explanation as a more general drive against education, success, globalization, and upward social mobility, emanating from the static and left-behind parts of the *Volk*.[23] The nation-state hence is being attributed a double function: mitigating the raging forces of modernity and keeping the *Volk* at bay. The vehicle to do so is the rule of law, and the condition for the state to fulfil this function is that it secures control over the borders and control over the composition of the inhabitants at any time. Only by preventing an uncontrolled influx of new carriers of modern uprootedness, it is possible to properly root–integrate–the newcomers and to reassure and take along the *Volk*.

These "liberal" ideas might at least partly motivate the strange topos of Merkel's alleged "loss of control" that has been dominating the discourse on "illegal" migration and on the so-called opening of the border. (The border was already open, due to the Schengen Agreement; Merkel just did not close it.) In order to keep the *Volk* reassured and to protect the imagined figure of the "integrated Jew"–a figure that one identifies with, feeling slightly uprooted oneself–it is necessary that the nation-state be intact, that state power be unchallenged, that the national population be halfway homogeneous, and that the borders be always under control.[24] Hence the curious phenomenon that so many educated and liberal Germans believe in cultural limits of Germany's "absorption capacity," even though they themselves identify as cosmopolites and do not practice a particularly "German culture" in their own lives at all. The benchmark for the "absorption capacity" is not formed by hard economic and social facts–by the labor market, the condition of the social security systems, the demographic development, and the like. Nor is it formed by cultural standards—will the newcomers play enough Brahms, appreciate asparagus, go to the Christmas market? But it is really formed by a political consideration: will Germany be able to "integrate the newcomers" and make them agreeable for the *Volk* quickly and thoroughly enough as to not give those who are perceived rightly or wrongly as the losers of modernization the chance to rise again and seize power?

The "migrant" and "refugee" is thus very closely tied to the threat of right-wing extremism. Identifying it as one, if not the main, cause for the outbursts of the *Volk*'s discontent with modernization, liberal discourse enters into negotiations with the right-wing discourse about access, control, integration, etc. The questions to be negotiated are mostly not tangible and practical but symbolic: unproductive claims that the immigrants are integrating well or will integrate soon or will not integrate or cannot integrate, equally unproductive demonstrations that the state and government are acting or not acting or cannot act or do not want to act, etc. A spiral of arguments is set in motion that pushes the liberals more and more into the defensive whereas the right-wingers get the lead. They can go on and on, as their demands are impossible to satisfy, as "integration" and "control" will never be completed, as the ambivalences of modernity cannot be solved, and as the worst human instincts in the *Volk* and the elites—greed, hatred, fear—get continuously rewarded instead of reprimanded, turning the supposed *Volk*'s potential Nazi threat into a self-fulfilling prophesy.

In 1993, the Social Democrats helped to alter the constitution and strip the right for asylum to bring down the numbers of "refugees," attempting to take the wind out of the sails of roaring antimigrant and extreme right-wing sentiments. Indeed, the numbers of protection seekers were reduced drastically through these and other measures, and, also, the numbers of antirefugee attacks were reduced. Since 2015, again, asylum laws have been tightened continuously, with SPD participation in government, and the numbers of protection seekers are drastically being reduced. While the numbers of antirefugee attacks also seem to be going down, albeit slowly,[25] there is no end in sight to the development of right-wing and xenophobic hate crime. "We'll hunt them down. We're going to hunt down Frau Merkel or whoever. ... We will chase the government," the top AfD candidate Alexander Gauland threatened the liberal establishment in September 2017 after the Bundestag elections, when the AfD became the third strongest party.[26] Indeed, even the Greens, originally fervently pro-refugee, have joined in the talk of the "rule of law" that allegedly needs to prove itself by executing deportations.[27] The desperate attempts to claim control over the borders and the foreign population, to thereby win back the *Volk* and to stop the rise of the right wing, have made the manifold violations of international law in

Europe's treatment of the "refugee," which are really happening, a negligible, acceptable factor.

The Germans' "refugees'" significance for the conditions of ambivalent modern and liberal existence in the nation-state, historically centered so much around sovereignty and homogeneity, will in the future rather increase than decrease.

Marion Detjen teaches history at Bard College Berlin and works as academic director of Bard College Berlin's "Program for International Education and Social Change." She studied history and literature in Berlin and Munich and received her PhD from Freie Universität Berlin with a dissertation on refugees from the GDR and people's smuggling after the building of the Berlin Wall. She is a regular contributor to the column "10nach8" at ZEIT-Online as part of its editorial team and is a cofounder of "Wir machen das" (We are doing it), a coalition of action focused on issues of forced migration in Berlin.

Notes

1. "BILD heißt Flüchtlinge willkommen!"
2. A follow-up study by a team of anthropologists under Werner Schiffauer, the chairman of the board of the Council for Migration, which in 2016 had done a mapping of the pro-refugee projects initiated in 2015, confirmed the persistence of the Welcome Culture until 2018. (Schiffauer, Eilert, and Rudolf 2018). Since then, the "helpers circles" frustrations have grown, due to politics; see e.g., "Integration im Alltag" (2019).
3. For the traps of methodological nationalism, see Glick, Schiller, and Wimmer (2003). I follow the theoretical concept of the Migration Regime developed by Frank Wolff and Christoph Rass that allows for scaling the analysis to all levels, from local to global, and my focus on Germany is a result of my questions, not of any kind of presuppositions about a German *Sonderweg*; see Rass and Wolff (2018).
4. See, on the "ethnonational dimension" of the German constitution, Klusmeyer and Papademetriou (2009: 22–29).
5. By 1950, only 11 percent of constitutions contained a right to asylum; see Meili (2018: 392).
6. The Federal Republic of Germany gained sovereignty in several steps between 1949 and 1990, the most significant one taken in 1955, and it only entered the United Nations in 1973 after the end of the Hallstein doctrine.
7. His article on "Racial Law and the Jewry," published in 1939, pointed to the "great dangers" of mixing "own blood" with "alien [artfremden] blood" and to the "drastic measures" that nations have been taking at all times to prevent racial alien infiltration [*Überfremdung*]; this racist discourse is not as opposed to his

admiration for the US constitutionalism as it appears to his biographers (Rohlfs 1997: 46–48).

8. Navid Kermani, a famous Iranian writer, was the first to draw attention to this fact in a speech delivered to the German Parliament in May 2014, celebrating the sixty-fifth anniversary of the constitution and ending with a memorable "Danke Deutschland!" (Thank you, Germany!); see "Jeder Zweite in Deutschland mit Migrationshintergrund?" (2015).
9. The interdependency between legal and illegal migration in German history is described by Karakayali (2008).
10. Foroutan (2013). For the gender implications of this development, see: Clarence (2009).
11. "Wahrnehmung und Realität" (2016).
12. For the racializing of the "foreigner," which not only affected German politics but also German historiography, see Alexopoulou (2018).
13. The full title of the law is: Gesetz zur Steuerung und Begrenzung der Zuwanderung und zur Regelung des Aufenthalts und der Integration von Unionsbürgern und Ausländern (Act to control and to curb immigration and to regulate the residency and the integration of EU citizens and of foreigners).
14. Steinbeis and Detjen (2019) offer a detailed reconstruction of the events and controversies around Merkel's alleged "opening of the borders" and its legal implications.
15. "Schäuble warnt vor Flüchtlings-'Lawine'" (2015).
16. Journalist Robin Alexander's (2017) number-one bestseller contributed significantly to this notion.
17. "Ein Pakt mit dem Teufel."
18. The double face shows itself in the "migration package," a series of nine legal acts that have come or are coming into effect between July 2019 and March 2020: on the one hand, the "Experts Immigration Act" takes significant steps toward further enabling immigration for well-educated migrants with knowledge of German and either a job or financial means; on the other hand, the "Orderly Return Act" not only eases deportation, it also forces the migrants to cooperate with authorities of their countries of origin, no matter how evil their governments are. See "Übersicht zum 'Migrationspaket'" (2019).
19. The government has promised to resettle 10,200 UNHCR refugees but is using public-private partnerships, in the so-called NesT-program, to get 500 of them financed through private persons, even though many municipalities have expressed their willingness to receive refugees. See "Kommunen als 'sichere Häfen'?" (2019).
20. The splinter parties Die Rechte, NPD, and Der III. Weg are openly Nazi. The Federal Office for the Protection of the Constitution estimated the numbers of persons with an openly Nazi orientation at around twenty-five thousand for 2018 ("Verfassungsschutzbericht 2018": 50).
21. Already observed by Kailitz (2015).
22. For the reactions of German-Jewish voices to the 1921 Scheunenviertel Pogrom, see Schneider (2017: 120).
23. See, as an example, Aly (2011).

24. The exploitation of the "integrated Jews" against the allegedly not integrable Muslims was one of the reasons why the young Jewish author Max Czollek wrote an angry polemic in 2018, raging against the German "integration theater" and "memory theater," where the Jews as "good victims" help to stabilize the Germans, and asking the Jews, the migrants, and whoever else to "desintegrate!" Czollek (2018).
25. "Straftaten gegen Asylunterkünfte nach Deliktsbereichen 2014–2018" (n.d.); "Chronik flüchtlingsfeindlicher Vorfälle" (2020).
26. "Wir werden Frau Merkel jagen" (2017).
27. "Wie die Grünen ihren Ton verschärfen" (2018).

References

Ahonen, Pertti, Gustavo Corni, Jerzy Kochanowski, Rainer Schulze, Tamás Stark, and Barbara Stelzl-Marx (eds). 2008. *People on the Move. Forced Population Movements in Europe in the Second World War and Its Aftermath.* Oxford: Berg.

Alexander, Robin. 2017. *Die Getriebenen: Merkel und die Flüchtlingspolitik; Report aus dem Innern der Macht* [The driven ones: Merkel and the refugee policy; Report from within the power]. München: Siedler Verlag.

Alexopoulou, Maria. 2018. "'Ausländer'–A racialized concept? 'Race' as Analytical Concept in Contemporary German Immigration History." In *Who Can Speak and Who Is Heard/Hurt? Facing Problems of Race, Racism and Ethnic Diversity in the Humanities in Germany*, edited by Mahmoud Arghavan et al., 1–21, Bielefeld: Transcript Verlag.

Aly, Götz. 2011. *Warum die Deutschen? Warum die Juden? Gleichheit, Neid und Rassenhass* [Why the Germans? Why the Jews? Equality, envy, and racial hatred]. Frankfurt am Main: S. Fischer Verlag.

Beer, Mathias. 2011. *Flucht und Vertreibung der Deutschen: Voraussetzungen, Verlauf, Folgen* [Flight and expulsion of the Germans: Conditions, course, consequences]. München: Verlag C. H. Beck.

Benz, Wolfgang. 2001. *Flucht aus Deutschland: Zum Exil im 20. Jahrhundert* [Escape from Germany: Exile in the 20th century]. München: Deutscher Taschenbuch Verlag.

"BILD heißt Flüchtlinge willkommen!" [BILD is welcoming refugees!]. 2015. BILD, 9 September. Retrieved 23 January 2020 from https://www.bild.de/regional/berlin/fluechtling/bild-berlin-heisst-fluechtlinge-willkommen-42502416.bild.html.

Buckel, Sonja. 2013. *"Welcome to Europe": Die Grenzen des europäischen Migrationsrechts* ["Welcome to Europe": The limitations of European migration law]. Bielefeld: Transcript Verlag.

"Chronik flüchtlingsfeindlicher Vorfälle" [Chronicle of attacks against refugees]. 2020. Mut gegen rechte Gewalt, ein Projekt des Magazins *stern* und der Amadeu Antonio Stiftung, last updated 13 January. Retrieved 23 January 2020 from https://www.mut-gegen-rechte-gewalt.de/service/chronik-vorfaelle.

Clarence, Sherran. 2009. "From Rhetoric to Practice: A Critique of Immigration Policy in Germany through the Lens of Turkish-Muslim Women's Experiences of Migration." *Journal of Social and Political Theory* 56(121): 57–91.
Comte, Emmanuel. 2018. *The History of the European Migration Regime: Germany's Strategic Hegemony*. London: Routledge.
Cremer, Will, and Ansgar Klein (eds). 2002. *Heimat: Analysen, Themen, Perspektiven* [Homeland: Analyses, themes, perspectives]. Bonn: Bundeszentrale für politische Bildung, Bd. 249/I.
Czollek, Max. 2018. *Desintegriert euch!* München: Carl Hanser Verlag.
Demshuk, Andrew. 2012. *The Lost German East: Forced Migration and the Politics of Memory 1945–1970*. Cambridge: Cambridge University Press.
Dufner, Georg. 2013. "Praxis, Symbol und Politik: Das chilenische Exil in der Bundesrepublik nach 1973." *Santiago-Berlin: Forschung und Meinung*, 20 December. Retrieved 23 January 2020 from http://santiago-berlin.net/praxis-symbol-und-politik-das-chilenische-exil-in-der-bundesrepublik-deutschland-nach-1973/.
Foroutan, Naika. 2013. *Identity and (Muslim) Integration in Germany*. Washington, DC: Migration Policy Institute.
Gatrell, Peter. 2013. *The Making of the Modern Refugee*. Oxford: Oxford University Press.
Gatrell, Peter, and Liubov Zhvanko (eds). 2017. *Europe on the Move: Refugees in the Era of the Great War*. Manchester: Manchester University Press.
"Geschätzte Anzahl der im Mittelmeer ertrunkenen Flüchtlinge in den Jahren von 2014 bis 2020" [Estimated number of refugees drowned in the Mediterranean in the years 2014 to 2020]. 2020. Statista, 8 January. Retrieved 23 January 2020 from https://de.statista.com/statistik/daten/studie/892249/umfrage/im-mittelmeer-ertrunkenen-fluechtlinge/.
Glick Schiller, Nina, and Andreas Wimmer. 2003. "Methodological Nationalism, the Social Sciences, and the Study of Migration: An Essay in Historical Epistemology." *International Migration Review* 37(3): 576–610. Retrieved 23 January 2020 from http://www.jstor.org/stable/30037750.
Göktürk, Deniz, David Gramling, and Anton Kaes. 2007. *Germany in Transit: Nation and Migration 1955–2005*. Berkeley: University of California Press.
Gosewinkel, Dieter. 2003. *Einbürgern und ausschließen: Die Nationalisierung der Staatsangehörigkeit vom Deutschen Bund bis zur Bundesrepublik Deutschland* [Naturalize and exclude: The nationalization of citizenship from the German Confederation to the Federal Republic of Germany]. Kritische Studien zur Geschichtswissenschaft, vol. 150, 2nd edn. Göttingen: Vandenhoeck & Ruprecht.
Heizmann, Kristina. 2012. "Fremd in der Fremde: Die Geschichte des Flüchtlings in Großbritannien und Deutschland, 1880–1925" [Strangers in a foreign land: The history of the refugee in Great Britain and Germany, 1880–1925]. PhD diss. Konstanz: University Kontanz. Retrieved 23 January 2020 from http://nbn-resolving.de/urn:nbn:de:bsz:352-0-294538.
Herbert, Ulrich. 1990. *A History of Foreign Labor in Germany, 1880–1980: Seasonal Workers/Forced Laborers/Guest Workers*. Translated by William Templer. Ann Arbor: University of Michigan Press.
Holler, Joanne. 1993. *The German Expellees: A Problem of Integration*. Washington, DC: Population Research Project of The George Washington University. Retrieved 23 January 2020 from https://hdl.handle.net/2027/mdp.39015016472857.

"Integration im Alltag: Was wurde aus der Willkommenskultur?" [Everyday integration: What became of the welcome culture?]. 2019. Ostsee-Zeitung, 8 February. Retrieved 23 January 2020 from https://www.ostsee-zeitung.de/Nachrichten/Politik/CDU-Fluechtlingsgespraech-Was-wurde-aus-der-Willkommenskultur.

"Jeder zweite Deutsche mit Migrationshintergrund?" [Every second German with a migration background?]. 2015. Mediendienst Integration, 7 January. Retrieved 23 January 2020 from https://mediendienst-integration.de/artikel/kermani-rede-jeder-zweite-hat-migrationshintergrund.html.

Kailitz, Steffen. 2015. "Rechte Kampagnen damals und heute" [Right-wing campaigns then and now]. Cicero, 13 November. Retrieved 23 January 2020 from https://www.cicero.de/innenpolitik/fluechtlingsdebatte-was-wir-aus-der-judeneinwanderung-der-20er-lernen/60106.

Karakayali, Serhat. 2008. *Gespenster der Migration: Zur Genealogie illegaler Einwanderung in der Bundesrepublik Deutschland*. [Ghosts of migration: The genealogy of illegal migration in the Federal Republic of Germany]. Bielefeld: Transcript Verlag.

Klusmeyer, Douglas B., and Demetrious G. Papademetriou. 2009. *Immigration Policy in the Federal Republic of Germany: Negotiating Membership and Remaking the Nation*. New York: Berghahn Books.

"Kommunen als 'sichere Häfen'? Abschlussdiskussion des Flüchtlingsschutzsymposiums" [Municipalities as "safe havens"? Closing discussion of the symposium on the protection of refugees]. 2019. Evangelische Akademie zu Berlin, 26 June. Retrieved 23 January 2020 from https://www.eaberlin.de/nachlese/chronologisch-nach-jahren/2019/kommunen-als-sichere-haefen/.

Limbach, Eric H. 2011. *Unsettled Germans: The Reception and Resettlement of East German Refugees in West Germany, 1949–1961*. Dissertation submitted to Michigan State University. Retrieved 23 January 2020 from https://d.lib.msu.edu/etd/1605.

Meili, Stephen. 2018. "The Constitutional Right to Asylum: The Wave of the Future in International Refugee Law?" *Fordham International Law Journal* 41(2): 382–424. Retrieved 23 January 2020 from https://ssrn.com/abstract=3126300.

Mommsen, Theodor. 1880. *Auch ein Wort über unser Judentum* [Another word about our Jewry]. Berlin: Weidmannsche Buchhandlung. Retrieved 23 January 2020 from urn:nbn:de:kobv:517-vlib-6261.

Neander, Joachim. 2008. "Das Staatsangehörigkeitsrecht des 'Dritten Reiches' und seine Auswirkungen auf das Verfolgungsschicksal deutscher Staatsangehöriger" [The citizenship law of the "Third Reich" and its effects on the fate of victims with German citizenship]. *Theologie: Geschichte* 3. Retrieved 23 January 2020 from http://universaar.uni-saarland.de/journals/index.php/tg/article/viewArticle/471/510.

Poutrus, Patrice. 2019. *Umkämpftes Asyl: Vom Nachkriegsdeutschland bis in die Gegenwart* [Contested asylum: From postwar Germany to the present]. Berlin: Ch. Links Verlag.

Rass, Christoph, and Frank Wolff. 2018. "What Is in a Migration Regime?" In *Was ist ein Migrationsregime? What Is a Migration Regime?* edited by Andreas Pott, Christoph Rass, and Frank Wolff, 19–64. Wiesbaden: Springer V.

Reents, Edo. 2019. "Festgemauert in den Phrasen" [Walled into stereotypes]. *Frankfurter Allgemeine Zeitung*, 1 June. Retrieved 23 January 2020 from https://www.faz.net/aktuell/feuilleton/wie-einfallslos-merkels-rede-in-harvard-war-16215400-p3.html.

Rohlfs, Angelo. 1997. *Hermann von Mangoldt (1895–1953): Das Leben des Staatsrechtlers vom Kaiserreich bis zur Bonner Republik* [Hermann von Mangoldt (1895–1953): The life of the constitutional law expert from the German Empire to the Republic of Bonn]. Berlin: Duncker & Humblot.
Schiffauer, Werner, Anne Eilert, and Marlene Rudloff (eds). 2017. *So schaffen wir das: Eine Zivilgesellschaft im Aufbruch; 90 wegweisende Projekte mit Geflüchteten* [This is how we manage: Civil society on the rise; Ninety groundbreaking projects with refugees]. Bielefeld: Transcript Verlag.
———. 2018. *So schaffen wir das: Eine Zivilgesellschaft im Aufbruch; Bedingungen für eine nachhaltige Projektarbeit mit Geflüchteten* [This is how we manage: Civil society on the rise; Conditions for a sustainable project work with refugees]. Bielefeld: Transcript Verlag.
Schneider, Julia. 2017. "(Für)Sorge–Die 'Ostjudenfrage' in der deutsch-jüdischen Presse" [Concern–The "Eastern Jewish question" in the German-Jewish Press]. In *Geflüchtet, unerwünscht, abgeschoben: Osteuropäische Juden in der Republik Baden (1918–1923)* [Escaped, unwanted, deported: Eastern European Jews in the Republic of Baden (1918–1923)], edited by Nils Steffen and Cord Arendes, 107–27. Heidelberg: heiBOOKS. Retrieved 23 January 2020 from https://doi.org/10.11588/heibooks.182.241.
Steinbeis, Maximilian, and Stephan Detjen. 2019. *Die Zauberlehrlinge: Der Streit um die Flüchtlingspolitik und der Mythos vom Rechtsbruch* [Sorcerer's apprentices: The controversy about the refugee politics, and the myth of the breach of law]. Stuttgart: Klett-Cotta.
Treitschke, Heinrich von. 1879. "Unsere Aussichten" [Our prospects]. *Preußische Jahrbücher* 44(5): 559–76. Reprinted in Karsten Krieger (ed.), *Der 'Berliner Antisemitismusstreit' 1879–1881*, 2 parts. Munich: K. G. Saur, 1003–2004, part 1, 10–16.
"Schäuble warnt vor Flüchtlings-Lawine'!" [Schäuble warns of a refugee "avalanche"]. 2015. Frankfurter Allgemeine Zeitung, 12 January. Retrieved 23 January 2020 from https://www.faz.net/aktuell/politik/fluechtlingskrise/wolfgang-schaeuble-warnt-vor-lawine-in-fluechtlingskrise-13907768.html.
"Straftaten gegen Asylunterkünfte nach Deliktsbereichen 2014–2018" [Offenses against asylum accommodations by area of offence 2014–2018]. N.d. Veröffentlichungen des Bundesministeriums des Inneren, für Bau und Heimat. Retrieved 23 January 2020 from https://www.bmi.bund.de/SharedDocs/downloads/DE/veroeffentlichungen/2019/pmk-2018-straftaten-gegen-asylunterkuenfte.pdf?__blob=publicationFile&v=4.
Sundhaussen, Holm. 1996. "Bevölkerungsverschiebungen in Südosteuropa seit der Nationalstaatswerdung (19/20. Jahrhundert)" [Population displacements in Southeast Europe since the emergence of the nation-states]. *Comparativ* 6(1): 25–40. Retrieved 23 January 2020 from https://www.comparativ.net/v2/article/view/1402.
Ther, Philipp. 2017. *Die Außenseiter: Flucht, Flüchtlinge und Integration im modernen Europa* [The outsiders: Escape, refugees, and integration in modern Europe]. Berlin: Suhrkamp Verlag.
"Übersicht zum 'Migrationspaket'" [Overview of the "Migration Package"]. 2019. Generalsekretär des Deutschen Roten Kreuzes, 21 August. Retrieved 23 January 2020 from Migrationspaket_20190821.pdf.

"Verfassungsschutzbericht 2018" [Constitution protection report 2018]. N.d. Bundesministerium des Innern, für Bau und Heimat. Retrieved 11 October 2021 from http://www.bmi.bund.de/SharedDocs/downloads/DE/publikationen/themen/sicherheit/vsb-2018-gesamt.pdf?__blob=publicationFile&v=10.

"Wahrnehmung und Realität 2016" [Perception and reality 2016]. 2016. Forschungsgruppe Weltanschauungen in Deutschland, 16 December. Retrieved 23 January 2020 from https://fowid.de/meldung/wahrnehmung-und-realitaet-2016.

"Wie die Grünen ihren Ton verschärfen" [How the Greens are tightening their tone]. 2018. Süddeutsche Zeitung, 19 December. Retrieved 23 January 2020 from https://www.sueddeutsche.de/politik/gruene-fluechtlingspolitik-argumentation-1.4259477.

"Wir werden Frau Merkel jagen" [We will hunt Frau Merkel down]. 2017. *Der Spiegel*, 24 September. Retrieved 23 January 2020 from https://www.spiegel.de/politik/deutschland/afd-alexander-gauland-wir-werden-frau-merkel-jagen-a-1169598.html.

Wolff, Frank. 2019. *Die Mauergesellschaft: Kalter Krieg, Menschenrechte und die deutschdeutsche Migration 1961–1989* [The Wall Society: Cold war, human rights, and inner-German migration 1961–1989]. Berlin: Suhrkamp Verlag.

Part IV
Refugee Agency

10

"Without It, You Will Die"

Smartphones and Refugees' Digital Self-Organization

Stephan O. Görland and Sina Arnold

Introduction

In European discourse, the year 2015 is referred to as the "summer of migration" (Hess et al. 2017). Starting from the numerous crisis hotspots in Africa and particularly the Middle East, even as far away as Afghanistan, a large number of people came to Europe, fleeing from war, starvation, inhuman systems, and persecution.

The images circulated on the internet and in global media from the various stations of the journey repeatedly showed exhausted people suffering from travel exertion. But looking closely at these images and comparing them to earlier refugee movements, something else was striking: smartphones were often the refugees' companions and became a media phenomenon that was constantly mentioned. The *New York Times*, for example, called the smartphone a "refugees['] essential"–alongside food and shelter (Brunwasser 2015). There were also countless reports and rising interest in the refugees' mobile phones in Germany, concluding that the mobile phone was replacing the bank account, the computer, and the landline phone (Meyer 2015).

Today's modern smartphone needs an essential prerequisite to fulfill this purpose: a connection to the World Wide Web. However, during the first phase of immigration in 2015, only very few refugee shelters had internet in private rooms or in the common room. However, starting from the observation that "for many, connectivity has become as essential for survival as food, water and shelter" (Accenture and UNHCR 2016: 11), more and more initiatives to further expand digital infrastructure have grown rapidly. In 2016, the German Federal Ministry for Economic Cooperation and Development (BMZ) highlighted this "unused potential" of digital infrastructure (Bundesministerium für wirtschaftliche Entwicklung und Zusammenarbeit [BMZ] 2016). Civil initiatives and even the German Federal Office for Migration and Refugees (BAMF) tried to address this digital development with their own strategies. The smartphone is thus increasingly becoming the focus of many integration initiatives.

In this chapter, we aim to illustrate the important role of the smartphone both for the migration and for the integration process in the country of arrival. In this sense, the smartphone is analyzed as a material object that is more than just a mobile phone, a context-sensitive tool for establishing translocal communication and situational community building. Accordingly, the smartphone is understood as a self-empowerment tool.

State of Research

Mobile media: never in the history of the world has a technology expanded faster (Görland 2020). More people now have access to mobile media like smartphones than to freshwater toilets. At the same time, telecommunication has become a major necessity in the context of the global migration movement. In the early 2000s, the emergence of low-cost global telephone and call shops was already described as the "social glue of migrant transnationalism" (Vertovec 2004). People were able to stay in touch at low cost and in real time. Today, this is even reinforced by permanent internet connection and the services associated with it, such as messenger apps, online social networks, and video calls. Dana Diminescu (2008) developed the image of the "connected migrant" as a convergence of social, digital and communicative developments. This concept is not free of criticism due to its common utilitarian interpretation as it assumes a great autonomy and speaks little about discrimination along the lines of gender and ethnicity (Awad and Tossel 2019: 12).

In general, it can be said that research has quickly turned its attention to this phenomenon. Even before the "summer of migration" there was a great amount of research in the international arena on the effects of mobile media during or after forced migration (e.g., Coddington and Mountz 2014; Harney 2013; Wall, Campbell, and Janbek 2015; Witteborn 2015; Accenture and UNHCR 2016; Andrade and Doolin 2016). In their meta-study on forty-three international (i.e., not exclusively European) studies, Mancini et al. (2019) differentiate five dominant topics on refugees' experiences and mobile phones (MP) between 2013 and 2018: "(a) media practices in refugees' everyday lives; (b) opportunity and risks of MPs during the migration journey; (c) the role of MPs in maintaining and developing social relations; (d) potential of MPs for refugees' self-assertion and self-empowerment; (e) MPs for refugees' health and education" (Mancini et al. 2019: 1).

Due to the emerging "crisis" in 2015 (as several European media have called it, further studies have been published on the relationship between migration and the smartphone in the European context. Most exhibit a duality of content (Arnold and Görland 2018): first, there is a description of media use during and after the migration process, followed by a comparison of these phases, which usually shows that "journey and integration in a host society represent two different processes" (Krasnova and AbuJarour 2017: 1796). The digital dangers in the migration process were also addressed; with the conclusion of a "dialectical tension" (Gillespie, Osseiran, and Cheesman 2018: 9): On the one hand, mobile media help with navigation and are thus self-empowering. On the other hand, mobile media also create danger: for example, if the German federal government orders smartphones to be read during the asylum application procedure (Chase and Dick 2017).

Most European studies have specific topics such as social integration into the new society (Krasnova and AbuJarour 2017), unaccompanied youth (Kutscher and Kreß 2015), mutual support via social media (Borkert, Fisher, and Yafi 2018), "decision-making" via social networks (Dekker et al. 2018), identity (Karnowski, Springer, and Herzer 2016), expectations regarding the host country (Richter, Kunst, and Emmer, 2016), and self-representation (Risam 2018). The topics and thus the various research interests are therefore manifold.[1]

All studies share the same emphasis on the importance of mobile and social media as well as connectivity for migration and diaspora communication, both for self-presentation and for integration into the arrival society. The smartphone, it seems, is an imminently important companion in everyday life.

This chapter wants to go one step further and focus on the self-empowerment character of the mobile phone through an actor-oriented perspective. For this purpose, we apply an approach that has not been used so far: logistics, an increasingly popular approach developed to study migration (Apicella, Arnold, and Bojadžijev 2018: 19; Thrift 2008 126).

Method

The following results are based on an empirical study conducted in Berlin between January and December 2016.[2] In Berlin alone, ninety thousand refugees arrived in 2015 (Nolan and Graham-Harrison 2015). In total, seventeen qualitative interviews with Syrian refugees were conducted in the project, and ninety-seven questionnaires were filled out in Arabic.

The qualitative interviews, conducted between May and September 2016, were focused on questions about the specific migration history of the interviewees and their media usage patterns—i.e., which media and social networks they used both before and after the migration process—but also included general questions about their life history and their future plans. We also asked how information had been shared and verified during the flight. The respondents were between the ages of sixteen and thirty-six (average age: twenty-eight), and their educational qualifications differed. Seven of them were male, eight female and all of them had arrived in Germany between August and November 2015. Most interviews were conducted in English; five interviews were conducted with the help of an Arabic translator. This fact necessarily resulted in a certain preselection with regard to the educational level of the interviewees.

The quantitative questionnaire was developed on the basis of the qualitative interviews. During this second phase of the project, we interviewed ninety-seven participants (average age: thirty, one-third female, two-thirds male) in November and December of 2016 in two different refugee shelters in Berlin. We worked with an Arabic-speaking research assistant who contacted potential interview partners, assisted them with unclear questions, and handed out shopping vouchers as a small reward. The questionnaires included questions on media use before, during, and after the migration, various (self-)assessments on topics related to (mass) communication, and questions on the use of so-called integration apps.

A reason for a relatively low response rate to the questionnaires that were distributed was "research exhaustion" during the survey period. In 2016, for example, there was a real boom in research on migration in Germany. However, according to the manager of a refugee shelter, many researchers proceeded insensitively, which led to many institutions not allowing any more research to be done there. The following figures are therefore not representative overall but do represent a first quantification.

Results

The phone is the only way to come here ... 99 percent you have to have a phone, and internet. Without it? You're lost, you will die! (M., twenty-two)

All of the refugees who were interviewed qualitatively or quantitatively had an internet-capable mobile phone, which they used both during the flight and in everyday situations in the country of arrival to coordinate essential areas of life. The connected migrants (Diminescu 2008) (i.e., the refugees who were fully connected via mobile media), were thus a reality in our sample. All interviewees, and this is confirmed by other studies such as those on media coverage, referred to the fact that smartphones are a routine item for refugees in Germany.

Quantitative Results

Even though we have supplemented the qualitative interviews with quantitative surveys in the study, we would like to use the results of the latter to give insight into the material first. The aim is to show to what extent the everyday life of refugees is "mediatized," because "media do not just add a new dimension to the phenomenon of migration, they transform it altogether" (Madianou 2014: 323).

As table 10.1 shows, the applications used by the refugees interviewed are dispersed and diverse; no major differences to German users can be observed.[3]

Above all, the social functions of the smartphone dominate: messenger services such as WhatsApp or Viber are used by four-fifths of those surveyed, and Facebook is just as popular. The telephone function was still used by 79 percent, but everyday aids (e.g., the map function), entertainment (e.g., music and games), information gathering, and religious needs are also very important. Of those surveyed, 45 percent said they had a digital version of the Koran on their smartphones, and 38 percent also used religious apps, which for example point out the direction of Mecca. Searching for contacts and relationships through apps such as Tinder or Lovoo is also a feature used by around 17 percent of our sample. In addition, young refugees in particular use media for entertainment—whether by watching films and series (43 percent) or playing games (38 percent)—in an everyday life that is often characterized by monotony and waiting.

Based on previous studies with a triple division into "before, during, and after migration" (e.g., Karnowski et al. 2016; Krasnova and AbuJarour 2017), we also asked for the five most frequently used apps in these different phases. Table 2 shows the results:

Again, individual adaptation to the specific requirements is obvious. Although the social networks WhatsApp and Facebook always rank within the first three places, it is clear that navigation apps became particularly important during the flight. After the migration, the focus shifted to language courses and the visual social network Instagram, a community in which images are exchanged.

Furthermore, we asked whether refugees use so-called integration apps, and if so, which ones. "Integration apps" are small, digital helpers (applications) that are supposed to help refugees to master everyday life in the host country by providing recommendations and small learning tutorials.

Table 10.1. Agreement to the Statement "I Use the Following Functions on My Smartphone" (n = 97).

Application	Agreement in percent
Messengers like WhatsApp	82 percent
Facebook	82 percent
Phone calls	79 percent
Voice messages	70 percent
Maps	69 percent
Reading news	65 percent
Camera	64 percent
Google	64 percent
Language courses	57 percent
Movies / TV shows	57 percent
E-mail	53 percent
Music	52 percent
Koran	45 percent
Games	38 percent
Praying App	38 percent
Instagram	36 percent
Online Shopping	31 percent
Twitter	20 percent
Online Dating	17 percent
Online Banking	14 percent
Snapchat	13 percent

Table made by Sina Arnold and Stephan O. Görland.

Often, they have been designed by government institutions on a federal or municipal level. The result was disillusioning: only eleven of ninety-seven people downloaded the relevant apps. The majority of them (six people) downloaded the app Ankommen (Arrive), which was launched in 2016 with great media attention by the BAMF. Digital dictionaries were used more frequently, as almost 28 percent of our sample (twenty-seven people) had downloaded one of the various apps, and 56 percent used online language courses. Of our respondents, 70 percent agree or fully agree with the statement that the smartphone helps them to learn German. This generally

Table 10.2. Most Frequently Used Apps before, during, and after Migrating to Germany (n = 97).

Ranking	Before migration	During migration	After migration
1	WhatsApp	WhatsApp	WhatsApp
2	Facebook	Maps/GPS	Facebook
3	Viber	Facebook	Different messenger
4	Different messenger	Viber	Language courses and translator
5	Phone calling	Phone calling	Instagram

Table made by Sina Arnold and Stephan O. Görland.

points to its high importance for informal learning: 59 percent of the respondents agree or fully agree that they use the device to learn German.

The respondents generally show a very high level of media competence and use media critically: 63 percent say they "do not" or "rather do not" trust what they read on Facebook, 67 percent do not or rather do not trust Arab media, and 36 percent do not or rather do not trust German media. Overall, trust in German media is the highest at 37 percent. Finally, the quantitative questions reveal the subjective perception of the smartphone as relevant for the migration process: 80 percent of the respondents agree or fully agree that the smartphone was a great help; more than a third think that the flight would not have been possible without the phone.

In summary, the quantitative data illustrates that all phases of migration—prior to, during, and after the flight—are highly mediatized. The smartphone has an enormous value for refugees and combines individual, social, and cultural practices in a new way. Refugees use these with the help of their high media competence. However, "top-down applications" like government-initiated integration apps are rejected.

Qualitative Results

As mentioned above, we want to describe the results using a logistics approach. We have chosen this approach given the idea that logistics is becoming the "central discipline of the contemporary world" (Thrift 2008: 126). Logistics in this sense goes beyond the mobility of goods, people, and information (Arnold, Bojadžijev, and Apicella, 2018 18): it includes networks and relationships and tries to make them material. A logistical perspective at an actor level allows the individual to become the individual logistician of planning and social organization (Arnold, Bojadžijev, and Apicella 2018: 19). It focuses on strategies regarding the anticipation of situations. A concentration on the actors in these coordination processes also provides a counterweight to current developments in European migration policy: the regulation of migration flows, the gathering of refugees at non-European collection points, and the increased inspection of refugees' smartphones all represent logistics "from above." They are counteracted at the individual level with logistics "from below."

We distinguished four different logistics of mediatized migration: maintenance logistics, coordination logistics, orientation logistics, and verification logistics. Based on these four areas, we will present the collected findings in detail.

Maintenance Logistics

> *I was afraid, because if it falls in the water, I'm gonna freak out. … So, I kept it and put it in plastic bags.* (M., twenty-nine)

Even though the smartphone plays a central role in migration processes mainly due to its digital functions, it is also a material object that requires maintenance of its functionality. All digital functions are therefore dependent on this materiality. In this context, the most important thing to maintain is the *battery level*. This maintenance had selective effects on the organization of the migration routes. In order to recharge their smartphone batteries, people adapted their routes to intersect with remote charging stations. Three-quarters of the respondents in our qualitative sample used external batteries, as these allowed greater independence from remote charging stations, which were usually multiple-outlet power strips at restaurants or cafés. However, some refugee camps, e.g., Idomeni on the Greek-Macedonian border, also provided charging stations or power strips where batteries could be recharged. Thus, Ahmed (twenty-four) declared: "Yeah, I have– I had alternative battery. Yeah, so every time when I went to the hostel or my place, I charged both with the battery, original one and the alternate one."

In addition to the physical factor of the energy level, it is also necessary to remain digitally *connected*. This is the second major challenge arising from maintenance logistics. For example, SIM (subscriber identity module) cards are helpful in the country of origin, but after crossing the next national border, one usually either has to pay high roaming charges, use the mobile internet, or buy a new SIM card. With one exception in our sample, all refugees bought different SIM cards during the trip in order to be reachable by SMS (Short Message Service) and for phone calls, to have access to the internet, or to navigate using map applications. Access to the internet played the more significant role since messenger services such as WhatsApp were usually more important than SIM-based services for both messages and calls. Technical convergence is useful in that modern smartphones are software based and most apps are device bound. This means that apps such as Facebook or WhatsApp do not change with a new phone number, so users do not have to provide new contact information with each new service. For example, N. (twenty-two) bought a new card in every country she crossed: "We bought in every country a new SIM card [sic]" A. (twenty-three) tried to act more economically and used the prepaid cards in roaming mode: "When I was in Turkey, I would–took a SIM card. It still worked until Greece, not all of it, some Greece. Then from Greece, I bought a Vodafone SIM card to continue until Serbia. From there, I also bought another SIM card from Vodafone until I reached Germany." Some of the interviewees even bought a phone that could hold two SIM cards before departure. This enabled them to keep their original number, which made it easier to contact their country of origin–especially in view of the often-interrupted internet connection there. In addition, depending on the country of transit, they were able to use another SIM card at the best local rates.

Protection is the third maintenance logistic. Because even if the smartphone is charged and the SIM card promises connectivity, there are still considerable dangers: robbery, blackmail, and damage to the phone represent very serious threats during the migration process. In our interviews, the crossing of the Mediterranean Sea was often mentioned, where capsizing and being in the water for any length of time were potential dangers. M. (twenty-two) reacted to this with the use of plastic bags: "So I kept it and put it in plastic bags. … Others … they were putting it in special plastic. Plastic bags or some kind of bag." Other refugees told us that they simply wrapped the smartphone in several layers of plastic foil. These three exemplary areas illustrate the challenges involved in maintaining a survival device, which functions as a necessary travel instrument in the migration process.

Coordination Logistics

The second type of logistics resulting from the challenges of the migration process are coordination logistics. These are first of all *navigation* practices, as refugees navigate through unknown terrain and often also unknown language regions. The smartphone has become subjectively indispensable for them: "Without it, I wouldn't move an inch," as A. concludes. M. shares a similar feeling: "The phone is the only way to come here. … 99 percent you have to [have] a phone, and internet and everything. Without it? You're lost, you die." It is certainly not surprising that for all of the refugees in our sample, apps like Google Maps, Here Maps, or Maps.me were the most used apps. "Yeah, Google Maps, absolutely Google Maps I used most," D. (twenty-seven) confirms. The use of these apps allows greater autonomy in the migration process, e.g., from traffickers or fraudsters. For example, a young refugee from Aleppo told us how she recognized maps on her phone and that a taxi driver in Greece wanted to drive her in the opposite direction from her destination, the Macedonian border. She was able to call him out and intervene, exemplifying how the use of navigation apps enables a form of self-empowerment even in unknown territories. Smartphones and apps thus have an effect on the users' well-being, making them feel less helpless. R. told us the following about his smartphone: "It has helped me to be more independent [in my journey] because you can't all the time ask the people, sometimes I need to know by myself to what should I do there."

However, coordination is not only achieved through map apps; *interpersonal exchange* and the use of mass media or Facebook groups are also important factors in coordinating the flight. A. (twenty-five) added: "My cousin communicated with a lot of other people how to go on ... WhatsApp and using the Global Positioning System (GPS). And this is the most important thing, of course, and all–and also, we said which city, which area we have to go. So, we wrote it in WhatsApp and sent it to the others and keep on." His statement illustrates the intertwining of interpersonal communication and spatiality. Repeatedly, our interview partners emphasized that they sent each other their locations in order to estimate distances on the one hand, but also to mark secure paths. One interviewee remembered how WhatsApp's "location" function enabled him to find his cousin in a chaotic situation on the Greek-Macedonian border, and the two of them were able to reunite in the middle of a large crowd of people, police, and a rapidly changing situation. Interpersonal exchange aided by the smartphone thus represents a mediatized in situ logistics with different levels of complexity and characteristics.

Orientation Logistics

The penultimate logistics are relevant mostly for the processes and challenges that refugees face in the country of arrival. We refer to these as orientation logistics, since orientation and guidance are central here. "Without it, I'm gonna be lost," says one interview partner (M.) about the role of his smartphone in Berlin. Another describes his concrete strategies: "I prefer my app. It is better connected. Its name is 'Here Maps,' and this connects everything. Maps, trains, navigator, everything is connected, better than Google maps. And it is international. And it shows you the numbers of the streets and houses. You can even download it and open it again when you have no internet" (O., thirty-two). O. illustrates the various challenges that occur in the country of arrival as well as the (digital) management of these difficulties. In his preferred app, several services converge, each of which would otherwise create its own challenges. For example, many refugees told us that they first had to come to terms with German street names and the public transport system (i.e., quite banal coordination of everyday life).

Here, digital services which can provide a *framework for orientation* can be helpful. Due to the use of the (same) Latin alphabet, it was much easier for English speakers to navigate in everyday urban life.

In addition to digital apps, the *camera* function was also frequently used. For example, interview partners described how they photographed and exchanged each other's location in order to be able to visually communicate their physical position. Combined with the WhatsApp "location" function, this was far more likely to be successful than simply mentioning street names. The camera also allowed a greater degree of control in a situation characterized by legal insecurity. For example, a Syrian woman reported how she photographed her own waiting number on the display at the former Berlin State Office for Health and Social Affairs (LAGeSo) so she had proof in case she would not be called in: something that had happened to other refugees previously.

In addition, mobile media are used for informal learning, demonstrating a global trend especially among children and young people (Hamm et al. 2014). For example, many refugees reported using language apps or digital language courses: "I have an app in Turkey I downloaded for learning languages" (P., twenty-seven). However, these language courses are usually so-called "freemium models," i.e., the basic functions are free, but in order to learn more vocabulary, one must subscribe or pay extra. This is difficult for many refugees, as they do not have a credit card, which is a requirement in most app stores. One way to avoid such models are YouTube tutorials. In this context, D. (twenty-three) explained to us: "I watch lessons on YouTube." In fact, there are several YouTube language courses that give aspiring learners a better understanding of the German language. These offers are mostly designed by amateurs or semiprofessionals, but they have a large following because of their appealing presentation and audiovisual character (figure 10.1).

Due to the lack of alternative media, the smartphone is not only used for communication or learning. It also provides spiritual support, for example via an app (Islamic Compass), that shows Muslims the direction of Mecca and prayer times using the GPS position, thus providing orientation. During the coordination phase, Facebook groups are also a great help when it comes to orientation needs: People exchange information about current developments and seek mutual assistance. For example, in the largest and best-known Syrian-German Facebook group "Syrian House" (البيت السوري) refugees and other Arabic-speaking Syrians support each other regarding their problems, whether they are issues with their residence status or finding accommodation. Communication with other refugees was equally as important as communication with families and friends in the home countries, and with those who had migrated and arrived in countries offering similar services (in our case, with one exception where relatives had located to Sweden, this was exclusively Germany).

Figure 10.1. YouTube Language Tutorial. Source: YouTube.

Verification Logistics

The study focused in particular on the question of how information is exchanged between actors. From a logistics point of view, there is the central question of anticipating and acting appropriately in different situations. For this purpose, the verification of information is essential. During the migration process, smartphones enable users to search for information about the journey and the countries of arrival; to navigate certain routes and avoid perceived dangers such as police, border patrols and robbers; to facilitate staying in contact with friends, family, and other migrants, and thus, smartphones become "digital travel companions." The emergency call functions give users a life-saving character, and at the same time this helps to reduce a dependency on traffickers. But where do migrants get this information from, and how does the verification process work? How exactly does this digital self-organization work? We were able to identify three different strategies:

The Chaotic Model

In example 1 (figure 10.2), dispersed communication practices were used for the groups: everyone gathered information and then decided how to proceed in joint discussions.

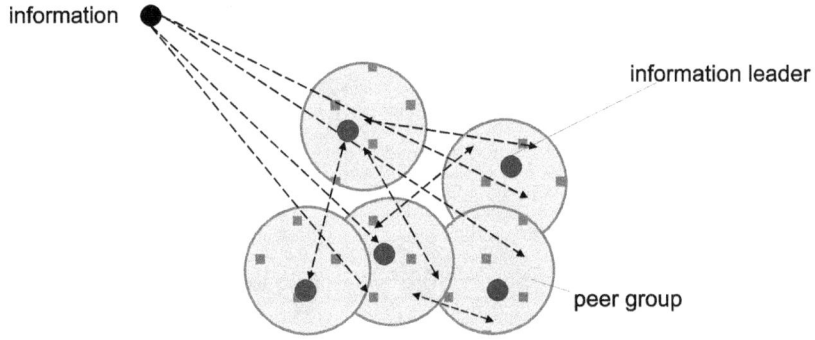

Figure 10.2. Verification of Information within the Chaotic Model. © Sina Arnold and Stephan O. Görland.

However, this grassroots model of verification turned out to be somewhat chaotic for many migrants. The fact that many people were gathering information at the same time resulted in a veritable information overload. Nevertheless, in this model, there were usually "information leaders" who decided how to proceed.

> But there's a leader. He leads the group. And those people, when they communicate, they have a lot of, yeah, connections everywhere. So any new information, they go to their leader. ... We informed us, and we should take this way or the other way. And [if] there are multiple confirmations or disinformation, then the leader in the group take[s] this way [MR1] (A., twenty-one)

The Hierarchical Model

Figure 10.3 shows a different strategy. In the summer and autumn of 2015, many refugees had to react flexibly to the insecure and constantly changing situations at European internal borders. Specifically, in these unreliable circumstances, digital media was a big help. One interviewee reported a change in the group size according to the changing circumstances. While a group of seventy people offered protection from predatory gangs in the border region of Macedonia/Greece, the subsequent division in Serbia was decided upon to avoid attracting attention from the police and state authorities. The group was divided so as not to appear suspicious: "But every group had someone [the group leader] who could use the internet and communicate with other groups" (H., twenty-two). Figure 10.3 also shows that the other

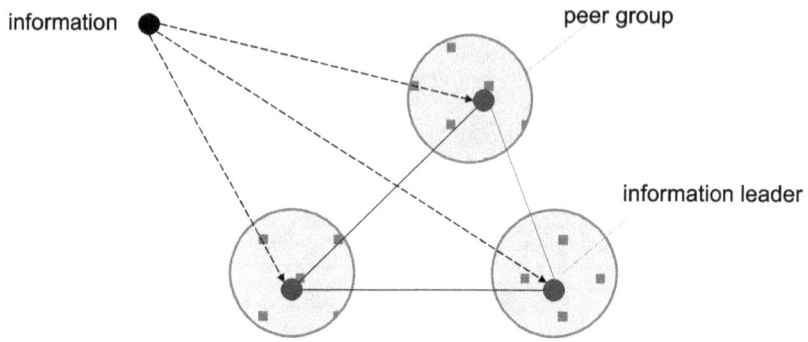

Figure 10.3. Verification of Information within the Hierarchical Model. © Sina Arnold and Stephan O. Görland.

group members switched off their phones to achieve an intended reduction in complexity. This reduction was based on the idea of possible monitoring by government agencies, e.g., by locating the devices. The groups wanted to ensure that they did not attract local attention. Group leaders were usually the people with the best language skills or the best mobile phone. These leaders continuously did their best to stay in touch, reporting back to their group members frequently.

The Gatekeeper Model

A third method of verification was the so-called gatekeeper model (figure 10.4). This describes a completely different approach to verification. Here, information is transmitted by a superordinate authority (i.e., the gatekeeper). This person constantly checks information on the migration route, the weather, and the latest news about the situation at the borders by obtaining it mainly from the destination country. This is partly done by acquaintances along the route, as well as by social media monitoring of known Facebook groups. A young refugee from Syria reported: "I called my father. My father and the whole family always look for everything in the news." Another interviewee agreed that his parents in the home country had done the same. The advantage of this method is obvious: by outsourcing the information search, it was possible to concentrate on the actual migration process. In addition, emotional support could also be given. For example, a young Syrian woman reported how she reached her family in the Berlin ref-

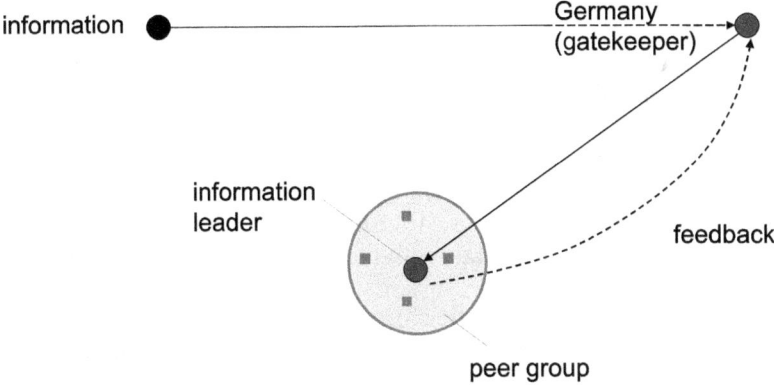

Figure 10.4. Verification of Information within the Gatekeeper Model. © Sina Arnold and Stephan O. Görland.

ugee shelter via Turkish roaming with her Syrian SIM card at the moment the engines of her boat stopped on the Mediterranean Sea. They engaged in a real-time connection and thus were able to provide emotional support in this situation.

On the basis of the logistics of verification, we see on the one hand individual patterns, which of course are also dependent on external circumstances and group size. On the other hand, all three models had a fixed peer group and chosen information leaders during the migration. One group offered protection and mutual support. The media always acted as an antenna to the rest of the group's converging world.

Discussion

Self-Empowerment via Smartphone: More Than a Feeling

All of the results, whether from quantitative surveys or qualitative interviews, show the great importance of the smartphone for refugees. The smartphone is their "window into the world," as one interview partner put it. The division in three different stages, before, during, and after the migration process (Karnowski et al. 2016; Krasnova and AbuJarour 2017), as has been practiced in many other studies, underestimates the importance of the smartphone in the everyday life of refugees. The general picture resulting from the different usage situations shows it as an object of self-empowerment, regardless of the situation in which the refugees find themselves. Often, the different stages are connected with each other: the refugees are planning their journey and downloading maps beforehand, so they can navigate offline while crossing different countries. One refugee told us how he prefers the label "traveler" instead of "refugee" because of the negative connotation of the latter. There are many interactions with crowds of "travelers" during the migration, the groups established in this way often maintaining contact for a long time after parting ways. After the arrival in the host country, the smartphone is still used to interact with family members and friends spread throughout different countries.

In summary, it can be said that the self-empowering character of the smartphone goes beyond the possibly directly intended character of the applications. Facebook, for example, was an important help in the migration. There were several different groups discussing the best path of migration, with names like "Travel to Greece from Izmir." Some of them had thousands or more members, often these discussions were short-lived. Some of them were run by traffickers, who sometimes presented themselves like a travel agency, with photos of happy "customers" arriving safely in the sunset. However, this online advertising also creates systems for comparing and monitoring prices and services; refugees were able to comment upon positive or negative experiences with certain traffickers. In addition, there are Facebook groups with names such as "Smuggle Yourself to Europe without a Trafficker," which help the "travelers" in navigating parts of the journey, especially overland routes, on their own.

Another example illustrates the self-empowerment character of the mobile phone. In September 2015, Hungarian police officers neglected to inform refugees traveling on a train headed to Austria and Germany that the Hungarian government intended for this train to return them to a refugee camp. Instead, the police gave wrong information (Nolan and Graham-Harrison 2015). The travelers still on the platform learned of the planned destination and were able to contact those on the already departing train, so that they could get off the train before the last stop and continue their journey to Austria on foot (Brunwasser 2015). Similarly, in the case of assaults, smartphones can assist in organizing help. One interviewee reported that after a robbery in Hungary, he was able to receive money from his uncle via Western Union's mobile money transfer service.

After their arrival in Germany, many refugees were surprised by the long time the German bureaucracy took to process their papers: the anticipated language courses had long waiting lists, and the allocation of private apartments instead of group accommodations took weeks, often months. Due to these circumstances, the smartphone became an "everyday companion," regardless of the gratification sought. For navigating in the new country, many refugees did "informal learning" via dictionaries, YouTube tutorials (figure

10.1), or other selected strategies; they tried to learn the German language as well as culture.

Based on the idea that digital networks are also a form of social practice that fits into real geographies (Trimikliniotis, Parsanoglou, and Tsianos 2015), refugees use digital technologies and social networks to participate in urban spaces. Digital platforms, for example, enable newcomers who are not yet part of an established civil society to access numerous services to communicate and interact within their new communities. As we were able to show, digital means can help in strengthening refugee organization vis-à-vis the state and bureaucracy. They can also assist in initiating meetings, finding self-help groups, or staging demonstrations for refugee rights. These platforms, put in use on the smartphone, thus help to instigate bottom-up processes of participation. If participation is power (Carpentier 2012), digital platforms help people without citizenship to assert their rights and become "digital citizens" (Isin and Ruppert 2015).

Our findings show that self-empowerment is definitely a bottom-up process. It is constituted through experiences and impressions but also through the specific logistical knowledge of the people concerned. As described, there are several so-called integration apps in Germany, initiated by state agencies. These are intended to help refugees acclimatize to the country. Out of ninety-seven respondents to the media consumption study, only eleven said that they had used such an app before, yet it lacked crucial services such as language translations, contact addresses, or assistance with healthcare. Instead, a young man noted that the apps have a strong focus on "cultural education." He criticized this focus, pointing to the fact that culture is something that is learned through everyday practice:

> I was like–they give you the information about integration in here. So it's like mostly talking about the cultures, how there are people living here. And when you are in the situation after ten months, nine months, you will see how people, they are living. And you would get used to these kind of groups. And maybe you can call that limitations or limit something like that. But you would get used to this, and you will understand that. It's something normal that happened to everybody. (M., twenty-nine)

Instead, as Gillespie et al. (2016: 14) have discovered, good practice proposals for designing digital resources for refugees need to be (1) user-centric, (2) secure and private, (3) accessible, (4) sustainable, (5) trusted, and (6) regularly updated. This undertaking is made easier if refugees themselves are participants in the design process as software developers and experts. Several initiatives, such as techfugees.com, have put these realizations into practice.

In summary, smartphone use among refugees highlights the high degree of (collective) self-empowerment that these devices enable, leading to greater independence from actors such as smugglers, state authorities, or border guards in different situations. In referring to an approach from critical migration studies that focuses on actor's agency (Mezzadra 2011), one could say that smartphones contribute to a certain "autonomy of migration."

Risks and Dangers

The increasing use of information technology during migration also brings "digital dangers," which point to systematic restrictions on participation attempts or even autonomy. The enforcement of European borders is partly aided by digital infrastructure. In an attempt to digitally control refugees, institutions like the United Nations High Commissioner for Refugees (UNHCR) have been using biometric data to identify populations on the move for well over a decade (Jacobsen 2015). In Europe, refugees have been registered in European Dactyloscopy (EURODAC), the European fingerprint database, since 2003. European expenditure on technological border control (drones, heat detectors, border protection robots, etc.) has increased in recent years (Proctor 2015). Gillespie et al. (2016: 29) report that soldiers asked refugees on the Syrian border for their Facebook passwords to find out if they were "regime friendly." In Austria, refugees are forced to hand in their mobile phones when applying for asylum; the mobile phone log files are then used to verify the applicant's identity (Young-Powell 2017). In Germany, mobile phones are increasingly playing a central role in these procedures as well, by means of new technologies that enable the Federal Ministry for Migration and Refugees (BAMF) to read out geodata (e.g., locations). In 2018, the mobile phones of 11,400 refugees were inspected for identity verification. The BAMF was able to find false information in only 2 percent of the cases (Lückoff 2019). In this context, Vassilis Tsianos and Brigitta Kuster (2010) spoke about "digital deportability," as the vulnerability and dangers that result from an increasing use of digital databases to monitor migrant movements become greater. Thus, the smartphone is a "double-edged sword" (Wall et al. 2017): it can be a potential source of danger if the data that enabled the migration process is subsequently read out and used against the asylum seeker.

Conclusion: Post-migrant Media Patterns

It is important to note that the use of media by new immigrants is hardly distinguishable from the media use of the majority society. Of course, there is a partial devotion to so-called "ethnomedia" that comes from the home country and deals with culturally related topics (Hepp and Düvel 2010).

However, this use is not exclusive but, rather, embedded in a broad media repertoire. Media culture is a global culture. Young people from Syria or Iraq are above all young people who are, in times of mediatized lifestyles, just as interested as their German peers in their stars on Instagram, the long-awaited update of a video game, or the latest action film with Jason Statham, all of which were reported to us during the qualitative interviews with young refugees. This puts into question notions on alleged homogenous "cultures of origin." On the contrary, young refugees' lifestyles are shaped by many different local and global factors, thanks to the digital world. This results in a cultural and identitarian mosaic that can be described as "post-migrant" (Foroutan 2016). The similarities of this global world–from Samsung through selfies to Skype–make it clear that the term "integration" is becoming increasingly fuzzy.

Stephan O. Görland is a postdoctoral fellow at the Centre for Media, Communication & Information Research (ZeMKI) at the University of Bremen. He studied communication science, psychology, law, and political science in Vienna from 2006 to 2011 and received his doctorate in 2018 at University of Rostock. His research topics are mobile media, social theory and media use, and migration and media use.

Sina Arnold is a postdoctoral researcher and lecturer at the Center for Research on Antisemitism/Zentrum für Antisemitismusforschung (ZfA) and the Research Institute Social Cohesion at Technische Universität Berlin, and an associate member of the Berlin Institute for Integration and Migration Research (BIM). She is a board member of the European Sociological Association's Research Network "Ethnic Relations, Racism and Antisemitism." A social anthropologist by training, she studied in Berlin and Manchester and has conducted fieldwork in Tanzania, Germany, Italy, and the United States. Her work focuses on antisemitism, social movements, anti-Muslim racism, "postmigrant" societies, refugees, and (post)national identities.

Notes

1. A good overview of the dynamic research in Europe since 2015 is illustrated, for example, by the *Sage Handbook of Media and Migration* (Smets et al. 2019).
2. The study was conducted as part of the research project "Solidarität im Wandel" (Changing solidarity) at the Berlin Institute for Migration and Integration Research (BIM) at Humboldt-Universität zu Berlin, funded by the Federal Commissioner for Migration, Refugees, and Integration of Germany.
3. For general mobile media usage data in Germany, see, e.g., Koch and Frees (2016).

References

Accenture, and UNHCR (United Nations High Commissioner for Refugees). 2016. *Connecting Refugees: How Internet and Mobile Connectivity can Improve Refugee Well-Being and Transform Humanitarian Action*. Retrieved 8 October 2021 from https://reliefweb.int/sites/reliefweb.int/files/resources/Connectingpercent 20Refugees.pdf.

Andrade, Antonio D., and Bill Doolin. 2016. "Information and Communication Technology and the Social Inclusion of Refugees." *MIS Quarterly* 2(40): 405–16. Retrieved 8 October 2021 from https://km4s.ca/wp-content/uploads/Informa tion-and-Communication-Technology-and-the-Social-Inclusion-of-Refugees-Diaz-Andrade-Antonio-and-Doolin-Bill.-2016.pdf.

Apicella, Sabrina, Sina Arnold, and Manuela Bojadžijev. 2018. "Logistik und Migration: Eine integrierte Perspektive für die empirischen Kulturwissenschaften" [Logistics and migration: An integrated perspective for empirical cultural studies]. In *Grounding Logistics: Ethnographische Zugriffe auf Logistik, Migration und Mobilität*, edited by Sabrina Apicella, Sina Arnold, Manuela Bojadžijev, 7–26. Berlin: Panama Verlag.

Arnold, Sina, and Stephan O. Görland. 2019. "Participatory Logistics from Below: The Role of Smartphones for Syrian Refugees." In *Media and Participation in Post-Migrant Societies*, edited by M. Stehling, T. Thomas, and M.-M. Kruse, 101–16. New York: Rowman and Littlefield.

Awad, Isabel, and Jonathan Tossell. 2019. "Is the Smartphone Always a Smart Choice? Against the Utilitarian View of the 'Connected Migrant.'" *Information, Communication & Society*: 1–16. https://doi.org/10.1080/1369118X.2019.1668456.

Borkert, Maren, Karen E. Fisher, and Eiad Yafi. 2018. "The Best, the Worst, and the Hardest to Find: How People, Mobiles, and Social Media Connect Migrants In(to) Europe." *Social Media + Society* 4(1). https://doi.org/10.1177/2056305118764428.

Bundesministerium für wirtschaftliche Zusammenarbeit und Entwicklung. 2016. *Entwicklung trifft Entwickler bei ICT4 Refugees-Konferenz* [Development meets developers at ICT4 Refugees Conference]. Retrieved 8 October 2021 from http://www.bmz.de/20160531-1.

Brunwasser, Matthew. 2015. "A 21st-Century Migrant's Essentials: Food, Shelter, Smartphone." *New York Times*, 25 August. Retrieved 8 October 2021 from https://www.nytimes.com/2015/08/26/world/europe/a-21st-century-migrants-check list-water-shelter-smartphone.html.

Carpentier, Nico. 2012. "The Concept of Participation. If They Have Access and Interact, Do They Really Participate?" *Fronteiras–Estudos Midiáticos* 14(2): 164–77. https://doi.org/10.4013/fem.2012.142.10.

Chase, Jefferson, and Wolfgang Dick. 2017. "Questions Surround German Government's Refugee Phone Surveillance Law." *Deutsche Welle*, 3 March. Retrieved 8 October 2021 from https://www.dw.com/en/questions-surround-german-gov ernments-refugee-phone-surveillance-law/a-38236850.

Coddington, Kate, and Alison Mountz. 2014. "Countering Isolation with the Use of Technology: How Asylum-Seeking Detainees on Islands in the Indian Ocean Use Social Media to Transcend Their Confinement." *Journal of the Indian Ocean Region* 10(1): 97–112. https://doi.org/10.1080/19480881.2014.896104.

Dekker, Rianne, Godfried Engbersen, Jeanine Klaver, and Hanna Vonk. 2018. "Smart Refugees: How Syrian Asylum Migrants Use Social Media Information in Migration Decision-Making." *Social Media + Society* 4(1). https://doi.org/10.1177/2056305118764439.

Diminescu, Dana. 2008. "The Connected Migrant: An Epistemological Manifesto." *Social Science Information* 47(4): 565–579. https://doi.org/10.1177/0539018408096447.

Foroutan, Naika. 2016. "Postmigrantische Gesellschaften" [Postmigrant societies]. In *Einwanderungsgesellschaft Deutschland*, edited by U. Brinkmann and M. Sauer, 227–54. Wiesbaden: VS Verlag für Sozialwissenschaften. https://doi.org/10.1007/978-3-658-05746-6_9.

Gillespie, Marie, Ampofo Lawrence, Margaret Cheesman, Becky Faith, Evgenia Illiou, Ali Issa, Souad Osseiran, and Dimitris Skleparis. 2016. *Mapping Refugee Media Journeys: Smartphones and Social Media Networks*. Retrieved 8 October 2021 from https://www.open.ac.uk/ccig/sites/www.open.ac.uk.ccig/files/Mappingpercent20Refugeepercent20Mediapercent20Journeyspercent2016percent20May percent20FIN percent20MG_0.pdf.

Gillespie, Marie, Souad Osseiran, and Margie Cheesman. 2018. "Syrian Refugees and the Digital Passage to Europe: Smartphone Infrastructures and Affordances." *Social Media + Society* 4(1). https://doi.org/10.1177/2056305118764440.

Görland, Stephan O. 2020. *Medien, Zeit und Beschleunigung: Mobile Mediennutzung in Interimszeiten* [Media, time, and acceleration: mobile media use in interim periods]. Wiesbaden: Verlag Für Sozialwissenschaften.

Harney, Nicholas. 2013. "Precarity, Affect and Problem Solving with Mobile Phones by Asylum Seekers, Refugees and Migrants in Naples, Italy." *Journal of Refugee Studies* 26(4): 541–57. https://doi.org/10.1093/jrs/fet017.

Hepp, Andreas, and Carolin Düvel. 2010. "Die kommunikative Vernetzung in der Diaspora: Integrations- und Segregationspotenziale der Aneignung digitaler Medien in ethnischen Migrationsgemeinschaften" [The communicative networking in the diaspora: integration and segregation potential of the acquisition of digital media in ethnic migrant communities]. In *Alltag in den Medien–Medien im Alltag*, edited by Jutta Röser, Tanja Thomas, and Corinna Peil, 261–81. Wiesbaden: VS Verlag für Sozialwissenschaften.

Hess, Sabine, Bernd Kasparek, Stefanie Kron, Mathias Rodatz, Maria Schwertl, and Simon Sontowski (eds). 2017. *Der lange Sommer der Migration* [The long summer of migration]. 2nd revised edition. Berlin: Assoziation A.

Isin, Engin, and Evelyn Ruppert. 2015. *Being Digital Citizens*. London: Rowman and Littlefield.

Karnowski, Veronika, Nina Springer, and Julia Herzer. 2016. "'I Was More of a Real Person. Now I'm Always on My Smartphone: Syrian Refugees': Use of Their Mobile Phones in and to Manage Their Journey to Europe." *ECREA Pre-Conference Media and Migration*. 7 November.

Koch, Von Wolfgang, and Beate Frees. 2016. "Dynamische Entwicklung bei mobiler Internetnutzung sowie Audios und Videos" [Dynamic development in mobile internet use as well as audio and video]. *Media Perspektiven* 9: 418–37.

Krasnova, Hanna, and Safa'A AbuJarour. 2017. "Understanding the Role of ICTs in Promoting Social Inclusion: The Case of Syrian Refugees in Germany." *Proceedings of the 25th European Conference on Information Systems (ECIS)*, 1792–806.

Kutscher, Nadia, and Lisa-Marie Kreß. 2015. *Internet ist gleich mit Essen: Empirische Studie zur Nutzung digitaler Medien durch unbegleitete minderjährige Flüchtlinge* [Internet is the same as food: empirical study on the use of digital media by unaccompanied refugee minors]. Universität Vechta. Retrieved 8 October 2021 from https://images.dkhw.de/fileadmin/Redaktion/1.1_Startseite/3_Nachrichten/Studie_Fluechtlingskinder-digitale_Medien/Studie_Fluechtlingskinder_und_digitale_Medien_Zusammenfassung.pdf.

Lückoff, Von J. 2019. "Viele Daten, wenig Nutzen" [Lots of data, little use]. *Tagesschau*. 16 February. https://www.tagesschau.de/inland/handydaten-fluechtlinge-101.html.

Mancini, Tziana, Federica Sibilla, Dimitris Argiropoulos, Michele Rossi, and Marina Everri. 2019. "The Opportunities and Risks of Mobile Phones for Refugees" Experience: A Scoping Review." *Plos One* 14(12). https://doi.org/10.1371/journal.pone.0225684.

Madianou, Mirca. 2014. "Polymedia Communication and Mediatized Migration: an Ethnographic Approach." In *Mediatization of Communication*, edited by Knut Lundby, 323–46. Berlin: De Gruyter. https://doi.org/10.1515/9783110272215.323.

Meyer, Von Christoph. 2015. "Handys sind für Flüchtlinge kein Luxus" [Cell phones are not a luxury for refugees]. *Süddeutsche Zeitung*, 11 August. Retrieved 8 October 2021 from https://www.sueddeutsche.de/panorama/vorurteile-warum-handys-fuer-fluechtlinge-kein-luxusartikel-sind-1.2603717.

Mezzadra, Sandro. 2011. "The Gaze of Autonomy: Capitalism, Migration and Social Struggles." In *The Contested Politics of Mobility: Borderzones and Irregularity*, edited by V. Squire, 121–42. London: Routledge.

———. 2017. "Digital Mobility, Logistics, and the Politics of Migration." *Spheres: Journal for Digital Cultures, Media and Migration* (4): 1–4.

Mezzadra, Sandro, and Brett Neilson. 2013. *Border as Method, or the Multiplication of Labor*. Durham, NC: Duke University Press.

Nolan, Daniel, and Emma Graham-Harrison. 2015. "Hungarian Police Order Refugees Off Train Heading to Austrian Border. | *Guardian*, 3 September. Retrieved 8 October 2021 from https://www.theguardian.com/world/2015/sep/03/budapest-station-reopens-no-trains-running-western-europe-migration-crisis-europe.

Proctor, Keith. 2015. "Europe's Migrant Crisis: Defense Contractors Are Poised to Win Big." *Fortune*, 10 September. Retrieved 8 October 2021 from http://fortune.com/2015/09/10/europe-migrant-crisis-defense-contractors/.

Richter, Carola, Marlene Kunst, and Martin Emmer. 2016. "Aus der Forschungspraxis: Flucht 2.0–Erfahrungen zur Befragung von Flüchtlingen zu ihrer mobilen Mediennutzung" [From research practice: Escape 2.0–Experiences of interviewing refugees about their mobile media use]. *Global Media Journal–German Edition* 6(1).

Risam, Roopika. 2018. "Now You See Them: Self-Representation and the Refugee Selfie." *Popular Communication* 16(1): 58–71. https://doi.org/10.1080/15405702.2017.1413191.

Smets, Kevin, Koen Leurs, Myria Georgiou, Saskia Witteborn, and Radhika Gajjala. 2019. *The Sage Handbook of Media and Migration*. Thousand Oaks: Sage.

Thrift, Nigel. 2008. *Non-representational Theory: Space, Politics, Affect*. London: Routledge.

Trimikliniotis, Nicos, et al. 2015. *Mobile Commons, Migrant Digitalities and the Right to the City*. London: Palgrave Macmillan.

Tsianos, Vassilis, and Brigitta Kuster. 2010. *Border Crossings*. Transnational Digital Networks, Migration and Gender. Retrieved 8 October 2021 from http://www.mignetproject.eu/wp-content/uploads/2012/10/MIGNET_Deliverable_6_Thematic_report_Border_crossings.pdf.

Vertovec, Steven. 2004. Cheap Calls: "The Social Glue of Migrant Transnationalism." *Global Networks* 4(2): 219–24. https://doi.org/10.1111/j.1471-0374.2004.00088.x.

Wall, Melissa, Madeline Otis Campbell, and Dana Janbek. 2015. "Syrian Refugees and Information Precarity." *New Media & Society* 19(2): 240–54. https://doi.org/10.1177/1461444815591967.

Witteborn, Saskia. 2015. "Becoming (Im)Perceptible: Forced Migrants and Virtual Practice." *Journal of Refugee Studies* 28(3): 350–367. https://doi.org/10.1093/jrs/feu036.

Young-Powell, Abby. 2017. "Asylum Seekers Will Have to Hand over Cash and Phones, Austria's New Coalition Says." *Telegraph*, 18 December. Retrieved 8 October 2021 from http://www.telegraph.co.uk/news/2017/12/18/austrian-far-right-sworn-government-amid-protests/.

11

Processes of Wage Theft
The Neoliberal Labor Market and Syrian Refugees in Turkey

Danièle Bélanger and Cenk Saraçoğlu

The unprecedented influx of Syrian refugees into Turkey since the onset of the Syrian civil war in 2011 has made this country home to the largest number of refugees worldwide. As of 2021, the number of registered Syrian refugees in Turkey reached 3.7 million (UNHCR 2021). The Turkish government, which does not grant official refugee status to war-displaced people from the Middle East, implemented the Foreigners and International Protection Law in April 2013.[1] Based on Article 91 of this law, the Turkish government issued a temporary protection regulation in 2014 that applied specifically to the conditions of Syrians who were designated to be in mass influx seeking immediate protection. This new regulation granted Syrian refugees access to services, including public education and healthcare. With return prospects diminishing after 2011, Syrians, who have been dispersed across various towns and cities, had to build a sustainable life in Turkey and, hence, had to participate in the labor market to generate income. Under these circumstances, an additional decree took effect in January 2016 that provided Syrians with the right to obtain a work permit. According to this decree, a registered Syrian refugee can obtain a work permit only in the province of registration (TEPAV 2018). Moreover, the number of employed Syrians in a workplace cannot exceed 10 percent of the total number of Turkish citizens at that workplace. As such, due to structural obstacles to formal employment, including strict rules, cumbersome and costly bureaucratic procedures, and language barriers, a very small percentage of employed Syrians were able to regularize their situation (Del Carpio, Şeker, and Yener 2018). As of the end of 2018, only 28,000 Syrians had work permits, which meant that most of them were employed informally without authorization.[2]

While a small segment of Syrians with sufficient capital set up businesses and became entrepreneurs, the majority of them, without capital and language barriers, had no choice but to sell their labor power on the informal labor market under precarious conditions in low-wage jobs in the textile, construction, agriculture, and food service sectors. It is estimated, as of 2018, that approximately 650,000 Syrians work informally (Erdoğdu 2018: 844; Erol et al. 2017). In this context, the Syrian refugee issue in Turkey can no longer be circumscribed to a legal relationship between the state and asylum seekers. Syrians in Turkey need to be treated not only as refugees but also as displaced migrant workers engaging in specific social relations with business and capital owners on the one hand and Turkish workers on the other.

The focus of recent academic studies has shifted from discussing Syrians' precarious legal status and limited rights to empirically documenting aspects of their lives, including labor processes (Bélanger and Saraçoğlu 2018; Canefe 2016; Danış 2016; Erol et al. 2017; Lordoğlu and Aslan 2016). By focusing on various sectors of the labor market where informal employment is prevalent for both local Turkish workers and Syrian refugees, these studies document how Turkish business and capital owners impose lower wages, longer working hours, greater control, and less secure conditions on the Syrian refugees compared to the Turkish laborers working under similar exploitative conditions in the same sector. These studies also suggest that, relative to other workers, Syrians are more likely to be the target of workplace abuses, including wage theft, sexual harassment, and physical violence.

The status of Syrians as non-citizen war exiles enables capital and business owners to impose such severe conditions on Syrians. The need to generate income forces Syrians to take on work under terrible conditions. Lack of monitoring, the indifference of state authorities toward workplace abuses, and the absence of support from Turkish workers who are also vulnerable in the context of the economic crisis contributed to Syrian workers' extreme precarity. Turkish capital owners are able to avoid legal and social safeguards and continue exploiting Syrian workers. In this respect, Syrian laborers fulfill a function for Turkish capital similar to that of temporary migrant workers and undocumented migrants employed in advanced capitalist countries and the Gulf region where the capital bypasses the domestic labor codes and regulations to exploit workers and accumulate capital (Hanieh 2015; Anderson 2010).[3]

As such, the conditions of the Syrian refugees in labor processes need to be situated within the context of their relations with capital owners, the state, and other workers. This vantage point opens new avenues to unravel the situation of Syrian refugees in Turkey. This research aims to further document these relationships by focusing on practices of wage theft or unpaid salaries that Syrian refugees commonly experience. Wage theft is by no means unique to Syrian refugees in Turkey, but Syrians are much more vulnerable to capital owners' utilization of it when they bypass social and legal limits to labor exploitation. An analysis of wage theft processes furthers the understanding of how the temporary protection regime equips the Turkish capital with more capacity to overcome domestic legal and social limits to exploitation and capital accumulation. In these very difficult conditions, some Syrians, however, deploy strategies to mitigate their precarious situation, albeit with very limited success. This analysis builds on fieldwork we carried out in Izmir between 2016 and 2018, which includes in-depth interviews with Turkish workers, business owners, and Syrian workers employed in different labor-intensive sectors.

Wage Theft: Definition and Cases

Wage theft falls under the broader practices of wage-related violations.[4] Because of its prevalence in certain jobs in both formal and informal sectors, it is often studied as a key indicator of labor standard violations and a severe form of labor exploitation. Wage theft is defined as the partial payment or nonpayment of wages that should have been paid to a worker for work already performed. Moreover, wage theft occurs when a standard wage (such as minimum wage) or the wage agreed to by an employer and a worker is not paid in its entirety in due time (i.e., weekly, bimonthly, or monthly). Other examples of wage theft include the following: mandatory unpaid probation or training periods, theft of tips, denial of rest or meal times, mandatory safety deposits (for instance, to prevent job desertion), mandatory unpaid or underpaid overtime work, unfair salary deductions (for example, fees for labor brokers or washroom use), and deduction or withholding of a portion of wages ("mandatory savings") to be paid (theoretically) only upon termination of employment (Dasse 2012; Taykhman 2016). In some contexts, employees who are victims of wage theft may seek redress, but often employers will hide assets in order to prevent employees who win their case in court from collecting judgments. Worldwide, numerous forms of wage theft are widespread and amount to very large unpaid sums. These violations entail very negative consequences for workers and their families.

An extensive body of research documents the endemic character of various forms of wage theft practices, particularly in low-wage jobs. In the United States, for example, a number of surveys done in large metropolitan areas, including Los Angeles (Milkman, González, and Narro 2010), Austin (Galvin 2016), and New York (Dasse 2012), provide evidence of systemic practices of wage theft toward workers in construction, hospitality, agriculture, and service sectors where monitoring is considered difficult to enforce (Fussell 2011). Studies on construction workers in countries such as Germany (Gibney 2000), Dubai (Buckley 2013), and Singapore (Charanpal 2015), for example, indicate systemic wage theft in this sector.

While widespread in all forms of employment, the occurrence of wage theft is higher, however, in the informal sector, the largest employment sector worldwide. Migrants with precarious status, including documented temporary migrants and migrants in irregular situations, are more likely to experience wage-related violations than others. According to research on the United States, undocumented Latino workers are particularly at risk of experiencing wage theft (Fussell 2011). Quantitative estimates based on survey data indicate that, nationally, nearly 50 percent of day laborers (many of whom are undocumented) reported at least one instance of underpayment of wages (Theodore, Valenzuela, and Meléndez 2009). Studies in the United States also indicate that gender matters: women are more likely to experience wage theft than men whether or not they are documented, American-born, Black, or working in specific sectors (Petrescu-Prahova and Spiller 2016).

Mechanisms for seeking redress exist, particularly for workers in the formal sector who are covered by labor codes and laws. Among precarious migrants, including those without a work and/or residence authorization, reporting wage theft is generally extremely difficult due to fear of retaliation from the employer. Being fired, reported to authorities, or illicitly detained are among common fears experienced by workers suffering wage theft. For undocumented migrants or migrants with precarious status, fear of deportation stands as the most critical concern: complaints or wage claims to the employer or a third party are nearly impossible when the migrant is deportable due to the unauthorized residence and/or employment.

In the case studied in this analysis, Syrians in Turkey have the authorization to reside in Turkey, but most do not have a work permit and, therefore, work informally. As non-citizens, their employment is unlawful, and thus they may suffer sanctions, including being caught by police and, in some cases, being deported. Despite such constraining environments, precarious workers who suffer from wage theft may deploy various strategies to mitigate their situations. For example, construction workers from South and Southeast Asia in Singapore who frequently experience deportation threats and physical and verbal intimidation use tactical accommodations when confronted with wage-related violations in order to obtain favors, including more hours of work or better jobs (Charanpal 2015). In Canada, temporary agricultural workers who suffer wage-related violations (not being paid hourly as they should be, for instance) may adopt compliant behavior to secure their jobs for the following agricultural season (Basok, Bélanger, and Rivas 2014).

In sum, the existing research on wage theft captures the contradiction between economic inclusion through employment and exclusion and marginalization due to the extreme forms of abuse these workers are subjected to, along with the very few avenues they have for claiming their rights and seeking redress (Sung et al. 2013). The study of experiences of wage theft among Syrian workers in Turkey contributes to understanding the stronghold capital and business owners have on them as well as the contradictory position workers find themselves in as legal residents but unauthorized workers.

Syrian Refugee Workers in Izmir, Turkey

This analysis is part of a larger project on relations within the Turkish society, including employers, citizens, nongovernmental organizations, and Syrian refugees. A total of ten field visits were conducted in Izmir in 2016, 2017, and 2018, as well as one in Gaziantep and Antakya in 2016. The first part of the project, based on seventy-eight interviews with municipality officials, NGO employees, business owners, and workers, focused on the governance of Syrian refugees and the relationships among these actors (Bélanger and Saraçoğlu 2018), the social construction of Syrian refugees among various groups in Turkish society (Saraçoğlu and Bélanger 2019b), and the political construction of the Syrian refugee crisis in Turkey (Saraçoğlu and Bélanger 2019a).

In 2018, we conducted in-depth interviews in Izmir, Turkey, with thirty Syrian refugees who had migrated to Turkey seeking refuge from the war that began in 2011 and were registered with state authorities under the Temporary Protection Regime. The first fifteen interviews were conducted on the premises of a nongovernmental organization that provides services to Syrians in Izmir. Our interviewees lived in the neighborhood when they first arrived in Izmir, and while some had moved, others were still living there. Some interviewees still used the services of this organization, particularly its Turkish language classes. The association introduced us to potential participants according to the criteria we provided, including gender, age, and work situation. The interview guidelines of the first fieldwork explored the participants' circumstances of leaving Syria, their trajectories, and their life and work experiences in Turkey. The second set of fifteen interviews were conducted with Syrians in a location of their choice, their home, or a public place (café, restaurant). For this group, the interview was more focused on insertion into the labor market, employment experiences, and working conditions. We asked questions about each employer as well the employment situation and history of family members, including children, spouses, and other cohabiting relatives. A few also provided information about close friends. All interviews were fully transcribed and translated to English by a native Arabic-speaking professional translator. Both authors of this chapter were present for all interviews. In total, we interviewed eleven men and nineteen women: nine were unemployed, one was working as a volunteer in a school, and the others were employed, full-time or part-time.

The theme of wage theft was not anticipated prior to the research, but it emerged as a very systematic experience of workers in low-wage jobs and loomed large in participants' narratives about their experiences in Turkey. This chapter primarily relies on the second set of interviews but is also informed by the first set, as well as all other interviews conducted as part of this project, including interviews with employers and NGO workers.

Making a Living in Izmir

Our sample of thirty interviewees indicates three subgroups with respect to work and income. The first group included families with unemployed parents (one in the case of single-parent families), who relied on their children's labor and, in some instances, received supplementary income from allowances donated by organizations, like the Red Cross and NGOs, on the basis of certain eligibility criteria. A strategy we noted in some families was to have some children in the home working to allow other children to remain in school. The second group was composed of families with at least one parent working for low wages in a labor-intensive sector. In these families, there were different configurations: both spouses may be employed, or one or more children may also be working. In the third group, we have a subset of families with one adult income earner holding a professional job. Most of these interviewees worked as teachers in temporary education centers and did not experience wage theft. Some of them, however, only worked a few hours a week, which resulted in a low but reliable income. Apart from the teachers, all others worked informally and only had a verbal agreement with their employer; among them, as we will see, wage theft was a very common experience.

Individual average monthly income among the eighteen interviewees who were employed was 1,500 Turkish liras (US$258). The household income of our interviewees varied between 1,700 and 4,800 Turkish liras per month, with an average of 2,600 Turkish liras (US$473/month). Average household size was 5.3 persons; thus, the average monthly available income per household member was 502 liras (US$89). These incomes are significantly below the legal minimum wage of US$418 per month and the national average household income per capita, which was US$3,604 in 2017. The poverty line set by the Turkish government for 2017 was 5,000 Turkish liras (US$861) per month for a family of four. The average household income of the Syrian families we interviewed was more than half below this threshold, and the average household size was above four.

Among the participants occupying low-wage jobs for whom we have detailed employment histories, fourteen reported an incidence of wage theft that happened to them or to a close family member (a few mentioned incidents that happened to a close friend). In total, the narratives provide information for twenty-six workers (participants and people close to them) who were subject to wage theft at least once, for a total of thirty-four cases/instances perpetrated by thirty-four different employers (some workers experienced it with more than one employer). Some interviewees did not elaborate on the work-related violations they suffered, so we underestimate the prevalence of wage theft among our interviewees and their family members. Nonetheless, stories of wage theft were recurrent and similar across interviewees in labor-intensive sectors, pointing to an existing pattern.

The most common types of wage theft occurred when workers' wages went unpaid, were delayed, and/or were only partially paid. For example, in some cases, employers told workers that a portion of their salary would be retained until the end of their employment. The following section of this chapter discusses the relationships that unfolded in instances of wage-related violations between employers, Syrian workers, Turkish workers, and state authorities. Unbalanced power relations are central to the dynamics that unfolded, due to workers' fear of being denied overdue wages, fired, reported to authorities (because of unauthorized employment), detained, or deported. The analysis shows how, among our study participants, the Syrian informal workforce in working-class jobs is used as a disposable workforce and, thus, experiences very severe forms of exploitation.

Processes of Wage Theft in Izmir

Processes and consequences of wage theft capture the extreme precarity of Syrian workers in low-wage jobs in the Turkish labor market. As noncitizens without authorization to work, they live in a liminal situation that exposes them to various forms of labor exploitation. We provide cases from our interviewees to illustrate the extent of the power imbalance and the consequences on workers and their families. In some cases, however, interviewees made attempts to seek redress when suffering from wage theft, but given their lack of access to legal recourse, their only option was to negotiate directly with their employer. As we documented elsewhere (Bélanger and Saraçoğlu 2018), NGOs are very careful in assisting workers in seeking redress because they fear exposing them as unauthorized workers. We interviewed NGO workers who instead focused on encouraging employers to obtain work permits for their Syrian workers. None of the Syrians we interviewed contacted nongovernmental organizations when experiencing work-related violations. As nonauthorized workers, they have absolutely no ability to claim workers' rights to state authorities.

As in many other countries, skilled workers also suffered from low wages because they could not obtain recognition for their skills. As unauthorized workers, they were, in addition, subject to frequent wage theft. Ibrahim was a professional truck driver in Syria and drove internationally to all neighboring countries, using an international driver's license he had obtained legally in Syria. He earned a good salary and enjoyed good working conditions. After he arrived in Turkey, he could not get a Turkish driving license, and his international one was not recognized by his employer.

> Ibrahim: They think that my driver's license from Syria is fake, so I have to bring them very old evidence to tell them that I am a driver with experience. I tell them to test me, but they don't believe me. They think that maybe I made fake documents. If someday they believe that my documents are authentic then they would give me the license for free. But they don't believe me because I am not a Turkish citizen.

In this case, Ibrahim is forced into a deskilling process whereby he is employed for other manual jobs requiring no professional skills and is frequently subject to wage-related violations. As many others, he felt powerless because he could not complain about this situation to anyone. This situation was felt by Ibrahim as a crisis of identity and masculinity because he could not adequately provide for his family. His wife expressed a desire to work, but Ibrahim refused, stating that he has to solve this license issue first and that his family would be fine afterward.

> Interviewer: When you weren't getting paid in Mersin did you think of going to a police station and filing a complaint or lawsuit against them?
>
> Ibrahim: No, it didn't cross my mind, and the trip would have been a waste anyways because they would have asked me for proof. Where is my proof? Where would I get any evidence from? There is no proof that my boss is not giving me any money. There are four employers here that scammed me. I was robbed of 5,000 liras. One of them took 1,200 from me, another took 1,100, and another took 700. The total is about 5,000, and no one paid me back that money. I went to one of them and told him that if he doesn't pay me the money then I would spill his oil. He told me to just go and there's nothing he could do. God will pay me back.

In his case, he even moved from Mersin to Izmir, hoping to find better working conditions, but he continued to face the same problems. Cases of internal migration within Turkey for finding better employment (in this case any employment, but with an employer that honors the verbal contract) was common among our study participants.

Bassam, who worked as a pastry cook and baker in Syria, found work in an ironing business where he was not paid at all during six months of work; the boss told him every time he did not have money and that he would pay him the following month. He then left for another employer, but the new boss underpays him, pays him late, and intimidates and threatens him.

> Bassam: I worked there for a while [six months without pay] and then I went around a few places until I found a place where they offered 400 liras for the same job [ironing]. But they treat me really poorly. They don't pay you what you deserve; they don't give me the money. Yesterday, I worked till 18:30 and I wanted to go home, but they wouldn't let me; they told me that if I went home then I shouldn't come back. "Go home but don't return." This happens every day.
>
> Heba (his wife): And he can't quit and find another job because they owe him money.
>
> Interviewer: How much does he owe you?
>
> Bassam: About 1,800 or 1,700.

Every payday, Bassam only receives about half of the promised income (200 liras instead of 400 (US$33 instead of US$66), and he is not paid for the overtime he is forced to do on a daily basis. His situation is akin to forced labor in a situation of servitude. His wife Heba explains:

> Heba: Working late is fine, but they don't pay them for it. They were supposed to pay him 400 liras on Saturday, but they only give him 200, and because they owe you money, they guarantee that you will come back. But they never give the money. Every Saturday we pray for them to give the money, but they never do. Everyone in the family is constantly praying to God, so he will be paid his salary.

Facing a very low and unpredictable income, Heba explains how she struggles with landlords to pay rent. The family wanted to move to another place because they could no longer afford their rent. After she found the place and agreed on the rent, the new landlord increased the rent before they moved in. This situation was experienced by other participants as well.

> Heba: When I went to pay the deposit before we moved, they said that we needed to sign a contract, and I saw that rent was 460. I told him that we want to move because we thought the rent was supposed to be 380, but he just said that it just increased. We told him that we couldn't pay that amount, so he reduced it to 440, but I told him that it's still too much. I asked him to reduce it to 400, but he refused ... and then he agreed to 425, but that he would increase the rent by 50 liras every year. And then he told us to register the electricity meter in our name and pay 300. We told him that we couldn't do

that, but he told us to come back next month when we can pay the rent and take care of the electricity. He tricked us and lied to us.

Teenage workers are particularly at risk for wage-related violations. When Mahmud was fifteen, he and his brothers could no longer go to school after they sought refuge in Turkey, and they worked in various small garment shops to support their family. They earned extremely low incomes (about US$30/week, so four to five times below Turkey's minimum wage), but these very regularly went unpaid or were partially paid. When workers complained, the boss fired them; in one instance, one boss just left the premises and "shut down" the shop.

Some employers hire Syrian labor as a "family." We had instances of these practices in two sectors: agriculture and retail. In one case, Nooran, her husband, and their seven children worked in agriculture in the region of Torbalı. They lived in tents alongside other Syrian families, had no access to showers, and received meager rations of cold food while they worked peeling, coring, and removing the pith of large quantities of oranges all day. Every month, their employer promised to pay them the following month. After six months of full-time work without pay, they had to run away because the husband was severely ill. They never received compensation for their forced labor.

Rahima's family worked in a store where wages were arbitrary and not paid regularly. The boss frequently complained they were not doing enough "as a family." After her son did not receive his wages, Rahima decided the whole family would leave the employer. She then found another job, offered by her landlord, but she found herself in another exploitative relationship.

Her case was similar to others because her employer was also her landlord.[5] In these cases, landlords directly retained wages in lieu of rent payment, although this arrangement was never discussed prior to the beginning of employment. Rahima was offered a job in her landlord's restaurant. After she began working, the owner withheld her salary, saying it was for rent and electricity. This dual dependence made her family particularly vulnerable to eviction and extreme poverty.

These examples illustrate that wage theft processes generally entailed nonpayment, partial payment, and late payment of wages, often combined with other dependencies, like access to housing, food, etc. In fact, verbal agreements rarely had any value. and only after some weeks of work could workers really know their employer's intentions. So much uncertainty resulted in very unpredictable incomes, and this had repercussions in all spheres of their lives. Women talked about the difficulty in providing adequate clothes and school material for their children, who then easily became the target of schoolyard bullies. The urgent need to find cheaper housing was also common for participants who could not secure a minimal steady income. As indicated above, some families migrated within Turkey, seeking less exploitative relationships. Nonetheless, despite bleak prospects for fair treatment, some workers, as we will see, actively sought to improve their situation, but any improvement did not come from solidarity with Turkish workers, who were themselves feeling precarious and/or threatened by the presence of Syrian workers.

Relationships with Turkish Workers

Most Syrians work alongside Turkish workers for the same employers. In some cases, the Turkish workers were also employed informally, and in others they had lawful contracts and other benefits. Hozan, for example, is the only Syrian worker in his workplace and suffers from partially paid wages from his employer of two years. His employer owes him more than 4,000 liras, which he will forfeit if he leaves his job. When asked about whether he receives support from Turkish workers, he says it is impossible since their communication is minimal.

In all cases, Syrians report knowing that they earned less than their Turkish counterparts doing the same job. When asked about forms of solidarity among them, Syrians report having cordial relationships, but, when problems arise, Turkish workers do not support or stand up for them.

> Interviewer: How much do the Turkish workers earn?
>
> Hozan: Honestly, they earn 150 liras more per day, and I work more hours than they do. The boss does this because we're Syrian.
>
> Interviewer: Do you talk with the Turkish workers about this? Do you ask them to stand by your side?
>
> Hozan: No one is standing by our side because we're Syrian.

In some larger workplaces with more employees, workers do not share the same socializing spaces. This spatial division maintained segregation and prevented the development of solidarity. In these cases, differences along national lines were reinforced, and communication was kept to a minimum. In one workplace, Syrian and Turkish workers did not eat their meals in the same place.

> Muhammed: The Syrians would drink tea together. When it came to food, Turkish workers had this special restaurant for them while we ate in the warehouse.

As indicated in our previous fieldwork (Bélanger and Saraçoğlu 2018), precarious Turkish workers employed informally feared being displaced by Syrian workers; hence, it was difficult to develop bonds of solidarity with them. Employers' differential treatment and special workplace arrangements further entrench divisions among workers. While both groups are marginalized in the Turkish labor market, employment practices and frequent negative discourse about Syrians from some employers together create a climate of divisive politics hampering collective claims for better working conditions. More politically engaged ethnic Kurdish and Turkish workers expressed empathy for Syrians, but, at the same time, they were so preoccupied with their own precarity and downward socioeconomic mobility, given the economic crisis, that it was difficult for them to overcome fear of displacement, which was, to some extent, already taking place in some workplaces (Saraçoğlu and Bélanger 2019b).

Workers' Strategies vis-à-vis Wage Theft

When confronting wage theft and other labor rights violations, workers deployed various strategies to mitigate the situation. An immediate change of employer was possible when workers had another job opening immediately. Some left their employer without another job because their family had more than one worker and they could survive through a period of unemployment.

Leila for instance, tells the story of how her husband was not paid after his first month of work. He changed jobs immediately.

> Leila: He was supposed to be paid a monthly salary, but he didn't get a salary the first month, so he quit and found another job. His first boss didn't pay him what he earned. But then he gave him 100 every once in a while, but he didn't get all of it. Over here if you don't manage to get your first payment at the end of the month then it is lost forever.

Some workers shared stories of attempts to report wage theft to the police, but all were told that they could not file a complaint of this type. For instance, Amira, whose husband was not paid at all for an entire month, explains why it was useless to go to the police.

> Interviewer: Have you thought of going to the police?
>
> Amira: No, we didn't.
>
> Interviewer: Do you think that going to the police would have helped you?
>
> Amira: My cousin, who's in Germany now, was living here with four children and worked as a tailor, and my other uncle lived with them as well, so they were five people in the house.
>
> Interviewer: Your uncle?

> Amira: Yes. They weren't paid their salaries for three months. He went to file a complaint at the police station, but they told him that he's a refugee and has no right to complain. This is why they went to Germany–illegally.

For Heba, not being able to complain stripped her of her agency and the ability to exert power over her life and destiny.

> Heba: If you go file a complaint, they will tell you that no one owes you anything, and you have no right to anything. If I try to take matters into my own hands then they will put me in jail.

Mothers with working children sometimes claimed their children's salaries. When her son, Asser, was not paid for his work, Rahima contacted his employer.

> Rahima: I went and spoke to Asser's boss and told him that he owed my son 300 liras, and I asked him why he wasn't paying him. He told me that he does give him money, but he saw that I am just an old concerned mother, so he told me that he only had 50 liras on him at that moment, so I asked him when he would pay us the rest, and he started saying to come back next week, but I said no. I said that I don't have time to come back here all the time, so I asked him to give me the money right now or in two weeks. I took some of the rest, but there was still 50 liras left. But at least I was able to get 250 liras. I went to his workplace in Çankaya twice as well, and I managed to get 200 liras, but they still owed him some money. I am glad that he's going to school now though, I'm just annoyed at what happened. Sometimes I consider immigrating somewhere else for their sake. For their future. I am learning English.

In workplaces where many Syrians worked together and the work required skills and experience to meet tight factory orders, Syrians had more ability to claim unpaid wages without fear of immediate retaliation. For example, Muhammed worked for some time at a factory assembling lamps where nearly twenty Syrians were employed. The boss very frequently withheld wages on payday. Whenever this happened, Syrians held a spontaneous strike to claim their salary.

> Muhammed: We did get a salary, but they constantly were late in giving them out. It was a monthly salary, and it was always late, so we, as Syrian workers, would go on strike because we wanted to know why it was late as the new month would begin. We held a strike against the owner asking him why he wouldn't give us our salaries. We formed a strike on the fifth of the month, and they would be as late as fifteen days into the next month even after the strike where we would ask "Where are our salaries? We need our salaries!" and so on.
>
> Interviewer: A strike?
>
> Muhammed: A strike where we would stop working because our salaries were late. Our boss was very difficult to deal with, and he was really mean. We

had to work for ten hours at a really high speed and productivity rate, and we never slacked. Work was going well, and we were hard workers and never slacked off, but then they would be late in giving out our salaries and cause these issues.

Despite the success of their protests, Syrian workers in this workplace still feared sabotage and arbitrary dismissal.

> Muhammed: It's not that he didn't like Syrians; it's just that if there was one bad Syrian, like if someone went and told him that one of the Syrian workers is bad, then he would just fire them without really knowing what happened. That's what he was like; everything was just according to his mood. There was no justice.

In response to wage theft and other work-related abuses, workers disciplined themselves to accept the situation to avoid problems. Many talked about not going out, avoiding public places, keeping a low profile, and self-excluding themselves socially, always fearful of exposing themselves to situations that could further harm them and their families. All interviewees had internalized the fact that they had no rights in Turkey; they could only survive and wait.

> Interviewer: When you were treated poorly by those Turkish workers did you discuss it among yourselves as Syrian workers?
>
> Roshan: Yes.
>
> Interviewer: What did you tell each other?
>
> Roshan: We told each other that we had to stay strong because we were in a foreign country and that we should be patient. This country welcomed us; there was nothing we could do. We had to just be patient, and life gets hard sometimes. *Hamdulillah* [all praise is due to God alone] that we have each other, but we just have to put up with it so that we can survive.
>
> Leila: The problem is that we are Syrian. He did think about doing this [complaining to the police due to unpaid wages], but we are Syrian and we want to do things, but we get scared; there is no one on our side

Amira explains:

> Interviewer: Do you have any experience dealing with the police? Or your husband?
>
> Amira: No. We never faced any issues. We just go from work to home, so we don't cause any problems with anyone. Same thing with the kids; they just go to school and come home; I don't let them go out.

In sum, strategies to claim wage theft were few, and most workers expressed fear of drastic consequences if they dared complain. Because they have absolutely no state protection as unauthorized workers, the only successes came when confrontations with employers resulted in better pay (closer to the agreed-upon salary) or more timely pay (closer to the agreed-upon payment schedule). Our cases indicate that the size of the business, the number of Syrian workers employed by one employer, the employer's ability to quickly replace the labor force (more difficult when workers require training, for instance, and the employer has tight production deadlines), and workers' willingness to take risks when claiming their rights together shape strategies and outcomes. Study participants who feel they have no choice but to accept the social exclusion their marginalization entails mention factors, such as developing self-discipline, possessing self-control, and adopting attitudes that are compliant, submissive, and obedient, as being important. Most had internalized their inferior status in Turkish society and even felt thankful to the Turkish government for giving them asylum and legal authorization to reside in Turkey.

Conclusion

Wage theft is a worldwide phenomenon. It epitomizes the exploitation of workers in an extreme form, leading to situations of servitude and forced labor in some instances. Workers with precarious status and limited or no access to labor rights are particularly at risk of experiencing wage theft, since capital and business owners enjoy impunity when dealing with these groups of denizens–people settled in a country who lack citizenship. In the era of global neoliberalism and global labor markets, labor circulates, and employers can hire workers with various residence statuses and national origins. As such, early capitalist forms of exploitation persist with the granting of precarious legal statuses to foreign labor or with the massive employment of undocumented residents (as in the case of the United States). Both groups become structurally incorporated in labor markets and provide new opportunities of expansion and accumulation to capital owners.

In Turkey, as elsewhere, capital and business owners employ precarious workers–in this case, Syrians who are employed informally without authorization to work. Because these workers are not protected by labor codes and are subject to social marginalization, employers can assertively and openly subordinate and exploit them. In this respect, the presence of Syrian refugees enables the Turkish capital owners to surpass some social and legal limits of labor exploitation in Turkey. Hence, Syrian refugee workers in Turkey are comparable to temporary migrant workers in some other countries where the domestic limits to capital accumulation are bypassed through the import of foreign workers with no citizenship rights. In this case, the fate of Syrians in Turkey relies largely on capital and business owners rather than on state institutions who fail to pay attention to work-related violations, including wage theft. Syrians' position in the Turkish labor market must, therefore, be examined from the point of view of employment relationships, the most critical determinant of well-being for Syrians who have practically no other safety net when it comes to survival. The paradox of economic integration and social marginalization already noted for undocumented labor is powerfully illustrated with the case of Syrians informally employed in Turkey. As put by Rajaram (2015), integration takes place through marginalization.

The consequences of systemic processes of wage theft, as Syrians we interviewed experienced, are numerous and tragic. Not being able to provide for one's necessities and being stripped of one's dignity as a worker and resident of Turkey together entail a cascade of negative effects, not only for Syrian families and communities but for Turkish society as a whole. Moreover, more detailed analyses need to be done to document inequalities among Syrians in the labor market, including factors such as age, gender, ethnicity, religion, class, place of origin, and place of residence in Turkey.

Danièle Bélanger is professor of geography at the Université Laval in Québec City and the holder of the Senior Canada Research Chair in Global Migration Processes. Between 1997 and 2013, she was professor of sociology at Western University, London, Ontario, Canada. Her research analyzes the relationships between policies and precarious migration status. Her projects have focused on temporary migrant workers, trafficked individuals, undocumented migrants, refugees, asylum seekers, and marriage migrants. She conducts fieldwork in Asia, Latin America, the Middle East, and Canada. Some of her recent migration research has been published in *The Annals of Social and Political Science, Current Sociology, Asian Population Studies, Asia Pacific Migration Journal,* and *Pacific Affairs.*

Cenk Saraçoğlu is a faculty member in the Faculty of Communication at Ankara University, Turkey. He received his undergraduate diploma from Bilkent University, International Relations Department, and earned his MA and his PhD degree in sociology from the University of Western Ontario, Canada, in 2008. He is interested in migration, nationalism, urban transformation, and ethnic relations, with a particular focus on Turkey. He is the author of the book *Kurds of Modern Turkey: Migration, Neoliberalism and Exclusion* (I. B. Tauris: 2008) and published several articles on Turkish society and politics in scholarly journals.

Notes

1. Turkey ratified the Geneva Convention and the 1961 protocol so that refugee status would be applied to European applicants only.
2. This information was revealed in December 2018 by Onursal Adıgüzel, a Turkish MP from the opposition Republican People's Party, in a press briefing. Retrieved 1 April 2019 from https://t24.com.tr/haber/chpli-adiguzel-son-uc-yilda-28-bin-suriyeli-calisma-izni-aldi,773713.
3. Elsewhere, we carried out a discussion comparing the conditions of Syrian refugees in Turkey and temporary labor migrants, especially in Gulf countries, around the concept of spatial fix (Saraçoğlu and Bélanger 2019c).
4. According to the International Labor Organisation 1949 Protection of Wages Convention (no. 95), which came into effect in 1952, wages are defined as "remuneration or earnings, however designated or calculated, capable of being expressed in terms of money and fixed by mutual agreement or by national laws or regulations, which are payable in virtue of a written or unwritten contract of employment by an employer to an employed person for work done or to be done or for services rendered or to be rendered" (Article 1, ILO: https://www.ilo.org/dyn/normlex/en/f?p=1000:11300:0::NO:11300:P11300_INSTRUMENT_ID:312240). Turkey ratified this convention in 1961. It is still currently in force. According to Article 2.1, the convention "applies to all persons to whom wages are paid or payable." The ILO recommends applying the standards of this convention to all workers, including those in irregular situations (https://www.ilo.org/wcmsp5/groups/public/—europe/—ro-geneva/—ilo-brussels/documents/genericdocument/wcms_177275.pdf).
5. Families we interviewed rented very low-end housing in poor neighbourhoods. Many spoke of unsafe, insalubrious, and promiscuous living conditions. Most paid between 380 and 500 liras per month for housing.

References

Anderson, Bridget. 2010. "Migration, Immigration Controls and the Fashioning of Precarious Workers." *Work, Employment and Society* 24(2): 300–317.
Basok, Tanya, Danièle Bélanger, and Eloy Rivas. 2014. "Reproducing Deportability: Migrant Agricultural Workers in South-western Ontario." *Journal of Ethnic and Migration Studies* 40(9): 1394–413.
Bélanger, Danièle, and Cenk Saraçoğlu. 2018. "The Governance of Syrian Refugees in Turkey: The State-Capital Nexus and Its Discontents." *Mediterranean Politics* 25(4): 1–20. https://doi.org/10.1080/13629395.2018.1549785.
Buckley, Michelle. 2013. "Locating Neoliberalism in Dubai: Migrant Workers and Class Struggle in the Autocratic City." *Antipode* 45(2): 256–74.
Canefe, Nergis. 2016. "Management of Irregular Migration: Syrians in Turkey as Paradigm Shifters for Forced Migration Studies." *New Perspectives on Turkey* 54: 9–32.

Charanpal, S. Bal. 2015. "Dealing with Deportability: Deportation Laws and the Political Personhood of Temporary Migrant Workers in Singapore." *Asian Journal of Law and Society* 2(2): 267.

Danış, Didem. 2016. "Konfeksiyon Sektöründe Küresel Bağlantılar: Göçmen İşçiler, Sendikalar ve Küresel Çalışma Örgütleri" [Global connections in the textile sector: Migrant workers, unions and global labor organizations]. *Alternatif Politika* 8(3): 562–86.

Dasse, Lauren K. 2012. "Wage Theft in New York: The Wage Theft Prevention Act as a Counter to an Endemic Problem." *CUNY Law Review* 16: 97–127.

Del Carpio, Ximena V., Sirma Demir Şeker, and Ahmet Levent Yener. 2018. "Integrating Refugees into the Turkish Labor Market." *Forced Migration Review* 58: 10–13.

Erdoğdu, Seyhan. 2018. "Syrian Refugees in Turkey and Trade Union Responses." *Globalizations* 15(6): 838–53.

Erol, Ertan, Ayla Ezgi Akyol, Cemal Salman, Ezgi Pinar, Gümüşcan İpek, Kıvanç Yiğit Mısırlı, Mustafa Kahveci, and Pedriye Mutlu. 2017. *Suriyeli Sığınmacıların Türkiye'de Emek Piyasasına Dahil Olma Süreçleri ve Etkileri: İstanbul Tekstil Sektörü Örneği* [The participation of the Syrian refugees in the Turkish labor market and its impacts: Istanbul textile sector]. İstanbul: DİSK Birleşik Metal-İş Yayınları.

Fussell, Elizabeth. 2011. "The Deportation Threat Dynamic and Victimization of Latino Migrants: Wage Theft and Robbery." *Sociological Quarterly* 52(4): 593–615.

Galvin, Daniel J. 2016. "Deterring Wage Theft: Alt-Labor, State Politics, and the Policy Determinants of Minimum Wage Compliance." *Perspectives on Politics* 14(2): 324–50.

Gibney, Matthew J. 2000. *Outside the Protection of the Law: The Situation of Irregular Migrants in Europe*. Refugee Studies Working Paper no. 6. Oxford: Oxford University Press.

Hanieh, Adam. 2015. "Overcoming Methodological Nationalism: Spatial Perspectives on Migration to the Gulf Arab States." In *Transit States: Labor, Migration and Citizenship in the Gulf*, edited by Abdulhadi Khalaf, Omer Al Shehabi, and Adam Hanieh, 57–76. London: Pluto Press.

Lordoğlu, Kuvvet, and Mustafa Aslan. 2016. "En Fazla Suriyeli Göçmen Alan Beş Kentin Emek Piyasalarında Değişimi: 2011–2014" [The changes in the labor market of five cities with the highest Syrian migrant population: 2011–2014]. *Çalışma ve Toplum* 49(2): 789–808.

Milkman, Ruth, Ana Luz González, and Victor Narro. 2010. *Wage Theft and Workplace Violations in Los Angeles: The Failure of Employment and Labor Law for Low-Wage Workers*. Los Angeles: UCLA Institute for Research on Labor and Employment.

Petrescu-Prahova, Miruna, and Michael W. Spiller. 2016. "Women's Wage Theft: Explaining Gender Differences in Violations of Wage and Hour Laws." *Work and Occupations* 43(4): 371–400.

Rajaram, Prem Kumar. 2015. "Common Marginalizations: Neoliberalism, Undocumented Migrants and Other Surplus Populations." *Migration, Mobility, & Displacement* 1(1): 67–80.

Saraçoğlu, Cenk, and Danièle Bélanger. 2019a. "Syrian Refugees and Turkey: Whose Crisis." In *The Oxford Handbook of Migration Crises*, edited by Cecilia Menjívar, Marie Ruiz, and Immanel Ness, 279–94. New York: Oxford University Press.

———. 2019b. "Loss and Xenophobia in the City: Contextualizing Anti-Syrian Sentiments in Turkey." *Patterns of Prejudice* 53(4): 363–83.

———. 2019c. "The Syrian Refugees and Temporary Protection Regime in Turkey: A Spatial Fix for Turkish Capital." In *Integration through Exploitation: Syrians in Turkey*, edited by Gaye Yılmaz, İsmail Doğa Karatepe, and Tolga Tören, 96–110. Augsburg: Rainer Hampp Verlag

Shneikat, Belal, and Chris Ryan. 2018. "Syrian Refugees and Their Re-entry to 'Normality': The Role of Service Industries." *Service Industries Journal* 38(3–4): 201–27.

Sung, Hung-En, Sheyla Delgado, Deysbel Peña, and Amalia Paladino. 2013. "Tyrannizing Strangers for Profit: Wage Theft, Cross-Border Migrant Workers, and the Politics of Exclusion in an Era of Global Economic Integration." In *Outside Justice*, edited by David C. Brotherton, Daniele L. Stageman, and Shirley P. Leyro, 247–67. New York: Springer.

Taykhman, Nicole. 2016. "Defying Silence: Immigrant Women Workers, Wage Theft, and Anti-retaliation Policy in the States." *Columbia Journal of Gender and Law* 32: 96.

Theodore Nik, Abel Valenzuela, and Edwin Melendez. 2009. "Worker Centers: Defending Labor Standards for Migrant Workers in the Informal Economy." *International Journal of Manpower* 30 (September): 422–36.

TEPAV. 2018. *Syrian Entrepreneurship and Refugee Start-ups in Tukey: Leveraging the Turkish Experience*. Retrieved 12 July 2019 from https://www.tepav.org.tr/upload/files/1566830992-6.TEPAV_and_EBRD___Syrian_Entrepreneurship_and_Refugee_Start_ups_in_Turkey_Lever....pdf.

UNHCR (United Nations High Commissioner for Refugees). 2019. "Syria Regional Refugee Response, Turkey." Retrieved 9 May 2019 from https://data2.unhcr.org/en/situations/syria/location/113.

———. 2021 "Operational Update, Turkey." Retrieved 30 October 2021 from https://reporting.unhcr.org/document/1010.

12

The Narratives of Syrian Refugees on Taking Turkey as a Land of a Long or Temporary Settlement

Samer Sharani

Introduction

In late 2011, when Syrians stepped into the Turkish lands after fleeing their country, they were perceived by the government as guests and Muslim brothers, not refugees (Memişoğlu and Ilgit 2017). As soon as increasing numbers of Syrians flooded into Turkey, the government legally put them under the temporary protection system: namely, their residency in Turkey was conditioned either on the conflict in Syria, whether it is settled to peace or not, or on their resettlement in a third country. Among those Syrians, more than ninety thousand have been bestowed with the Turkish nationality according to *selective* criteria (Akçapar and Şimşek 2018).[1] The others, more than 3.6 million Syrians (UNHCR 2019), are either still under temporary protection or live illegally in Turkey.

After nine years of the ongoing civil war in Syria, one can eagerly ask the questions regarding a possible home return[2] of Syrian refugees from Turkey or of refugees seeking asylum in Europe. Indeed, refugees' repatriation increasingly forms a heated debate in academia and policymaking fields (İçduygu and Nimer 2019). However, this chapter does not approach this issue via legal or practical lenses; rather, it digs into how Syrian refugees comprehend and cognitively see home return in an "ideal" imagined situation, regardless of the legal and practical realities.

I discuss the intentions of Syrians in Turkey, whether they desire to stay permanently or for a long time, to seek refuge in Europe, or to return to Syria. I aim to find the underlying mechanisms of such intentions. In other words, what does each of these three alternatives mean to them? And, via a sociopsychological lens, how do they meaningfully constitute each alternative?

In doing so, this chapter presents the contexts and conditions where Syrian refugees live and where they can relocate, namely, Turkey, Europe, and Syria. Then it reviews the literature on repatriation and home return; four main theoretical approaches are classified in this study as the most prevailing theories and theoretical frameworks in literature. In order to surpass contradictions or inconsistencies between these approaches and to have a comprehensive model of home return, two concepts are extracted to form the fundamental blocks of the suggested model: identity-agency and place.

To test and develop the designed model, I adopted a narrative analysis method and conducted twenty-one interviews with Syrian refugees in Turkey, Germany, and Sweden. After explaining the methodology, I depict the analyzed narratives in detail, answering the research questions. Finally, I end the chapter with conclusions and recommendations for further research.

Syrians' Inclusion and Exclusion: Future-Syria, Europe, and Turkey

Three durable solutions are addressed by the United Nations High Commissioner for Refugees (UNHCR) for refugees: (1) home return, which is the most preferable because it refers to bringing the situation in the country of origin to its "natural," prewar situation; (2) local integration in the current country of settlement, Turkey in this case; and (3) resettlement in a third country, which is usually a Western country (UNHCR-Kenya 2019). Regarding the 3.6 million Syrians in Turkey, how do the contexts in Europe, Turkey, and Syria affect their possible intentions of the three alternatives?

After nine years of war, the situation in Syria remains ambiguous and uncertain. Violence oscillates between higher and lower levels from month to month; the economic conditions are deeply devastated; the infrastructure is poorly maintained; and the security/legislation question is not concretely reestablished. Therefore, between 2015 and 2018, only 103,000 Syrians repatriated voluntarily, which constitutes 2 percent of the Syrian refugees who live in the neighboring countries, including Turkey (World Bank 2019). Bearing that in mind, this study questions the *intention*, not the actual action of home return. Today, no one can assure that the basic needs of Syrians are met or able to be met in case of repatriation, either legally, socially, or economically. And no developmental strategic plans have been established to make the home return possible (World Bank 2017). Syria now is not suitable for home return, at least, for the reasons mentioned.

Regarding Syrians in Europe, the refugee crisis that has hit the European Union since 2015 (Khiabany 2016; Scipioni 2018) negatively affects Syrians, making them more prone to uncertain fates, in spite of the well-intentioned refuge system (Zisser 2019). The refugee-triggered crisis in Europe is a key "stressor" on the European Union, threatening its very identity (Mitzen 2018); hence, the Syrian refugees there are depicted as a potential threat (or at least a topic) of a deep cleavage between European actors (e.g., parties, states, and EU institutions). Syrian refugees form a symbolic field of battle, which is represented and narrated daily in media and in banal conversations between people (Boswell, Geddes, and Scholten 2011). Therefore, whether or not they are thinking of leaving Turkey to Europe, this negative (or, say, conflicting) picture is not absent from the Syrian refugees' awareness in Turkey.

Although this policy is the basic attractive element for Syrians to take refuge in Europe, the integration policy in Europe causes tensions within refugees' identity. Schinkel (2018) criticizes the integration policy in the West as constituting a type of neocolonialism. For him, the integration policy–in its very nature–frames the newcomers, who are Muslims generally, as strangers forming an "ethnicity" within the Western countries. The newcomers have to integrate by adopting the mainstream values and lifestyle of the Western modernized countries. More precisely, any Western country is seen as a pure, constant society, unchangeable over time, while the newcomers will be, and will always stay, the *minor* ethnicity who must integrate to some extent, more or less. Refugees are at best integrated but not "citizens." Discrimination, therefore, against the "integrated" refugees is inherent in their lives in the new society. Thus, their self-identities and self-esteem can be strained.

For example, "gender equality" is used in the Western countries as a tool of discrimination and stigmatization against Muslim refugees, as Yurdakul and Korteweg (2013) argue. A woman's body turns into a measurement of integration into the "Occident" society; the "Oriental backward" Muslim refugees have to adopt the "hosts' way of doing things," including the ways of women body practices (Ruby 2013). In this vein, Syrian refugees in Europe, who are exposed to that kind of policy, might feel that they are excluded from the society's mainstream.

These issues, the refugee crisis of the EU and the problem of integration, affect the intentions of Syrians in Turkey about whether to take the arduous roads to Europe or to stay in Turkey. Notwithstanding this negative image, Syrians can get a better refugee status in the EU than in Turkey, as they have more rights and their lives are much comfortable due to the "full" refugee-status in the EU,[3] whereas they have limited rights and less beneficiaries under the temporary protection in Turkey (Baban, Ilcan, and Rygiel 2017; Kutlu Tonak 2016). This positive side of the picture is also, of course, present in the Syrians' minds when they make their intentions.

The refugees' situation in Turkey, on the other hand, forges a mixed and contested picture. Syrians in Turkey have some social rights, while they are prevented from others. According to the 2013 Law on Foreigners and International Protection, Syrians have the right to stay in the Turkish lands, to freely register children in the public schools, and to get work permits. However, many Syrians cannot send their children to schools because of the language barriers and economic difficulties, which makes the right of education unattainable in practice (İneli-Ciğer 2017). Additionally, Syrian workers and employees rarely apply for work permits because of the rigid system and its inflexible conditions. Therefore, the majority of Syrians work illegally with significantly lower wages than their Turkish peers (İneli-Ciğer 2017). Syrians face other obstacles, such as restricted mobility between provinces even if they are registered under the temporary protection system. All these factors hamper a successful integration of Syrians in Turkey (Baban, Ilcan, and Rygiel, 2017; İçduygu 2015; Kutlu Tonak 2016; Memişoğlu and Ilgit 2017; Şimşek 2018). It is worth adding that endowing exceptional citizenship to some Syrians in Turkey has not enhanced their integration. Indeed, Turkish locals continue to picture Syrians as a demographic threat and a competitive bloc over public services (Akçapar and Şimşek 2018; Memişoğlu and Ilgit 2017).

Nevertheless, at the grassroots level, many Syrians find Turkey a continuous cultural-religious sphere of their home. On the one hand, the historical relationship between the Ottoman Empire and present-day Syria (which was a part of it) is one reason for this cultural familiarity. On the other hand, the huge number of Syrians who flooded into Turkey early have created a kinship network, on which later Syrian newcomers relied (Kaya 2017). These factors contribute to making Turkey a good place of integration for Syrians, culturally at least.

The question of integration and marginalization, inclusion and exclusion for Syrians in Turkey underlies the refugees' desire to stay, go to Europe, or return home. Previous studies on Syrian refugees in Turkey have shown scattered results regarding home return. A study in 2019 found that the majority of Syrians (90 percent) desire "ideally" to return home, *conditioning* this return on prosecuting human rights violators (Fabbe and İnmazdemir 2019). Other studies found that the longer Syrians stay in Turkey, the less desire they show to repatriate (Balcılar and Nugent 2019; Kivisto and La Vecchia-Mikkola 2015). However, a deeper mechanism behind these results has not been explored.

To sum up, inclusion/exclusion of Syrians in Turkey and the EU is multi-dimensional. Syrians are more included in Turkey on some dimensions, such as culture (e.g., wearing headscarf is seen as normal in Turkey, praying in mosques is easy since there are many), and excluded on other dimensions. The same is to be said on inclusion/exclusion dimensions in Europe. According to some scholars, the "gender equality" policy in Europe plays an exclusive role against Syrians when it is seen via the lens of multiculturalism. These complicated factors should be taken into account when analyzing the Syrians' narratives on their future plans.

Theoretical Approaches to Refugees' Home Return

Literature on home return is wide. The current study addresses four main approaches that cover this topic: failure-success, integration, transnationalism, and homemaking. They overlap in some parts and contradict each other in other parts. Generally, inconsistency is prevalent among these four approaches. Reshaping these approaches in a whole, compatible, coherent model is the intention of this study. Such a model must surpass the inconsistencies among these approaches and configure a systematic theoretical view out of them. To achieve this purpose, this study will first depict the concepts of these approaches, then it will extract the relationships between these concepts, reshaping a coherent model (a method of theory building; e.g., Finfgeld-Connett and Johnson 2013).

Two concepts (more precisely, conceptual umbrellas) should be delineated before presenting and analyzing the four approaches: *place* and *identity-agency*.[4]

Place is not a material container where people live, act, and communicate. Place is a *soft entity* enrooted within the material environment: it is a milieu to create meanings of human beings' lives. Social communication, normative behaviors, cultural symbols, and everyday economic activities are actualized *by* and entangled *with* place (Devine-Wright 2009; Devine-Wright and Lyons 1997; Di Masso, Dixon, and Pol 2011; Dixon and Durrheim 2004, 2000). People are, generally, attached to their places because place is a framework that coalesces the fragmented events, memories, and social and political objects in one coherent whole, with which people define themselves (Djenar 2016).

Drawing on this concept, both the host country, where refugees live, and home, the original country of refugees, should not be understood as merely geographical territories. Place is a practice on multilayer dimensions.

Identity-agency is another conceptual nexus that needs to be clarified. On the one hand, self-identity (or identity) refers to an answer to the question, "Who am I?" including my values, goals, and belongings to different social groups, ethnicities, or collectives (e.g., Breakwell 2014; Cieciuch and Topolewska 2017). Agency, on the other hand, points to the individual potential freedom, the capacity to choose among alternative conditions, and the ability to act (Alkire 2005; Giddens 1991, 1984; Hitlin and Elder 2007). Agency, in other words, is about having control over our own lives and over the deeds we need or want to do. It is entangled with identity since "who I am" is sought through being able to achieve "my" morality as well as my needs and goals, i.e., through my agency (Nilson 2001).

Failure-Success Framework

Failure-success framework is a theoretical approach of home return based on migrants'[5] *economic performances* in host countries. What determines the refugees' intentions to return home or not is simply their economic performances. Three different theories compete within this framework: neoclassical economic theory of migration (NE), the new economics of labor migration (NELM), and the diaspora trap (Nzima and Moyo 2017).

The NE theory focuses on the individual-migrant, and it evaluates her/his success or failure in the host country according to the monetary gains. When the money s/he earns in the host country does not significantly differ from that in the home country, or when s/he fails in her/his endeavor to achieve the money s/he sought before emigration, then home return will be the logical outcome of the migration process (de Haas 2010; Cassarino 2004). Simply put, when a migrant fails in the economic performance, s/he decides to return home.

The NELM theory, contrary to the NE theory, contends that migrants return when they succeed in their *general* economic performance. NELM focuses on the household or family level not on the individual level as the NE does. So, any migration process is seen as a family action, which starts from the decision to migrate and ends when the family's "sent" members achieve the family's goals. These goals are not monetary gains only—as in the NE—but achievement of better livelihood conditions as a whole in home. Hence, as migrants cannot improve the livelihood conditions of their families, they stay in host countries for a longer time, hoping to achieve their goals in future (de Haas 2010; Cassarino 2004).

The last approach within the failure-success framework is the Diaspora Trap. This approach accounts for a set of complicated factors that affect the decision of emigration and home return. According to this approach, an economic success in host societies does not necessarily mean returning to home because the economic conditions at home could be harsh and unsuitable for migrants, who get used to high standards of life. Also, failure in host countries does not necessarily lead to a home return as migrants could feel socially pressured and ashamed because of the failure, so they prefer to stay abroad (Nzima and Moyo 2017).

The failure-success framework's subtheories are divergent in terms of the assumptions on what makes migrants return to their homes. These theories, however, draw on similar theoretical assumptions. First, the host country is the place where refugees achieve their goals, while home is passively depicted as merely a place of return. Second, the economic performance is the focal point of home return intentions. What formulates such intentions is the refugee's agency, the ability to act and achieve her/his goals.

Integration

Integration does not have one generally accepted definition. It can be understood as a process targeting refugees in multiple domains grouped into four categories: (1) guaranteeing the necessary means of refugees to live well in the new society (having access to education, healthcare, housing, and work); (2) including refugees within the new society by enhancing their connection with the native people; (3) guaranteeing safety, stability, and cultural and linguistic skills for refugees; and finally (4) granting citizenship at the end of the integration process (Ager and Strang 2008). In other words, integration is essentially designed to give refugees, who are expected to stay in a host country for a long time, the ability to be active and self-reliant in their new societies (European Commission 2016).

In line with the failure-success framework, studying the relationship between integration and home return is also complicated without a general accepted theory. Pierre, Martinovic, and de Vroome (2015) studied this relationship throughout multiple dimensions of integration. Refugees' *social* integration into a host society (i.e., having social networks and connections with the natives) and *cultural* integration (adopting the core values of a host society) are positively associated with refugees' identification with and integration in their host countries. This results in less desire to return home. Nevertheless, they also found that the *more* cultural integration and *structural* integration (i.e., economic integration and the level of education fulfilled in the host country) are achieved, the *more* discrimination is perceived by refugees, which in turn leads to a greater desire to return. These findings are in line with the "integration paradox" idea: namely, higher levels of integration within a host society lead to *more* perceived discrimination. That is, well-integrated refugees have intensive connections with natives, they expect more rewards for their economic and educational achievements, and they become more sensitive to less respect, simply put (de Vroome, Martinovic, and Verkuyten 2014). Home return then becomes a way to avert discrimination and a failed integration.

In light of this approach, home is not simply a place to where refugees go back when they fail or succeed economically in the "host." Refugees continuously evaluate their home situations and their integration level in the "host." If security, economic conditions, and the political climate at home are unsatisfying for refugees, they will likely refuse to repatriate regardless of their situation in the "host," whether they are well integrated or not (Chimni 2002; Essuman-Johnson 2011; Fransen, Ruiz, and Vargas-Silvam 2017; Muggeridge and Dona 2006; Rabinowitz 2010).

Intention of home return is shaped by evaluating both the home and the "host," while in the previous approach, the "host" matters more. Home is important because returning is not identical with "going back," but it is a new integration *into* home (Heimerl 2005). Returnees may suffer from discrimination in their own home, and they may lack the necessary ability to sustain an acceptable level of well-being because of "local" skills they have lost in the refuge country (Fransen, Ruiz, and Vargas-Silvam 2017). For example, a returnee may not find a house to dwell in, or s/he may not fit into the education system in the case of a long stay abroad (Ecke et al. 2016; Omata 2013). Factors in both home and the "host" are subsequently evaluated by refugees.

Although the integration approach assigns equal weight to home and the "host," it conceptualizes the boundary between these two places as clear-cut and fixed: a refugee is either totally here or there. The home and "host" are seen as separate places.

On the contrary, the integration approach does not limit the intention of return to refugees' agency (e.g., economic performance) as the failure-success framework does; rather, it also accounts for self-identity. When a refugee's self-identity is threatened, her/his integration will fail in the host society, and s/he will have more reasons to repatriate (Kivisto and La Vecchia-Mikkola 2015). For example, perceiving discrimination in the host society implies refusing the refugee's own values and culture, which leads to an exclusion that mainly strains the refugee's self-identity.

Transnationalism

Under the umbrella of the transnational approach, refugees in a host society develop diasporic, transnational spaces where they evoke their homes, practice their cultures on the base of everyday life, and create their own communities outside the homes' borders (Savaş, 2010). For example, they pursue having traditional food, visiting mosques (for Muslims), or attending their own cultural clubs to practice the home language and music. Thus, a communal memory and a collective identity would be sustained and endorsed in exile. In other words, refugees practice two lives, here (in the host country) and there (at home), at the same time while living–actually–in the "host." This is what is called transnationalism, which is implemented through *social transnational spaces*. Social transnational spaces, in turn, are home-related places and *activities* held in the host country. In this regard, assembling around a traditional dinner table in a living room, gathering in a cultural organization to sing or to discuss political events, and even dressing in a traditional way (e.g., wearing headscarf by Muslim women) are all social transnational spaces linking the "alien" hosting place/culture to home (Al-Ali, Black and Koser 2001a; Anthias 2016; Levitt and Schiller 2004; Roudometof 2005).

In light of transnationalism, home return is increasingly seen as a political-social action, especially in a context of war-torn countries. Home return is a "social contract-*remaking*," as it means that refugees repatriate because a *new* relationship binds them with their state (Long 2011). This political action in host countries by refugees entails that they impact their home's situation while they are far away from it (e.g., via remittance and political lobbying).

Intentions to return home or not are deeply imbued with a political meaning. And this meaning–itself–is not limited to refugees who live in a host country but is also made by a continuous "re-composing" of their experiences *before* fleeing from home and *during* residency in a host community (Einhorn 2000). Refugees reshape their identities, their social norms, their goals, and future plans by continuously bridging two shores, life in the home and life in the host countries. Put differently, the past and present on one side and home and host countries on the other side function simultaneously to carve out intentions of home return or not (Al-Ali, Black, and Koser 2001a, 2001b; Şimşek 2019). As a result, a remote home itself is recreated within these transnational social spaces through complicated dynamics of bridging both the home and the "host" (Brown 2011; Capo 2015). The place from where refugees escape is not perceived anymore as the same place to where they might return.

The relationship between transnationalism and integration is highly contested; for some scholars, transnationalism enhances integration in host countries, while others think of transnationalism as hindering integration (Şimşek 2019). The latter contend that transnationalism pushes refugees and migrants to feel as if they live neither there (home) nor here (host country), which ignites anxiety (Nukaga 2013). This case has been described as "liminality," whereby refugees do not abandon their past status–as belonging to home–nor do they identify themselves as belonging to the new place and its culture. Briefly, liminality is to live between places or in no place (Daskalaki, Butler, and Petrovic 2016).

Dwelling on what has been mentioned, mechanism of home return as seen through the lens of transnationalism is not decisive. Such mechanism is dynamic, whereby the boundaries between home and "host" are highly blurred, and both are under dynamic configuration. The idea of home manifests via refugees' daily lives in their host countries, socially, culturally, economically, and politically, while the relationship with the "host" (i.e., integration) varies from one case to another, either enhanced or worsened. We can see that the concept of self-identity and the question of belonging play a more important role (Huizinga and van Hoven 2018)–in this approach–compared to the two previous approaches, integration and failure-success. That is, refugees' pursuit to maintain their identities is what explains their transnational activities, partially at least. It is worth mentioning that integration in the "host" and returning to home are not mutually exclusive as they were in the previous approach; rather, they coexist as two fluid processes, within the frame of transnationalism. Return/nonreturn forges a complex mixed process (Capo 2015; Omata 2013).

Homemaking

Finally, the homemaking approach refers to home as a continuously reloaded concept with meanings. In this approach, being out of or within homelands does not matter that much, contrary to the previous approaches. Home is an *abstract* space, whose boundaries are themselves changeable, negotiable, and reshapeable as refugees' identities are always constructed. Homemaking, then, is directly related to meaning making of belonging and identification (Liu 2014; Tete 2012). Differently stated, home is a multiple and fluctuant concept, apart from being a constant territory, culture, or idea.

Homemaking not only "omits" the boundaries between host and home places but also trespasses the concept of home itself. Home turns into a blurry place (not just its boundaries) and becomes an essential element of negotiating and forging the refugees' self-identity in a context of a continuous loading of meanings (see Identity Process Theory: Breakwell 2001; Timotijevic and Breakwell 2000; Vignoles, Chryssochoou, and Breakwell 2002). Hence, self-identity surpasses agency in shaping the intention on return in this approach.

The four approaches are not mutually exclusive, despite the fact that they are presented separately. We can find some of them presented together in one study. For example, Tezcan (2019) demarcates three factors to predict the desire of home return: the experienced xenophobia and identification with host and home countries (integration approach), economic success (NE theory, failure-success approach), and transnational activities (transnationalism approach). He found that xenophobia experienced in a host country, identification with home, failure in making economic success, and engaging in transnational activities are all positively associated with a stronger desire to return home.

In the next section, I show how these four approaches can be coherently coalesced.

Table 12.1. The Four Approaches and Their Conceptualization of Place and Identity-Agency in Terms of Shaping the Home Return Intention.

The Approach	Place: Home and the "Host"	Identity-Agency
Failure-success	Only the "host" matters	Only agency matters
Integration	Both are important	Agency matters as does identity
Transnationalism	Both are important and are practiced together (regardless of the distance)	Agency and identity matter equally
Homemaking	The two are melded, forming one "conceptual" unit	Self-identity matters the most

Table made by Samer Sharani.

Building a New Model on Home Return

After presenting the similarities and demarcating the differences between the four approaches, identity-agency and place are the wide concepts I am using in order to build a comprehensive model. Place is linked to agency since it enables a wider or narrower range of an individual's alternative tools and objectives. For example, infrastructure in one place could be widely deteriorated while it is developed in another (Pretty, Chipuer, and Bramston 2003). Place is also linked to identity by giving meaning to a person's life and anchoring her/himself to a specific culture, norms, and social identity that dwell in that place (Cuba and Hummon 1993; Kumsa 2006).

As table 12.1 shows, the four approaches differ in terms of how they conceptualize place and identity-agency. Patently, either identity is weighed more than agency, they are equally important, or agency is what shapes the intention of returning home more than identity. Place differs across these approaches according to how they conceptualize the boundaries between home and the "host"; are the boundaries fixed between two separate places (home/host) or blurred as the two places are almost obscured together in one "abstract" place?

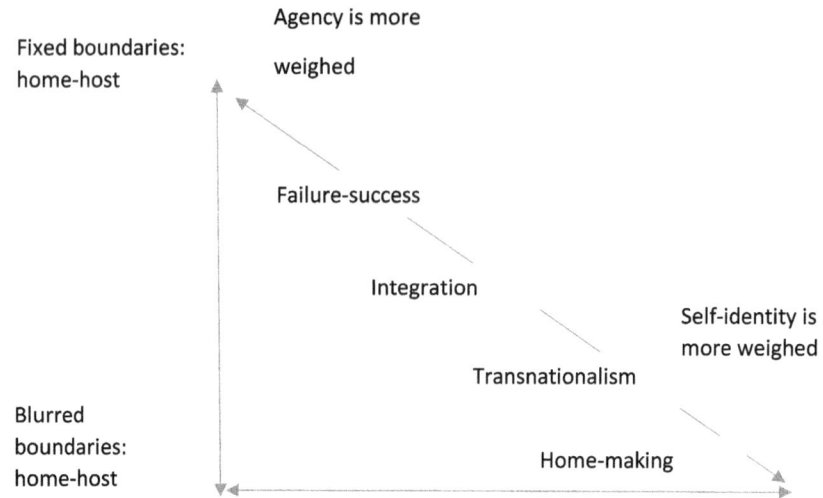

Figure 12.1. Projecting the Four Approaches on Two Dimensions, Place and Identity-Agency. © Samer Sharani.

By projecting these approaches on the place and identity-agency concepts, on the one hand, we find that the more an approach dwells on the concepts of identity and blurry boundaries of home/host, the more it is close to the *pure* homemaking approach. On the other hand, the more an approach gives heft to the concepts of agency and clear-cut boundaries of home/host, the more it is close to the pure failure-success approach (figure 12.1).

At this point, we can think of identity-agency as a nexus with two poles. The agency pole becomes more weighted when refugees carve their intention by asserting terms such as *ability, capabilities, control, livelihood, guaranteed future, efficacy,* and *security*. Whereas, asserting themes of *belonging, one's group, ethics, nostalgia, self, nation, religion, values,* and *belief-system* shifts the balance to the other pole of the nexus: self-identity. Place also can be pictured as a nexus with two poles: blurry or fixed boundaries of home/host (figure 12.2).

After explaining the methodology, I will analyze Syrian refugees' narratives as hinged on these two nexuses.

Methodology and Narrative Analysis

This study uses narrative analysis in its endeavor to answer the research question. Narrative analysis, and qualitative methods generally, allows for going forward and backward between different concepts and across different

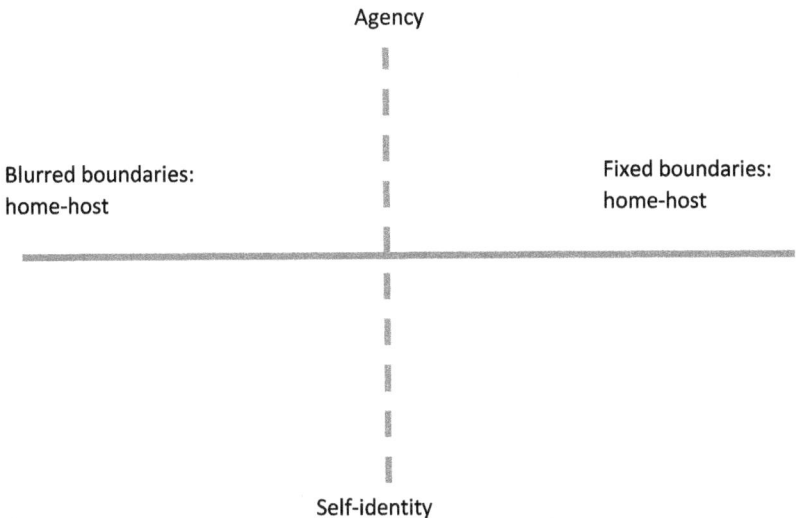

Figure 12.2. The Four Poles of the Two Dimensions. © Samer Sharani.

levels of depth during data collections. The topic of this study is complex. It lacks a general acceptable framework, and the different approaches and theories used to tackle it have resulted in divergent and–sometimes–contradictory conclusions. The picture of refugees' home return in the context of civil wars is, therefore, fuzzy, especially considering that the civil war in Syria is still ongoing.

I conducted twenty-one interviews (individual narratives) with Syrians in Istanbul, Germany, and Sweden between February and September 2019. All the interviewees are Syrian refugees who live or had lived in Istanbul in the wake of the civil war's breakout in 2011. The sample consisted of two types of Syrians, those who still live in Istanbul and those who had lived there and moved to Europe later. The sample is purposive, yet I sought to make it represent different Syrian groups in terms of gender, religion, educational level, and age (for more details on the sample, review the appendix). In total, every interview lasted between thirty and seventy-five minutes and was conducted face-to-face, via WhatsApp or Skype. Interviews were held in Arabic, recorded, and transcribed, then *thematically*[6] analyzed (Clarke and Braun 2017; Fereday and Muir-Cochrane 2006; Tuckett 2005). No translation was needed since the researcher's native language is Arabic.

The collected data are narratives. *Narrative* is defined as a story told by a person on his or her own life and experiences, but it is not merely an alignment of events in a time sequence; this is a chronicle, not a narrative (Nilson

2011). A story intended to be a narrative should (1) depict the events and experiences lived by the narrator and (2) filter the most salient events to be narrated. That is, someone cannot tell everything s/he has been exposed to; rather, s/he selects what s/he thinks the most important events to tell in terms of her/his identity, worldview, and morality. Narrative also includes (3) interpretive elements of the experienced events and life. Finally, (4) narrative puts lived fragmented events, ideas, and emotions in a connected, meaningful whole (Brockmeier 2001, 2000; Bruner 2001; Josselson 2006; Mankowski and Rappaport 1995; Nilson 2001). Narrative analysis, I argue, is better than conducting (semi)structured interviews because it enables the respondents to speak freely, as if they are telling stories.

In this regard, it is noteworthy to determine the precise type of narrative this study pursues, the "small story." *Small story* is defined by Georgakopoulou (2006) as an umbrella term covering a gamut of shared events: future events, ongoing events, and *deferral of tellings and refusal of tellings*. Small stories can be narratives of small events in terms of period or imagined events that did not happen yet but are expected to in the future. The small story concept paves the way for researchers to dig deeply into the narrator's self.

Deferred and refused-to-tell *small stories* or narratives are important because they unearth contradictions within the narrator's self. Traditionally, narrative is seen as a *coherent* whole, clean from discrepancies; even if the narrator has many contradictions within her/himself, s/he narrates in a coherent way (Hanninen 2004; Kraus 2006; Schank and Abelson 1995). In this traditional vein, coherence in narrative is a critical criterion because narrative functions as a conveyer and generator of meaning, making life seem nonrandom and reasonable (Baumeister and Newman 1995; Bruner 1998). Thus, having incoherence within a narrative is indicative of meaningless elements within the narrative, which negates its function. Nevertheless, other scholars have argued that we analytically can find incoherencies within blatantly coherent narratives (Hermans 2000). Precisely, *untold stories* (small stories) are the places where incoherencies exist (Schank and Abelson 1995). These incoherencies are unavoidable. First, the self is not a pure unit; rather, it is multiple-selves (Kraus 2006); second, self-narrative is not confined to the inner-self but is interwoven with various others. The other members of the community do matter essentially as they–with the individual narrator–form the cultural repertoire (Bruner 1998; Nilson 2001), and self-narrative itself borrows its elements from this repertoire (Feldman 2001).

Digging within incoherencies of narratives becomes a source of rich information to be analyzed. It could channel the analyst to the source of these incoherencies, going beyond the "superficial" coherent narrative and trying to unearth the schemata or structure of the narrative, which is important to grasp a deep understanding of the complicated, fleeting reality (Brockmeier and Harre 2001).

Syrians' Narratives in Turkey: Staying, Resettlement, or Home Return

In the rest of this study, I will analyze Syrian refugees' narratives, which fit into two broad categories: first, their perceptions of Turkey and Europe as two alternatives of refuging; and second, their perceptions of home per se, their intentions to return or not, and the ways by which they justify their intentions.

Turkey vis-à-vis Europe

All the interviewees narrated their experiences in Turkey (more precisely, Istanbul) in light of comparing them to their real experiences or imaginations of Europe. This case could be attributed to the fact that being in Turkey invokes a potential ability to take refuge in Europe, so both Turkey and Europe form a domain of refugeehood. Deciding to stay in Turkey or leave for Europe is justified by this comparison. Such justification is necessary because it alludes to choosing the place where the refugees' identities and agencies will be exercised, where to live is an essential decision for human lives.

Out of the twenty-one interviewees, nine have presented Turkey as a mere *passage* to Europe. Turkey is a place to be passed–they either passed to Europe or could not. Delal, a thirty-year-old woman who lives in Sweden now, said, "Turkey was a window only. ... I decided to travel to Europe before I came to Turkey. ... There [in Turkey], I felt suffocated and stranger ... no one was around but two Syrians. ... I had to stay for two years there because I needed money to send to my family [in Syria] and to save for smuggling to Europe."

Turkey is a passage to Europe not only because of its geographical proximity but also because people can find jobs in Turkey, save money, and send it to their families (remittance), which all play an important role in the migration process. Interestingly, those who described Turkey as a passage focused on the difficulties they had faced there and attributed these difficulties to the place, Turkey, which helped them only to pass through, not to stay. Most of these difficulties are in line with what was mentioned early, such as the absence of monthly allowance, the practical difficulties of getting job permits, and the lack of full refugee status.[7] Ahmad, a Syrian Kurdish refugee who has been living in Turkey since 2013 said, "I am at thirty-three, but I feel that I am at twenty-three ... not because I feel younger but because I lost ten years in Turkey." Maed, another Syrian who had lived in Turkey for two years before migrating to Sweden, said, "If I had felt safe with a guaranteed future in Turkey, I would have never left it." Another refugee, the thirty-five-year-old Zehlan who lives in Germany now, described the beauty adherent to Istanbul, although he was forced to leave: "In Turkey, I was able to eat, but I always felt pain because I can eat while my parents cannot. So, I was in deep sadness. ... Istanbul is a beautiful city, I miss it. There were a lot of activities that bounded me to the city, but there was no support [state support] for us, then I traveled to Berlin."

For refugees such as these, agency is weighed over identity because they assess Turkey in terms of what enables or restricts them, and they establish their arguments on the potential place where agency (not identity) could be better fulfilled, i.e., Europe. Identity does not seem important in their referring to Turkey or to Europe, or in making the decision of staying or leaving. Regarding the notion of place, as having blurred or fixed boundaries between Syria (the home) and Turkey (the passage), these refugees implicitly tend to see places with fixed boundaries, in spite of some transnational activities such as remittance. Refugees are neither engaged in *serious* transnational activities nor actively involved in narrative practices to define home or even question it. This is expected since identity is almost absent in the narratives about Turkey as a passage. Additionally, this fixity of perceiving the place might help the refugees to keep the home astray far enough from their thinking as much as possible, because home is basically narrated as a trauma (however, we will see later that identity is kept silent but not absent). Delal asked me during her narrative, "Could you write down cursing words ... I want to say about Syria?" and Zehlan described his experience in Syria just before coming to Turkey as, "When I left Syria, I was in big trouble. ... Because I was kidnapped ... I was mentally and emotionally destroyed."

Contrary to those who pictured Turkey as a passage to Europe, others presented Turkey as a better place for exercising agency and identity compared to Europe. In this case, a voluntary stay in Turkey has ensued. Transnational activities, which are available for Syrians in Istanbul, such as meeting in Syrian social centers, working in Arabic schools, and attending Arabic-speaking mosques, compose *one* factor satisfying agency and identity exercises. The other factor is, ironically, engendered by the *absence* of a robust integration policy toward refugees in Turkey, such as compulsory attendance of language schools, monthly allowance, a policy of integration in the job market, and a policy of housing. This absence gives refugees a wider space to prime their morality as being self-dependent, hard workers to survive, and freer to exercise their identity. Arwa, a twenty-three-year-old woman who has been living in Turkey since 2015, clearly expressed, "Here [in Turkey] you convey Syria with you because no one cares about you [state does not care]. However, in Europe it is not the case; you must integrate, then either you do not and become isolated or you integrate without thinking and you will become skinned out from the Syrian community."

For Arwa, transnational activities in Istanbul made her more confident, giving her higher self-esteem: "The first time I got out of my home I went to a social center for Syrians run by an American woman who helped me a lot. I learned English, then I enrolled in a university, which gave me a great hope; later I met a Syrian girl studying with me, so I did not feel alone anymore. ... I work in an Arabic school, and I am very successful in my work. Now, I have progressed very much. ... I am in a place (position) and my peers, in Syria, are in a far lower place."

Twenty-eight-year-old Mohammad explained that his identity is safer in Turkey than in Europe, and he can successfully fulfill his agency: "Here, I discovered that every day I develop ... also, here you can practice your religion because there are religious lessons in Arabic in the near mosque, and all my [Syrian] friends are here with me. ... But you know in Europe, you will be alone, and there is very much sexual freedom, so you know ... you can do a sin... this is not the case in Istanbul."

Alep, who is twenty-six years old and living in Istanbul, made a short and clear statement to express his idea about the great opportunity for fulfilling his agency in Turkey: "In Europe you are refugee-refugee, here you are productive-refugee [namely, you need to work to live since there is no state-supported aids]." Similarly, Alaa, a thirty-four-year-old man in Istanbul, explained, "Here I am struggling a lot, it is difficult, not as in Europe where everything is easy. ... Nevertheless, after years you will be proud that you have done a great job in your exile [in Turkey]."

These quotations show that those refugees can exercise their morality (related to self-identity) and their jobs and capabilities (related to agency) in one place, where both identity and agency are facilitated by less restrictive integration policies and more transnational activities. By the "one place," I mean that refugees perceive the notion of place as having blurred boundaries; Turkey (the host) and Syria (the home) are blended and cognitively brought together throughout transnational activities and via identifying the self-identity as better fitting in Turkey (e.g., through Islamic practices).

Bai, a thirty-three-year-old Syrian woman in Istanbul, did not *directly* express the exercising of her identity and agency *in* Turkey as the others did; rather, she expressed this exercising *vicariously* through Europe as a place of agency*less-ness*. In other words, Europe is what gives meaning to her self-identity and empowers her agency exactly because she did not go there: "Turkey was a nice place, a new place, an attractive place to be digested [by a newcomer], but as a Syrian escaped the war, you cannot [enjoy the place]. ... Of course, I was happy with [the provided] electricity, water, and internet ... but still, fear was a big title, we did not have the luxury to buy a bottle of water for one lira. ... In Turkey I am not a refugee, and I do not have the right to be a refugee in Europe; others have this right more than me. ... Europe is for these people ... not me ... even if I failed in Turkey, I would come back to Syria, not go to Europe."

Bai exercises her morality and agency by refusing to take a European "seat" from an "eligible" refugee who is more vulnerable than her. Bai's account implies that Europe is perceived as a place for agencyless people because of the provided livelihood there.

By looking at the narratives of Syrian refugees who described Turkey as a mere passage and applied for asylum in Europe, I argue that their agencies are not fully fulfilled *if* they perceive the place concept as fixed. Differently put, refugees' agency in Europe is based on self-contradiction and *inconsistency* between their identities and agencies. Delal, in Sweden now, described the most preeminent moment of her agency fulfilment as following: "When I was in Germany, in the camp, I made a revolution there, I led seventy-five men behind me ... do you know why? Because they [German employees] cut off our salaries [allowances], so we demanded our rights. Later, the authority thanked me and invited me to speak in the [local] parliament ... because you know ... I am a woman, from Syria, I am supposed to be suppressed there. In spite of that, I made a revolution."

The importance of this moment in Delal's narrative is generated from (1) being a woman from Syria, helpless and agentless, and (2) having the law violated in Germany by the employees. Therefore, her agency is *not* exercised *within* the German system/place, but *out* of this system/place, i.e., her agency is expressed by the contradiction between in-system and out-system, between Syria and Germany. Her agency emerged in that moment because of a crack in applying the German law, which is not normal in the German system.

Another Syrian refugee in Sweden, Maed, expressed another contradiction between the job he does not like and the safety ensuing from this job: "Look! Here you have nothing to fear ... I work in a tough job, I do not like it, but I am ready to work even in garbage because here you work to guarantee your future ... because they will pay for you when you are old or jobless." Maed perceives his agency as contingent on vulnerability, which implicitly stems from being a Syrian (he said before that he would have not left Turkey, had Turkey guaranteed his future).

To sum up, Syrians, who narrated Turkey as a better place than Europe, perceived the notion of place as blurry, not fixed. Thus, the boundaries between Turkey and Syria–as places–are porous (socially, culturally, and economically), and refugees' identities and agencies are "well" expressed and exercised within these blurry places (figure 12.3a). On the contrary, Syrians who narrated Europe as a better place perceived the place as more fixed, Europe vs. Syria, with a clear edge between them. Furthermore, their agencies and identities are inconsistently expressed (although unconsciously); that is, they seek agencies' fulfilment in Europe while they still identify themselves as Syrians (while Syria is framed as an abhorrent place). More importantly, their agencies are preeminent (or just exercised) as much as they are poor and weak Syrians. Simply put, agencies of those who preferred Europe *are* in a place, Europe, and their self-identities *are* in another *separately fixed* place, Syria (figure 12.3b).

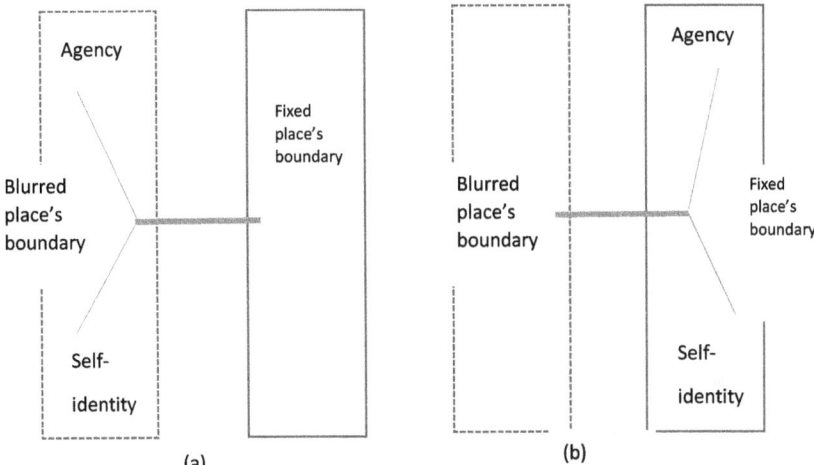

Figure 12.3. Representing the Narratives: (a) agency and self-identity exercised in the same place, Turkey (blurred boundaries between Turkey and Syria), and refugees prefer to stay in Turkey; (b) agency and self-identity exercised in different places, which have fixed boundaries (between Europe and Syria), and refugees prefer to leave for Europe. © Samer Sharani.

Home: Return or No Return

After presenting how Syrians comprehended Turkey and Europe, I will now bring the notion of home to the analysis's foci. Syria is negatively described by all of the interviewees: it is the place of fear, pressure; it meant nothing to some refugees; and it is stripped from being a "land," shrinking to be merely a social network. However, we cannot induce whether these refugees belong to Syria or do not. They, more importantly, *contradictorily* picture the home, as we will see.

Must, a twenty-five-year-old Syrian man who has been living in Istanbul and Edirne since 2014, said, "I do not feel any nostalgia. ... all my friends are killed or emigrated. ... All people who have stayed in Syria are forced to stay; they all prefer to leave it." Latif, a twenty-five-year-old Syrian man in Istanbul, had a similar feeling: "Look! I had lived for twenty-five years in Syria, where is it now? Gone! I belong to people not to place [land]."

Family occupies a special position among the social networks that give home its meaning. Zehlan, who now lives in Germany, said, "In Istanbul, early, I did not care about Syria, it meant nothing to me, only my family meant something to me. ... I even wished my mom die soon to relieve my pain, to relieve my Self, to cut all the relations with Syria."

And for Ahmad, Syria has no legitimate existence as he explained, "Syria has no history. I do not recognize something called Syria. What is Syria? Who controls Umayyad Square [the center of Damascus] controls Syria [he points to military coups]." Another interviewee, Arwa, had her own tragedy, bloodier than the others as she allegedly claimed: "The [Syrian] army attacked the town, they raped women, and threw them from windows, they killed men, and even they split a man into two parts ... a savage pain and fear my family experienced is what contributed to our decision to leave Syria."

Nevertheless, Arwa refused to leave at the beginning of the civil war; she said that people have paid huge amounts of money to leave the country. She blamed them because she thought, "We were in a revolution. We should have never left. ... How can we leave in the critical moment? They cannot kill all of us."

The place of Syria, seemingly, expels Syrians *by its "nature"* more than by political and other related circumstances, speaking at the fundamental level. Clearly according to Bai's saying, "We are the Syrians who cannot live in Syria, that is our identity," it is the identity that pushes Syrians out, more than other political or economic factors. Also, in Arwa's narrative above, the people and not the attack by the army per se are blamed for leaving the country. This view of home could be attributed to the nature of civil war, as circumstances become inseparable from the place itself. If it is the case, how could Syrians come back? And to which "Syria" may they return?

Tracing the "short narratives" allows for detecting the contradictions within narratives. Contradictions were present in most of the narratives when the interviewees highlighted the notion of home, describing it inconsistently along their narratives, sometimes *consciously*. Zehlan, for example, who lived in Istanbul for two years and then smuggled himself to Germany, denied "Syrian" as an identity when he was in Istanbul: "Syria meant nothing to me," he said. But, later during the narrative he consciously showed a contradicted conceptualization of Syria and re-narrated the home as following: "Syria is the place of my tortured childhood, it is the place of bullshit passing down from a generation to another. ... Its historical sites are where people pee, these sites are your identity [O Syrian!] This pain is in my bag I carry ... Syria has changed ... I miss the strong, warm hug, I miss Syria."

Bai consciously expressed, "I do not long for Syria, but when I started to forget the aspects of Damascus, I felt afraid." And Alaa has an unconscious contradiction regarding the home: "Feeling of home is dead," later he said, "the memories in home link me to there." Then he added after relating some other details, "I am proud of being a Syrian." Another Syrian, thirty-three-year-old Zeir, living in Istanbul, unconsciously expressed similar contradictions: "Who asks me, 'Who are you?' I say Muslim, human. I am not Syrian, I am not proud of being Syrian." Later he adds, "I long for my room,

I miss my parents, friends, the farms." Then he says, "But I cannot go back, I have children, so I have to look after them, it is a must, you know ... Syria will not be a good place ..."

Zeir's narrative shows that (1) he would like to return to (2) a place he hates, (3) but he cannot because he must raise his children away from the "bad" place. This contradiction in narrating home is, I argue, generated from perceiving identity and agency as exercised in separately fixed places, the host country and the home country. Agency is fulfilled in the "host," while identity is formed and anchored in the home, and both places are fixed in boundaries (that is why they are separated). Literature strongly discerns agency and identity as distinguishable from each other but entangled (Giddens 1991, 1984; Hitlin and Elder 2007). Therefore, distancing them generates this type of contradiction. Practically, we notice that lacking transnational activities and "home-making" thinking fuel this distancing.

When this contradiction is unconsciously experienced, some refugees express a very clear liminal status, as Samiha, a 34-year-old woman living in Istanbul, said: "You do not want to stay in Turkey, but you do, you want to go to Europe, but you cannot, you long for memories in Syria but you are far away. You live in three places at the same time, and at the same time you live in no place."

However, others do not have this strong and clear status of liminality when they are more engaged in transnational activities, more identified as Muslims, and less distanced from their identity as Syrians. In other words, identity and agency tend to be anchored in the *same* place, which is defined as a place with blurry boundaries–Turkey is almost blended with Syria. The religious Mohammad, who is satisfied with his agency in Istanbul and with his identity by attending, for example, religious Arabic lessons, said, "If I bring my mother here, I will never go back, because 90 percent of the Syrians in Syria are bad persons ... but if Turkey annexes Aleppo, I will go back to Aleppo." Later he added, "But even if I take the Turkish nationality, I will teach my children that they are Arab Syrians."

Despite his engagement in transnational activities, Mohammad has a latent contradiction in picturing home, to some extent. As in the cases of Mohammad and Samiha, refugees who unconsciously embed contradictions in their narratives of home are either not sure about home return or they are certain of non-return.

On the contrary, those who explicitly extracted the contradiction to the surface of their narratives consciously (such as Bai; see below) expressed their deep desire to return home, but not as a simple movement. Rather, home return is a project that contributes to rebuilding the home. Bai, for example, said, "I plan to go back to rebuild. Before the war there was no hope, but after the huge damage, hope could exist. You can be active, even those who are in Europe must build bridges to Syria. ... I mean everyone should invest in Syria."

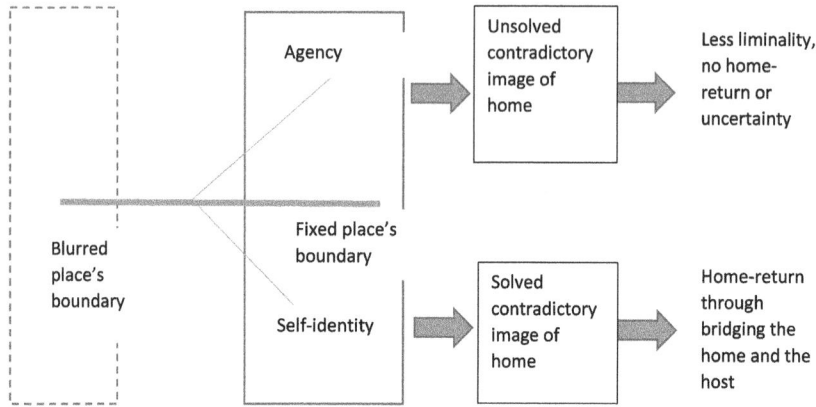

Figure 12.4. The Mechanisms of (Non)Home Return Desire. © Samer Sharani.

Zehlan said something similar: "I will come back only with strong knowledge. I will go back to invest in the society." Both of them try to solve the contradiction between identity and agency by investing more in homemaking. Thus, places are conceptualized as *actively* blurry; Bia and Zehlan laboriously bridge the two places. Home return then becomes a result of this solved contradiction mechanism.

To sum up, every interviewed refugee expressed a level of contradiction in picturing home. Those not engaged in solving this contradiction expressed various levels of liminality and showed no desire for home return or were uncertain. By contrast, those engaged in solving the contradiction showed a desire to bridge the host and home and to make a home return (figure 12.4).

Conclusion

Syrian refugees in Turkey have three alternatives: staying in Turkey, moving to Europe, or returning home. This study sought to probe into how Syrian refugees accomplish their intentions about these three alternatives.

By using a theory-building method, synthesizing different theoretical frameworks on home return—as a wide theme—this study suggests a theoretical model used to analyze refugees' narratives. This model consists of two nexuses: identity-agency and place. Identity-agency nexus is composed of two dimensions, self-identity and agency. Although they are inextricable, someone can assert one at the expense of the other while shaping an intention and practicing his/her identity and agency at the everyday level. Therefore, these two dimensions appear as opposite poles on one axis. The other nexus, place, is defined as an abstract container that coalesces social and cultural norms, infrastructure, social relationships, and the like. In other words, place contains what makes the self-identity and agency possible to be exercised and actualized. Also, this nexus has two opposite poles: fixed boundaries between places (the "host" and the home) and blurred ones. The fixed comprehension of place deals with the "host" and the home as two separate places; you are either there or here. By contrast, a blurry place means that the "host" and home could be practiced and experienced at the same time through transnational activities and engaged in home-making practices.

Analyzing the narratives that were collected from Syrian refugees (who are still in Turkey, or who once lived in Turkey before moving to Europe) resulted in what follows. First, those who highlighted their identities and agencies equally and pictured the place's boundaries as blurry preferred to stay in Turkey over fleeing to Europe, while those who primed their agencies over self-identities preferred Europe over Turkey. Second, among Syrian refugees in Europe, some of them pictured the place's boundaries as fixed, splitting the "host" from the home, which resulted in establishing their agencies on a self-contradictory ground. S/he fulfils her/his agency as much as s/he is a weak Syrian, whereas her/his self-identity as Syrian is denied. This study tried to show that integration per se is not what impacts the refugees' decisions but a mechanism lurking behind it. How refugees "interpret" an integration policy is due to how they understand their agencies, self-identities, and place.

Third, regarding home return, all interviewees depicted the home negatively. By talking about the home, Syrians showed various levels of contradiction, which again emanate from representing place's boundaries as fixed and anchoring the self-identities and agencies in the two separated places (home/host). This contradiction sometimes was cognitively pulled to the surface of narrative and sometimes was kept silent and unrecognized. Those who recognized this contradiction and tried to solve it expressed a clear desire to return home, contrary to the others who were unaware of this contradiction. It is worthy to mention that home return was understood as a complex and laborious process that inherently includes efforts to bridge both the home and host places, the place of agency's fulfilment and the place of self-belonging.

Finally, this study is not without limitations. Besides the small sample, which threatens the results' generalization, operationalizing the concepts is an arduous task. Future research may devote more efforts to find more concrete themes that denote the concepts of fixed/blurred place's boundaries, bridging host and home places, and the relationship between self-identity and agency. More importantly, this study ignores those who have lost *forever* their houses and properties in Syria due to compensation or damage. Accounting for the complex situation in Syria will be necessary for future research to illuminate a more precise picture on Syrians' intention of home return.

Appendix: The Research Sample

The research sample is a purposive sample, consisting of twenty-one Syrian refugees. They range between twenty and fifty years old. During interviews, I assured them that their personal information would not be shared or revealed to anyone or to any institution. Besides those who shared their names with me voluntarily, I did not ask for their full names. This procedure is important in the Syrian context, making the respondents feel comfortable. All the interviews were recorded and kept in a safe place. The interviews were transcribed immediately, then the original voice record was deleted. Only, the transcribed interviews were kept for further analysis on the researcher's personal computer. All these procedures were explained to the respondents.

The respondents' ages range between twenty and fifty years old. The rest of their personal attributes are presented in the table below.

Table 12.2. Personal Attributes of Syrian Refugees.

		Sex		Education			Occupation		Religion and ethnicity		
	Total	Female	Male	Primary	Secondary	Tertiary	Unskilled	Skilled	Sunni Arab	Sunni Kurdish	Minorities, unknown, or atheist
Refugees Number	21	8	13	2	12	7	4	17	12	1	8

The sample's distribution between Turkey, Germany, and Sweden is as follows:

	Total	Turkey	Sweden	Germany
Refugees Number	21	11	2	8

Table made by Samer Sharani.

Samer Sharani was born in Syria in 1986 and studied at Damascus University in 2005–12. He has been living in Istanbul, Turkey, since 2014. He finished a master's program in conflict analysis and resolution at Sabancı University in 2020. He is now a PhD student in political science and international relations at Sabancı University.

Notes

1. Syrians who are highly educated (doctors, engineers, etc.) and who have established businesses in Turkey are more likely to get Turkish nationality.
2. Although literature usually uses "repatriation" instead of "home return," I prefer the latter term because the European Union began to use the term "effective return" to indicate sending refugees/migrants back to their homes (see European Council: EU Migration Policy https://www.consilium.europa.eu/en/policies/migratory-pressures/).
3. For example, the European Uniont asserts that successful integration of Syrians (and refugees generally) is much less costly than failed or no integration. So, the EU member states apply effective policies to help refugees integrate in the educational system and the job market, supporting them with housing, monthly allowance, and the like (European Commission 2016).
4. Methodologically, it is worth noting that I did not come up with these two concepts prior to the analysis of the four approaches. Rather, these two concepts were extracted after making the analysis, i.e., they are ex post not ex ante concepts. However, I elaborate on them prior to the analysis to ease the reading.
5. This framework focuses on migrants, not refugees (i.e., on those who had emigrated for economic reasons, not because of persecution). Nevertheless, refugees and migrants are two overlapping categories (Erdal and Oeppen 2018).
6. Thematic analysis refers to revealing patterns of meanings that systematically unfold across the qualitative data. It allows the researcher to adjust the theoretical model after immersing it in the data, i.e., it allows for deductive-inductive method.
7. As mentioned earlier, Syrians in Turkey are under the Temporary Protection System, and they are not generally considered refugees as the case in Europe.

References

Ager, Alastair, and Alison Strang. 2008. "Understanding Integration: A Conceptual Framework." *Journal of Refugee Studies* 21(2): 166–91.

Akçapar, Şebnem Köşer, and Doğuş Şimşek. 2018. "The Politics of Syrian Refugees in Turkey: A Question of Inclusion and Exclusion through Citizenship." *Social Inclusion* 6(1): 176–87.

Al-Ali, Nadje, Richard Black, and Khalid Koser. 2001a. "Refugees and Transnationalism: The Experience of Bosnians and Eritreans in Europe." *Journal of Ethnic and Migration Studies* 27(4): 615–34.

———. 2001b. "The Limits to 'Transnationalism': Bosnian and Eritrea Refugees in Europe as Emerging Transnational Communities." *Ethnic and Racial Studies* 24(4): 578–600.
Alkire, Sabina. 2005. "Subjective Quantitative Studies of Human Agency." *Social Indicators Research* 74(1): 217–60.
Anthias, Floya. 2016. "Interconnecting Boundaries of Identity and Belonging and Hierarchy-Making within Transnational Mobility Studies: Framing Inequalities." *Current Sociology* 64(2): 172–90.
Baban, Feyzi, Suzan Ilcan, and Kim Rygiel. 2017. "Syrian Refugees in Turkey: Pathways to Precarity, Differential Inclusion, and Negotiated Citizenship Rights." *Journal of Ethnic and Migration Studies* 43(1): 41–57.
Balcılar, Mehmet, and Jeffrey B. Nugent. 2019. "The Migration of Fear: An Analysis of Migration Choices of Syrian Refugees." *Quarterly Review of Economics and Finance* 73(c): 95–110.
Bar-Tal, Daniel, and Ilai Alon. 2017. "Socio-psychological Approach to Trust (or Distrust): Concluding Comments." In *The Role of Trust in Conflict Resolution: The Israeli-Palestinian Case and Beyond*, edited by Ilai Alone and Daniel Bar-Tal, 311–36. New York: Springer.
Baumeister, Roy F., and Leonard S. Newman. 1995. "The Primacy of Stories, the Primacy of Roles, and the Polarizing Effects of Interpretive Motives: Some Propositions about Narratives." In *Advances in Social Cognition*, vol. 8: *Knowledge and Memory: The Real Story*, edited by Rober S. Wyer, 97–108. Hillsdale, NJ: Lawrence Erlbaum Associates, Inc.
Boswell, Christina, Andrew Geddes, and Peter Scholten. 2011. "The Role of Narratives in Migration Policy-Making: A Research Framework." *British Journal of Politics and International Relations* 13(1): 1–11.
Breakwell, Glynis M. 2001. "Mental Models and Social Representations of Hazards: The Significance of Identity Processes." *Journal of Risk Research* 4(4): 341–51.
———. 2014. "Identity Process Theory: Clarifications and Elaboration." In *Identity Process Theory: Identity, Social Action and Social Change*, edited by Rusi Jaspal and Glynis Breakwell, 20–37. Cambridge: Cambridge University Press.
Brockmeier, Jens. 2000. "Autobiographical Time." *Narrative Inquiry* 10(1): 51–73.
———. 2001. "From the End to the Beginning." In *Narrative and Identity*, edited by Jens Brockmeier and Donal Carbaugh, 247–80. Amsterdam: John Benjamins Publishing Company.
Brockmeier, Jens, and Rom Harre. 2001. "Narrative: Problems and Promises of an Alternative Paradigm." In *Narrative and Identity*, edited by Jens Brockmeier and Donal Carbaugh, 39–58. Amsterdam: John Benjamins Publishing Company.
Brown, Jennifer. 2011. "Expression of Diasporic Belonging: The Divergent Emotional Geographies of Britain's Polish Communities." *Emotion, Space and Society* 4(4): 229–37.
Bruner, Jerome. 1998. *Acts of Meaning*. Cambridge, MA: Harvard University Press.
Bruner, Jerome S. 2001. "Self-Making and World-Making." In *Narrative and Identity*, edited by Jens Brockmeier and Donal Carbaugh, 25–37. Amsterdam: John Benjamins Publishing Company.
Capo, Jasna. 2015. "Durable Solutions, Transnationalism, and Homemaking among Croatian and Bosnian Former Refugees." *Refuge* 31(1): 19–29.

Cassarino, Jean-Pierre. 2004. "Theorising Return Migration: The Conceptual Approach to Return Migrants Revisited." *International Journal on Multicultural Societies* 6(2): 253–79.
Chimni, Bhupinder S. 2002. "Refugees, Return and Reconstruction of 'Post-Conflict' Societies: A Critical Perspective." *International Peacekeeping* 9(2): 163–80.
Cieciuch, Jan, and Ewa Topolewska. 2017. "Circumplex of Identity Formation Modes: A Proposal for the Integration of Identity Constructs Developed in the Erikson-Marcia Tradition." *Self and Identity* 12(3): 37–61.
Clarke, Victoria, and Virginina Braun. 2017. "Thematic Analysis." *Journal of Positive Psychology* 12(3): 297–98.
Cruickshank, Jorn, Winfried Ellingsen, and Knut Hidle. 2013. "A Crisis of Definition: Culture versus Industry in Odda, Norway." *Geografiska Annaler: Series B, Human Geography* 95(2): 147–61.
Cuba, Lee, and David M. Hummon. 1993. "Constructing a Sense of Home: Place Affiliation and Migration across the Life Cycle." *Sociological Forum* 8(4): 547–72.
Daskalaki, Maria, Christina L. Butler, and Jelena Petrovic. 2016. "Somewhere In-between: Narratives of Place, Identity, and Translocal Work." *Journal of Management Inquiry* 25(2): 184–98.
de Haas, Hein. 2010. "Migration and Development: A Theoretical Perspective." *International Migration Review* 44(1): 227–64.
de Vroome, Thomas, Borja Martinovic, and Maykel Verkuyten. 2014. "The Integration Paradox: Level of Education and Immigrants' Attitudes towards Natives and the Host Society." *Cultural Diversity and Ethnic Minority Psychology* 20(2): 166–75.
Devine-Wright, Patrick. 2009. "Rethinking NIMBYism: The Role of Place Attachment and Place Identity in Explaining Place-Protective Action." *Journal of Community & Applied Social Psychology* 19(6): 426–41.
Devine-Wright, Patrick, and Evanthia Lyons. 1997. "Remembering Pasts and Representing Places: The Construction of National Identities in Ireland." *Journal of Environmental Psychology* 17(1): 33–45.
Di Masso, Andres, John Dixon, and Enric Pol. 2011. "On the Contested Nature of Place: 'Figuera's Well,' 'The Hole of Shame' and the Ideological Struggle over Public Space in Barcelona." *Journal of Environmental Psychology* 31(3): 231–44.
Dixon, John, and Kevin Durrheim. 2000. "Displacing Place-Identity: A Discursive Approach to Locating Self and Other." *British Journal of Social Psychology* 39(1): 27–44.
———. 2004. "Dislocating Identity: Desegregation and the Transformation of Place." *Journal of Environmental Psychology* 24(4): 455–73.
Djenar, Dwi W. 2016. "That's How It Is There." *Narrative Inquiry* 26(2): 402–29.
Ecke, Jonas, Geetor Saydee, Joseph W. Nyan, Kalilu Donzo, Mackie K. Dolo, and Richard Russ. 2016. "The Subjective and Economic Well-Being of Repatriated Liberian Refugees from Ghana." *Refugee Survey Quarterly* 35(3): 119–43.
Einhorn, Barbara. 2000. "Gender, National, Landscape and Identity in Narratives of Exile and Return." *Women's Studies International Forum* 23(6): 701–13.
Erdal, Marta Bivand, and Ceri Oeppen. 2018. "Forced to Leave? The Discursive and Analytical Significance of Describing Migration as Forced and Voluntary." *Journal of Ethnic and Migration Studies* 44(6): 981–98.
Essuman-Johnson, Abeeku. 2011. "When Refugees Don't Go Home: The Situation of Liberian Refugees in Ghana." *Journal of Immigrant and Refugee Studies* 9(2): 105–26.

European Commission. 2016. *The EU Integration Action Plan of Third-Country Nationals*. EU: The European Commission
Fabbe, Kristin, and Tolga İnmazdemir. 2019. "Reflections on the Geopolitics of Refugees and Displaced Persons: Syrian Refugees in Turkey and the Politics of Post-conflict Reconciliation." *Review of Middle East Studies* 52(2): 249–62.
Feldman, Carol F. 2001. "Narratives of National Identity as Group Narratives." In *Narrative and Identity*, edited by Jens Brockmeier and Donal Carbaugh, 129–44. Amsterdam: John Benjamins Publishing Company.
Fereday, Jennifer, and Eimear Muir-Cochrane. 2006. "Demonstrating Rigor Using Thematic Analysis: A Hybrid Approach of Inductive and Deductive Coding and Theme." *International Journal of Qualitative Methods* 5(1): 80–92.
Finfgeld-Connett, Deborah, and E. Diane Johnson. 2013. "Literature Search Strategies for Conducting Knowledge-Building and Theory-Generating Qualitative Systematic Reviews." *Journal of Advanced Nursing* 69(1): 194–204.
Fransen, Sonja, Isabel Ruiz, and Carlos Vargas-Silvam. 2017. "Return Migration and Economic Outcomes in the Conflict Context." *World Development* 95: 196–210.
Georgakopoulou, Alexandra. 2006. "Thinking Big with Small Stories in Narrative and Identity Analysis." *Narrative Inquiry* 16(1): 122–30.
Giddens, Anthony. 1984. *The Constitution of Society: Outline of the Theory of Structuration*. Berkeley: University of California Press.
———. 1991. *Modernity and Self-Identity: Self and Society in the Late Modern Age*. Stanford, CA: Stanford University Press.
Hanninen, Vilma. 2004. " A Model of Narrative Circulation." *Narrative Inquiry* 14(1): 69–85.
Harre, Rom. 2001. "Metaphysics and Narrative." In *Narrative and Identity*, edited by Jens Brockmeier and Donal Carbaugh, 59–73. Amsterdam: John Benjamins Publishing Company.
Heimerl, Danieal. 2005. "The Return of Refugees and Internally Displaced Persons: From Coercion to Sustainability?" *International Peacekeeping* 12(3): 377–90.
Hermans, Hubert J. M. 2000. "The Coherence of Incoherent Narratives." *Narrative Inquiry* 10(1): 223–27.
Hitlin, Steven, and Glen H. Elder Jr. 2007. "Time, Self, and the Curiously Abstract Concept of Agency." *Sociological Theory* 25(2): 170–91.
Huizinga, Rik P., and Bettina van Hoven. 2018. "Everyday Geographies of Belonging: Syrian Refugee Experiences in the Northern Netherlands." *Geoforum* 96: 309–17.
İçduygu, Ahmet. 2015. *Syrian Refugees in Turkey: The Long Road Ahead*. Washington, DC: Migration Policy Institute.
İçduygu, Ahmet, and Maissam Nimer. 2019. "The Politics of Return: Exploring the Future of Syrian Refugees in Jordan, Lebanon and Turkey." *Third World Quarterly* 41(3): 415–33.
İneli-Ciğer, Meltem. 2017. "Protecting Syrians in Turkey: A Legal Analysis." *International Journal of Refugee Law* 29(4): 555–79.
Josselson, Ruthellen. 2006. "Narrative Research and the Challenge of Accumulating Knowledge." *Narrative Inquiry* 16(1): 3–10.
Kaya, Ayhan. 2017. "A Tale of Two Cities: Aleppo and Istanbul." *European Review* 25(3): 365–87.

Khiabany, Gholam. 2016. "Refugee Crisis, Imperialism and Pitiless Wars on the Poor." *Media, Culture & Society* 38(5): 755–62.
Kivisto, Peter, and Vanja La Vecchia-Mikkola. 2015. "The Integration of Iraqis in Two European Cities: Emotions and Identity Work." *Emotion, Space and Society* 16: 90–98.
Koinova, Maria. 2018. "Diaspora Mobilization for Conflict and Post-conflict Reconstruction: Contextual and Comparative Dimensions." *Journal of Ethnic and Migration Studies* 44(8): 1251–69.
Kraus, Wolfgang. 2006. "The Narrative Negotiation of Identity and Belonging." *Narrative Inquiry* 16(1): 103–11.
Kumsa, Martha Kuwee. 2006. "'No! I'm Not a Refugee!' The Poetics of Be-Longing among Young Oromos in Toronto." *Journal of Refugee Studies* 19(2): 230–55.
Kutlu Tonak, Zümray. 2016. "Endless Escape: From Syria to Turkey, Then to Europe." *Studies in Ethnicity and Nationalism* 16(1): 121–34.
Levitt, Peggy, and Nina Glick Schiller. 2004. "Conceptualizing Simultaneity: A Transnational Social Field Perspective on Society." *International Migration Review* 38(3): 1002–39.
Liu, Liangni Sally. 2014. "A Search for a Place to Call Home: Negotiation of Home, Identity and Senses of Belonging among New Migrants from the People's Republic of China (PRC) to New Zealand." *Emotion, Space and Society* 10: 18–26.
Long, Katy. 2011. "Refugees, Repatriation and Liberal Citizenship." *History of European Ideas* 37(2): 232–41.
Mankowski, Eric, and Julian Rappaport. 1995. "Stories, Identity, and the Psychological Sense of Community." In *Knowledge and Memory: The Real Story Advances in Social Cognition*, edited by Robert S. Wyer, 211–26. Hillsdale, NJ: Lawrence Erlbaum Associates, Inc.
Memişoğlu, Fulya, and Aslı Ilgit. 2017. "Syrian Refugees in Turkey: Multifaceted Challenged, Diverse Players and Ambiguous Policies." *Mediterranean Politics* 22(3): 317–83.
Mitzen, Jennifer. 2018. "Anxious Community: EU as (In)Security Community." *European Security* 27(3): 393–413.
Muggeridge, Helen, and Giorgia Dona. 2006. "Back Home? Refugees' Experience of Their First Visit Back to Their Country of Origin." *Journal of Refugee Studies* 19(4): 415–32.
Multeciler Dernegi. 2019. 19 September. Retrieved 19 October 2019 from https://multeciler.org.tr/.
Nilson, Hilde Lindemann. 2001. *Damaged Identities, Narrative Repair*. New York: Cornell University Press.
Nukaga, Misako. 2013. "Planning for a Successful Return Home: Transnational Habitus and Education Strategies among Japanese Expatriate Mothers in Los Angeles." *International Sociology* 28(1): 66–83.
Nzima, Divane, and Philani Moyo. 2017. "The New 'Diaspora Trap' Framework: Explanation Return Migration from South Africa to Zimbabwe beyond the 'Failure-Success' Framework." *Migration Letters* 14(3): 355–70.
Omata, Naohiko. 2013. "The Complexity of Refugees' Return Decision-Making in a Protracted Exile: Beyond the Home-Coming Model and Durable Solutions." *Journal of Ethnic and Migration Studies* 39(8): 1281–97.

Pretty, Grace H., Heather M. Chipuer, and Paul Bramston. 2003. "Sense of Place amongst Adolescents and Adults in Two Rural Australian Towns: The Discriminating Features of Place Attachment, Sense of Community and Place Dependence in Relation to Place Identity." *Journal of Environmental Psychology* 23(3): 273–87.

Rabinowitz, Dan. 2010. "The Rights to Refuse: Abject Theory and the Return of Palestinian Refugees." *Critical Inquiry* 36(3): 494–516.

Roudometof, Victor. 2005. "Transnationalism, Cosmopolitanism and Glocalization." *Current Sociology* 53(1): 113–35.

Ruby, Tabassum Fahim. 2013. "Muslim Women and the Ontario Shari'ah Tribunals: Discourses of Race and Imperial Hegemony in the Name of Gender Equality." *Women's Studies International Forum* 38: 32–42.

Saint Pierre, Francesca Di, Borja Martinovic, and Thomas de Vroome. 2015. "Return Wishes of Refugees in the Netherlands: The Role of Integration, Host National Identification and Perceived Discrimination." *Journal of Ethnic and Migration Studies* 41(11): 1836–57.

Savaş, Özlem. 2010. "The Collective Turkish Home in Vienna: Aesthetic Narratives of Migration and Belonging." *Home Cultures* 7(3): 313–40.

Schank, Roger C., and Robert P. Abelson. 1995. "Knowledge and Memory: The Real Story." In *Advances in Social Cognition*, vol. 8: *Knowledge and Memory: The Real Story*, edited by Robert S. Wyer, 1–85. Hillsdale, NJ: Lawrence Erlbaum Associates, Inc.

Schinkel, Willem. 2018. "Against 'Immigrant Integration': For an End to Neocolonial Knowledge Production." *Comparative Migration Studies* 6(31). https://doi.org/10.1186/s40878-018-0095-1.

Scipioni, Marco. 2018. "Failing forward in EU Migration Policy? EU Integration after the 2015 Asylum and Migration Crisis." *Journal of European Public Policy* 25(9): 1357–75.

Şimşek, Doğuş. 2018. "Integration Processes of Syrian Refugees in Turkey: 'Class-Based Integration'." *Journal of Refugee Studies* https://doi.org/10.1093/jrs/fey057.

———. 2019. "Transnational Activities of Syrian Refugees in Turkey: Hindering or Supporting Integration." *International Migration* 57(2): 268–82.

Tete, Suzanne Y. A. 2012. "'Any Place Could be Home': Embedding Refugees' Voices into Displacement Resolution and State Refugee Policy." *Geoforum* 43(1): 106–15.

Tezcan, Tolga. 2019. "Return Home? Determinants of Return Migration Intention amongst Turkish Immigrants in Germany." *Geoforum* 98: 189–201.

Timotijevic, Lada, and Glynis M. Breakwell. 2000. "Migration and Threat to Identity." *Journal of Community and Applied Social Psychology* 10(5): 355–72.

Tuckett, Anthony G. 2005. "Applying Thematic Analysis Theory to Practice: A Researcher's Experience." *Contemporary Nurse* 19(1–2): 75–87.

UNHCR (United Nations High Commissioner for Refugees). 2019. "Registered Syrian Refugees." Retrieved 15 October 2019 from https://data2.unhcr.org/en/situations/syria/location/113.

Vignoles, Vivian L., Xenia Chryssochoou, and Glynis M. Breakwell. 2002. "Evaluating Models of Identity Motivation: Self-Esteem Is Not the Whole Story." *Self and Identity* 1(3): 201–18.

Yurdakul, Gökçe, and Anna C. Korteweg. 2013. "Gender Equality and Immigrant Integration: Honor Killing and Forced Marriage Debates in the Netherlands, Germany, and Britain." *Women's Studies International Forum* 41(3): 204–14.

Zisser, Eya. 2019. "The Syrian Refugees–Left to Their Fate." *British Journal of Middle Eastern Studies* 46(2): 293–309.

Concluding Remarks

Erol Balkan and Zümray Kutlu Tonak

As of September 2020, there were nearly 80 million forcibly displaced people worldwide (UNHCR 2020). Among them were 5.6 million Syrians who fled their country. Turkey, together with Lebanon and Jordan, are the leading host countries for Syrian refugees. While millions of Syrians remain displaced within their own country, those who have found a way to overcome increasingly sealed borders are struggling with anti-immigrant measures, xenophobia, mounting racism, and limited access to basic human rights. The pandemic of racism and intolerance has a longer history than that of Covid-19; at this writing, however, both are in full swing.

When we started working on this book, the growing population of refugees the world over was already facing challenging conditions; the criminalization of asylum seekers and restrictive measures taken against them by the wealthy states of the North, limited access to basic rights in the host countries, and protracted incarceration in refugee camps with inadequate facilities were very much in evidence. An increasing number of refugees were defying European borders, and Europe was thus forced to pay more attention to them due to a simple accident of geography. Most of the discussion taking place there concerned potential ways to keep the refugees near their countries of origin. Europe's immediate periphery turned into a buffer zone, whose function was to keep the refugees out of the European Union itself. Southern and Eastern European countries began to grapple with an unprecedented influx of refugees. In the meantime, limited humanitarian relief and assistance were offered by the wealthier members of the European Union so that the already economically struggling host countries were forced to shoulder an increasing share of the burden.

People do not become refugees as a result of individual actions in specific settings. Rather, the refugee problem is the inevitable result of the international state system in which we live (Haddad 2008). The increasing emphasis placed on aligning rights with belonging points directly to the international context in which the refugee problem has arisen. The current focus on security and policy has suppressed any possibility of addressing the actual reasons for which refugees become refugees. Although the motivation for seeking refuge is often a war, the causes of that war are not questioned. Everyone agrees that refugees experience unbearable and inhuman conditions in their home countries, but providing them with humanitarian relief is preferred to taking direct political action that might address the war that made such relief necessary.

Focusing on Syrian refugees in Europe and Turkey, the chapters in this book offer a variety of perspectives and research results. The authors mainly address the challenges that refugees face in different localities and make us think of, and question, the international context. Rising nationalism in Europe, conditions prevailing in refugee camps in Greece, the criminalization of asylum seeking, and the working conditions faced by Syrian refugees are just some of the topics addressed by this book. Furthermore, although these issues certainly remain important and relevant, conditions have worsened with the ongoing pandemic, the economic crises, fires, closed borders, and an increasingly harsh anti-immigrant and racist political climate.

We believe this book contributes to furthering the public's understanding of the current state of affairs for refugees. Once a hero and now a criminal, the refugee has seen their image evolve in recent years in accordance with the changing political interests of concerned governments. But refugees are, first and foremost, our neighbors, our friends, our families; hearing their stories, understanding the causes that have forced them to leave their homes, and showing solidarity with them must be our primary response.

Erol Balkan is professor of economics at Hamilton College and visiting professor at Sabancı University in Istanbul. His current research focuses on the impact of the pandemic on refugee communities.

Zümray Kutlu Tonak is lecturer at Smith College. She received her BA and MS in sociology from Middle East Technical University, her MA in theory and practice of human rights from the University of Essex, and her PhD in political science from İstanbul Bilgi University. Her teaching and research focus on refugees, urbanization, and human rights.

References

Haddad, E. 2008. *The Refugee in International Society*. Cambridge: Cambridge University Press.

UNHCR. 2020. "Figures at a Glance." Retrieved 12 December 2020 from https://www.unhcr.org/figures-at-a-glance.html.

Appendix

Statement from the Association of Bridging Peoples

It Is Not a Refugee Crisis, It Is a Secret War against Refugees

Cem Terzi

Who We Are?

I am writing this statement on behalf of the Association of Bridging Peoples. Thus, it would be best to start by describing the association, which was set up in İzmir, Turkey, in 2014 to establish public solidarity and friendship between peoples based on the principles of equality, justice, and freedom. As a volunteer coalition, we consider ourselves a solidarity group rather than a nongovernmental organization. We do not hold back from politics because we do not separate life from politics, and we are on the side of life. We strive to build a public space for the politics of friendship, striving for a society free of hate, fear, isolation, conflict, and enmity toward one another. We work on a voluntary basis and believe in collective efforts without seeking parochial interests.

We have been working for and with refugees since Turkey, in general, and İzmir, in particular, have become major destinations for people escaping war and insecurities in their home countries. Our association includes a large health group consisting of nurses, midwives, dentists, healthcare workers, dietitians, psychologists, and doctors, including a field group that scans the streets and neighborhoods; a translation/interpretation group with experts in Arabic, Kurdish, and Farsi; and an art and culture group that organizes events for adults and children. We have carried out a wide range of activities in different neighborhoods and with the participation of hundreds of volunteers. People from different professions and backgrounds contribute with their labor. Our volunteers also include musicians, actors, lawyers, teachers, students, workers, unemployed people, and, most importantly, refugees. We hold no executive committee meetings. Activities are organized and run through public meetings open to all. Membership is not a necessary condition for attending the public meetings. Everyone has equal voting rights—irrespective of membership status. People contribute what they can, without having to compromise on who or what they are. Since day one, we have never turned our back on any of the refugees who sought our help. We have met more than 150,000 refugees face-to-face and treated or helped to find treatment for more than 7,000 refugee patients.

The Association of Bridging Peoples is not in the business of preparing "projects" for the United Nations (UN) or the European Union (EU). We think the conventional "project" approach is conducive to quasi-professionalism and undermines the spirit of voluntary work. Voluntary work enables us to escape the trap of market relations and protects us against the degeneration of our labor into a market good. We do not accept any monetary donations from any state(s) or national or international institution. We value our independence and the capacity to question shared wisdom. We carry out our mission supported by small voluntary donations and membership fees.

We believe in solidarity—not in charity. In fact, we think charity is dysfunctional because it is momentary, and its reach is person specific. Charity creates a culture of dependency conditional on the will of the wealthy and powerful. The equitable dispensing of charitable donations may not be taken for granted. Financial support cannot substitute for collective social, economic, and political responsibilities or for the public good. Charity can only have a complementary function. Therefore, we have always called on the government and its officials to carry out their duties. For each work field and health intervention, we have written detailed reports and submitted them to the governor's office, health directorates, and public health directorates. We have produced the information of the streets, informed the public, and democratized the production and dissemination of information.

Solidarity corresponds to rights-based struggles. It is not limited to the provision of healthcare, food, or clothing. It is based on community objectives, specifically regarding refugees, and acting together with them. Solidarity precludes conceptions of the refugees as helpless victims and requires support for their united voices and political entitlements. It involves participation in the fight they lead for their just rights. It precludes incorporation into the state(s)' vertical politics of command. It means questioning the political consequences of state actions. We embrace solidarity as the "politeness of the oppressed" and as the oldest and most precious institution of humanity.

The West and the Rest–Reasons of Migrations

Besides, from the military interventions in the Middle East, the economic and political understanding that we call "the West and the rest" is the main reason for the chaos and the violence in the Middle East, Africa, and Asia. Neoliberalism has seriously boosted inequality between the North and the South, which has caused fragile social structures in the Global South. A significant number of people from all around the world, especially from war-torn regions, are looking for a new life because of desperate structural problems. The main reasons for the migration movements in the world today directly relate to global economic powers, political pressures, economic marginalization, discrimination, and the ugly face of globalization. The globalization that makes capital and commodities transcend all the borders does not offer equal opportunity for either the refugees or the migrants. European countries, such as Turkey, criminalize refugees and militarize borders, yet they have a vested interest in their open-air prison system for these people. It was the Western intervention in Libya that threw the country into chaos. It was the US attack on Iraq that created the conditions for the rise of Islamic State. The ongoing civil war in the Central African Republic between the Christian south and the Muslim north was not just an explosion of ethnic hatred; it was triggered by the discovery of oil in the north: France and China fight for the control of resources through their proxies. It is necessary to understand that the first reason for the recent refugee issue lies in the fact that the current turbulent, violent, and unstable context in Africa and the Middle East has brought together migrants and refugees from different origins, all seeking a better life in Europe. Perceiving refugees as a threat to security initiated the European anti-migration policies, such as criminalizing refugees, militarizing the borders, and transferring refugees to subcontractors, that have been prevailing for years. The main reason for the rise of boat incidents and the dead bodies washing ashore are the migration policies of the EU. Europe asks Turkey to ban the crossings to Europe, to keep the refugees in Turkey, and to protect "the Fortress of Europe"; the plan is to turn Turkey into an open-air prison for refugees.

We, the Association of Bridging Peoples, do not define the situation as a "refugee crisis" per se in our position papers. Identifying the situation as a singular identity crisis hinders a critical comprehensive analysis and the establishment of a rational ethical position. We approach the situation as a humanitarian, political, historical, and economic crisis.

Migration of Syrians

Since April 2011, approximately seven million Syrians have been forced to migrate, and almost four million came to Turkey because of the civil war, which was intensified by intervention of several states. The Syrian uprising followed a range of uprisings in the Arab world. We witnessed the process of the uprising turn into a proxy war with sectarian overtones. The People of Syria are not defeated in Syria and eventually forced into massive migration; instead, the People of Syria are defeated in Washington, Paris, Riyadh, Ankara, Doha, etc., in the competitive nature of the power struggles of the international system to secure the markets, possess energy and resources, control energy, and continue the "realization-evaluation" cycle in the military industry.

In 2016, the Aegean Sea became the passageway used by human smugglers to transport nearly one million people from Turkey to Europe. This crossing resulted in thousands of deaths on irregular migration routes. The main reason for the rise of boat accidents and the dead bodies washing ashore indirectly relates to the migration policies of the European Countries and the European Union. Within the EU, emerging political responses to the problem have been crafted largely on national rather than union perspectives.

The main concern in European countries has been keeping the influx of migrants under control. Nearly all governments in Europe have built long razor-edged fences along the borders and forced the refugees to change their route, intensifying their attempts to reach the Eastern Aegean Islands. In Europe, right-wing groups have emerged in opposition to migration, and many forces are exploiting this hostile mood.

The responses and responsibilities of the neighboring countries were disappointing as well. In July 2015, Turkey's open-door policy started to change, and finally, Turkey closed the borders as well and built a long wall on its Syrian border. Now, although the war is still going on, Syrians are no longer allowed to migrate to Turkey.

Turkey has 4.5 million refugees, of which 4 million are Syrians. Only 10 percent of Syrians are living in 25 refugee camps located in 10 Turkish provinces close to the border region with Syria. Other Syrians, scattered in other parts of Turkey, are struggling daily with their own resources by begging for food, finding employment in the informal and temporary job sector, or getting social aid.

Turkey refuses to grant legal refugee status to refugees from outside Europe, thereby depriving them of the rights and benefits they would otherwise have as registered refugees. The treatment of refugees as "guests" and the new national legal framework, "temporary protection," offer the government great flexibility and freedom of action. Syrians living in Turkey are considered "guests" with temporary protection status and a lack of permanent residence permits. Turkey's approach to the problem has always been charity based rather than rights based. The management of Syrians in Turkey is based on ideological and political reasons and on the faulty assumption that their stay in Turkey would be of a short duration (three months!). However, due to the uncontrollable dimension of the mass inflow and the absence of a strong infrastructure in the Turkish asylum system to deal with it, all politics related to Syrian refugees has failed. Because of the number of Syrian refugees, Turkey has been greatly affected in terms of not only foreign affairs but also domestic issues.

Turkey is giving neither Syrians nor other refugees official refugee status; thus, it is not a safe country for them. They are not under the cover of international law in Turkey without an official refugee status. Those who enjoyed temporary protection are not allowed to apply for individual refugee status determination, so they do not have any chance to be resettled in a third country by the United Nations High Commissioner for Refugees (UNHCR) in the same way as other non-European refugees do. This accords unlimited freedom to the Turkish government to make decisions concerning the lives and future of four million Syrian refugees. If the government decides that they constitute a risk to the security of the country or a threat to public order, the refugees can and will be deported.

What Should Turkey Do?

The simplest fact is that millions of people flee their countries and lose their rights based on national citizenship, and thus, as refugees, they struggle to survive in a foreign country where they are deprived of basic rights, including the right to citizenship. In this regard, the people in the host nations, as they welcome refugees and migrants, should adopt an unconditional and ethical approach that goes beyond the conjectural needs of nation-state or limitations of international hegemonic powers and institutions.

We, the Association of Bridging Peoples, express our desire to establish a relationship with the oppressed, refugees, and migrants who are marginalized above and beyond the legalistic and institutional view of the world. By doing so, we open a pathway to protest injustice and exploitation in pursuit of human rights. The Association of Bridging Peoples says "Welcome" unconditionally to all refugees and migrants, without any ifs, ands, or buts!

The "right to rights" for these people who are stripped of all basic rights upholds their right to exist without being pushed around or absorbed by dominant politics and powers. It is in fact a right to self-determination and political existence. No government should be allowed to strip the refugees of their political rights and take away their national identities as their own political subjects. We believe that being a political subject begins with having the right to self-determination of one's own life. This right can be achieved internationally if political subjects receive their rights to full refugee status and access to citizenship in the host nations. Without hesitation, we demand the granting of refugee status and the right to citizenship to all refugees and migrants in Turkey.

For these reasons, we should remember the conditions in which foreigners live in Turkey and the fact that Syrians are not the only ones who are deprived of citizenship rights. Foreigners in Turkey come from many countries such as Iraq, Afghanistan, Pakistan, Iran, Romania, Ukraine, Russia, Bangladesh, and Georgia. Even before the Syrian refugees arrived, all of these people have been exploited in the labor market without any rights and protection. They have been living on the streets in Turkey with neither recognized visibility as humans nor the status of refugees.

While capitalism and capitalist nation-states continue to produce the conditions, which provoke cross-country migrations, migrants themselves continue to be used as cheap and "flexible" labor for increasing profits. When the core capitalist states' cheap labor markets have been saturated, late capitalist states, like China, India, and Turkey, have opened their economies to cheap migrant labor. Turkey has accommodated over one hundred thousand migrant workers in the last twenty years. Just like core capitalist states, Turkey has intentionally accepted many irregular/undocumented migrant workers and fed its growing economy with their cheap and flexible labor power. It is believed that almost one million foreign workers are underpaid and without any insurance or union support in various industries, including textile production and mining, agriculture and construction, tourism and entertainment (including the sex industry), domestic work, and elder care. Owners of small and medium-sized businesses are especially happy with this new army of slaves of global capitalism. By not paying the minimum wage, by employing underpaid, undocumented, and unprotected migrant workers, such companies make extra profits.

Based on these facts, we challenge those who view the Syrian workers as the cause of low wages, unemployment, and poverty. Employers forced Turkish workers to endure exploitative working conditions long before the Syrians arrived. For these reasons, our call for the right to citizenship is not just for Syrians but also for all migrants in Turkey. We recognize that social, political, and economic injustices have created the systemic and structural exploitation of human life. As part of the international framework of rights, we demand the granting of full refugee status to all migrants and refugees and the banishment of segregation between citizens and foreigners, and we demand that all migrants be granted the right to citizenship.

The Right to Citizenship and Discrimination

We reject the conditions and criteria put forward for granting citizenship, such as skills, education, and economic status. These are elements of class-based discrimination. Those most oppressed require the most protection. We stand in solidarity with the poor, the women, and the children. It is those neglected children missing their vaccinations and all types of healthcare, the exploited Syrian child workers laboring ten to twelve hours a day, the underpaid seasonal farm workers, the exploited "Syrian brides" married to Turkish men as second wives, the sick and elderly, and the Syrian LGBTI members who most deserve the right to citizenship.

Our call for the right to citizenship is not a glorification of the nation-state or the borders that encircle it. On the contrary, we call for people fleeing wars and economic conditions to do so knowing "no borders." We also stand with the continued hope of refugees to return to their own countries. We stand in solidarity with their claim and their fight for their freedom and existence on their own land. We define the nation as a collective of people willing to live together in an enriched society of diversity rather than enforced singularity. Our call for citizenship is not about glorifying nationalism here but about fostering a world that supports human rights for all people.

We call on the refugees: if you want to become an equal part of this nation, we stand in support with your demands and your right to live here.

At this point, we call on all asylum seekers, refugees, and migrants on this land: we defend your right for free, safe passage to this country. In accordance with your wishes, we demand the right to citizenship. We do not see citizenship as a form of social integration that swallows and eliminates you or your identity, uses you for economic exploitation, or categorizes you based on your background, nationality, religion, or ethnicity in the name of social engineering projects. We see you as our partners in the struggle for a new society of democracy, freedom, and equality. With the hope of knowing and understanding "one and all," we say "Welcome" to people of all nations.

We were all foreigners at some stage, and in the future we could be foreigners in another country. That we were born on this land does not make us its owners. All land is for all people. Hence, real hospitality is about internationalism. The fight for internationalism will transform and change us all.

Utopian positions are also forces that change reality. In fact, we require this utopia as much as you do to be and stay human. We need this equity for a democratic world and a democratic nation-state.

By rejecting the definition of citizenship as being part of national identity, we also reject the ethnic and religious totalitarianism of nation-states. Instead, we see nations as a political form that intends for us to live together in a diverse society that welcomes the newcomers. "Civilization" began with settlement. By taking away people's rights to settle down, you take away their humanity. A nation is a collective of people settled together. Newcomers are not a danger or a threat to the nation but rather a cultural enrichment.

Conclusion

Migration is a major social issue of our times. Migrants are and continue to be important political actors of the future.

In addition, many movements of social solidarity with migrants/refugees are occurring all around the world. Despite Europe's policy toward migrants, people of various countries, from Greece to Germany, have seriously and unexpectedly supported and aided refugees in crossing the borders. The antimigrant wave in Europe is not a new phenomenon. Solidarity of the people and the peoples' friendships will be an obstacle toward the antimigrant atmosphere in Europe that causes fascist organizations to grow.

The existing conditions of today, with migrants risking their lives to seek protection, makes the EU asylum system unsustainable. Instead of signing new readmission agreements with other countries, the EU should focus on preventing the desperation that leads to suffering and avoidable deaths.

The EU-Turkey "Readmission Agreement" should be abrogated: refugees must not be returned to the countries where they might face persecution.

European and other countries, especially those who are militarily active in the Middle East, should take responsibility for the refugees as much as the neighboring countries.

Providing political prerogatives and financial aid to countries such as Turkey for keeping refugees away from Europe should be halted.

Legal and safe passage should be ensured to those who want to go to Europe.

Anti-immigrant border policies that cause deaths and human rights violations should be denounced.

As a good role model for other countries, Turkey should go back to its "open-door policy"; subsequently, the deal to send migrants back to Turkey or refugees back to their countries should not be accepted, as fear of persecution for political or religious beliefs exists for these people.

Our Concluding Statements to the Turkish Government

All migrants, refugees, and foreigners, including Syrians, should be given full refugee status.

All willing migrants, irrelevant of their class, ethnicity, or religion and without any discrimination, should be given the right to citizenship.

Turkey should not turn into a refugee prison to please the EU. All refugees willing to go to other countries should be allowed to do so.

Syrians should not be systematically discouraged from hoping to return to their homeland in the future.

The future of millions of people in the region, including people in Syria and Turkey, depends on Turkey's politics and policies to be humanitarian, realist, pluralist, and democratic.

Cem Terzi graduated in 1984 from Ankara University Medical Faculty. He is professor of surgery at the Dokuz Eylül University Medical Faculty, Izmir, Turkey. He is the chairperson of the Board of General Surgery of European Union of Medical Specialists (UEMS) since 2014. The Association of Bridging Peoples was founded by Professor Terzi and his colleges in 2014, and he is still president of the association. This association works for refugees, especially providing them with health services.

Index

A
Adana, 41
advanced countries, 14, 27, 31
Aegean Islands, 4, 161, 163, 168–70, 172, 177–79
AfD, 223–25, 228
Afghan civilians, 33
Afghan National Army forces, 33
Afghan refugees, 5, 118, 134, 140–43, 152–53
   Iran and Pakistan, 135, 138–43, 152
   registered, 140
Afghanistan, 15, 33, 63, 133, 135, 140, 142–43, 152–53
Africa, 20, 35, 67, 84, 174, 178, 239, 316
   sub-Saharan, 15, 167
Agamben, Giorgio, 65, 189, 203–4
agriculture, 21, 39, 42, 45–47
AKP government, 52
   electoral defeat, 180
Alevi
   government of Assad, 34
   minority, 34, 36
   state, 49
American Revolution, 29
Amman, 41
Ansar-Muhajir fraternity, 49–50
Arab Spring, 33–35, 38, 44, 145
arbitrary arrest, 193–94, 206
Arendt, Hannah, 187, 190, 195–97, 200–203, 205–7
armed conflicts, 32, 34, 36, 38
Association of Bridging Peoples, 314–16

asylants, 218–19
asylum, 14–16, 28–30, 37, 44–45, 48, 50, 53, 56
   first, 135, 145
   governance, 97, 106
   grant(ed), 14, 29, 215, 226
   laws, 228
   mass-scale, 30
   overburdened, 179
   overstrained, 220
   policies, 148
   procedures, 168
   process, 179, 188
   seeking, 14, 16, 28–29, 97, 187, 205, 281
   transitioning, 147, 153
   of unprecedented numbers of refugees, 204
   US news media portrayal, 64, 69
Auerbach, Erich, 14
authoritarianism, 43

B
Bahrain, 33–34, 36, 39
Bashar-Al Assad, 34, 49, 146, 180, 210, 223–24
Beirut, 41
Bild, 212
borders, 2, 4, 6, 140–41, 178–80, 191–92, 210–11, 223, 227–28, 316–17
   dilemma of visual excess, 66–67
   dystopia of physical borders, 65
   image as border concept, 65–67

C

capital, 15, 17–18, 20–26, 31, 39–40, 42, 49, 82, 263, 276
capital accumulation, 4, 17–18, 21–24, 26, 31, 170, 264, 276
capitalism, 17–19, 21, 23, 38, 40, 43, 50, 319
capitalists, 17–18, 24, 26–27, 41
   class, 22–24, 26
   economies, 17–19, 22
CEE (Central and Eastern European), 111, 117, 119–21, 123
   anti-immigration sentiments, 123–27
   cultural conflicts, 127
   public opinion on migration, 117–23
   welfare nationalism, 113–17
child labor, 47–48, 51–53, 101
Chios, 162, 170–73
citizens, 14–15, 22, 25, 27, 43, 56–57
civil war, 16, 28–31, 34–35, 40, 133, 143–44, 146, 148, 293, 300, 316–17
colonialism, 14, 21
   white settler, 21, 23
colonization, 23, 67, 84–85, 202, 213
convergence between migrants and refugees, 28, 31
Council of Europe, 197–98
crisis of governance, 163–65, 169, 182

D

Daqneesh, Omran, 67, 73, 84
detention, 6, 173, 180, 186–95, 200, 203–6
   administrative, 191
   arbitrary, 187, 204
   indefinite, 186–87, 189, 203–5
   migration related, 6
   offshoring, 189
   U.S context, 203
   use of, 187, 205
Disaster and Emergency Management Presidency (AFAD), 49, 54, 151–52
displaced persons, employability, 93–95, 98–105
Dublin Regulation, 162, 210, 220, 221

E

Eastern Bloc, 42
Egypt, 33, 35–36, 39–40, 45
11 September 2001 attack, 203–4
empire
   Ottoman Empire, 99, 284
   Russian Empire, 226
   Soviet Empire, 218
employability of refugees
   host countries' challenges, 93–95, 98–99, 102–3, 105–6
   structural and agency constraints, 93–95, 102
   Syrians in Turkey (case study), 96–106
   UNHCR statistics, 103
employers, 41, 43, 49–50, 53, 56–57
employment
   extremely irregular, 19
   finding, 317
   formal, 262
   informal, 176, 263
   legal, 93–94, 142, 153
   low, 43
   massive, 276
   responses apropos, 98
   securing long-term, 103
   unauthorized, 268
   unregistered, 51–52
   wage-earning, 98
Erdoğan, Recep Tayyip, 34–35
ethnic cleansing, 16
Europe, 14–15, 23, 28–31, 35, 38, 42, 54
European Agenda on Migration, 162–63, 177–78
European Commission, 162, 171
European integration, 166–67, 219–20
European refugee crisis, 63
   economic model, 170–71
   EUTF, 174, 176, 178
   EU-Turkey deal, 148, 161–63, 168, 171–74, 177, 179–80, 321
   and the Greek debt crisis, 165
   "hotspot approach" on five Aegean islands, 172–73, 181
   Joint Action Plan, 171–72
   Jordan Compact, 168, 175–78

Juncker Commission, 171
Khartoum Process, 176
Lebanon Compact, 176
life on Kos, 161–62, 173
market and democratic principles, 165–67
new externalization measures, 174–77
policy innovations, 162–64, 179, 181
Single Market concept, 169
Syrian refugee crisis of 2015, 167–69
technocracy *vs.* democracy, 177–78
2016 London Conference, 175
European Union, 15, 19, 34, 36, 46, 163, 165–69, 171, 219, 283, 312, 315, 317
EU-Turkey Agreement/ Statement, 2, 148, 161–63, 168, 171–74, 177, 179–80
Operation Sophia, 224
European Union Trust Fund for Africa (EUTF), 174, 176, 178
Europeanization, 219
exile, 14, 29, 43
expellees, 214, 216–17
exploitation, 38, 43, 50–51, 264, 268, 276, 318
externalization, 174
 agreements, 180–81
 of migration, 174, 178
 programs, 171

F
Fanon, Franz, 37
fascist movements, 25
food
 prices, 39, 43
 security, 58
Foreigners and International Protection Law, 262
France, 22, 25, 30, 33, 35, 42
Frantz Fanon, 13
French Revolution, 29, 213

G
Gaddafi, Mu'ammar, 35
gang criminality, 28
Gaza Strip, 36

Gaziantep, 41, 52, 54, 56–57, 151, 266
gender issue, 16
Germany
 Chilean refugees, 217–18
 colonization movements, 213
 constitutional right for asylum, 215–16
 exclusion and "integration," 220–21
 expellees, 216–17
 forced migration, 214
 GDR citizenship, 215, 217–18
 immigration law, 212
 "Kölner Sylvesternacht," 222
 labor migration, 218–20
 partition of, 214
 refugee crisis, 209
 right of asylum, 215–16
 right-wing extremism, 225–29
 solidarity issues, 221–24
 "Summer of Welcome," 211–12, 221
 under Merkel's leadership, 210, 221–23
 West German constitution, 214–15
globalization, 18, 38, 40
Great Depression, 25, 27, 79
Greco-Turkish exchange of populations, 30
Greece, 2, 35, 42, 119, 123, 162–63, 165–66, 168–70, 172–73, 177, 179–85, 219–20, 223, 247–48
Guatemala-Mexico border, 28
guest workers, 136, 218–19
Gulf countries, 39, 43, 47

H
Haiti, 20
hate speech, 58
Hayata Destek, 52, 58
Hezbollah, 34, 36, 47
homicide rates, 28
Honduras, 28
hospitality, 211, 265
hostile environment, 6, 187–90
hotspot approach, 6, 162–63, 168, 171–72, 174–75, 177, 179, 181–83
hotspot islands, 162, 171, 174
human movement, 187, 196

Human Rights Watch, 53
human traffickers, 15–16
human trafficking, 35, 41
humanitarian assistance schemes, 93, 99
Hungary, 63–64, 112, 117–22, 124–31, 210–11, 254
Hussain, Amal, 67, 77, 82, 84–85
Hussein, Saddam, 33
hydrocarbons, 35–36, 39

I

identity, 65, 71, 177, 283, 285–86, 289–92, 294–98, 300–303
    politics, 13
images, 4, 63–86, 161, 168, 200, 209, 226, 239–40, 243
    of suffering children, 4
imperialism, 14, 70, 85
industrial reserve army, 17–21, 26, 29
inequalities, 16, 37, 43
informal jobs, 48, 176
informal sector, 4, 101, 264–65
insecurity, 25, 27, 43, 47–48
integration, 136, 138–39, 149–50, 153, 166–67, 228, 241, 283–85, 287–91
    of refugees, 5
    social, 5–6
Internally Displaced Persons (IDPs), 140–41
International Labor Force Law (ILFL), 100–101
international migration, 16, 18, 22, 25, 28, 31, 112
International Refugee Organization (IRO), 196–97
IOM, 178
Iran, 34, 36, 103, 138–42, 147, 152–53, 319
Iran-Iraq war, 36
Iraq, 33, 36, 43, 45
Islam/Islamic, 30, 32, 81
    civilization, 49
    Compass, 249
    element, 49
    front, 49
    fundamentalist, 81
    grassroots level, 49

NGOs, 49
    practices, 297
    regime, 140
    territory, 49
    world, 36
Islamic Republic of Iran, 103
Islamic State, 32–34, 316
Islamist ideology, 49
Islamization, 15
Islamophobia, 81, 211, 212, 224
Israel, 34, 36
Israeli-Palestinian conflict, 46
Istanbul, 14, 30, 37, 39, 52, 58
Italy, 22, 25, 33, 35, 42
Izmir, 2, 7, 254, 264, 266–69

J

Japan, 19
Jews, 29–30
job security, 50
joblessness, 26
jobs, 14, 26–27, 40, 42, 46–48, 50–51, 54, 57
Joint Action Plan, 171–72
Jordan, 41, 45–46, 53, 58, 162, 175, 177, 312
Jordanian Compact, 46, 163, 167
juridical non-personhood, 202–3

K

Kilis, 41, 54
Kızılay, 56
knitting industry, 45, 52, 55–56
Kurdi, Aylan, 67, 72–73, 84
Kurdish/Kurds, 14, 30, 35, 55, 147, 150, 304, 315
    workers, 51, 55–56
Kuwait, 42–43

L

labor, 17–18, 20, 22–24, 27, 40, 42, 44, 48–49, 51, 53, 57
    cheap, 31, 40–41, 43, 50–51, 56
    market, 17, 38–41, 45–46, 48–51, 53–57
    migration, 40–41, 51
    supply, 18, 22, 41–42, 48
    unregistered, 39, 45

labor migration, 40–44, 51, 93, 191, 286
  women's role, 50–52
Latin America, 20, 67, 84
Lebanon, 34, 41, 45, 47–48, 53, 58, 175, 312
Lesvos, 162, 169–74, 179
Libya, 16, 33, 35, 39–40, 167, 210, 224, 316
logistics, 241, 245–47

M
Maastricht Treaty, 165, 170
Macron, Emmanuel, 164
Malik, Charles, 194
Marx, Karl
  as asylum seeker, 29
  on capital accumulation, 17
  capitalism in agriculture, 21
  on reserve army of labor, 17–20, 23
mass destruction, 15, 33
mass exodus, 28, 30
mass flows of refugees, 134, 179
  permanency *vs.* temporariness in settlements, 135–39
mass influx, 95–96, 99–100, 104–5, 262
  vulnerable permanency, 133–57
MENA (Middle East and North Africa), 32–36, 133
Merkel, Angela, 209–10, 222–23, 227
Mersin, 54, 151, 269
Meza, Maria, 82, 84–85
Middle East, 15, 32, 35–36, 38–39, 41–43, 49, 54, 133, 316
migrants, 16, 28, 30–32, 35, 37, 41
  categories, 28, 31
  seasonal labor, 44–45
  undocumented, 42
migrant workers, 7, 42, 55, 136, 319
  displaced, 263
  irregular/undocumented, 319
  unprotected, 319
migration
  and asylum, 37, 50
  colonial and racialized gaze, 76–81
  fundamental reason, 40
  humanizing and dehumanizing images, 69–75
  international, 16, 18, 22, 25, 28, 31
  liberal theories, 40
  new wave, 38
  people's view, 117–22
  photographs, explanatory power, 65–68, 71–73, 76–79, 82–85
  political economy of, 13–37
  proximate causes, 31
  racialized children's suffering, examples, 64–65, 68–69, 71–73, 77, 81–82, 84
  suffering images, 64–68, 71–73, 77
  systemic violence by Western nations, 81–84
  violent border enforcement, 64
  visual raciontologies, 81–84
  welfare nationalism, 113–17
  women and children, 76–77
migratory movements, 16–17, 38–40
mobile media, 241
mobile phones (MPs), 204, 239–41, 254, 256
Muhajir, 49–50
Muslims, 30, 32–33

N
nation-states, 21, 97, 210, 213–16, 224, 226–27, 318, 320
neoliberal labor market, 262–77
New York Times, the, 77–79, 82, 84–85, 196, 239
1951 Refugee Convention Relating to the Status of Refugees and the Additional Protocol of 1967, 136–37, 214–15
1967 Protocol, 98, 141
Non-Governmental Organizations (NGOs), 5, 27, 32, 46, 77, 106, 204, 267–68
non-personhood, 186–87, 189, 191, 195, 200–203
North Africa, 15, 36

O
Obama, Barack, 35–36
Orientalism, 76
Osama bin Laden, 33

P

Pakistan, 5, 15, 30, 86, 103, 134–35, 138–42, 152–53
Party of Kurdistan (PKK), 36
path dependence, 95–97
Patriot Act, 203–4
pauperism, 19–21
permanent settlement, 5, 134–35, 139–40, 152–53
PKK (Party of Kurdistan), 36
political economy of migration
  capitalist phenomenon, 16–21
  concept of servitude, 15
  immigration restrictions, 24–25
  MENA region, wars in, 32–37
  populism movements, 25
  refugee category, 28–31
  US-Mexican border, 14
Portugal, 15, 22, 42, 124, 219
poverty, 26, 39, 42–43, 58
Powell, Colin, 33
production, 18, 20–21, 37, 39, 43, 54–55
proximate causes for migratory movements, 31–37
proximity, 52, 63, 295

Q

al Qaeda, 32–33

R

race, 66, 69, 76, 82, 86
racism, 86, 211, 225, 312
  institutionalized, 205
Ramirez, Valeria, 85
Rancière, Jacques, 205–6
Reception and Identification Centers (RICs), 162, 179
redistribution mechanism, 223
refugees, 14–16, 21, 28–32, 35, 37, 42, 44–45, 47–52, 54, 56–58
  experiences, information technology
    Ankommen (Arrive), 244
    chaotic model, 250–51
    digital dangers, 256
    gatekeeper model, 252–53
    hierarchical model, 251–52
    integration apps, 243–44
    media usage patterns, 242
    self-empowerment via smartphone, 253–56
    smartphone, 239–41, 243–50, 253–56
  status, 15, 24, 28–30
  workers, 48, 52, 56
refugee status determination (RSD), 137–38, 141, 147, 318
reserve army of labor, 4, 18–20, 22–24, 26
right to citizenship, 318–20

S

Saudi Arabia, 34, 36
Schengen agreement, 64
self-empowerment, 241, 248, 253, 255
sex workers, 16
Shia, 33, 36, 47
smartphone
  coordination logistics, 247–48
  maintenance logistics, 246–47
  migration relationship with, 241
  orientation logistics, 248–49
  refugees' experiences, 239–41, 243–50, 253–56
  verification logistics, 250
social classes, 3, 14, 16, 54, 82, 116
social policies, 3, 5, 83–86, 95–97, 102, 106, 120–21, 142, 148–50, 162–63, 167–68, 177–81, 196, 283, 296
socioeconomic integration, 46–47, 93–96, 99, 102–3, 105–6
Souda camp, 173
Spain, 30, 42, 219
special economic zones (SEZs), 175, 177
suffering of Others, 70–71, 77, 85
Sunni, 30, 33–34, 36, 304
SuTP, 100, 106
sweatshops, 26, 50, 53
Sweden, 7, 124, 249, 282, 293, 295, 298, 304
Syria, 33–36, 39–41, 47, 49–50, 52–57
  domestic and international conflicts, 145–47
  "failed state" status., 145–46
  humanitarian crisis, 67

political restructuring, 151–52
Syrian immigrants
  in day labor markets, 54–55
  future threats, 55–58
Syrian refugees, 31, 41, 45–51, 55–56, 58
  and deportees, 210
  in Europe, 283, 303
  in labor processes, 263
  workers, 46, 52, 266, 276
Syrian refugees into Turkey
  failure-success framework, 286–87
  home return approaches, 285–86
  homemaking approach, 290
  inclusion and exclusion, 282–85
  integration and home return, 287–88
  in Izmir (wage theft examples), 268–72
  labor processes, 262–64
  narratives, 295–303
  neoclassical economic theory of migration (NE), 286
  new economics of labor migration (NELM), 286
  place and identity-agency., 291–92
  relationships with Turkish Workers, 272–73
  temporary protection, 2, 58, 95–96, 100–101, 104, 106
  transnational spaces, 288–90
  Turkey's policy reactions, 147–49
  wage theft, 264–66, 272–76

T
technocracy, 165, 171
Temporary Protection (TP), 2, 58, 95–96, 100–101, 104–6, 137, 147–48, 150, 153–55, 262, 264, 266, 284, 317–18
textiles, 39, 45–46, 52, 55
Trump, Donald, 25, 36
Turkey
  harmonized unemployment rates, 103–4
  liberalization of migration policies, 149–51
  Syrian children in schools, 52–53

Syrian participation, labor market, 48–49
See also Erdoğan, Recep Tayyip

U
UAE (United Arab Emirates), 34, 36, 42
UN Global Compact for Migration, 175
unemployment, 17, 19, 26, 34, 39, 41, 43, 45–46, 48, 52, 55, 57–58
UNHCR (United Nations High Commissioner for Refugees), 32, 45–47
United Kingdom, 6, 22, 33, 42, 187, 189, 191, 194, 202, 204–5
  illegal migration, 187
  indefinite detention for non-citizens, 187–90
United Nations, 32–33, 196, 199, 214–15, 219, 315
United Nations High Commissioner for Refugees (UNHCR), 32, 45–47, 101–3, 137, 140, 142–43, 240, 256, 312–13, 318
United Nations International Children's Emergency Fund (UNICEF), 52–53, 101, 150
United Nations Relief and Rehabilitation Organization, 196
United Nations Relief and Works Agency, 32
United States, 23, 26, 32–37, 67, 82–84, 86, 189, 191, 194, 205, 226, 264–65
  "due process," immigrant detention, 192
  Immigration Act of 1891, 191
  Patriot Act, 203–4
Universal Declaration of Human Rights (UDHR), 70, 187, 192–93, 215
Universal Declaration of Human Rights, 193–95
US-Mexico border, 83, 85, 205

V
violence, 41, 43–44, 48
visual anthropology, 66
visual economies, 67, 73, 76, 81

W
wage theft, 262–80
wages, 17, 19, 24, 26, 39, 47–48, 50–51, 56–57
War on Terror, 33, 64
welfare nationalism, 112–13, 115–17, 123–29
Western audiences, 67–69, 71, 74, 76, 79, 84
work permit, 46, 100, 262, 265
Workers Party of Kurdistan (PKK), 36
working class, 7, 19–20, 23–27, 41
World Bank, 47
world capitalism, 16, 22, 26
World War I, 29
World War II, 38, 41, 145, 168, 193, 205, 213–14, 216, 227

Y
Yemen, 33, 36, 39–40
Yugoslavia, 22, 42

Z
Zaatari Refugee Camp, 45

www.ingramcontent.com/pod-product-compliance
Lightning Source LLC
Chambersburg PA
CBHW070802040426
42333CB00061B/1787